Archipelago

A READER

Archipelago

A READER

Edited by

NICHOLAS ALLEN

and

FIONA STAFFORD

THE LILLIPUT PRESS
DUBLIN

First published 2021 by
THE LILLIPUT PRESS
62–63 Sitric Road, Arbour Hill
Dublin 7, Ireland
www.lilliputpress.ie

Paperback ISBN 9781843517825

A CIP record for this title is available
from The British Library.

10 9 8 7 6 5 4 3 2 1

The Lilliput Press gratefully acknowledges
the financial support of the Arts Council/
An Chomhairle Ealaíon.

Set in 11pt on 16pt Galliard
Printed in Poland by Drukarnia Skleniarz

Contents

SCOTLAND

OTHER WORLDS

ENGLAND

WALES

AFTERWORDS

'It is not down in any map, true places never are'

HERMAN MELVILLE (THREE)

Editors' Note

Nicholas Allen and Fiona Stafford

Archipelago was an occasional magazine of literature and art edited by Andrew McNeillie and published for twelve issues from 2007 until 2019. Its origins were complex and many, and anchored firmly in McNeillie's own experiences on the Aran Islands as a younger man, described in the memoir of his earlier years, *An Aran Keening*, which was published by the Lilliput Press in Dublin. Lilliput's first publication had been a pamphlet by the cartographer, writer and artist Tim Robinson, whose art set the co-ordinates for an emerging body of coastal writing around the Irish and British isles, and further beyond. *Archipelago* gathered this flotilla in safe harbour and set it to sail into the environmental, cultural and political storms of the early twenty-first century under McNeillie's steering eye, which, if not always steady, was fiercely intent on charting the deep tides that make for history and place at the sea-struck edge.

Archipelago was from the beginning a collaborative project. McNeillie first thought of the journal on a family holiday in Spain, where he found a ready associate in his daughter Gail, who became a regular contributor to the magazine. He soon sought opinions of the possible project from the many writers and artists he knew from his decades of work in publishing. They were all for it, as the exceptional contributions to the first issue attest. Launched by Seamus Heaney in the Bodleian Library, Oxford, *Archipelago* soon attracted a dedicated readership. In doing so, each issue gathered a network of associations that together provided material for the deep consideration of particular places in relation to each other. Some of these sites were more familiar to the literary and visual traditions than others. McNeillie's innovation was to make of *Archipelago* an atlas of found places, the flotsam of centuries of interactions by the sea found with the jetsam of an artist's life. The results were astonishing. *Archipelago* was consistently interesting, provocative and gifted with a complement of artists and writers who summoned together an entirely new vision of land and sea, and this from the intractable material of a long-broken union whose fragmentation is ongoing.

Part of *Archipelago*'s charge was, of course, to show that such political arrangements have no natural purchase in the lived reality of the seaside place. The timescale in which the contributors to *Archipelago* worked ranged from the thrum of the wild bird's rush to the deep rumble of the sea on the islands' rocky promontories. Through this were threaded stories of bird, fish, animal and human, sometimes freighted with a historical moment, as in the meditations by Ivor Gurney on the Severn, and sometimes afloat from them, as in the many, and all remarkable, etchings by Norman Ackroyd of blustery weather offshore. This selection of key contributions also includes new material: hand-drawn maps by Malcolm Sparkes; notes and afterword by Chris Fletcher and James Macdonald Lockhart; poems, artwork and an essay by Andrew McNeillie. Fletcher writes about the journal's archives in the Bodleian Library, an early source of support for the journal (and one of the ironies of this coastal enterprise is the energy it took from the landlocked community of Oxford). Macdonald Lockhart, the author of *Raptor* was, along with Katherine Rundell, *Archipelago*'s associate editor. His reflections on the experience are an afterword and prelude to McNeillie's own record – half-memoir, half-manifesto, all individual – of his hopes for the journal.

As each issue of *Archipelago* had its own ecology, geography and relations, it would be impossible, and misleading, to separate out any particular set of essays, poems or images as representative of a larger whole. This might, in fact, be damaging, in a way that Tim Robinson warned about in his own writing of the West of Ireland, which paid attention to the particularity of its subjects and became, in the process, a series of correspondences whose braiding together in prose was the substance of his style. When asked to collect a record of *Archipelago* in book form, to mark the journal and its achievements and provide a frame for future readers, we decided to arrange the collection in strands of association that trace imaginative journeys around the isles. The journeys and places pivot around an Other Worlds that gesture towards *Archipelago*'s consistent attempt to look beyond the known horizon. The separation of other sections is not a demarcation, but a map of possible departures and resting places. Given the riches of *Archipelago*'s twelve volumes, some of the essays have had to be reduced in length and we have had to leave many excellent pieces within the pages of their magazines. We offer this selection as one possible choreography of *Archipelago*'s serial complexity, in the hope that it may give the journal's regular readers fresh ways into familiar pieces, and new readers, now and in the future, a sense of its exceptional contents, and of their unfolding possibilities.

In collecting the materials, we were confirmed in our belief that *Archipelago* marks a creative and intellectual turn towards the coast, the sea, and the endless declension of water as the matter, embodied and imaginary, of our shifting relations, among these islands and beyond. We were reminded too of the pleasure of reading and the promise of looking. As Andrew McNeillie invited the reader to join the complement of his crew in the first issue, so we extend the invitation to readers old and new to sail these imaginary isles in the company of artists whose works point to the far shores of new understanding, all the closer now through *Archipelago*.

‘What is the future of a place, if no one remembers its name?’

TIM ROBINSON (SEVEN)

A Note on the Archive

Chris Fletcher

'This whole string of incantation of places' could be a description of the *Archipelago* project. It was a phrase used by Norman Ackroyd at the start of a reading for the journal held by the Bodleian Library in 2013. The politically contentious space of Convocation House, used by both Cromwell and King Charles during the Civil War, could hardly be further from the sea. Yet it was to the margins of the land that Ackroyd took us, from Muckle Flugga to Skibbereen. His unscripted litany of islands and coastal places traced a parabola across the occident from his point of origin in Elmet. In his mind's eye he revisited the fishing boat trips from which he painted in preparation for work on his rich and intense etchings darkly drenched in the chaos of the sea and set alight with its birds. He invoked the actually loved, the known and the marvellous. As I said, just like *Archipelago.*

The Clutag Press and the Bodleian were early collaborators. An earlier event in 2007 brought together young poets like Paul Abbott, who riffed out his long piece *Flood*, alongside master makers including Seamus Heaney. It captured what was to be the last, I think, recorded sound of Mick Imlah, reading *Muck*. Other readings included Andrew

McNeillie, Kate Rundell and Tom Paulin. All of these events have run alongside a project to capture the written record of the Clutag Press, through the acquisition of tranches of its archive. This has given the Bodleian an important slice of contemporary material. All of the writers and artists who have sailed in Andrew's boat now form part of what Francis Bacon described as 'an ark to save learning from the deluge'. The modest funds requested by Andrew for the papers helped to keep the enterprise afloat.

My friend Richard Ovenden – Bodley's Librarian – and I have had some jolly Oxford lunches and dinners with Andrew, both in the early days of the press and since. We shared our love of the land and seascapes he set about celebrating through our Scottish connections and appreciation of British neo-romanticism of the 1940s and '50s, in photography, art and writing. Being librarians, this was not all a case of beer and skittles. We have benefitted from the connections Andrew brought to us. Alongside the Clutag archive itself we have, with the generous support of his executors and family, received the donation of Mick Imlah's papers. Norman Ackroyd has promised us his; others might receive a letter from me at some point.

Andrew has murmured to me a few times that the project is taking a rest. But like the sea, it is restive. I suspect the archive will grow and the events will happen again. The last time I was with him was on a visit to Norman's London studio in Morocco Street. The massive etching press anchors the warehouse; a floor up, ink dries and work finds a frame. Climbing again we reach living quarters, grand and homely all at once, with notable unglazed art nailed to the wood surrounding an orderly mass of archives, beaten up yet cherished kitchen utensils, brushes and empty fag packets. We stood on the little balcony, looking out at The Shard. Landlocked again, but it felt as if we were afloat.

IRELAND

'Or perhaps the landscape saw me coming'

TIM ROBINSON (SIX)

Derek Mahon (ONE)

Insomnia

Scratch of a match
fierce in the dark. The alarm clock,
night-vigilant, reads twenty minutes to four;
wide awake, as so often at this dead hour,
I stare down at the lighted dock,
trawlers and crated catch,
as if on watch.

The bright insects
of helicopters drop to the decks
of gas-rigs ten miles out in the heavy waves,
their roaring rotors far from our quiet leaves,
before midnight; and the ship that shone
at dusk on the horizon
has long since gone.

Nothing stirs
in garden or silent house,
no night-owl flies or none that we can hear;
not even the mild, traditional field-mouse
runs nibbling, as you'd expect, under the stairs.
Boats knock and click at the pier,
shrimp worship the stars.

The whole coast
is soporific as if lost
to echoes of a distant past –
the empty beach-house with no obvious owner,
an old hotel like a wrecked ocean liner
washed up one stormy night
and left to rot.

The woman from
the Seaview, a 'blow-in'
of some kind from a foreign shore,
seems out of her element and far from home,
the once perhaps humorous eyes grown vague out here.
What is she? A Lithuanian, or a Finn?
We've met before

beside some flat
road bridge or bleak strand road,
two men in black at the corner staring hard,
far off in the stricken distance perhaps a shipyard,
chimneys, power plants, gasometers,
oil refineries, Gothic spires
and things like that –

where a cloud climbs
and swirls, yellow and red,
streaking the estuary, and a soul screams
for sunken origins, for the obscure sea bed
and glowing depths, the alternative mud haven
we left behind. Once more we live in
interesting times.

Bernard O'Donoghue (ONE, TEN)

Geese Conversations

i.m. Ian Niall

It would have been about this time of the year
that we watched the field-geese near Macroom
grow restless, preparing to call out
to the Canada geese flying overhead
to regions of thick ribbëd ice, far away
from the Lee Scheme's kindly reclaimed stretches.

Ballybeg Priory

for Brian Friel

Writing from Lisbon in 1705,
the Bishop of Cloyne lamented how
'oxen and asses ruminate
under the shadows of the Austins' church
at Ballybeg, the stone coffins of the monks
their watering troughs, and the tombs
where rest the bones of abbots are their byres.'

By now you might expect to find in place
an instructive interpretative centre,
explaining how the columbarium
provided guano which the friars sold
as fertiliser because it was better
for herb gardens and cloth making
than the droppings of the farming stock.

But there are no display-cases here:
no art-objects or explanations.
The close is untended, and the walls
go on crumbling. And in the field around
are tinkers' ponies: piebald, skewbald,
ungroomed, unshorn, stumbling blindly
on their overgrown, unfarriered hooves.

Norman Ackroyd (SIX)

Kilkieran Bay, Co. Galway, Golam Head

Moya Cannon (SEVEN)

Bees under Snow

In a field beside the dark wood,
this year there are fifty-two beehives –
orange and blue cubes with zinc lids,
raised on long girders.

Last winter, under a foot of snow,
they were square marshmallows in a white field.
By a miniscule door lay a few dead bees
and one or two flew about distractedly
but the bees inside hovered in a great ball
shivering to keep warm, to stay alive
moving always inwards towards the globe's centre
or outward towards its surface.

As much as their hunt for sweetness
or their casual work of fertilizing the world's
petalled, coloured, scented flowers
to bear fruit for all earthbound, airborne creatures,
this is part of their lives,
these long months of shivering, of bee-faith.

Tim Robinson (NINE)

The Gods of The Neale

For reasons not worth rehearsing, when I set out to begin my map of Connemara, in 1979, it was from the humdrum little town of Claremorris in the flatlands of south Mayo. Slightly nervously I wheeled my over-laden bike out into the busy street and wobbled off in the direction of the mountains that formed a long rim to the western horizon. The day was perfect April, compounded of sun and breeze; the roads were almost empty of traffic, the countryside very quiet. As I approached the village called The Neale I noticed a small pyramid or ziggurat of nine stages in a field by the road, and went to look at it. A largely illegible inscription seemed to identify it as 'Templum Fortunae' and date it to 1750 or 1760. Back on the road, I overtook a lady walking between two sticks, who told me that she was paralysed on one side after a brain haemorrhage. I asked her about the monument, and she was very informative. Lord Kilmaine, she said, had been one of the good land-lords, and had employed the farmers ('such as they were') on building this folly as well as a small round Greek temple visible in the distance. I should go and see 'The Gods of The Neale', since I was interested in things like that. She could not explain what these Gods were, but I would find them, she said, by taking a turning to the left just ahead.

The turning sent me down a little road with a tall demesne wall along its left-hand side, overtopped by old trees. Unable to identify anything that might be a God or Gods, I spoke to some children playing football in a little schoolyard on the right, who directed me onwards to a hole in the wall, which I was able to jump through. I spent some time wandering around the low remains of the mansion, tumbledown outhouses and overgrown gardens, and finally came across a monument, perhaps ten or twelve feet tall, set against a thicketed bank. Three medieval-looking rectangular bas-reliefs were inserted in its frontage; the lowest of them, horizontal, represented a slender four-footed creature, a lion to judge by its curly mane and fierce claws, with a long whip-like tail ending in what looked like a hand of three fingers and a thumb. Above that the other slabs stood vertically and side by side: on the right, an angel in a long dress, facing forwards and holding a small shield or perhaps a book against its breast; on the left a horse, perhaps a unicorn, which appeared to be sitting on its tail and looked to me as if it should have been set horizontally. Below these carvings was a broad limestone plaque with a long inscription of an eighteenth-century appearance, which in this shadowy retreat was hard to make sense of. Some phrases stood out that were given resonance by the obscurities in which they were embedded and the empty-echoing mansion nearby:

> The Irish characters on the above stone import that in this cave we have by us the Gods of Cons … Lett us follow their stepps sick of love with FVLL confidence in Loo Lave Adda … the Shepherd of Ireland of his era … These images were found in a cave behind the place they now stand & were the ancient Gods of the Neale which took its name from them. They were called Déithe Fhéile or the Gods of Felicity from which the place in Irish is called Ne Heale in English The Neale LL reigned AM 2577 PD 927 AHTE C1496 and was then 60: CEDNA reigned AM2994 & 64 of Edna was wel 50 CON MOIL was ye son of Heber who divided this kingdom with his brother and had the western parts of this island for his lott all which was originally called from Con Conovcht or Cons portion and his son LOO LAVEADDA who found the Druids was thought to have drawn all his knowledge from the SVN Thus the Irish history. N.B.

> the smaller letters on the upper part of the great plinth import that it was erected by Edna Loos Gods were adopted by Con and Edna of the line of Heber established their worship there 1753.

Whether myth is the consolidated sediment fallen out from the ceaseless perturbed flow of folktales, or folktales the crumbled remains of forgotten myth, scholarship conditions us to prefer deeper layers to later ones. So, to clear away some of the misidentifications of earlier misidentifications, I add here my findings, fruit of subsequent rummaging in archives and reference books.

Con is clearly Conn of the Hundred Battles, the king who divided Ireland with Eoghan Mór (not his brother), and took as his portion the part known from him as Connacht. Heber is probably Éibhear, the mythical leader of the Gaels, who ruled over the southern portion of Ireland for a year. Loo Laveadda is a phonetic attempt at Lugh Lámhfhada, Lugh of the long hand, in origin a Celtic deity, hero and master of all the arts; he was not the son of Con. Lugh led the otherworldly Tuatha Dé Danann to victory in the fabulous Battle of Moytura, said to have occurred a few miles west of The Neale. Edna or Edana was a poet and prophetess of the Tuatha Dé Danann. The jumble of figures in the middle of the inscription are dates; AM stands for Anno Mundi, the 'year of the world' in the system based on the date of Creation, 4004 BC, concocted by Bishop Ussher in the seventeenth century; what the other abbreviations stand for I do not know. The old idea that the village name, The Neale, is an anglicisation of the Irish An Fhéile, the festival, felicity or generosity, is not favoured by placename experts nowadays.

Estate records of The Neale say the various follies were designed by Lord Charlemont, whose sister married Sir John Browne, later to become the first Baron Kilmaine, in 1764. But Charlemont was an enthusiast for classicism (the Casino at Marino in Dublin was his pleasure house, and his main residence, Charlemont House, is now the Dublin City Gallery), so even if he is responsible for the symmetrical form of the monument, which tapers upwards stepwise to a little pedestal bearing a stone sphere (now missing), he would not have approved either the style or the substance of the garbled inscription. The first investigator to transcribe the plaque was seemingly the travel writer and actor Richard Hayward in 1941 or 1942; a unionist with nationalistic sympathies, he dismisses the monument as a whim of the irresponsible landlord class: 'a more absurd conglomeration of unrelated objects never confronted the eyes of man.' In stark contrast, the archaeologist Peter Harbison writes:

> The inscription and the whole monument should be seen not just as a piece of romantic dilettante erudition, but also as an extraordinary piece of reverence to the Celtic past by a member of the landed aristocracy in the west of Ireland.

Is it possible then that the date 1753 at the end of the inscription refers to a re-establishment of the worship of the ancient Irish gods by members of the landlord's family? What trace, what presence, might such a cult have left in the atmosphere of this ruinous and overgrown corner? Looking around me, I thought of M.R. James' *Ghost Stories of an Antiquary*. All the props of an incipient tale in his vein were here: the unfrequented ruin, the puzzling inscription, the premature dusk gathering under the trees. I did not linger, but found my way back to the hole in the wall and scrambled out into the coolly rational summer afternoon.

*

The above account is an accurate reflection of this curious experience, written in a B&B in Connemara five or six hours later, bulked up with some material from subsequent research. But before I looked it up in my diary my clear and unarguable memory of the episode was somewhat different. Soon after leaving the commonplace little town I became aware of the absence of traffic. The broad, shallow farmlands breathed a disquieting silence. The first person I saw on the road was an elderly man on a bicycle; I caught up with him just as we passed the monument with nine tall steps leading up to nothing. I asked him what it was, and he told me about the landlord who had had his hungry tenantry build it in the famine time. Then he went on to urge me, insistently, to visit the Gods of 'The Neale', the nature of which entity he could not articulate. A little further on we passed a small community hall that, he told me, was named from a young republican killed in 1921 by the Black and Tans in the Tourmakeedy ambush. We went on to talk of the troubles in the North, which were at their most murderous at that time. Recognising that I was English, he hastened to tell me that the history being taught nowadays made the present IRA think they were emulating the old IRA of the War of Independence, which they were not; I was not to think that Irish people in these parts had any sympathy for those people.

When we parted he continued westwards and I turned down the lane he had told me would lead me to the mysterious Gods. The children in the village school playground pointed me on my way; I climbed from sunlight into tree-shadow through the broken-down demesne wall with a sense of achievement, of escape from the everyday net of public ways, into the realm of the unexpected. The monument reared up before me as I parted the rampant vegetation. I took out my notebook and set myself busily to transcribe its inscription, perhaps to disperse the rather oppressive eeriness of its unfrequented and neglected setting. I could only make it out in parts and by degrees, but this much was clear: '… Lett us follow their stepps sick of love with FVLL con dence in Loo Lave Adda … the Shepherd of Ireland of his era …' What exactly did that mean? What did 'sick of love' mean in the eighteenth century? Are we tired of loving our old ways, or overcome by love of these new or rediscovered gods?

The antique stones had nothing to add. I dismissed as over-imaginative a twinge of anxiety, a faint premonition of nightmare, of failing to rend the hole in the demesne wall. The birdless shrubbery, the ivy weaving its nets around the fallen masonry of the old mansion, suggested politely but firmly that I should now leave, and allowed me to do so without difficulty.

On reaching the main road again I turned westwards towards Connemara, the mountainous boundary of which reared up from the plain more and more decisively as I progressed. A few miles beyond the village I saw a figure standing in the road with a bicycle; as I approached, I realised it was the man I had met earlier. He had waited for me, he said, because he wanted to be sure I would not miss the site of the Battle of Moytura. He indicated a number of huge boulders among a few trees at the further end of a low rise in a roadside field, and having pointed out my way, or put me out of my way, once again, took himself off. I strayed among the ancient stones for some time, wondering why he had so insisted on my making this detour. I knew little about the epochal battle that took place, or has been staged by ancient story-tellers, here. Later I read it up in *Lough Corrib, Its Shores and Islands*, by the nineteenth-century antiquarian Sir William Wilde, who had his country home nearby. Putting together local folklore and the witness of medieval manuscripts, Wilde gives a detailed account of the battle between the magical invaders, the Tuatha Dé Danann, or People of the Goddess Danu, and the native Fir Bolg, which raged for four days, involved a hundred thousand on either side, and left its memorials in the form of the numerous cashels, cairns and standing stones to be seen in the sleepy countryside around The Neale. Lugh, son of the Dé Danann king Nuadu, was killed in the third day's fighting and is said to be buried under one of the standing stones near the village. But in the end the Fir Bolg were defeated and took refuge in the Aran Islands, where they built the great clifftop fort of Dún Aonghasa.

However, there is a grander corpus of myth concerning another Battle of Moytura, usually said to have been fought at another Moytura in Sligo but frequently – and certainly in my mind – conflated with the Battle of Moytura in Mayo. This second battle pitched the divine Tuatha Dé Danann against the Fomhóire, a grim race of sea-pirates, and its pivotal event was the confrontation between Lugh and his grandfather Balor, a giant, perhaps a thunder god in origin, who had a single lightning-flashing eye which it took four men to open. Lugh flung his spear, or a slingshot, at this baleful eye and knocked it through to the back of his head so that it looked upon Balor's own soldiers and, according to Mayo folklore, turned them into the stones I was wandering among, somewhat empty-mindedly, that day of my journey.

Why was I here? Not one of the boulders had a word to say. The sky was darkening, and I still had a long way to go. I returned to my bike and set off again westwards.

*

I broke out through the rapidly diminishing hole in the wall, breathless, my heart racing. The shrieks of the children drove me back to the junction with the main road, where I saw that the old man riding away on his bike was still only a few dozen yards distant; it was as if I had spent no time at all in the demesne, or none of the time of this world. I laboured on my bicycle but I could not catch up with him, although he seemed to be pedalling at a normal easy rate; it was because the road was slippery with blood, and my long hand impeded me. Soon he was far ahead and waiting for me near the circle of stones. The hedges for miles around were full of the sound of iron on skin, iron on flesh, iron on bone. He towered among the thunderclouds forming on the mountain rim of Connemara. In the middle of his forehead is the mark I must aim at.

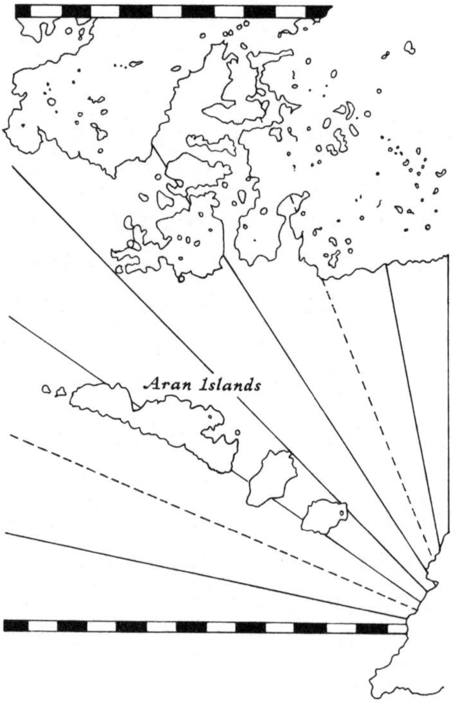
Aran Islands

Deirdre Ní Chonghaile (TWELVE)

Greim an Fhir Bháite

Drownings are imagined as an eternal feature of island life. Whether we are affected by them personally, or hear about them in the news, we recognise that we are powerless before the sea. The lighthouse on the horizon, the life-ring on a waterside railing, the model lifeboat cum charity box on a pub counter, all dare to inspire hope that seafarers can and will return home. For most of us, however, drownings are simply stories. Most of us do not know a life lived, day in, day out, with this terminal hazard.

A single drowning can prove a last straw, not alone to the bereaved but to an entire community. Drownings can trigger evacuations and the abandonment of islands. A unique way of life relocates to the realm of island diaspora, and into dreams – of memory, regret, or hope for what might yet be. As Marina Warner has observed of tragedy, some narratives of drowning are so shocking, they have the potential to 'seize attention' and to 'obscure rather than reveal'. At their most extreme, they can be seen in terms of social Darwinism – essentialist nightmares of decline in rural areas and in indigenous populations and cultures worldwide.

Yet drownings can and sometimes do spark more positive action, the epicentres of which are often local: for example, in Britain and Ireland, the Royal National Lifeboat Institute and LAST – Lost-At-Sea Tragedies. The supportive work such bodies provide to island communities eager to make a case for their long-term sustainability is rarely acknowledged in the wider world. This is where writers and teachers, historians and critics, and a publication such as this, have a campaigning role to play. They can assist by revealing and countering fatalism and the normalising power of the word. They can help lead communities and their authorities to a deeper understanding of how perniciously narrative can operate, press them into critical awareness, and spur them to take responsible action to reduce risk.

The common and generalised depiction of small island demographics and island life is, unsurprisingly and justifiably, one of contraction or decline. But close studies of individual island populations and demographics reveal the shortcomings of such a generalised depiction. There are always local anomalies to take into account: peripatetic islanders, for instance, people who come and go beneath the radar as a matter of routine; and the population of Inis Oírr, the smallest of the three Aran Islands, which has been growing in recent years – against common assumptions and trends. Such data is scattered and seems rarely to inform decisions taken by regional authorities and central government, suggesting a failure to engage with such detail. The challenges facing island communities, the complexities of their demographics and social structures, tend to remain invisible to the majority. Ignorance reigns and remains, unquestionably, the greatest challenge facing those committed to reform and improvement.

Island narratives of drownings are typically tales from lives as labour, stories of people – mostly men – extracting a living from the sea: lightkeepers, as were my uncle and granduncle; naval ratings, as was my great-grandfather; sailing traders, as was my great-great-grandfather; coastguards, as was my great-great-great-grandfather; and especially, the most numerous, fishermen, who have the most complex relationship of all with the sea – my brothers, father, grandfather, great-grandfather, fishermen all.

The unpredictability of the sea's moods is more acute and abrupt than that encountered by, say, a farmer eyeing the fruit of his/her husbandry. The fisherman's fear of the sea is, perhaps, closer to the miner's fear of the coalmine. Those who extract resources from ocean and earth are equally and rightfully distrustful of the elemental storehouses they are exploiting. Acknowledging the impossibility of possession, the respectful raiders cultivate a vocabulary of guardedness and superstition, shoring up their banks of hard-won knowledge to equip themselves for their future navigations.

Tales of near-drownings and near-crushings provide proscenia for heroism, the necessary aspiration of challengers and champions. But, where the deep, dark, dusty danger of the mining life holds little affirmation beyond a wheezing wage, the seafaring life holds the promise of untold adventure and bounteous reward – fresh air, swollen nets, bellies full of health-giving fish, and the awe-inspiring, mesmerising beauty of the sea. At once a mother and a lover, nursing all manner of desire, it holds the promise of a thrilling intimacy. Such promises and prayers inspire the resolve we witness among seafaring communities to return to sea even after disaster strikes.

*

Ideas of island decline augment the sense of adversity implicit in narratives of drownings, and suggest that islanders are doomed to inherit a worsening situation. The climax of the 1934 film *Man of Aran* exploits the mystique and danger of the marine environment in its portrayal of the islanders' encounter with the ocean, mythologising their struggle via *tableau vivant*. After Robert Flaherty persuaded an Aran crew to row through a storm for his camera lens, his biographer Arthur Calder-Marshall observed: 'Those three men in the curragh fighting through the storm became a little bit bigger than life size. They became characters out of one of their own heroic legends, a saga of themselves.' Islander Pat Mullen – who was Flaherty's right-hand man in Aran and who helped persuade the curragh-men to take on the perilous challenge

– wrote about their feat in his book *Man of Aran* (1934), which includes a drawing depicting their epic voyage:

> Patcheen and his men were drenched with sweat and brine, but their blue eyes were lit up with fire, and a great thrill of wild pride shot through me as I looked at them, for here had been a trial of some of the old, old stock, and the blood still ran true.

Flaherty said later: 'I should have been shot for what I asked these superb people to do, all for the sake of a keg of porter and five pounds a piece.' But Mullen's account can also be read as a justification for the role he played; and, indeed, in the wake of the act of daring being rewarded with immortality, as a forceful expression of faith in the future of his community.

Flaherty observed that the relationship between an islander and the sea is no vague piety or idle romance. He stayed a year and eight months in Aran, waiting to capture those awesome storm scenes, now iconic in the canon of sea-lore not only of Aran, but also of Ireland, and of islands. Flaherty understood that the drama rested in necessity: 'The Aran Islander in order to survive has to fight the sea.' Episodes of defiance and deliverance at sea such as he constructed, in collaboration with islanders, are grounding reminders of the social and cultural contract of a marine life. But we need not rely on the fictional alone to remind us of the risk that comes with that particular contract. There are a myriad of real-life examples all along the west coast. Among the most potent is that of the Cleggan Disaster of 1927 (famously retold by Richard Murphy). Preserved in local memory farther north in Mayo's Mullet Peninsula is the story of the loss in that deadly storm of ten young men aged between sixteen and thirty-three years, the lifeblood of the twin islands of Inishkea. There is also a tale of the survival of two brothers from Inis Gé Thuaidh, Anthony and John Meenaghan.

They had pulled their valuable nets into their three-man curragh and were able to use the nets as a form of sheet anchor to slow their progress. Their craft was washed ashore near Tiraun [Torán], directly opposite on the mainland. The seawater that had entered their boat had also assisted them by acting as a form of ballast. Anthony badly gashed his head as they tried to get ashore. The two brothers finally stumbled into the licensed premises of Mrs Conalty in Aghleam [An Eachléim, two miles away]. One of them still had the bailer from the boat in his hand.

'Greim an fhir bháite' – the grip of the drowned man.

Visual and physical evidence of the contract of a marine life appears in Brian Dornan's book *Mayo's Lost Islands*, from which the above account is taken. Dornan shares three arresting illustrations including a meteorological chart of the storm – which would not have then been available to those who needed it most – and diagrams of devices that offered little defense against the approaching danger: a primitive barometer, and a straimpín, a release rope for a boat anchor. Photographs accompanying Tom Cork Kenny's international scoop on the Cleggan Disaster go farther: an image of coffins in a mass grave is printed next to an image of a bereaved widow and her children. Eight years later in November 1935, when nineteen people were drowned en route home to Arranmore Island, Co. Donegal, newspaper photographs taken there show the coffins open to reveal the drowned, positioning the images somewhere between memento mori and shock tactic. Both sets of photographs accompanied pleas for action to help the plight of poorly resourced west coast islanders, challenging fatalistic responses to the incidents.

> How jovial their minds and contented
> While skillfully sorting their old torn gear,
> Hoping to land some small catches
> Of fish that were temptingly near.
> Signs of storm appeared, but they ventured
> To gather a crust from the sea,
> All other resources denied them
> In a wilderness far from being free.

While the drownings that occurred that October night in the Inishkea islands were a crushing blow for the local community, the straw that broke the camel's back was the double-drowning that occurred two years later. That aftershock set into motion the eventual abandonment or evacuation of the islands a few years later. This pattern is echoed in another island farther south, Inishark in Co. Galway, which was evacuated in 1960. While the loss of the two Lacey brothers, Martin and Michael, and their cousin Peter Lacey on Easter Sunday 1949 sounded the death-knell for Inishark, it was ultimately the next tragedy a few years later that kick-started the final evacuation: a young man died after a three-day illness during which bad weather left him without a doctor or a priest. As the population then numbered less than 100 people, the island community had been denied a telephone line, so they resorted in that emergency to lighting a bonfire to signal for help.

The song 'Thomas Lacey's Last Stand' – which was composed by Mike Walsh from Inishturk and commemorates how the father of the Lacey brothers remained alone for one last night on the island after everyone else had left – draws on the memory of evictions and nineteenth-century transportation to express the violence inherent, psychologically, in the islanders' dispossession and displacement. Pouring scorn on 'Tara's Hill' – the mythical seat of ancient Irish kingship representing the contemporary Irish establishment – Walsh sounds the depth of betrayal:

> The day we spent in merriment 'til it was growing dark,
> We gave three cheers for Ireland and lovely Inishark,
> 'Twas there we met Tom Lacey, that chieftain bold and true,
> Who fought against Victoria's troops and the Tans he did subdue,
> He led his men both fierce and grim and conquered many a foe
> Until he came to Tara's Hill which proved his overthrow.
>
> 'Twas there he was surrounded by the Land Commission men
> 'Surrender now, my boys,' they said, 'or we will shoot to kill
> And have you all transported to the rocks of Fountainhill.'

Resettled from their respective island homes, Mike Walsh and Tom Lacey had become neighbours in the inland village of Fountainhill, Co. Mayo.

*

On Irish islands, narratives of sea disasters and their consequences do not confine themselves to the past nor even to the present. In Cill Éinne, Árainn, which has the strongest historical link to Aran's fishing industry thanks to its reliable harbour, there stands a memorial erected to remember all islanders who are known to have drowned. Its northern, seaward face is strikingly empty, waiting for the names that could – some would say 'will inevitably' – be carved therein in the future. This blank space brings the sense of foreboding to the paradox of living with and from the sea – 'the delight and the dread,' as the folklore scholars Patricia Lysaght, Séamas Ó Catháin and Dáithí Ó hÓgáin put it in the book *Islanders and Water-Dwellers*. It speaks to a sense of expectation and also to an acceptance of a particular level of risk, which the Health & Safety Authority has recently measured. In Ireland, where construction is seven times more dangerous than the average industrial job and agriculture is eleven times more dangerous, fishing is forty times more dangerous. Reports from the Marine Casualty Investigation Board reveal that around forty fishing boats have sunk in the twenty-one years from 1995 to 2016 and, with those forty boats, thirty fishermen have drowned. When government officials remain deaf to the concerns of industry and of constituents, and blind to how ignorance and convenience impact their decision-making, we witness how resignation has been built into this way of life from all sides.

While the frighteningly stubborn level of mortality present in the fishing industry remains and continues to call into question the risk assessment procedures and the morality of government officials, narrative emerges as chief prompter of concessions to ignorance and convenience, helping to preserve the status quo. Take, for instance, the beguiling element surrounding this drama – water – and people's relationships with it. Ever-changing, unpredictable and treacherous, its potential to mesmerise and to mystify cultivates and even encourages ignorance. Human engagement with water is usefully contextualised in *Islanders and Water-Dwellers*:

> … water highlights the manner in which environmental peril and environmental necessity are intertwined to constitute a hugely productive dichotomy in the lore concerning seas, lakes and rivers.
>
> … This essential and enduring, yet dangerous, substance touches upon human life in so many ways, and its expanses are so impressive and mystifying, that it calls forth all kinds of emotion. It is probably the symbol most suited for the disintegration and reintegration which is experienced as an essential part of life.

That disintegration and reintegration call forth another narrative: the inevitability of mortality itself. The disruptive potential of mortality increases when given a watery context and is augmented once again on the open ocean. In Inis Meáin in the autumn of 1901, the funeral of a young man, whose body was washed ashore some weeks after he was drowned, haunted Synge: 'As they talked to me and gave me a little poteen and a little bread when they thought I was hungry, I could not help feeling that I was talking with men who were under a judgment of death. I knew that every one of them would be drowned in the sea in a few years and battered naked on the rocks, or would die in his own cottage and be buried with another fearful scene in the graveyard I had come from.' Such feelings of helplessness and hopelessness generate the inertia of resignation.

There is also the audacity of seafarers. In their milieu, courage in the face of adversity is understandably celebrated, as upholding that ideal could mean the difference between living and drowning. Imagining themselves to such a pantheon means challengers are readily mythologised, as are the *Man of Aran* curragh crew. This factor also suggests seafarers develop a higher tolerance for adversity, which may cause some of them to suffer in silence or to carry on regardless of what hand Fate deals them. For such resolute, steadfast seafarers, to yield to a life ashore could trigger an existential crisis.

The prospect of surrender imbuing each of these three narratives makes them seductive; but islanders fighting decline and the death of community, and who are all too familiar with the cost of ignorance and convenience, have yet to succumb. Faced with the prospect of effectively vanishing off the map – as recently depicted in an animation sequence in a TG4 documentary about Inis Bigil, Co. Mayo, population 25 – they choose defiance. They choose to defend their way of life, not simply because it is theirs, but because they know it to be worthwhile. While continuing to battle the elements at sea, they are now battling ignorance ashore. They are drawing on the economics research of Nobel-winner Elinor Ostrom to argue for the sustainability of their communities. They are marshalling technology and media, including documentary film-making, and accessing political networks in order to deliver their message to those in power and to their fellow voters. They are organising: island fishermen have formed IIMRO, the Irish Islands Marine Resource Organisation, which is currently shepherding through the Irish houses of parliament a bill to secure heritage licences for Irish island fishermen.

Defiance is resource-dependent, and diminishing populations struggle to keep up the fight. Its potential human cost is captured graphically in a testimony from the Blasket Islands. There, in January 1947, the death of Seáinín Neain Ó Cearna at twenty-four years of age precipitated the eventual evacuation of the island in 1953. The tragic circumstances of Seáinín's death of meningitis, at a time when the battery-operated telephone provided by the government to the islanders had failed yet again, made the islanders, and the Ó Cearna family in particular, bitterly angry. His brother Maidhc wrote in his 2013 memoir:

> When we got into the island, poor Seán, I couldn't look at him. He was lying dead on the bed in my father's bedroom. He had been dead for three days. Cáit had cleaned him up, washed his body with soap and water, and dressed him up, but decomposition had already started to set in. Everybody was crying. We put Seán in the coffin and nailed the lid shut. There was no wake; there was no time. The lifeboat was waiting. …
>
> When we got to Dingle, the medical people said they had to determine the cause of death. My father told them to write down that the government killed him. He was very angry and so was I. We felt that the government should have installed a better radio system or provided a

> motorboat – anything to improve the safety of the people living on the island. This was just the kind of situation we warned could happen.

Tragedies like these and their ramifications are rightfully remembered and commemorated and serve to forewarn future generations of the impact of ignorance and negligence and of daring to live on an island in their shadow. But there are also more positive narratives of resolve, resilience and renewal to forearm them for the road ahead, e.g. Jerry Early's song 'I'll Go' about the courageous Arranmore Lifeboat rescue of eighteen Dutch sailors in 1940; sales of the single (via iTunes) continue to raise money for the upkeep of a newly erected monument. Each type of narrative serves to consolidate the attitudes of islanders who weave through the fabric of their existence the tales that help them to survive and thrive. Their lesson is that, while the price of island life may be high in monetary and emotional terms, so too are its rewards.

Norman Ackroyd (ELEVEN)

Inishbofin Sound

Andrew McNeillie
(CLUTAG BLOG, 2018)

Richard Murphy

Between our roads, a handful of years,
and then the past all round these shores
haunted by the ghost of the *Ave Maria*
telling the epic of the Cleggan Disaster,
holding today up to yesterday's mirror –
the world kept afloat by running repairs.

The landlady of Oliver's Seafood Bar
calls – from a tale or song of long ago? :
'Your heart beats when you hear my name,'
she laughs and tells it him again, 'Joe, Joe,
your heart beats when you hear my name.'
So Cleggan resounds, the day set fair

waiting for the ferry. And my head full
of memories of sailing to an island –
of corncrakes in the month of June
grinding out their tuneless tune:
such unlikely music. My heart unmanned
to hear it once more, to hear it still

on Inishbofin by Cromwell's fort
and the blind tower, as the ferry departs
and leaves me caught in '68 and '69 again,
days on the cusp of violence as they were,
reminded of all those broken hearts
from 'Droit de Seigneur' to Aughrim –

holding yesterday up to today's mirror
and reading in its guilt-edged frame
the old story of a poet's prescience
who saw tomorrow the day before.
Small wonder then that I should say:
my heart beats when I hear his name.

Richard Murphy (ELEVEN)

from *The Price of Stone Notebooks*

Connemara Quay

23 April 1982

There's always an excuse for not writing … either I've slept too little or too long … wake up and look at the garden, where the yellow flowers of dandelions are turning into clocks whose time will be blown away before tonight … now is the time to retrieve some of the nothing that remains of the past, by writing words that lead from place to place across the sands of memory … Rosleague, the Diamond Mountain, the Quay at Letterfrack … follow those words down to the shore where other words may bring other memories to light … such as razor-fish that stick up their shells in the sun on a beach at low water … but go gently … or else, as you approach to catch them, they will sink and vanish in the sand.

Focus on the mystery of fishing boats that had never put to sea or caught a fish, but lay rotting in skirts of seaweed at the Quay where, led by your brother, you escaped on bicycles from Rosleague and Nanny's desire to keep you spotlessly clean to explore their foul decay … lifting a slimy hatch to peep into the murk of an engine room that every high tide would fill with salt water, which, on every ebb, would spout and weep from bilges through planks eaten by worms.

'Those engines,' they say, 'have not been started since before you were born' … why ever not? … the big house, looking down its nose with the complacency of not-so-old money, blames the ignorance and laziness of the people, and the de Valera government for destroying their markets and paying the Irish to speak Gaelic to their children … but the Gaelic speakers blame the crowd in Dublin, the lawyers, the banks and the businessmen, who sent back word to the Sergeant and the Postmistress in Letterfrack that the boats were to stay where they were and no one was to take them out fishing on pain of imprisonment for contempt of court.

So it remains a mystery as to why a fleet of fishing-boats should lie idle at a quay in Connemara, year after year of misery for the families of fishermen, boats eaten by creatures of the sea they were designed to harvest.

That summer of my eighth birthday – Chris was a year and eight months older – our 'frail but indefatigable mother', so 'delicate' that we boys were told to be careful not to upset her with our bold and selfish behaviour, went to England, waving goodbye with tears in her eyes from Aunty Kay's brown Humber Tourer with the canvas hood down, to receive a medal from King George the Fifth at Buckingham Palace, for saving countless lives during the great malaria epidemic, which, thanks to Nanny's care and, don't forget, God's help, we had survived in Ceylon the previous year … and we were thrilled when our mother brought back to Ireland her MBE with cuttings of her picture in the newspapers.

So the question arose, as it often did, with her and with Nanny, thinking of our future:

> What do you want to be when you grow up? … you can't spend your life playing the fool in Connemara, getting nowhere … you might end up like one of those boats that never caught a fish, obstructing the quay that was built to relieve dire poverty but never did any good … the people are hopeless here and their children will have to emigrate … you'd better

> become a doctor and save the sick from dying … remove lead pellets from their stomachs if they've swallowed them by accident … discover a cure for TB, typhoid, diphtheria, blood poisoning or lock-jaw, all the diseases you are most afraid of catching … that's why you are going to boarding school … so when you grow up you can do something useful, as your father has done for twenty-five years, helping the natives in Ceylon to be better educated and to govern themselves in the future … if you work hard you could win medals and become famous … if you can, if you can, if you can … you'll be a man, my son.

I knew by heart most of Kipling's poem 'If', which Nanny had bought in Colombo and hung instead of a picture above my bed … the capitals decorated on a cardboard print … 'If you can keep your head when all about you … Are losing theirs and blaming it on you.'

Sat 24 April 1982

Why did the figure of eight impress me so gravely in a dream that I have remembered it since the day before yesterday? … image of equipoise and completion, of things that add up, of evenness and grace … a male number described in a female form … beautiful as the flight of a fulmar off its nest in a cliff on High Island.

She rang from the North … said she liked 'Planter Stock', which I read to her on the phone … may not come back until Monday … said the poems are beginning to fit together like a jigsaw puzzle, each one makes a bit more sense … so keep going deeper into self-discovery.

If only I can go on … how near the brink of failure I came last night in having a row with my friend over his coming home late from the city centre … how precarious the balance of passion and control in the figure of eight … if there's a fault, it's less likely to be in my friend than in me, so I should not explode.

If I calm down, a poem might come from a dream of what ought to have been achieved by the erection of that stone quay … a phallic symbol forever hard but impotent stuck in the estuarine vulva of the motherland … dream of the halibut and cod that might have been caught on deep shoals that had not been fished for three hundred years

… of the sea's riches that would fertilise the impoverished land and feed the poor … of the teeming shoals of words I would haul into epics of the sea that had kept me in a Connemara dream, as if in Tír na n-Óg, combating failure and a feeling of estrangement in my heart by writing poetry, much of which was rejected, for a long time of obstinate unfruitful perseverance … years blown away like the seed of a dandelion propagating weeds.

The Quay might be personified in the poem, whose span may extend across my failure to live up to the promise expected of me in my youth … now including my failure to marry my lover in spite of her producing a son.

Fishermen personify their boats as women … their companions on board are exclusively men, but every part of the boat is sexualised and treated with affection as female.

The poem could be about the failure of a marriage promised between the young green earth and the old grey sea … a flawed enterprise causing craft to be wasted in idleness, desire frustrated by the law, confidence lost in despair brought on by abandonment … and the turning of that abandonment, lost confidence, illicit desire, and a dream of marriage that failed into a work of art … some of this might be condensed with ambiguity into the sonnet.

Tues 27 April 1982

Dream last night … along a river bank in Devon I am wading through long wet grass that might be corn, through which yellow and blue flowers are thrusting their copious heads … I should not be trespassing here, trampling the crop before it is harvested … but O the joy of seeing such fertile beauty springing from the ground … not far from here, Ted Hughes has a secret place, a tree-hut or a lime tree bower, where he hides himself away to do his writing … with an unlisted telephone number you would not dream of asking him for, not even in this dream.

She returned with her child yesterday evening. I cooked some haddock here, and brought it down to her house for supper. Still hates the place. Wants to sell it as soon as it can be got ready for sale, and move abroad. A new but not unexpected disturbance. Hates me for not letting her live with me 'happily ever after'. I wish I could.

Connemara Quay

I should have done this, that and all those things
Goodwill intended when I was designed
To end the poor land's hunger. Failure brings
Catches that slip through nets too close to mind.

Men stood me up here, promising that I'd be
Their godsend: ocean would provide more food.
The green earth should have married the grey sea,
But fell foul of her storms, her moody tide.

Attached by strings of warps to my stone head,
Fine wooden craft came, to be overcome
By torpor. Keels took root in silt of seabed,
Ribbed frames rotted in a frayed hemp dream.

You played in these hulks half a century ago.
What did you think you might do? Now you know.

27 Apr 1982

Pier Bar

4–13 Oct 1982

Tall grey barrack of rendered stone, three storeys high … old as the fishery dock that its white sash windows dominate … watering-hole of islanders weather-bound in Cleggan … 'No boat will reach Bofin today … maybe not for a week … with the seas going to the skies over the Stags … dark clouds ready to pour out of the heavens … fill them up, Major!'

That's what Major liked to hear … pensioner of World War One … said to have returned from Mesopotamia with his back bent in the shape of a curragh ... might not be true ... others say he started to bend his back after the war in order to gain a British army pension ... married a teacher and bought the Pier Bar for next to nothing ... previous owner out of luck ... the fool had thrown a customer's fishing nets that were drying on the Pier Bar fence into the sea.

A former sergeant major, Major could bark orders ... he didn't like to hear a carpenter whine, 'I'll fix your door-lock now in a minute, but give me time' ... there was plenty of time in those days ... saving it got you nowhere unless to England or America ... he ran the bar with his daughter, who adored Dada so much that she never got married ... her tongue could sting a drunk man like a wasp ... sweet as honey to a tourist.

Trammel nets hung from the ceiling ... fishermen, when there were fish, would squander money here ... boys and old men, heroes of tiller and foredeck ... seldom a woman, unless a tourist, entered the bar ... mothers and wives, sisters and daughters, waited at home for father or brother or son to return from the sea or the pub ... families often deprived if not bereaved ... Major, like a grizzled old bird of prey perched on a barstool, kept a calculating eye on the boats landing people or fish on the pier ... counting the boxes brought up from the *St John*, a small converted hooker in which he owned a share.

But mostly the pier was idle ... worm-eaten boats tied up in the dock or abandoned to rot on the ground ... old men in the bar, deploring the present, would glorify the past when thousands of barrels of salted herring were sold in Cleggan to buyers from New York and St Petersburg ... when forty nobbies, each crewed by seven men who were never afraid to go out, would moor side by side at the pier ... good times that will never return, now that foreign trawlers are allowed to suck up the fish with machines like vacuum cleaners sweeping the ocean bed ... 'that can't be right'.

Picture yourself disguised in a skipper's cap and yellow oilskins ... sailing the *Ave Maria* from Cleggan pier to Inishbofin with a cargo of anglers or trippers, day after day, summer weather permitting ... tourists you indulge for seven hours on the boat in the sun, the wind and the spray, on tide rips and shoals, reeling up pollock and mackerel on ten-feathered jigs, becoming ankle deep in fish … after their safe return imbued with the buoyancy of the sea, you join them in the Pier Bar for more entertainment … with fish scales on your sleeves and boots … a wad of fishy bank notes in your pocket.

Now I must try to distil a beery flow of words into a sonnet that gives a touch of bar-room pleasure … a feeling for the danger, the love, and the intoxication of the sea … as Dr Johnson wrote, 'The only end of writing is to enable the readers better to enjoy life, or better to endure it.'

I hated business, but got embroiled out of necessity and the wish to belong, to impatriate myself in that distant impoverished bleak corner of Connemara … the whole question of who or what is a tourist, who or what is a native, becomes questionable in the Pier Bar … truly I was a native, though a drunk nationalist once accused me of having forged my birth certificate … but I spoke like a tourist acting the part of a fisherman, becoming a voice for the fishermen … and became, in the eyes of journalists, the Cleggan fisherman-poet … a maritime figure attracting tourists to visit a rugged impoverished land-and-seascape … having written the copy and arranged for ten thousand brochures advertising the *Ave Maria* and the *True Light* to be printed at the Dolmen Press, publishers of my poetry … earning as epitaph, 'Murphy put Cleggan and Inishbofin on the map.'

Trying to simplify the complexity of my life … becoming a fisherman in order to write poetry from experience of the sea … and wearing the mask of a fisherman to conceal the poet I wanted to prove myself to be … much duplicity in living that split level life … and counter-cultural obstinacy in trying to revive the art of narrative poetry that Joyce was said to have killed, though he reinvented it, with *Ulysses.*

Bring the sea into the bar … sea rhythms and sounds … boat rhythms … pressure and kick of the tiller under my arm and the hard roundness of its carved oak knob in my hand … smell of oakum and tar … name the boats … *True Light* … *St John* … *Topaz* … *Volunteer* … *Star of the West* … not for nostalgia … there's more to say than to sigh about the sea at this crossing of a boundary in my life … my literal transgressing.

> 'What time will the mail boat leave for Bofin?'
> 'When she's ready to go, if the weather is fit. You'd better be aboard, because she won't wait.'
> 'How will we know when she's ready?'
> 'You'll see her leaving the pier.'

That's how it was in Cleggan in the early nineteen-sixties … the black pint of Guinness XX stout cost one shilling and four pence, when men earned twenty shillings equal to £1 a day on the roads, and the doctor charged the same to see a patient for ten minutes … sawdust on the floor of the bar … Major tapping a barrel … cooper's art dying out … Galway hookers almost extinct … trying, how hard I tried, to revive the past … digressing down backward lanes of hawthorn and hazelnut that might lead to glory or desolation … in a moribund place with much talk of the dead … 'he went fast, the poor man' … 'better men than you tried that and failed, you're wasting your time' … 'our plumber hadn't his new car a week but he'd taken his wife to seven funerals'.

'Fill them up, Major!' … that's what Major liked to hear … looking back at myself in the Pier Bar mirror, I seem determined to stay afloat the more they predicted 'Murphy will sink the *Ave Maria* and drown everybody aboard' … as I nearly did … trying to prove another kind of potency after my marriage had failed … by succeeding in a difficult action of no importance but dare devil risk … wallowing in troughs of waves with a boy whose forceful courage saved me from sinking on the open sea … a digression of joy in a life of digressions, as the sonnet may sing.

'Fill them up, Major!' … again and again … till the wind is shaking the door like an angry drunk locked out on a winter's night … who above all were you hoping to see, coming from London, to turn the sad faces, sunk in their weather-bound torpor, bright with the prospect of fishing again, but Tony White? … redeemer and prime entertainer … who made you all feel better by his presence … who, when talking to you in a crowd, without offending others who may have hoped to catch his eye, could make you feel his eyes on you alone.

Pier Bar

For donkey's years I've stood in lashing rain
Unbudgingly, casting a fish-hawk eye
On dock-tied hookers. How could we regain
Lost native custom tourist cash would buy?

Snug in my torporific trammelled air
Of a dream village roped to a lifeless quay,
I can help you play with an old craft, but your
Ten-feathered jigs will get fouled up at sea.

What brings you back to me, having said goodbye
To bull-head shillings in my handcarved till,
Unless to greet, reflected through my dry
Distillery, the dead friend whose glass I fill?

Why drown so carefully with mosshung chain
On sound moorings? Rig me. I'll entertain.

13 Oct 1982

New Forge
13–20 Oct 1982

Now to the New Forge … the house that embedded me in Connemara for thirteen years … built by my neighbours in Cleggan after my father died. He had spent most of his life in resplendent British colonies, while I chose to live under clouds among Irish Catholic nationalists near his and my mother's roots … on the ocean edge of his father's large desolate Church of Ireland parish of Omey. The shock of his death confirmed my desire to build a house of local granite … where poetry could make rubble fragments of my life integral as random stones in a course of masonry … stone bonded by stone.

Warm pink to dark red colours of the granite ruins of cottages dating back to the famine in our neighbourhood reminded me of the walls of a tavern in a small Breton fishing village, where shortly after Patricia and I had met as mature students in Paris, she brought me to stay in the gloom and gales of December 1954 … the wine was dark and rough as the sea … and there we decided to marry.

Six years after our divorce, wanting to build a larger house in Cleggan, where I was living up a narrow lane behind the Pier Bar in a cottage called the Old Forge, I found and bought the granite of seven ruins … saving it from burial in foundations of new roads.

The widowed mother of my mates on the *Ave Maria* and the *True Light* gave me a site next to the forge garden commanding an easterly view over the village and across Cleggan Bay as far as the Diamond Mountain above Letterfrack. A Scottish architect, with roots in Dunfermline and a London practice, who chartered the *True Light* for a family holiday each August, designed the house fulfilling my wish for the façade to reconcile the romantic charm of an Irish cottage with the classical grace of an Anglo-Irish house in a demesne. Our mason modelled his dry stonework on the style of an early Celtic oratory.

All this detail will not fit in a sonnet … too much rain on a mountain turns a waterfall into a gush … but memories need to be refreshed before a few may be channelled and compressed into sonnet form.

The walls of my new house in Cleggan rose while I was a guest for two months at the Colonnade Club on the Lawn of the University designed by Jefferson in Virginia. Before the house was roofed with sea-green slates from Cumbria, Ted Hughes, who was staying with Assia and the children at Cleggan Farm across the bay, had suggested calling it the New Forge. For ten years I enjoyed living there, feeling that now I belonged in a house that belonged to me … the rock and shell of my forged identity as a poet … where I finished *The Battle of Aughrim* followed by *High Island* … until shaken by the sudden death in February 1976 of Tony White … and in September the following year Patricia's suicide.

Notebooks written during that interval remind me of how my passion for building in granite, combined with my love of the beautiful ceramist, our engagement, and her desire to live with me, but my need for a split-level union, resulted in my decision to build a pottery studio for her in my garden at the New Forge … and how the rising tension of the rising cost, combined with my faithlessness, resulted in the breach of our engagement … and how, while finishing the studio for my books and writing, I was forced to sell the Hexagon.

Among notes of desire, conflict, anger and remorse, written at the New Forge in the month between my fiftieth birthday and the shocking death of Patricia from an overdose of alcohol and barbiturates, there's a poem of one continuous sentence in long lines of free verse. I composed it in the twilight of the 18th August 1977 under a skylight in a small bedroom, two nights after I had given up the habit of drinking pints of stout in the Pier Bar before or after dinner, and was feeling a thirst for alcohol. Sitting on the edge of the bed with the notebook open on my knees, regretting that I had ever started to build the studio, and feeling harassed by the process of building, I finished this poem in twenty minutes without a correction or a break, and called it 'The Price of Stone':

> How much it hurts me to tidy up when all my papers are
> heaped on the desk in a three-month mess,
> To regain control of this drift of days I've lost in
> my passion for building in granite,
> And face the bills I must pay by leaving the house
> that has cost me too much to enlarge,
> Where I passed the time too quickly preparing a place for
> the future to work within soundproof walls,
> So never had a moment in the present for writing about
> the moments that were passing away:
> How much it hurts to see the destruction that all good
> building, even the best, must cause,
> Not only the hedges that had to be first cut down
> before the foundations were dug,
> But deeper cuts through veins in the mind that carried

the blood of memory through the brain:
How much it hurts me to have neglected all this summer
the friends whom I might have seen,
But for my mad obsession of building more rooms
to entertain them in time to come:
Because these times are apt to elude us, we die, or our
friends drop dead before we can say
I'd love you to see and enjoy the house whose construction
has kept us entirely apart.

Dennis [O'Driscoll] now thinks 'The Price of Stone' would be a good title for the sonnets as a sequence ... and in that case I must think of another title for my spontaneous overflow of powerful feelings in twenty-four lines ... such as 'Stone Mania'.

Here at Knockbrack, a flimsy house on granite foundations, I have tried to sublimate my passion for building into the making of sonnets ... often harassed by the labour ... and the paradox that inspiration cannot be forced, nor will it flow without work ... so now I must labour to vocalise the building that became a carapace I had to shed to grow.

After putting the New Forge in the hands of a Dublin auctioneer, I felt vulnerable as a crayfish coming out of its barnacled shell ... there's a technical word for this process – exuviate – which sounds just as awkward as its meaning ... when rain lashed the walls that sheltered me in the house, the granite glowed like the shell of a crayfish in a wicker pot hauled from the seabed on to a deck ... I loved that house but I had to move ... never to be integral again but to grow more articulate with age ... so 'New Forge' will be a poem of metamorphosis, from stone into poetry.

There were many obstacles to selling in 1979 ... a strike cutting off our telephone and mail for four months, no petrol for two, no bids at an auction except off the wall ... until chance brought a large family on holiday in July ... who, seeing a red granite gable rising above 'pleasure ground' garden walls with a sign reading HOUSE FOR SALE, bought into a dream from which I was waking. But when they woke from their dream, after schools for their eight children reopened in September, they leased the house for a peppercorn rent to the Brothers of Charity, who ran a home for the mentally handicapped seventy miles away.

Since then, the New Forge, designed for writing poetry under an attic skylight above an oasis of books in a desert of literacy, has been changed into a weekend retreat for men with the minds of toddlers ... why? ... because failures caused by my folly in split-heartedness compelled me to obey the haunting injunction of Rilke, 'You must change your life.'

Leaving the west and settling in south county Dublin gave me the stimulus of conversation with poets and critics, especially Dennis. Finding a house that faced mountains and turned its back on the sexually liberated city, whose lights beckoned in the ten miles distant dark, gave me freedom to write poems of displacement and estrangement set in the modern world ... exposed to the city's moral radiation.

But how strong the pressure of Connemara to bring me back to where I was deeply implanted ... even this morning on my run in the dark before dawn to the top of Killiney Hill and around the Folly clockwise I thought of offering the buyers a bargain if they would exchange the New Forge for Knockbrack ... umbilical cordite.

Predators around a crevice ... waiting for the carapace to be shed ... starlings infesting shrubbery at nightfall ... brain-damaged men filling the vacated shell with nonsensical noise ... trampling heather and rue from Slieve Donard across the border ... twittering of ghosts in my ear on a pillow.

Random stone laid without mortar in regular courses gives most musical pleasure to the eye ... with crevices deep enough for blue tits to nest in safety between the stones ... sparkle of mica in a sunbeam on granite after rain ... stone bonded by stone making symmetry out of fragments ... alternative housing for ambiguous needs ... in a crevice or on a crag.

New Forge

From derelict huts of Cleggan rock I grew
To look most natural here, though I began
Strangely; your Breton stone design drawn through
A London architect's Dunfermline plan.

For thirteen years this perfect place to write
Creviced you in my Galway garden bond;
Green Cumbrian slates letting in attic light;
Slieve Donard heather's white crossborder stand.

Why did you sell me? Did you feel trapped here,
Compelled in cold blood to exuviate
My hard pink shell? A Dublin auctioneer
Hammered you free to grow articulate.

Our union was split level. Now I'm used
To keep old men with infant minds amused.

Wed 20 Oct 1982

Andrew McNeillie (FOUR)

Where Art Meets Sea: Ackroyd, Heaney, Murphy, Dunn

For a while I thought to dip into my pocket for one of his Aran etchings, for obvious reasons of personal association. But in the end I plunged like a gannet, head-on, for the tumultuous wonder that is 'Inishbofin Sound'. I was in the best place in the world to do so: the inland equivalent of Bass Rock for all members of the archipelagic species, all Ackroydal *islomaniacs*, like myself: 1 Morocco Street, Bermondsey, the converted warehouse-workshop-gallery and penthouse residence of the man himself, in London's old leather market district.

So now I own two Ackroyds, the other being 'Postscript' (a gift from the artist). In that work, as you see, Seamus Heaney's poem of that title is ghosted over an etching of a trinity of island, mountainous dark clouds, and a scattering of soaring and plummeting white seabirds. The location is presumably somewhere down 'the Flaggy Shore' of Co. Clare. A reproduction of 'Inishbofin Sound' may also be found in the Royal Academy publication *A Line in the Water* (2009), a collaboration with the poet Douglas Dunn, while 'Postscript' appears in the catalogue to *Irish Etchings 1987–2008*, a touring exhibition that came inland in March this year at The Fine Art Society, New Bond Street.

As 'Postscript' suggests and as *A Line in the Water* confirms, poetry is important to Ackroyd. He loves the word. There are photocopies of favourite poems pinned up about his studio. And he likes to collaborate with poets, to pair poem and image. (*A Line in the Water* is not his first major collaboration with Dunn. Their *Pictish Coast* dates back with their friendship twenty-five years.) Otherwise, his work is silent (plug your ears against the storm) and as free from narrative as an individual work of art can be (but button up your 'oiler', as they used to call an oilskin on Inis Mór, pop a couple of *Sea-Legs*). He doesn't do what the late Kyffin Williams, another great sea- and landscape artist (and fellow Royal Academician), could seldom resist doing: that is, supplement the self-sufficient image with a verbal account. This is a point *A Line in the Water* underlines. Its etchings, interleaved here and there by fifteen new poems by Douglas Dunn, bear neither title nor caption. No words stand between the work and the viewer. If you want to know the title or location of what you have seen, rather than continue looking into the form and texture of what is before your eyes, turn to the gazetteer and thumbnails at the back.

Above all Ackroyd wants your first encounter to be with the image, and not for you to say, 'Oh, that's a beautiful picture' of High Island, say, or of Black Sod Bay. The subject is the land- or seascape as framed from the world, for the occasion. Instressed into its inscape are the elements, the drama of light and shade, wind and rain, and shine, and storm or calm at sea, first snatched from the air, into a working sketch-book, or etched on the spot. Ackroyd's great subject is quite as much 'weather' as 'place', as Douglas Dunn has remarked. Equally involved, too, is the way the etching process is as fickle and spectacular in its effects as the weather itself. The result typically seems nothing short of miraculous, and irreducible. Look into an Ackroyd image and know there is no critical attention it won't weather, no matter the marked absence of the human figure. The viewer is the solitary human presence in these images. In the visual arts, perhaps only ceramics, or the casting of bronzes, come near to etching for immediate hazard and serendipity.

Ackroyd's is also an art that knows how diving gannets may best be represented as being as black as cormorants. There are, real art always tells us, startling ways of being true to life, and light. At the same time, he wants to embrace the word, in a sister art and to juxtapose, even conjoin the two. Of course, whether we come to image or poem, we do so with baggage, none the less. *We* are not innocent. I dived into my shallow bank account, at risk of breaking my overdraft, if not my neck, to buy 'Inishbofin Sound', not simply for the incontestable beauty of it, but because its subject also prompted me to remember the poetry of Richard Murphy.

I came a little late to discovering Norman Ackroyd's work, as things turned out, yet life had schooled me for the moment for decades. I grew up in sight of islands, and wheeling seabirds, and near-islands, like the Great Orme's Head, and classic coastal promontories like Penmaenmawr. I sailed to islands and fished round them. And I read about them, as from the day in my mid-teens I first set eyes on J.M. Synge's account of Aran, to life-altering effect. I have been an island-dweller. As to Ackroyd, the moment of true encounter had gone on ahead to lie in wait to run me aground again, to float me off …

Or not quite *the* moment. For I have to say, the first Ackroyd I ever saw, on an otherwise bare white kitchen wall, was 'St Catherine's Hill above Winchester' (1982). It did not have the means or the subject to bowl me over. That can't be said of Richard Murphy's first collection of poems *Sailing to an Island* (1963). It swept me away on a current of excitement the moment I opened it, in Green's Bookshop, hard by Dublin's Trinity College, in 1965, just after my nineteenth birthday. It swept me away. It made me green with envy, with its sea-green typographical jacket, its beautiful typography (with those raised, double-limned capitals opening each poem, such as next year were to be found in Heaney's *Death of a Naturalist* (more green sorrow and delight)). Murphy's title poem, his 'Last Galway Hooker' with its occasional internal rhymes and bold alliteration, his 'Cleggan Disaster', all metamorphosed the dream before my eyes into a vision of astonishing beauty. But then *Sailing to an Island* was a key book for Norman Ackroyd too, and Richard Murphy's spiritual adventure is not so far from being a version of Ackroyd's own. As is that of Tim Robinson, the great Proustian master of our new *islomaniacal* and liminal chorography.

But Ackroyd chooses not to live the liminal or reclusive life. He may well be 'a force of nature' as Douglas Dunn describes him but he works the margin from the centre. He is a metropolitan force too, and, by birth and upbringing in South Leeds, an urban man in his soul. So he sees beauty in, and loves to haunt, has no perceivable aversion to, that isle of dogs, the city of London.

I reflected on this last March as I stepped down New Bond Street, to the private view of 'Irish Etchings'. Here was a prospect of the world turned inside-out, among the *cognoscenti*. I'd already received a listing of works exhibited and I relished the prospect of inspecting in the flesh 'High Island from Inishbofin – Force 10' (having known at first hand, such west coast conditions, perilously); and I dwelt on Murphy's lines about: '... the boat that belched its crew / Dead on the shingle in the Cleggan disaster' ('Sailing to an Island'), having known and lamented two men lost at sea, personally; and recalling, from Murphy's elegy to the Cleggan tragedy, how:

> From the village of Rossadilisk they lost sixteen
> And from Bofin nine.

How 'one man above all' among them was left blind, and all that felt as ancient as Greece. And I thought how far such experience is, and ever will be, from London's Mayfair, Norman Ackroyd notwithstanding.

*

The 'private view', in a small gallery at least, is a peculiar convention in which neither viewing nor privacy prevail. I turned from the street into a gannetry of gabble, beaks and elbows, of meet-and-greet and gargle, like a book-launch on a choppy sea. Everyone wants to buttonhole and congratulate the artist, to corner the hero of the hour, the famous one, hitherto perhaps only admired from afar, like the first solitary gannet you ever saw. Now for once he's down on the rock, among the crowd.

As in a whirlpool, energies are less concentrated at the edge of things, where the pictures hang. By the time I arrived most of the viewing seemed to have been done and I was able to go round the walls twice with only the occasional impatient peck at (and from), other latecomers, or devotees of true stamina. So here was 'High Island from Inishbofin – Force 10' (2007). It blew me away. 'Extraordinary obliteration of white wave-surge,' I jotted in my notebook. As if to prove, if not the inadequacy of words, the inadequacy of *my* words. Here too, before 'Study of Sun & Rain Galway Bay' (1999), I noted 'the pyramid trope', of sheer light. It recurred in the staggering achievement of 'The Three Sisters, Dingle' – as black pyramids of seemingly disembodied and frangible, geology. However brilliantly they are reproduced for publication, as in *A Line in the Water*, nothing, and certainly no digital image on a screen, can begin to recreate the texture and scale of the thing itself.

Ackroyd is a celebrant. In many ways he sings from the same hymn-sheet as Heaney. Though Heaney is grounded otherwise, Antaeus-like, in the dark side of human aspiration and struggle, on a European scale. Still, both Ackroyd and Heaney can, in Heaney's words, 'catch the heart off guard and blow it open' too. It takes visionary courage and a special awareness of life's mystery and human limitation to celebrate life, and it takes a certain humour too and wit. Heaney crosses the page here for a very good reason. The version of 'Irish Etchings' I saw at The Fine Art Society Show, included 'Postscript'. But what delayed me more, more I confess than any other work in the exhibition, was the piece entitled 'West Coast', another nod in the poet's direction, scarcely oblique.

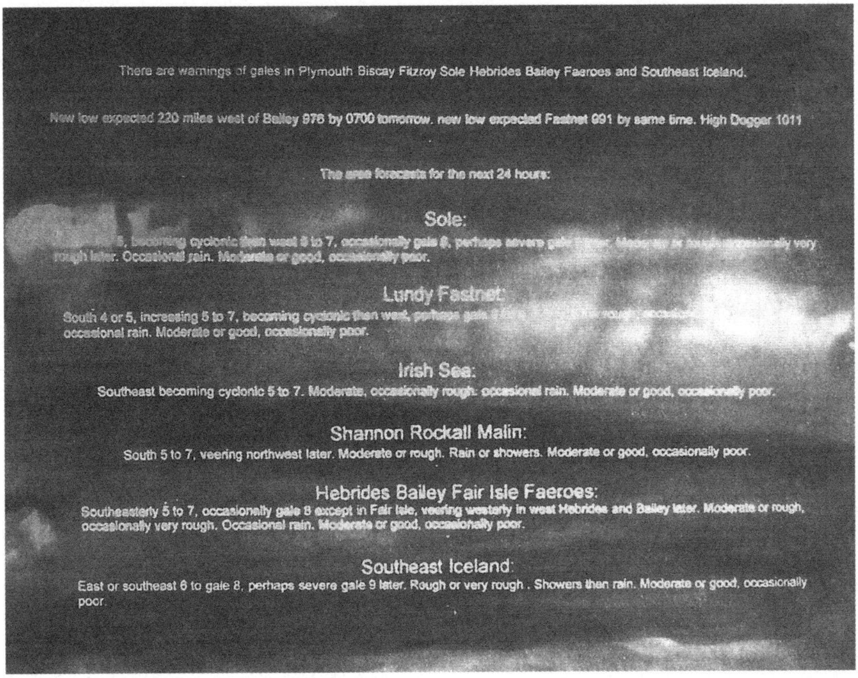

West Coast

In the manner of 'Postscript', 'West Coast' uses the ghost of a text too. This time, as you see, the words appear to derive from an actual 'Shipping Forecast' bulletin, or else have been very convincingly contrived to imitate one: 'There are warnings of gales in Plymouth Biscay Fitzroy Sole Hebrides Bailey Faeroes and Southeast Iceland / New low expected 220 miles west of Bailey 976 by 0700 tomorrow. new low expected Fastnet 991 by same time. High Dogger 1011.' Stare at the ceiling in the dark and imagine it, imagine your way on the stormy airwaves, riding out life's journey, life's storm. Gaze into this picture. Consider the 'area forecasts for the next 24 hours'. You know and don't know it by heart. As if to prove it, Ackroyd obliterates some of it in white waves, like radio interference. So that what's in store for 'Sole' doesn't all come through: '[text whited out] … becoming cyclonic then west 5 to 7, occasionally gale 8, perhaps severe gales'. So it continues, with: 'occasional rain. Moderate or good, occasionally poor'.

Had I not broken my bank already, here, I thought, was the Ackroyd I'd buy there and then, that evening.

As we all know, it wasn't that Heaney invented this found-sound poetry. It was invented by the Air Ministry in 1924 for decidedly practical not poetical purposes. If you can in reality put a sheet of paper between such things. Those in peril on the deep, as a way of life, have their own theology and poetics, and don't you doubt it. But the power of Heaney's poem derives precisely from the fact that scarce a person living in our islands does not know what the Shipping Forecast is and how it's rhythmed. This is what Heaney saw and saw into. He seized upon a common burden, in the language of the tribe, whether its members be landlocked at Mossbawn or in the English midlands, or seaward-bound from Kilronan or Tarbert. For the majority of us, our lives being so remote from those of the Met Office's intended audience, the forecast might as well be an incantation in Latin, or a prayer before bedtime, at the brink of the foundering dream element, nightmare on the rocks increasing gale 8, perhaps severe gale 9 later. For those potentially in peril its shorthand doesn't beat about the bay but gets straight to the point, where the peril is. To those of us more securely cabined ashore, it can acquire a comic touch. So parodists like to show, fitting to its marine-morse echo-soundings and rhythms any number of airy nonsenses. But here in Heaney's poem are wit and potential tragedy cast away together, in movingly redeemed cliché.

'West Coast' delayed me and it made me smile to myself. It reminded me of storm-force winter nights on Inis Mór, the island plunging into the Atlantic, holding her course, as if labouring to ferry us to exile in America. Next I was distracted by more words among the images, as my sonar picked up on the talk in the tide of private viewers … 'Best smoked haddock in town …!' from someone in a smart blazer and cufflinks, several sheets to the wind, who'd been where? Sailing close to the bottom of a bottle. 'Oysters to die for …' from Galway Bay. '… Sick as a dog, off Skellig Michael … Never again!' from one who'd accompanied Ackroyd on a sketching trip, perhaps. So ran a chorus of well-voyaged Ackroyd devotees, now nose-diving like gannets into their wine-glasses, safe as houses in Mayfair … tottering about, 'moderate or good, occasionally. new low expected by 0700 hours tomorrow'. And here was the artist himself, as I eavesdropped him, describing an incident at Black Sod Bay to an enquiring lady. 'The wind was so strong it raised the water up' – to speak biblically – 'hundreds of feet in the air' and his car parked above 'moved on its suspension, alarmingly, to and fro …' – motion even more disturbing than Heaney's 'big soft buffetings', but of the same kind.

Seamus Heaney and Norman Ackroyd in the Quod Bar of the Old Bank Hotel, Oxford, 2007.

*

I speak of Heaney, for obviously pertinent reasons. But the poet of the occasion, the chosen one, the true, active collaborator, is Douglas Dunn. Aware that Douglas and I know each other, Norman rang me one day to ask would I like to join them at the Royal Academy. They were to spend as long as it took to co-sign the various editions of *A Line in the*

Water (Deluxe limited, Limited and Standard), with a break for lunch. So there I found myself one Tuesday morning in the holy of holies, the Academy's General Assembly Room (in which Darwin first presented his *Origin of Species*), while a team of five people, two sporting blue rubber gloves, against damaging the books as they opened them at the signing page, organised a kind of assembly line, along and around the great table, and tried to police it, not entirely successfully, against confusion.

So unsigned books were unboxed at one end and re-boxed at the finishing line, the Deluxe ones with a signed insert to boot. Norman walked along the row of opened books signing them as he went, and talking; and Douglas ('given more to meditative stasis' as one of his poems puts it), sat as they were fed along to him. After the first ten copies were processed, he had a point when he turned sympathetically and suggested it was hardly a spectator sport. But as they signed, and Norman sang and extolled the genius of Haydn, or told us how lovely it had been yesterday to take a day off for once ('to be in the city with nothing to do while everyone else is working'), to visit St Mary Wolnoth (in Lombard Street) and St Magnus (at the Bridge Foot), and a courtyard where a beautiful Brazilian girl was selling coffee ... as they signed and talked, I sat distracted by the book. I gazed into its images, and brooded over Douglas's subtly fathoming poems, and found myself hooked deep by them. They led me to reflect on those observers 'In Whalsay's only pub' who know 'They're watching the real thing, the nerve of it, / The speed, the daring skill, sheer verve of it' as Norman seizes the day in his sketchbook. Like those folk on Whalsay, I knew I was also in the presence of the 'real thing', of two real things. Forget the famous ghosts on the walls, with the possible exception of a Constable: 'Rainstorm Over the Sea. *c.* 1824–28', like an ur-Ackroyd, in which, the caption explained: '... thunderous black clouds and torrential downpour have been painted rapidly to capture the fleeting nature of the scene.' (But it is Turner who is Ackroyd's acknowledged master, late Turner above all. And the late Francis Bacon the contemporary and friend whose work and philosophy of art he admires most.) Even when I wandered off, to browse the private galleries a while, I was drawn back, reminded of Whalsay (via MacDiarmid) by Fuseli's monstrous 'Thor Battering the Serpent of Midgard'.

Anyway, here I was, with these two, just off Piccadilly, at the heart of London's west end bustle. Hardly could we have been farther from the concerns of the Shipping Forecast, or from:

swaying kelp forests,
Undersea jungles, an ecologist's
Submarine visions of the Hebridean
Seabeds, the Minch's deep, dark, seldom seen
Submarine botanical landscapes, sea-trees
Waving farewell for ever to the sea's

Surfaces, to landfalls, daylight, sky, stars,
Always waving. Midnight oceanographers,
Improbable in diving suits – Good Lord,
He's smoking! – but we boot our way toward
Undersea dreamscapes, surreal, eel-fathomed
Depths in the super-dark, the silent, dumbed,
Unpainted and unwritten floors
Of the visionary deep, the great outdoors,
Geology, botany, sky, sea, birds, fish,
So commonplace to here it's just outlandish.
Now, listen. Here's what I heard today –
A corncrake in the Hebridean hay.

That from 'Working with Norman'. In his introduction Dunn calls their collaboration 'a slightly odd pairing', in terms of temperament as well as modes of expression. Slightly odd or not, it's a pairing that finds its own harmony, and all the stronger for the way in which the two men have pursued their task. Each has gone his way. There is no strained denial here of 'a basic difference between two grammars'. Time has passed between them, the poems coming in late, after deliberations and musings at a different set of horizons of thought and method, of history, past and present, of geology, archaeology, legend and semantic burden. It might be that Dunn is no *islomaniac* (the coinage derives from Lawrence Durrell) in the driven way that Ackroyd is, whose greater project extends to include even the Galapagos. But he speaks 'island' and its coastal dialects fluently. 'Remote,' he writes, 'unpopulated landscapes and seascapes convey a fundamental, bedrock timelessness, as well as a flavour of mutability that is simultaneously benign and chastening.' Today they secure us and anchor us, perhaps more than ever, havens of the mind, places of respite and recovery, in the face of a hectic and brutal world.

Do not forget either that Dunn is the author of *St Kilda's Parliament* (1981), with its 'poetry of ghosts' and of survivors looking 'across the stern / Of a departing vessel for the last time / At their gannet-shrouded cliffs'. He is the poet too, who, in that same volume, in the meditation 'Remembering Lunch', tells us: 'I long for more chances to walk along depopulated shores.' So this pairing with Ackroyd is not so odd at all. The poems in *A Line in the Water* stand alone, but they also marry with Ackroyd's images, and sing to them as groom to bride with perfect pitch, and nowhere better than in the poem 'A Coastal Wedding' (on the occasion of an actual wedding), the second, last stanza, of which reads:

> This coastal wedding reaches out beyond
> Private significance. It seeks to bond
> In meaningful water, that hard element
> Budged only by the Moon and astral powers.
> A moonlit highway on the Firth of Forth
> Includes reflected stars like water-flowers,
> Your wide night-view's nocturnal aquatint.
> For you are lovers of the East and North,
> The West, and waters, and your arts' no-place,
> Invention's home, that better place to be.
> You live in an estuarial embrace
> And there the sea meets art, and Art meets Sea.

Richard Sharland (TWELVE)

Photographs of the Ave Maria *Awaiting Restoration*

Robert Macfarlane (THREE)

On Tory Island

The painter Derek Hill was once asked how he imagined death. 'Probably,' he replied, 'it will be like going on a trip to Tory Island.' Halfway through the crossing to Tory from the Donegal mainland, I thought I understood what he meant. A Force Five was blowing, and our boat was whacking up off the waves in big bronco leaps and rolls. One of my companions, the artist Norman Ackroyd, was standing easily in the bow, a cigarette stuck to his lower lip and a paintbrush in his hand, knocking off a watercolour of the approaching island. Whereas I – well, I was kneeling queasily on the port-deck, hugging the side-rail, retching purple into the Atlantic and feeling at least halfway to death.

On reflection, though, I suspect Hill was thinking less of sea-sickness and more of sunshine when he made his comparison. For Tory is famed for the qualities of its light: its clarity, candour and amplitude. On the island, you recognise John Berger's description of the light on the Irish west coast as 'a weir pouring over the edge of Europe'. To sail to Tory is therefore to journey towards the light – and in this way might be said to resemble death.

*

Tory is three miles long and about a third of a mile wide. It lies eight miles or so off the coast of North Donegal, which makes it Ireland's most distant island. Seen from the south, it looks in profile like a bather floating on his back, skull to the east and feet bobbing in the west. During the biggest northerly gales, wave-spray is carried clear over the island by winds that, as one islander put it to me, 'could beat the head off you'.

Like most of Ireland's western islands, Tory was settled by early Celtic Christians. Today around 160 people live there, despite the efforts of the Irish government to lure the population back to the mainland, leaving them free to turn the island into a prison, a firing-range or a quarantine zone.

*

I'd come to Tory to begin a possible collaboration with Ackroyd: his images and my text. Ackroyd is Britain's most renowned etcher. He has spent the past twenty-five years travelling and etching the wild places of Britain and Ireland. The body of work he has produced is, to my mind, the most important artistic record of these landscapes since those of William Daniell and J.M.W. Turner in the early 1800s. Ackroyd's plan was that we explore the Donegal coast together this summer, and then travel to the Outer Hebrides next year: Barra, Lewis, St Kilda and the gannet-island of Sula. My seasickness on this short crossing boded ill for those far longer sea-journeys, if I joined him for them. But soon after landing I felt well again, and so we spent that afternoon exploring the island on foot. I walked and wrote, Ackroyd walked and sketched.

The north coast of Tory is a precipitous, wave-smashed theatre of pink and white granite: echoey sea-caves, two-hundred foot rock-stacks, and bird-filled zawns. Our path followed the cliff edge as neatly as a hem-line. Once or twice we flopped onto our bellies and peered over the brink, looking down to where the green sea shampooed the red rocks, kittiwakes described their cat's-cradle flight paths and gannets arrowed past.

Here and there, Ackroyd stopped to paint. Watching him work was a joy. He moves swiftly: with extreme concentration but without urgency. Ten minutes for each picture, rarely more. First he clamps his sketchbook to a backboard of wood, using a Myers bulldog-clip with rusty screws. Then he rummages in deep pockets for a candle stub or a white wax crayon to prepare the page. Rummage again: out comes a soft pencil or a fountain pen, to 'get the first lines off'. Dash, scribble, stab. He likes to hold his fountain pen back to front, so that the curved side of the nib releases wide smears of ink. Once the ink or lead is on the page, he then works it. Smudge, smear, wipe, using his nicotiney fingers, or a scrap of tissue, or a shred of sponge. Then the paint on top, if needed. All the while he smokes.

And suddenly the image emerges, like a plot resolving itself. What seemed to be scribble shimmers into a landscape: as though the image had been latent in the paper, and Ackroyd merely washed it over with a developing fluid. The work is done, he gives a grunt, and throws his sketchbook down with a slap onto the grass to dry.

Ackroyd is an artist of weather, above all. Rain, snow, smirr, spume, the complications of light on water and steep rock, these are what fascinate him, and what he renders better than any living artist I know. In a sense, he's a painter *with* weather, for he'll often dab his brush into a pool of rain-water on a boulder or capstan, and work that into the image.

That afternoon on Tory, rain-water was in abundance. A black rain-squall hit us at about 3 o'clock. Within seconds my notebook pages were an indigo blur. Ackroyd painted on, but soon the rain was so heavy that the paint had bled off, the colours mixing into a reddish stream that poured from a corner of the sketchbook. 'You can sometimes get in the shade from rain,' Ackroyd said as he clapped the book shut. 'But not today.'

The rain was still hissing down at 7 o'clock that night, when a shout went up in the lobby of the one hotel on Tory Island: 'There's a dolphin in the harbour!' I ran down to the jetty, to find an astonishing sight. A Labrador was in the water, barking and paddling in circles, while around it played an eight-foot dolphin, blue in hue when on the surface but green-grey at depth.

So I joined them, stripping down to my boxer shorts, *hooh*-ing and *haah*-ing my way into the frigid sea off the harbour steps. And for a magical quarter of an hour I swam with the two creatures. The dolphin was curious, familiar. It lay on its side beneath me, nuzzling my ankle, or bottled up to watch me through black cheeky eyes. Once it retreated to a distance of ten metres, then disappeared, before rising up sharkishly beneath me. Its skin, in the cold water, felt blood-warm to the touch, and smooth as neoprene.

Afterwards, I shivered uncontrollably for an hour or so: the deep body shiver induced by seawater. But it had been more than worth it: a wonderful, accidental event, freely given, that I wouldn't ever forget. Padraig, the owner of the hotel, told us that the dolphin had been coming to the harbour for a year and a half now, seeking company after the death of its mate, whose corpse had washed up dead on Tory's south shore. He also said that he had once seen 'upwards of a thousand dolphins' in Tory Sound, all heading westwards. The parents and their children leapt together in perfect synchrony, he said, 'as though each child were stuck to its mother's side'.

Our remaining days on the island were spent exploring by boat and on foot. The dolphin returned the following day, and I swam again with it in sunshine. One morning I lowered myself down a cliff in a northern cove, and fished from sharp rocks tasselled with thong-weed, while the sea slopped hungrily at my feet. I caught two big pollack on light tackle, and felt the happy fear of being alone in a wild place.

Gradually, I also came to notice not just the wildness of Tory but also its tarnish. For, like any modern inhabited island, Tory's sea-scrubbed purity is an illusion, at least in part. It's hard to get rubbish off the island, so abandoned cars lie around, grass growing through their wheel hubs. Many of the northern ravines are rank with fly-tipped garbage: shredded magazines, swollen chipboard, sofa cushions. On the footpath verges, exotically named plastic bottles vie for attention with exotically named flowers: Montbresia, Volvic, Eyebright, Lucozade. And out near the lighthouse, seabirds swoop low over empty cider cans: fulmars over Bulmer's. On Tory, the abject and the sublime are never far apart – but then this is part of its interest.

The day we left Tory was windy and bright. We blasted back across a choppy Sound. Diesel fumes, salt spray, engine roar, sunlight. Our wake showed green and cream. Norman painted the retreating island. We passed a basking shark wallowing on the surface. Shoals of mackerel brought the sea to the boil, rising up after sand eels.

And the sand eels also drew the gannets, who made long surveillance glides, or slammed down into the water like rockets. Gannets have gleaming white bodies, but their necks are discoloured a strange nicotine-yellow. Their plumage thus alludes both to purity and pollution, and in this way, it seemed to me that morning, they were the perfect guardian birds of Tory.

Norman Ackroyd (THREE)

Malin Etchings: From Malin Head; Tor Rocks, Malin

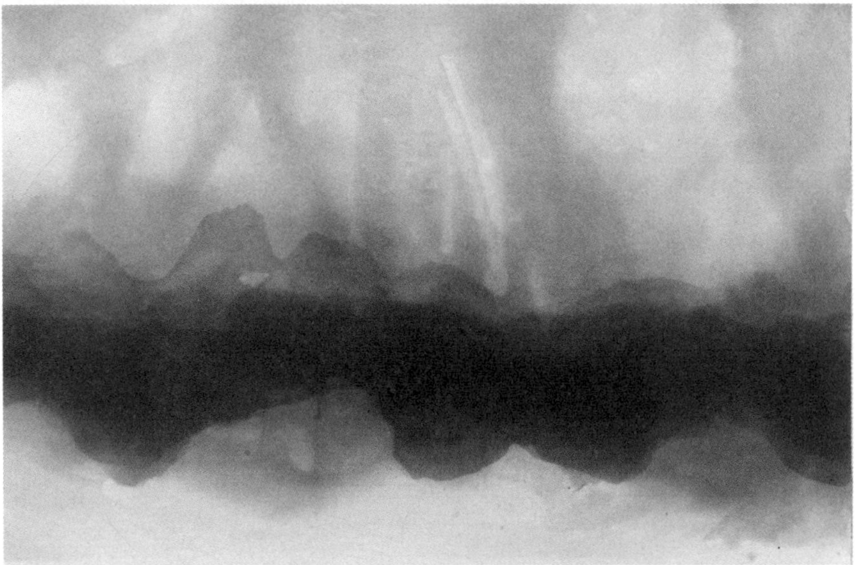

Seamus Heaney (TWO)

Loughanure

i.m. Colin Middleton

Smoke might have been already in his eyes
The way he'd narrow them to size you up
As if you were a canvas, all the while

Licking and sealing a hand-rolled cigarette,
Each small ash cuticle flicked off
As white as flecks on the horizon line

Of his painting of Loughanure, thirty guineas
Forty odd years ago. Whitewashed gables
Like petal stripped from hawthorn, heather ground

A pother of Gaeltacht turf smoke. Every time
He came to the house, he would go and stand
Gazing at it, grunting a bit and nodding.

*

So this what an afterlife can come to?
A cloud-boil weather on a wall
Like murky crystal, a remembered stare –

This for an answer to Aligheri
And the man of Er? Who saw the immortal souls
Choose lives to come according as they were

Fulfilled or repelled by existences they'd known
Or suffered first time round. Saw great farseeing
Odysseus in the end choose for himself

The destiny of a private man. Saw Orpheus
Because he'd perished at the women's hands
Choose rebirth as a swan.

*

That purplish, stone wall, Donegal tweed plain
And fuming sky he caught so perfectly,
That mystery of the usual unenhanced

Yet entered, at once unveiled and veiled –
For him it was unusual, who preferred
To go in by the door of the surreal,

Through a grain of linseed or of Lough Neagh sand
To the spéirbhean in the flax beet or the granite
Groin of Silent Valley high in Mourne.

Or up a Jacob's Ladder to an angel stranded
Like a ragdoll left by firemen who'd long since
Scooted away in their toytown scarlet engine.

*

Another way in: legs apart, to stand
Back to the motif, and then bend down
Until the hills in their perpetual light

Were framed in his fork like a Tuscan scene
Through a slender columned arch,
His inverted face an arse-kisser's contorted

In a vision of the damned. Or he'd read the Wake
And giggle. Or William Blake. Anything
To open those same doors of perception.

Even, nearer home, Kavanagh
With his 'light that might be mystic or a fraud',
Shutting his eyes to see the way to heaven.

*

Had I had sufficient Irish in Rannafast
In 1953 to understand
The seanchas and dinnsheanchas,

Had heard the tale of Caoilte and the fawn
He hunted from Tory Island to the door
Of a fairy hill where he wasn't turned away

But led to a crystal chair on the hill floor
Where he saw warriors seated with their women
On one side of the house, while a girl with yellow hair

Harped and then drank from horns they handed her,
The horizon might have lightened and the far
'Lake of the yew tree' gleamed in that cloud-swabbed air.

*

Not all that far, as it turns out, now
My brazen car can cover those few miles
In almost as few minutes, Mount Errigal

On the skyline the one constant thing
As I drive unhomesick, unbelieving, through
A grant-aided, renovated scene, trying

To remember the Greek word that signifies
A world restored completely: that would include
Hannah Mhór's turkey-chortle of Irish,

The swan at evening over Loch an Iubhair,
Clarinco Murray's hard iced caramels
A penny an ounce over Sharkey's counter.

Terry Eagleton (TWO)

West Is South

I live part of the time in a remote corner of north-west Ulster under a mountain called Benevena, where St Patrick and St Colum Cille (Columba) are rumoured to have roamed. Patrick is thought to have employed a priest from our local village to wait on his table. We even know his name: Cattan. It is strange to think that the first writer against slavery in Western history (Patrick had been a slave himself) actually had a butler in tow. Colum Cille writes nostalgically from exile about Benevena, then known as Foibne Hill:

> O Son of God, it would be sweet,
> a lovely journey,
> to cross the wave, the fount in flood
>
> to Eolarg Plain, by Foibne Hill,
> across Loch Febail,
> and listen there to the matching music
> of the swans.

Another local lad was St Aidan, nephew of Colum Cille, to whom a holy well across the road is dedicated. So this is a salubrious spot for a writer, since the well's waters are said to be good for eyestrain. Those afflicted with skin complaints evidently find it equally therapeutic. The authenticity of Aidan's grave nearby is not beyond doubt, unless the saint was buried several centuries after he died and his bones kept in the meanwhile in the medieval equivalent of a biscuit tin. High up on the mountain is a Mass stone, where Catholics during the eighteenth-century penal era, forbidden to assemble in churches, would gather in secret to celebrate the Eucharist. As if in homage to its monkish history, the mountain itself is tonsured, its bald summit rising with mildly comic dignity through a thickly tressed circlet of pine and fir.

Temporally speaking, however, this terrain is as complex and disjunctive as any other. The arable lands over which ancient Benevena broods, with their fertile stretches of lough-dank soil and networks of laconic, hard-headed Ulster farmers, are historically very recent, reclaimed from the waters of Lough Foyle in the early twentieth century. The Big House opposite me, home since the seventeenth century to the landowning Gage family, is now in the hands of a Belfast garment manufacturer, a petit bourgeois who the patrician Gages would hardly have allowed through its portico. One of the last of the family, having nothing much else to do, shot himself with a rifle. His ancestors had been awarded the land around here in the Ulster Plantation, once it had been confiscated from the native Magilligans. One of the Magilligans' strongholds was the now-ruined thirteenth-century Dunluce castle, which visitors to the Giant's Causeway may recall glimpsing from the car window. The Magilligans had a stab at snatching their lands back in the uprising of 1641, but succeeded only in having more of it seized by the Crown.

The well-groomed estate of the Big House over the road carves space into figures of symmetry, elegance and proportion. It is everything that the struggle between the Gages and the Magilligans was not. The house is set well back and can't be seen from the road – partly, no doubt, to avoid offering an insolent provocation to the surrounding small tenantry in earlier times. But to own space is also to buy privacy;

and a cunning crafting of such space allowed the landowner to be, like God, present but invisible. Perhaps this was a minor compensation for the fact, that unlike the English industrial proletariat, Irish tenant farmers knew where their boss lived, and occasionally came marching uninvited up his drive.

In the early middle ages, this slender tract of Ulster was a hotbed of Celtic spirituality. Protestant Ulster has prided itself in modern times on its industrial efficiency and paid-up modernity, in contrast with the feckless papist Micks; but Ulster was also the most traditionalist region of Ireland, the last redoubt of a time-honoured Gaelic culture. In the fifth century, Patrick founded a church and abbey on the road where I live, one of the wealthiest and most celebrated spiritual powerhouses in the province, with an immense library. Some of the books were salvaged from invading Danes by being concealed in a box which, according to legend, could be opened only by one who had never been born, mounted on a white foal never foaled. Bishop Hervey of Derry, of whom more in a moment, claimed with characteristic panache that he was the man in question, since both he and his horse had been born by Caesarian section. But if Hervey was lying, which he almost certainly was, he got his comeuppance for thus disgracing the cloth. He is said to have discovered at Duncrun a collection of Druidic writings, and was so fearfully disturbed by their occult contents that he went wandering off around Europe with his mind unhinged. In fact, he needed no excuse at all to gallop off to the Continent at the drop of a mitre. In any case, there are those who would claim that his mind was unhinged from birth.

Like all natural landscapes, but rather more than most, the one that encircles me is held in a web of mostly invisible geopolitical forces. If I look to the west I can see Lough Foyle, apparently only a stone's throw away, and behind it the misty black mass of the Inishowen hills. The Irish playwright Brian Friel lives on the far side of the lough, and the two of us are almost close enough to communicate by semaphore. But what I am looking at as I gaze westward is a country as officially foreign to Northern Ireland as Slovenia or Peru, with its own distinct language, currency and system of government. Though only a brief ferry journey divides them, my shore of the lough lies in the United Kingdom, while Friel's side is in Donegal in the Republic of Ireland. In these conciliatory times, an ancient ferry across the water has resumed its services. It is said to have been blessed by Colum Cille, who predicted rather rashly that none of its passengers would ever be drowned, and who with impeccable even-handedness cursed the nearby Benone river, with the result that it is sorely bereft of salmon. These days, Northern Irish Protestants make their way for the first time with mild apprehensiveness to the shores of Donegal, a crossing that literally speaking takes five minutes but politically speaking has taken several centuries. Similarly, Catholic Gaels from the Donegal shore set a faltering foot for the first time on Northern Irish soil, gratified and faintly bemused to discover that its people have more or less as many limbs as they do.

From where I'm standing, then, west is south and east is north. The blurred landmass pockmarked with ugly white bungalows over the lough is what some of the British still like to call 'southern' Ireland, even though this so-called southern nation-state stretches a considerable way north of Belfast into the mossy Irish-speaking regions of north-west Donegal. Friel, for his part, looks across from his window at 'Northern' Ireland – though the terrain before his eyes is actually south-east. Many things on this island are topsy-turvy. Political and geographical cartographies are surreally askew: though an invisible frontier uncouples my side of the Foyle waters from the other, both territories form part of Ulster, an ancient land mass which seditiously refuses to acknowledge partition. (There have been even so, 'partitionist' geographers in Belfast who have discovered a preternaturally sharp contrast between the geology of Irish Donegal and that of British Antrim.) On my side of the lough, *beg* means *big*, given the Ulster-Scots habit of pronouncing *i* like Standard-English *e*. Over the water, however, 'beg' means 'small' in Irish. So three cultures at least interlock here, not just two. From just round the corner, close to the Giant's Causeway, you can sometimes just about glimpse Scotland's Mull of Kintyre a mere twelve miles away, though semaphore with Paul

McCartney would require unusually fine weather. The legendary Irish giant Finn MacCool used to step across to Scotland from the Giant's Causeway. Walter Scott stepped the opposite way a couple of times, and is said to have visited the house I live in, since he knew the rector there.

All natural landscapes are deceptive, since they tend to appear innocent of the semiotic traces which history has inscribed upon them. Space has a trick of obliterating time, or at least of homogenising it. In a tract of land, different strata of time are stacked spatially cheek-by-jowl, obscuring their divergences. And since much of the natural world is still and solid, it has an aura of permanence about it which can belie the truth of human change and disruption. Thomas Hardy knew that natural terrains were faded texts, to be patiently deciphered for the half-effaced human meanings which score them through. In this culturally patchworked country around Lough Foyle, different cultural spaces are overlain, alternative time-schemes tug apart and interpenetrate, geography is history, the past invades the present and common ground can serve simply to sharpen contrasts.

Tucked into the groin of Lough Foyle is the city of Derry, or Londonderry as Unionists would call it, where two different cultures overlap and spring apart in a single signifier. Smart business enterprises, fearing to alienate potential customers on either side of the politico-religious divide, have solved the problem literally at a stroke with the brightly meaningless 'L/Derry'. Twenty years ago, the town lay in ruins; nowadays it has risen phoenix-like in its bright-eyed, Blairite way to become the second most economically unproductive urban centre in the United Kingdom, which is where it is said to be situated. Not all the semiotics of this landscape, however, demand much subtle decipherment. If Benevena lies in one direction when I look out, in the other directions stands a prison, once full of political inmates, and an army base. The area, in other words, has continued to be a hotbed of religious devotion, proudly maintaining its medieval legacy. It is just that Aidan gave way to the armalite.

Since I live in a nationalist enclave, the clattering British army helicopters from the nearby base tend to fly particularly low, not least around bedtime. No doubt we shall soon be shot of them. A mile or so down the road the pavements are painted red, white and blue, and there are pubs I wouldn't venture inside with my arty beard and poncy English accent. At my age and with my unathletic build, I have no chance of being mistaken for a British army officer. The more assertively the Union flags flap, the more anxious and enraged the loyalists who run them up the telegraph poles. Your identity is secure only when you don't feel the need to flaunt it. By what curious geopolitical conjuncture, a stranger to the region might wonder, do the Israeli and South African flags come to be fluttering in the streets of a remote Ulster village alongside the banners of St George and St Andrew?

Patrick's ruined abbey, the Mass rock, the Big House, the prison, the ferry, the army base, the pronunciation of 'big' as ' beg', the ambiguous title of the local city: these are all disjointed segments of the same turbulent history. Or rather they belong to conflicting historical narratives which knot in the sinews of this landscape. If it is by no means a seamlessly coherent story they recount, neither is it a mere heap of unrelated fragments. There is another culture in the area as well, however – a wedge of European civility jammed incongruously into the gaunt North Antrim coast. This is Downhill, the ruined palace of Frederick Augustus Hervey, eighteenth-century Bishop of Derry, Earl of Bristol, scion of the Bristol cream sherry dynasty, sometime Viceroy of Ireland and megalomaniac. One of the great Anglo-Irish eccentrics, Hervey had a pile in Suffolk, but was determined to build on the Northern Irish coast road a cliff-top palace to outdo Blenheim itself. His magnificent library, the Mussenden Temple, remains intact, perched precariously above the Atlantic. Watching ships toss and sailors drown from a safe haven was the kind of pleasurably vicarious terror known to eighteenth-century aesthetics as the sublime, and to the modern age as sado-masochism.

Hervey stuffed his palace with paintings by Rubens, Correggio, Raphael, Van Dyck, Tintoretto and others, all garnered on his frequent jaunts around the Continent. Everywhere in the county he clapped elegant spires on plain churches. He was determined to overlay all this bare Derry basalt with the trappings of high European culture, and did not mind being thought mad for building in such an egregiously inhospitable place. On the contrary, it was the sheer ludicrousness of the project which seems to have delighted him. His idiosyncrasies were as familiar to the Florentines as to the plain people of Derry. Staying one night in an Italian inn, he is said to have heard the sounds of a papist procession in the street outside, and throwing open his bedroom window emptied the contents of his chamber pot on the Eucharistic host as it was borne solemnly beneath him. He was chaplain for a time to George III, about whose court he wrote a slanderous, salacious memoir, and had also been bishop of Cloyne, where he drained the Great Bog.

Admired by Voltaire and Boswell, this prince of the church had the honour of being lampooned as Sporus in Alexander Pope's *Epistle to Arbuthnot*, as well as being cited in John Gay's *The Beggar's Opera*. As a keen geologist, it was he who first popularised the Giant's Causeway. Despite being a notorious libertine himself, he would scatter flour on the floor of the servants' quarters at Downhill to keep track of who was sleeping with who. He would force the local clergy to race each other on horseback on the sands below his palace, awarding the winner with a fatter living. It was said that the Church of Ireland curates, being better paid and thus better fed than their lean Presbyterian colleagues, tended to be the victors. In his latter years he was dangerously mad (those Druidic books, perhaps), and was imprisoned as a spy in Italy by Napoleon's troops, dying near Rome in 1803. It was said that the world consisted of men, women and Herveys.

So there are traces of a cosmopolitan culture here as well, as there are everywhere in Ireland. From medieval missionaries to modern corporate executives, the Irish have always looked to Europe. Yet it was not a culture wholly at odds with the Mass stone, the prison and L/Derry. For Hervey was a great European liberal and reformist, who commissioned a road for famine relief which runs just above my house, and is still known as the Bishop's Road. He then had part of the road destroyed and rebuilt to provide further relief work for the poor. When

Catholic priests were smuggled in on the ferry from Donegal in penal times, it was Hervey the Protestant prelate who allowed them to say Mass in the crypt of his library. He also provided food for the priest and fodder for his horse. He played a leading role in the campaign against the penal laws, and supported Catholic Emancipation. Placed at the head of the Irish Volunteers, he had himself drawn in a sumptuous carriage at the head of his troops, dressed in purple with gold tassels and diamond buckles, in a splendid procession through the capital. But he was beaten to the post by Lord Charlemont, and consoled himself by building another palace. The fact is that he was too radical for the Volunteers, whose ranks he considered should be open to Catholics. That he has not been the subject of a major Irish novel or drama is astonishing.

These are secret affinities inscribed in this landscape, then, as well as rifts and ruptures. Little though they probably knew it, those who reopened the ferry across Lough Foyle some years ago were the spiritual progeny of the Hervey who helped smuggle in papist clerics to this region. So it is fitting after all that ferry and palace, prison and holy well, should all be held together in the same encompassing space.

Les Murray (SEVEN)

All of Half Way

i.m. Sue Ridley

As I was going to Coleraine
a man in Bewleys said to me
I wouldn't wear that green cap up there,
and I snatched it off –

colours aren't yet mortal in Australia.
It was only our equestrian team cap
that you had given me, but
I took the warning, folded, to Coleraine.

There I found hospitality
and Bushmills and the Giant's Causeway.
No bush near the Mills
but a coracle sea and the Giant's columns

massing on out, a basalt grandstand
of rain-cup pillars, crimped like Rubiks
from cooling their rock floor
all of half way from America.

SCOTLAND

‘Now, listen. Here’s what I heard today –
A corncrake in the Hebridean hay’

DOUGLAS DUNN (FOUR)

Norman Ackroyd (ONE)

Ailsa Craig

Mary Wellesley (TEN)

Ailsa

'Hearken, thou craggy ocean pyramid!' begins John Keats's sonnet 'To Ailsa Rock', in the vocative mode the Renaissance called 'epideictic', the paean of praise or blame. I am sure I didn't know what epideixis was, aged fifteen or so, when I came across the poem while nosing around in a bookshop, during a time after school when I should reasonably have been doing some homework. Nor had I – most likely – registered the fourteen lines as the first signs of a sonnet. What I did know, as I let my eye scan idly over the index of the *Complete Works of Keats*, was the island that was the subject of his poem. In fact, I knew it well. I would have said I loved it, even.

It is hard to describe the eerie beauty of Ailsa Craig, which lies off the coast of Ayrshire (the south-westerly nub of Scotland that sits nose to nose with Northern Ireland). The island is an extinct volcanic plug, nine miles out to sea and around a thousand feet tall, its sides rising steeply from the sea. It is no more than a few miles in circumference, a mountain in the ocean, sitting alone and seemingly impassable in the Firth of Clyde. In its history it has supported a modest human population. But, when the island's lighthouse was automated in 1990, the island was deserted. It is now uninhabited but for 23,000 nesting pairs of gannets (about 5 per cent of the global population of the bird) that visit and breed there in the summer. There are also other fauna, but Ailsa is by rights the gannets' place now. Ailsa sits on the welded join between sky and sea. Sometimes, on clear days, the hilly Isle of Arran and the long shoulder of the Mull of Kintyre can be seen behind it in hazy backdrop, but generally it sits all alone: a great, dark, ocean pyramid. At night, its once-manned lighthouse sends out a lonely, rotating beam across the Firth.

Every summer of my life, I've visited the part of Ayrshire that claims Ailsa in its dominion. For me and my family the island is a kind of talisman. Out walking on the moors, it's a reflexive gesture for us to turn our heads out to sea in her direction. The promise of a sight of her, out in the Firth, brings us – short of breath – to the tops of hills, scrambling round the corners of rocky coves and draws us regularly from our homes in the South. We've endowed her with false wisdom. As such, we are all strangely convinced that the clarity of her shape on the horizon is a reliable indicator of the weather (which is famously fickle in Ayrshire). If she's invisible, we expect a torrential downpour, but days when you can see every heathery undulation on her sides, are days when the sun is sure to be out until evening. I always feel a sense of sadness when she's invisible. And the moment when I first catch sight of her from a car or train window is the moment I have arrived properly in Ayrshire. She anchors me to a landscape and seascape that I love. Sometimes late at night or in the early inklings of the morning, when I cannot sleep, I listen to the Shipping Forecast and wait – expectantly – for 'Malin'. Then, I imagine Ailsa's steep sides, her tenacious sea-birds and her abandoned dwellings and I wonder about that lonely place.

Visiting Ailsa by boat is a journey of an hour and a half. The last time I went, we saw three basking sharks, so close to the boat we could see the creamy-white insides of their giant, gaping, benign mouths. (On being told about them afterwards, my niece asked if they really did have baskets.) The boat trip goes from Girvan harbour, which is roughly the closest point on the mainland to the island. So Ailsa is seen straight on from the moment you leave the Ayrshire shore, its shape slowly filling an ever larger space on the horizon in a quietly ominous sort of way.

Half of the island is made up of steep cliffs with tiny ledges formed by basaltic pillars, on which the gannets and guillemots make improbable and cheerless nests. Their eggs are nearly conical in shape so that on a flat surface they only roll in a circular direction. It's an evolutionary quirk that allows them to breed successfully in such precarious surroundings. Approaching the island, even at some distance, all you can hear is the birds' keening. Then, as you near the cliffs, the sky becomes a boil of birds circling above. They form a noisy mass overhead, while all around you the gannets put on an aeronautical display, diving – arrow-like – from heights of seventy feet, with sharp-beaked precision, into the Firth. Bird species abound on Ailsa. There are kittiwakes, razorbills, guillemots, little auks and puffins, to name only the most charismatic. This latter species, which nests in accessible burrows, not on the cliffs, was decimated by introduced rats in the twentieth century. Mercifully, the rat population was eradicated over several years in a project overseen by the RSPB, whereby three tons of rat poison had to be flown in by RAF helicopter. Finally, in 1991 nesting pairs of puffins began, slowly, to return to the island. All of these bird species have a rich lexicon of local and archaic names. Gannets were known as solan geese, guillemots as tarnathans, razorbills were called strannies and puffins were once known as paties, albunacs or Ailsa cocks, and a Scots name of Tammie Norries is still in use in parts of lowland Scotland.

The sea-birds once made Ailsa a prized piece of property. They were harvested for their eggs and flesh throughout the summer. A 1404 charter granted by King Robert III, confirming the possessions of Crossraugel Abbey mentions 'item, insula de ailsay cum pertinenciis'. The Medieval Latin phrase, 'cum pertinenciis' means 'whatever belongs with it'. The 'pertinenciis' crucially would have included the sea-birds. In a description of Carrick of 1696 by William Abercrummie, Episcopal Minister of Maybole, it is said that the local population have 'store of solan-geese in so great plenty, that the very poorest of the people eat of them in their season, at easie rates: besides other sea-fowls, which are brought from Ailsa'.

Just as Ailsa was exploited for its sea-fowl throughout its history, in the nineteenth and twentieth century it was exploited for its stone. The island's granite, with its distinctive pillar-like formation and beautiful copper-oxide green speckles made it a prized quarry for stone to make curling stones. The demand for curling stones has fallen in this century, but to this day, Ailsa is one of only two quarries that supply all curling stones world-wide. There are accounts of its granite being used from 1805, but since the founding of Royal Caledonian Curling Club in 1838 (it was originally the 'Grand Caledonian') Ailsa Craig granite has been the official gold standard in curling. In 1842 on a royal visit to Scotland, Prince Alfred and Queen Victoria were presented with a pair of silver-handled stones at the Palace of Scone and in London in 1851 Ailsa curling stones formed part of the Great Exhibition at Crystal Palace.

Quarrying the stone from the island (the blasted chunks of granite were known as 'cheeses') and bringing it to the mainland was a dangerous and tricky business. In 1899 Andrew Girvan, the son of the island's quarryman, was killed in an explosion at one of the island's quarries. He was twenty-three years old. The island did not get a telegraph until 1935, which meant that in the event of an accident (of which, sadly, there were several) carrier pigeons had to be dispatched for the mainland. A small rusted railway at the island's base and a series of ruined buildings are a testament to a once-bustling industry of curling stone production that supported a population of nearly fifty people in 1911, in the heyday of the quarrying operations.

Of course, my family and I aren't the first people to be captivated by Ailsa's mysterious and lonely beauty. Sitting between the Irish and Scottish coasts, the island has woven itself into the literature of both cultures. The island has fanciful names in Irish Gaelic, Scottish Gaelic, Scots and English. 'Ailsa Craig' is said to mean 'fairy rock', allsie creag, but it might also just mean 'rocky isle', 'aill' meaning cliff and the 'a' suffix meaning 'island', like Sanda or Islay. It's also apparently known as creag enlasaid, 'Elizabeth's Isle' and Paddy's Milestone, on account of its position on the crossing route between the Scottish and Irish coasts. In Ireland in the nineteenth century it was supposedly called 'Brian's Stone', after a story that King Brian Boroimhe (*c.* 941–1014) took possession of it in *c.* 1000.

The island is called carraig Alasdair, 'Alistair's Isle' when it makes its earliest appearance in literature, in the *Buile Suibhne*, a medieval Irish poem about the legendary King Suibhne (anglicised as 'Sweeney'). The poem only survives in a manuscript copied in County Sligo in the 1670s, but the work is much older, dating in some form from the thirteenth century, with elements of a much, much earlier tradition that dates back to the Battle of Rag Math in Moira in 637. The poem dramatises the flight of the cursed and exiled King Suibhne, who travels over the landscape of both Ireland and Scotland. Each of his stopping places occasions a poetic reverie on his plight.

The text was translated and re-configured by Seamus Heaney as *Sweeney Astray* in 1983. Heaney's poem is characteristically crisp and economical. The passage that deals with Ailsa tells us that Sweeney spent six weeks on the island. Weakened and bleeding, Sweeney reflects on his place of exile:

> But to have ended up
> lamenting here
> on Ailsa Craig
> A hard station!
>
> Ailsa Craig,
> the seagulls' home,
> God knows it is
> hard lodgings.
>
> Ailsa Craig,
> bell-shaped rock
> reaching sky-high
> snout in the sea –

it hard-beaked,
me seasoned and scraggy:
we mated like a couple
of hard shanked cranes.

Later Sweeney, bereft and alone, dreams of the wooded shore: 'I need woods / for consolation.' Ailsa is a desperate refuge, porcine and unhomely. The mating of the 'hard shanked cranes' is an ironic metaphor for Sweeney's lack of human comfort.

Buile Suibhne is the first in a long tradition of literary accounts of Ailsa. In *The Grey Man*, by S.R. Crockett, a fanciful nineteenth-century novel of local colour, there are extensive stories of Ailsa Craig as a site of recusant treason, and a home of smugglers and vagabonds. The story of recusant treason is probably not entirely untrue. In 1597, a recusant Catholic, Hugh Barclay hatched a plan to take possession of Ailsa and make it a haven for Catholic dissenters. His scheme was frustrated by a Protestant minister, Andrew Knox, who had already stationed himself on the island and was waiting for the unfortunate Barclay. In his 1656 *Compleat History* of the reigns of Mary I and James VI of Scotland, William Sanderson describes the circumstances of the treasonous plot. Sanderson's account is recognisably anti-Catholic and, thus, not entirely trustworthy. He writes,

> There was discovered a practice of surprizeing the Isle of Elsay in the West Seas for receiving forces resolved upon by the Spaniard [presumably Philip II] to be sent thither. The contriver of this design was Barklay the Laird of Ladyland … [who had] secretly gotten to this Isle, being a high rock four miles compass, and thereon an invincible Tower somewhat ruinate of difficult access which he meant to victual. But was sodainly surprized by one Knox, who landing on the shore, Barklay was walking down the Hill to take view of the Company; not mistrusting to be known. And finding that he was thus betrayed, ran into the sea and drowned himself.

After this, the island was entrusted by its owner, the Earl of Cassilis (ancestor of the modern day Marquis of Ailsa) to one Thomas Hamilton to protect it from further recusant colonisation. The Hamilton arms are still visible, carved above the lintel of the island's 'ruinate' keep – an upright rectangular building that perches around two hundred feet above sea-level in gannet-nest-style on the side of Ailsa's heathery foreshore, facing the mainland that can only be reached by a goat-path that defies all but the most determined. There is also another account of a certain 'Lord Maxwell', ten years earlier, in 1587, who was being pursued by representatives of James VI on account of his recusant faith. He fled 'in ane cokboit to Ilslaiy' (in a cock-boat – a kind of small vessel – to Ailsa). On his return to the mainland, Maxwell was captured. I'd like to believe that these stories are true, that Ailsa might have been at the centre of internecine treasonous plots, but I'm inclined to think that Ailsa is just a metaphor for these Protestant revisionists: that this desperate island is an allegory for the desperation of choosing the Catholic faith and plotting treason.

The island has also fascinated many a traveller. Many of those who have taken the coast road that snakes its way north from Stranraer towards Girvan have been struck by the sight of Ailsa Craig out to sea. That was exactly what John Keats did in the summer of 1818 on a walking tour with his friend Charles Brown. They had begun their journey in June, in the Lake District. Keats's letters at the start of the tour are filled with optimism. On 27 June, in Cumbria, he wrote, exultant, reflecting on the beauty of the landscape surrounding him: 'I shall henceforth write more than ever, for the abstract endeavor of being able to add a mite to that mass of beauty which is harvested from these grand materials.' Yet the journey was tinged with fear form the start. Before leaving, Keats had written to Benjamin Bailey, 'I am not certain whether I shall be able to go on any journey, on account of my Brother Tom, and a little indisposition of my own.' His brother was suffering from tuberculosis, a disease from which Keats would himself die three years later. In the end, the 'little indisposition' proved greater than he could handle and the walking tour was cut short. The pair had planned to walk to John O'Groats, but the experience of climbing Ben Nevis 'brought things to a crisis', as Andrew Motion observes. Keats wrote to Tom that attempting to climb Ben Nevis in his condition was 'like a fly crawling up a wainscot'.

By the time Keats reached Ayrshire, there had been some disappointments: Keats's hero, Wordsworth, was not at home when they called on him at Rydal Mount, while in Ireland Keats had written desperately of the 'worse than nakedness, the rags, the dirt and misery, of the poor common Irish'. Moving out of the lee of the Rhins of Galloway, after disembarking from the ferry from Ireland and making their way north, the pair saw the island. Keats wrote 'in a little time [we] descried in the sea Ailsa rock ... the effect ... with the peculiar aspect of the sea in connection with the ground we stood on, and the misty rain then falling gave me a complete idea of a deluge – Ailsa struck me very suddenly – really I was a little alarmed'.

The curious thing about Ailsa Craig is that it changes shape. Glimpsed from the south, near the port town of Stranraer, it is the shape of a looming dunce's hat out to sea. And yet, as you progress up the coast, its shape softens and it flattens. By the time you have passed Girvan (the nearest point to it on the mainland) and get to Turnberry, the island is an unthreatening muffin shape, filled out at the edges: a lady in advanced middle age. There is, I think, a tone of puzzlement in Keats's letter, written from Girvan where they had stopped for the night, that the island had produced such alarm at first. Perhaps he looked out to sea and saw its softer shape and wondered at his initial reaction. Keats wrote his sonnet in his letter to his brother, in a little drawn-off area in the top left-hand corner of the verso side. He calls it 'the only sonnet of any worth I have of late written':

> Hearken, thou craggy ocean pyramid!
> Give answer by thy voice, the sea-fowls' screams!
> When were thy shoulders mantled in huge streams?
> When from the sun was thy broad forehead hid?
> How long is't since the mighty Power bid
> Thee heave to airy sleep from fathom dreams?
> Sleep in the lap of thunder or sunbeams,
> Or when grey clouds are thy cold coverlid?
> Thou answer'st not, for thou art dead asleep;

Thy life is but two dead eternities –
The last in air, the former in the deep;
First with the whales, last with the eagle-skies;
Drown'd wast thou till an earthquake made thee steep –
Another cannot wake thy giant size!

The island for Keats hangs precariously between the infinities of sea ('with the whales') and sky ('eagle-skies'). The poem is framed as a series of questions, but frustrated questions that remain unanswered. Keats, like many Romantic poets, was famously inventive with the sonnet form. At risk of labouring the point with technical detail, the 'volta' or turn, which is when the rhyme scheme changes in the course of the sonnet, comes at the beginning of the ninth line, beginning 'thou answer'st not'. In using the poem's form in this way, Keats indicates a sharp change in tone after this point, emphasising that the island remains unreachable, his questions unanswered, and the final lines of the poem become a meditation on the rock's ancient age. I think there's something quite sad about the poem, something in its frustrated questions and in Keats's sense of distance from the island. There seems something melancholy in Keats's desire to 'add a mite to that mass of beauty which is harvested from these grand materials', which seems unfulfilled, his imploring appeals to the silent island on the horizon remain unanswered.

The version of the sonnet in Keats's letter to his brother Tom reads 'thy life has been two dead eternities' and also 'thy life will be'. I like these early drafts, which suggest that Keats thought of the island as poised, precariously between eternities of time as well as space, somewhere in a magical liminal space between the two.

In 1819 when the poem was published in Hunt's Literary Pocketbook, Blackwood's Edinburgh Magazine derided Keats for 'standing on the sea shore … cross-questioning the Craig of Ailsa', missing the subtlety of his use of the sonnet form, and apparently blind to the way that Keats was responding to the alluring mystery of Ailsa's ominous and unreachable shape out to sea. Robert Burns's only mention of the island is in his poem 'Duncan Gray', which contains the line 'Meg was deaf as Ailsa Craig', again gesturing to its silent, impervious appeal.

During an eclipse of the sun in 1833 William Wordsworth passed Ailsa in a steamboat and afterwards wrote a sonnet of his own about it. His preface to the poem describes some 'persons of the poor and labouring class' who were also on deck with him. 'Not one of them,' he spluttered, 'seemed to notice the magnificent objects with which we were surrounded.' It's difficult not to hold this against Wordsworth and resent his sonnet somehow. In his poem, which I have a hunch is influenced by Keats's (it describes the island's 'forehead' amongst other things), Wordsworth genders the island male, 'Still is he seen, in lone sublimity.' His focus is not on the sounds of the island, its imagined voice and absent reply, as Keats's is, but more on its appearance, and how it towers over passing ships. Perhaps seeing the island up close from the steamboat, Wordsworth had less of a sense of the island's ethereal presence on the horizon, as Keats did, observing it from the shore. His sonnet seems more pedestrian to me, missing some of the magic. This is something my aunt is actually afraid of. She has never visited Ailsa in a boat, having looked at it from the shore all her life. Encouraged by friends to take a boat trip around the island a few years ago, when the boat neared the island she said she just could not look. She turned her back and looked back towards the Ayrshire shoreline.

In his introduction to *Sweeney Astray*, Heaney writes that his connection to Sweeney was a topographical one. Heaney lived in south County Antrim and north County Down, 'in sight of some of Sweeney's places and in earshot of others', places with musical monikers, like Slemish, Rasharkin, Benevenaugh, Dunseverick, the Bann, the Roe, the Mournes. He recalls a family of tinkers, called Sweeney, who camped in the ditchbacks along the road he took to school. He writes, 'one way or another he seemed to have been with me from the start'. Heaney's point is the way that landscape is the hinge that connects us to our past, whether it is a literary or a historical past. He also pays tribute to the way that landscapes, the figures within them and their place-names sometimes take on the quality of literary characters, and how we carry the feeling for these places with us, wherever we go. And Ailsa is that for me. The island has taken on the status of a literary character in my imagination, it is the hinge that connects me to the past. I carry the idea of her with me, and sometimes I actually carry a little piece of her, a smooth, green-flecked granite pebble weighing down my pocket seams.

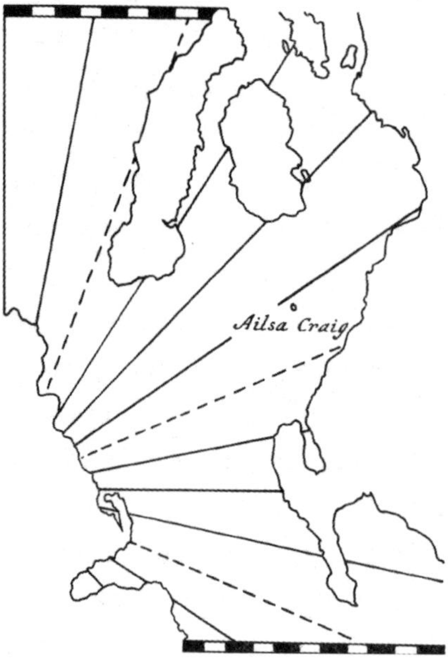

Alan Riach (TWELVE)

Scotland: Drawing a Line

In *Here Is Where We Meet*, published in 2005, John Berger remembers his mother saying to him, 'Everything in life, John, is a question of drawing a line, and you have to decide for yourself where to draw it. You can't draw it for others. You can try, of course, but it doesn't work. People obeying rules laid down by somebody else is not the same thing as respecting life. And if you want to respect life, you have to draw a line.'

Scotland, in the course of the twelve issues of *Archipelago* from 2007 to 2019, has had its share of lines drawn and crossed, lines of demarcation, lines of association, connections made and promises broken. Commitments have been renewed and investments have been taken further, both in what people put into the country and what others take out of it. Yet increasingly the idea of the archipelago has deepened and enriched our sense of what Scotland is in the global or even the universal context. I mean this literally. The Caribbean laureate Derek Walcott in 'The Schooner *Flight*' says it like this: 'Open the map. More islands there, man, / than peas on a tin plate, all different size, / One thousand in the Bahamas alone …' Then he says this:

The bowsprit, the arrow, the longing, the lunging heart –
the flight to a target whose aim we'll never know,
vain search for one island that heals with its harbour
and a guiltless horizon, where the almond's shadow
doesn't injure the sand. There are so many islands!
As many islands as stars at night
on that branched tree from which meteors are shaken
like falling fruit around the schooner *Flight*.
But things must fall, and so it always was,
on one hand Venus, on the other Mars;
fall, and are one, just as this earth is one
island in archipelagos of stars.

For if looking out and up shows you 'the cold sea rippling like galvanize / and the nail holes of stars in the sky roof' and gives you the prospect of journeys and connections and navigation by the constellations, then standing firm on the earth also gives you a sense of compass points, of responsibilities, of time's currents and the borders of our deepest concerns and loves.

Walcott in the West Indies knew that archipelagic world intimately, just as Sorley MacLean, Iain Crichton Smith, Aongheas MacNeacail, Derick Thomson and Meg Bateman know the Outer and Inner Hebrides; Edwin Muir and George Mackay Brown know Orkney; and Hugh MacDiarmid, William Tait, Christine De Luca and Jen Hadfield know Shetland. Taking ourselves around the borders of Scotland, from what Norman MacCaig called the 'capital-in-waiting', Edinburgh, to the northern then the western isles, returns us by another Celtic 'commodious vicus' beyond Joyce's remit, to the Solway's tidal estuary and what it might portend.

Let's say it starts with what's given, in that Gaelic word *dùthchas*, which is threefold: land, people and culture. And here 'land' includes islands, seascapes, whale roads. There is no Gaelic word for nation, prioritising the legal limits of the nation-state, but *dùthchas* gives you a relational identity: three things that work with each other to create something unique to a place, related across time to what we would call a nation, open and porous to the coming and going of people, over time, for better or worse, and characterised by, interpreted by, represented to others by its own cultural production, things to be accepted and approved or resisted and changed.

A series of evocations, to remind ourselves of this various terrain and its different seas, is what Alexander Moffat, Ruth Nicol and I began with in the work that has gone into the touring exhibition *Landmarks: Poets, Portraits and Landscapes of Modern Scotland*. The show opened in the Lillie Gallery, just north of Glasgow, in January 2018, then went to Montrose on the east coast, and then to St Andrews, and further. Moffat's portraits of the great Scottish poets were complemented by Nicol's landscapes, each evoking their respective territories, and poems of my own, along with biographical essays and 'encounters'. The literary authority of the poets was itself complemented by the oral, folk traditions of music and song, collectively evoked in Moffat's painting 'Scotland's Voices' (2017), a partner to the famous 'Poets' Pub' (1981) from the Scottish National Portrait Gallery. The central point about the show was that the work of the poets should be understood in the contexts of the places where generations since have lived and live now, the carrying stream that runs into futures we'll never know. Some of the inhabitants of these various places honour their poets and artists by reading and looking at their work, drawing what lines they will to connect them, to keep them distinct from others, and fresh for the future.

Yet 'Scotland's Voices' complements the literary tradition of the poets with the oral and folk tradition of the singers and musicians, many of whom were women, and these considerations open and extend our sense of the lines of connection and the distinction of the patterns they help generate, the cradle they become of the life of the future. This is what makes the nation. It arises, not from rules laid down or imposed from above or outside and obeyed, but through reading, performing and respecting what life is, what these lives were and continue to be, and give. And if it is a nation, it exists because of its distinction. So let's take all that as a given, a place or condition from which everything arises.

Within this place or condition, this variously populated, geologically differentiated, historically rich area or terrain or territory – call it what you will – there are co-ordinate points. That's why we called the exhibition 'Landmarks': these are the most secure places, sites from which you can navigate your way around the country from place to place, and explore its history, and go back in time through different languages. In Gaelic, Scots and English, these depths of time and distances of space are held in a perpetually changing, somehow stable equilibrium. Demographics are never enough.

In Edinburgh, the city MacDiarmid called 'a mad God's dream', look north from the Castle terrace to Columba's other island in the Firth of Forth, not Iona but Inchcolm, where the music of the Inchcolm Antiphoner was probably written at the end of the thirteenth and beginning of the fourteenth centuries, drawing on a whole archive of Celtic Christian plainchant. This marks the first of our locations. Inchcolm was founded in 1123 by Alexander I and the Antiphoner contains music commemorating Columba which would have been performed in the monastery there dedicated to him, and which may have come from inherited material originally sung and perhaps recorded in older manuscripts from Iona itself. The two islands balance each other on either side of the country and take us from the sixth to the twelfth centuries. Now come forward and go north. Take a line north-east to Catterline, Joan Eardley's seascapes, paintings we cannot neglect. Looking at 'January, Flow Tide' (1960), 'The Wave' (1961) and 'Summer Sea' (1962) can leave you breathless.

It's difficult to say why without becoming pedantic, talking about technique, the clutch of the paint at grasses, blown straw, scraps of living things, or melodramatic, talking about the scale and overwhelming authority she is acknowledging here. Eardley, like Turner and McTaggart, both confirms and defies the authority of nature. This is maybe most apparent in the sequence of five small pastels, 'Approaching Storm' (1963), tiny sketches on paper, not dependent upon the scale of the great seascapes, but equally urgent and dramatic in their rapidly executed depictions of cloud and sea. Once seen, these are permanently lodged in the visual imagination. They are works which remind you of an absolute imperative, just as Wallace Stevens's 'Snow Man', winter-minded, a listener, listening in the snow, 'beholds / Nothing that is not there and the nothing that is'. In his book, *Dear Sibelius*, Marshall Walker describes what the great composer captures in the icy chill of the tone poem 'Tapiola': 'spears of wind and shards of light glittering from icicles, reflected by snow-caked branches along interminable corridors of quintessential cold'. Stevens and Sibelius evoke winter forests, but Eardley turned to an even greater austerity, the sea, 'an apotheosis of unpeopled nature': 'purely and impersonally itself, as far from considerations of human reason as the iceberg that sank the *Titanic*'. That's what Eardley saw, looking at the North Sea off Catterline.

Go further north, and the line crosses over the edge of the sea: Orcadia. The cobbled streets in deep dark winter and the high, eternal skies of long warm breezy summers. Here's George Mackay Brown, recording the voyages of his people, living till, at the very last, in the hours before his own death, he said that he could see all the ships now leaving the harbour. He wrote: 'The children of time, their roof-trees should be strong.'

And further north, to Shetland: to the farthest limits of what Scotland means, to Unst, to Yell and Whalsay, where MacDiarmid lived in the 1930s. You can walk down from the house where he and his wife Valda and their young son Michael lived, and come to the well in the field, down the slope from the bod. It was covered over when I was there but still you could lift the stones and panels, wave the green weed to the side and drink the replenishing water.

Come back south now, cross the sea again, to Sutherland, Lochinver and Assynt like a sugarloaf shouldering high, with its unmappable streams and lochs and lochans and elusive little trout. Norman MacCaig's favoured territory. This is walkable land, where the whole shapely skyline changes every hundred yards, as if you were on a ship at sea. Horizons are deceptive. The schoolmaster looks through the classroom window and reads the land and sea out there with one Greek eye and one Latin one, while 'a boat rounds the point in Gaelic'.

Go south-west now, to Skye and over to Raasay, the waterfall below Hallaig, with flat-topped Dun Cana rising above. Then back to Skye, to Braes, round the winding valley road from Portree, the Cuillins in the distance in their dignity and imposition. And Sorley MacLean, looking over the sea to Screapadal in north Raasay, saying of the factor Rainy, who cleared fourteen townships, that he left the place without people, without houses or cattle, only sheep: 'but he left Screapadal beautiful; / in his time he could do nothing else'. Seals lift their heads, a basking shark its sail,

> but today in the sea sound
> a submarine lifts its turret
> and its black sleek back
> threatening the thing that would make
> dross of wood, of meadows and rocks
> that would leave Screapadal without beauty
> just as it was left without people.

The threat is vivid here, of tragic, irreparable loss, the fact of the loss that has happened, the worst of things that have been and may come. And in the Outer Isles, in Lewis, Derrick Thomson's 'An Tobar' or 'The Well', tells us of 'an old woman' who speaks to the poet, and asks him to deliver some water from the well to her, 'even a thimbleful /to bring back the colour to my cheeks' – but going to the well, the poet finds 'only bracken and rushes, /and the old woman's eyes are closed /and a film has come over their merriment'. This is the territory, Iain Crichton Smith reminds us in 'Poem of Lewis', where people 'have no time for the fine graces / of poetry, unless it freely grows / in deep compulsion, like water in the well' – begging the question, how deep must such compulsion be? Will 'the barren rock' still give 'a value to / the bursting flower'? Liz Lochhead describes this, in 'Another Life' in her second collection, *Islands*:

> From each dour house
> always this always black

and white dog comes to stand stock still.
He's only ruffled by the wind.
He doesn't waste a bark.

From such true austerities, resilience and resistance arise. These strengths are measured and tested by the vulnerabilities and sensitivities of the living, women and men. So south, now, to Oban and Taynuilt and Glen Etive: the landscape of the lovers, Deirdre, Naoise, beautiful in sunshine, hard in the snow. The deer on the high hills show you where to go. As Deirdre sings in her last farewell to Scotland, 'I would never have come here and never have left, were it not for my one true love.'

Anyone wishing to discover more of the sense of this in music might find John Purser's CD, *Dreaming of Islands* (JWP010) and listen to 'Creagan Beaga', a setting of a MacLean poem for soprano, clarsachs and cello, and 'Tha Thu Air Aigeann M'Inntin' – 'You Are at the Bottom of My Mind' – a setting of a Crichton Smith poem for two cellos and soprano. And there is an unforgettable setting of 'Deirdre's Farewell' on the double CD set, *Scotland's Music* (LINN CKD008). The music itself takes you deeper.

The poets and writers and artists and composers of modern Scotland, to some degree like Derek Walcott in the Caribbean, engaged with a diversity of terrains, a range of different seascapes, a world of archipelagos as vividly realised, as closely explored, and as essential to our understanding of the human story as those of Homer and the ancient Greeks. There was Philoctetes, with his suppurating wound, waiting with his bow, knowing that in time, Odysseus must return for him, for without him the war will never end. This world had been divided. The dividedness conjured hostility, as it always does. In Scotland, maybe more than elsewhere, this happened over centuries. But all the arts welcome otherness, make enquiries into it with all the intrinsic optimism of curiosity.

Whatever the hand holds: camera, paintbrush, pencil, pen
the fingertips upon the laptop's keys, the paper, screen or canvas

and the air the senses carry in – make traces, tracks, a patterning
that moves out from the place and its location on the clock,
to be caught, glimpsed, held on, whatever that may be,
and at whatever time, but never trapped. That is what work we do.

The lines that connect differences are what all of us make, as we write, draw, paint, score, as surely as we make the attempt to keep these worlds safe and accessible to those who respect the life of them. And protect them against those who don't.

Mountains are permanence. Rivers are change.
Rocks and stones will build your bones.
Words are what we live by.
And water is what moves us all, even now, the carrying stream.

So to the Border, where we draw the line. MacDiarmid saw and heard three lines, in Langholm, three long rivers, moving, and said he could tell where he was, as a boy, just by the sounds of the water moving, running fast and walloping, or flowing slow and charming. Still, you can turn your head and one ear leaves the sound behind, while the other picks up another. You know where you are, you can navigate between the vital, vitalising, liquid co-ordinates, the points and lines that give co-ordination.

These poets of modern Scotland lived in the tidal wake, receding, of the First and then the Second World Wars. And Ireland, and Russia. And another tide advancing, the rising of another war, on knowledge, on reason, on life. The truths these poets give us are perennial but each has its own geography, and place on the cosmic clock. And they bring us back. Something unplanned, intuitive, relaxed, working in the bones and muscle, way below the memory of things: abstraction, yet as real as salt spray that hit you like a shower switched on when the ferry smashed the cross-wave and a blast of blue and green turned white as frost and drenched you in a sudden cold – as if all resolution, steel and ice were sensitised. This is what sharpens your vision, allows you to see what has changed and what remains, and by whatever chance and will should be, what's drawn back by magic. Edwin Morgan, writing in the

1960s, in 'Glasgow Green' tells us that 'the beds of married love / are islands in a sea of desire': the rare things that need to be valued and the vulnerable things that need to be cared for. Which brings us to the Solway, at last.

In a recent excellent collection of critical essays all related to the central concerns of *Archipelago*, *Coastal Works: Cultures of the Atlantic Edge*, edited by Nicholas Allen, Nick Groom and Jos Smith, Fiona Stafford has a remarkable essay, 'The Roar of the Solway', provocatively connecting Walter Scott, John Ruskin, Matthew Arnold and Ciaran Carson. I'd like to draw to a close with her reading of a key passage in Scott's *Redgauntlet* (1824). To quote Fiona Stafford, 'Much of the action of *Redgauntlet* takes place around the Solway, but the most dramatic moment occurs *in* the Firth itself, when Darsie [the central character and narrator of much of the novel] is forcibly taken at night from a fishing hut on the Scottish coast. He is injured, bound and helpless, lying in a cart in the darkness and only able to guess where he might be. Gradually, the slow movement of the cart, "sinking" and "sticking", makes him realize he is in "the formidable estuary which divides the two kingdoms", mired in the mudflats, surrounded by quicksands. This is a place of meeting and division – where rivers meet the sea, where earth meets firth, where Scotland meets England, north meets south – and where the estuary divides all. In the darkness, Darsie's normally sharp sight becomes redundant, and as the surrounding sounds are accentuated, he hears first the sudden, alarmed dispersal of his mysterious captors, and then the terrifying approach of the tide.'

Stafford then quotes Scott, and these are Darsie's words: 'There lay my native land – my own England – the land where I was born, and to which my wishes, since my earliest age, had turned with all the prejudice of national feeling – there it lay, within a furlong of the place where I was; yet was that furlong, which an infant would have raced over in a minute, a barrier effectual to divide me for ever from England and from life. I soon not only heard the roar of this dreadful torrent, but saw, by the fitful moonlight, the foamy crests of the devouring waves, as they advanced with the speed and fury of a pack of hungry wolves.'

Stafford comments: 'There is nothing reassuring about the sound of the Solway. The ancient impulse to animate the physical phenomena seems as natural as the fear inspired by the sound of the approaching tide. This is an image of terrifying inundation, as the waves are transformed into a wolf pack, roaring hungrily. The vivid focus on the hapless figure, whose struggle for personal identity against overwhelming external forces drives the entire narrative, enables Scott to convey the formidable power of the estuary, where at one moment the waters part to allow crossings, but at the next, the unstoppable sea charges inland, engulfing everything in its path.' Scott's Solway, she notes, 'is a border region, a place of the in-between, dangerous, full of secrets, where strange things shift over sands by night'.

Edwin Morgan, in his sequence *Sonnets from Scotland* (1984), evokes a different picture. This is another vision of the Solway and its potential to establish Scotland itself, with all its various voices, as part of a literal archipelago that it takes a leap of faith to make more than imaginable. 'The Solway Canal' is not the first nor last in the sequence but it was the first to be written and its symbolic power is both a memorial to past lives and a prospect of future possibility in a Scotland where the line has been drawn literally. Morgan's space- and time-travellers sail on their hydrofoil slowly through the Cheviot hills at dawn, under the high steel bridge at Carter Bar, in fog, quietly, past wet rock walls on either side 'and scarves of dim half-sparkling April mist':

> a wizard with a falcon on his wrist
> was stencilled on our bow. Rough waterfalls
> flashed on that northern island of the Scots
> as the sun steadily came up and cast
> red light along the uplands and the waves,
> and gulls with open beaks tore out our thoughts
> through the thick glass to where the Eildons massed,
> or down to the Canal's drowned borderers' graves.

We are with these voyagers, cruising along this humanly created border, not a wall but a waterway, not an end but a source of renewal and a form of connection, respecting life, honouring the dead, touching nature, valuing warmth, sensitive to the wet, wild, wilderness world, but confident enough to draw the line, to take the risk, to delineate, to inhabit such a territory, a modern, future fiction with commitment strong enough to one day make it real. That line has not reached its endpoint yet. And when it does, it will be only another beginning.

David Douglas and Angus Macmillan (EIGHT)

Mūjo

Up on moorland at six hundred feet above sea-level, in the Stewartry district of Galloway, the ground is wet, and first a trickle then a torrent of burns runs into the loch. At its south-west corner, a small burn runs out. It is the start of the River Urr. All about are wild rush, sedge, moss and moorland grass, variously waterlogged, according to season and rainfall. When the sun shines, as it does even here occasionally, the meaning of the moorland's Gaelic name becomes clear: Moneybuie derives from *Monadh buidhe*, the yellow moorland. All around the moor is the half-turned evidence of long-gone occupation – cairns, battered tumuli and, in the loch, a *crannog* or man-made island, with its submerged causeway and, recently discovered, the rough-hewn remains of an oak canoe. In geological terms, in the language of deep time, the loch lies at the centre of a ground-down cirque, surrounded on three sides by the hard-rock greywacke of the hills nearby.

Every place is unique, as somewhere Thoreau says, and this is no *terra nullius*. Like many another obscure territory of the kind, the Urr and its catchment is rich in presences and absences, traces of early and more recent settlement, occupation and struggle, all inflected by a haunting linguistic history. The river runs from the loch of its name some thirty-five miles to the sea. South towards Corsock, it passes Crogo Mill – a medieval manor house and chapel – and the old mills of Corsock. Then down beyond Areeming Pool, it swings suddenly east, helter-skelter roll-rock through a series of rapids, before turning south again, past the Brig of Urr (once a milltown) and the planned estate of Kings Grange. Next, on it dashes or glides past Spottes (mansion house and mill), the Haugh and the Motte of Urr (medieval motte and bailey), to Buittle or Bottle (tower house home of Devorgilla, celebrated wife of the no-less celebrated John Balliol). Here the Urr becomes tidal, meandering past the Dub o' Hass (Old Scots: the pool at the throat), the old port at Dalbeattie, to the silt-lined estuary at the port of Palnackie, once a smugglers' retreat.

Just by Buittle the river valley reaches its narrowest point, and between Dalmone Hill and Barsolus, both masses of indurated greywacke, heated and made rock-hard by the granite to form low hills, the river punches through like a stream of once-departed ice, to open a hairline crack in the margin of the Criffel-Bengairn pluton. This is a vast mass of granodiorite stretching some twenty miles along the coast from New Abbey to Auchencairn and at its highest point reaches just short of two thousand feet. Beyond Palnackie is a granite-lined indentation to the coast, the estuary of the Urr and the Rough Firth, which leads past Almorness, an elongated rocky nose, full of granite sculptures in mire and midden scrapes, to the Solway and the Irish Sea beyond.

*

The area is fertile ground for researchers, with placenames reflecting the interplay of languages and the shifting of political power. It is likely that Scots came to replace Gaelic as the language of the upper strata of society, with Gaelic clinging on in the rural areas amongst those who worked the land. The push and pull of languages is readily observed in Scottish words such as 'doon', a re-working of the Gaelic *dùn*, for 'fort' or 'hill', while Kirklebride, an old graveyard by Margley, is a mixture of Scots *kirk*, Gaelic *cill* for 'church' and the name of the saint, Bridghe. There was a church to St Brigid, long since disappeared, and a holy well – all dry dust now – by Blaiket Plantation (Scots: *black oak*). Almorness reflects the elision of Gaelic and Norse – *àl mor*: Gaelic for *great rock*, and *nes*: Norse for *nose*.

Most of the placenames in the Urr catchment and wider vicinity, to east, north and west, are rooted in Gaelic, reflecting the extent to which this was the language of Galloway in earlier times, and its survival into the 1500s. The word Urr itself derives from the Gaelic *oir* meaning 'edge' or 'boundary'.

What is it an edge to, what boundary does it mark? The charter of the twelfth-century abbey of Holm Cultrain tells us the Urr was the border between old East and West Galloway, in the reign of Fergus, one that in later times shifted westward to the River Cree (Gaelic *crioch*, another word for 'boundary') which flows down through the town of Newton Stewart and into Wigtown Bay. Every type of marauder has had their day in this peninsula, stuck like a ragged isthmus at the south-west margin of Scotland, pointing on towards Ireland. They have all conquered here: Romans, Irish Gaels, Scots Gaels, the Picts, the Angles, Norse and Danes, the Normans, the Scots, and after wresting their bit of land would eventually intermarry and settle down. Within modern times it was the waves of Irish, escaping the potato blight misery of their homeland, who settled. In the 1860s, 30 per cent of the next county to the west, Wigtownshire, and fifteen percent of the county through which the Urr flows – the Stewarty – was Irish.

There would have been a time when the landscape was peppered with the dense particularity of naming required by those who actively worked the land and moved livestock around. Placenames would have been one facet of an oral culture, held in memory and given life in daily exchanges and regular talk. There is some resonance in such places with Bruce Chatwin's accounts in *Songlines* of how aborigines 'sang' the landscape and its features into being, with a sense of the land itself, with all its features, being encoded in the melody and rhythm of the song.

Around the Urr area, as in many other rural settings, when the use-dependence of the name faded away, along with the valuing implicit in it, so did the name itself: what now remains is often skeletally Gaelic, often corrupted into a map-maker's nonsense syllables.

Many names, once deciphered, bring descriptive colour to the landscape – names such as Dunjarg: *Dùn dearg* – red hillock; Drumwhirn: *Druim chuirn* – ridge of the cairn; Glaister's Hill: *Glas tir* – green land. Others hint at ways of living and practices long-gone. Elrig Moss is derived from the Gaelic *eileirig,* which refers to a deer trap in which the animals would be herded through a narrow defile and then shot with arrows. East of Dalbeattie, Craignair, from *Creag an àir* – crag of the slaughter, probably described a similar setting. Areeming, from *àiridh meadhan*, middle shieling, suggests the practice of transhumance, in which animals would be moved away to summer grazings – the shieling was the simple building which housed those looking after the animals. Knockvennie, from *Cnoc a bhainne,* the milking-hill, envisages a spot where the cows would be gathered each morning and evening. There are many more examples. And always, once the ghosts of meaning emerge, the name infuses our seeing.

*

The history of human habitation here is rich and complex and we are still learning about it. Notable in this respect is a series of what appear to be Iron-Age hilltop forts, some twelve to fourteen in all, paired on either side of the river. This stretches the idea of *oir* or boundary back beyond the so-called Dark Ages. Apart from the Mote of Mark, fifth century and Anglian, by the mouth of the river close to Scaur or Rockcliffe and Rough Island, the forts, surprisingly, have been very little explored. They stretch on opposite sides of the river from the Solway at Mote of Mark/Cocklehaen to Moyle Hill/Ramshorn Wood, to Buittle, to Waterside/Camp Hill (where one of us lives at the Haugh of Urr), to Mote Hill, Clarebrand/the Doon of Urr; Glenroan/Margley and possibly Arkland/Monnydow Mote. No dates have yet been assigned to them. They are sited on the hilltops on either side of the valley, making use of the old *drumlins* – shaped mounds deposited in the last Ice Age. The summit of the Doon of Urr, about thirty feet high and a hundred feet long, resembles an upturned boat, with a surrounding ditch, and rampart which would once have been palisaded round with tree trunks. In place of the rampart today, is an elliptical plantation of oak, elm and Scots pine. If you peer from between the trees it is possible to see up and down the valley to the scarp-shaped mound of Screel, and the conical Bengairn, to the south-west, in the Criffel range. To the west, about a mile and a half away is the next fort on the other side of the river at Mote Hill, Clarebrand. Similarly, to the north-west upstream, Glenroan is just visible on the other side of the low rise to the valley. The pairings and strategic positions of the forts suggest that the river served as a boundary many centuries before the Holm Cultrain scribe so described it, into a time of warring tribes camped either side of a border zone – the river – and keeping an eye on each other.

While placenames are clues to ways of living on the land, what is of greater interest to the archaeologist are the more substantial remains. Of these, the Motte of Urr is the best example, home to a vassal of Uchtred, son of Alan of Galloway, from the twelfth century. It stands an upturned pudding bowl of a motte, plainly visible for miles up and down the valley, and located about a mile downstream of the Haugh. Yet even here, the past gets lost. There was an excavation in the early 1950s – we have a photograph of twelve of the diggers, all kitted up in thei ex-army shorts, tackety boots, the odd beret that probably originally saw service in North Africa, the men sucking their pipes, the women linking arms. Unfortunately, the notes to the expedition got lost. Its leader, Brian Hope-Taylor, left them on a train. Only a few years ago they turned up and, if rumour is to be believed, the findings are soon to be published. Given that the Motte of Urr is generally admitted to be the most impressive example of a motte-and-bailey castle in Scotland, it is surely remarkable that we still await the report.

*

If landscape may be considered as a system of signs planted by persons not cognitively dissimilar to us in the past, then reading and rereading it is to decipher, remember and perhaps come to understand some sort of textual palimpsest: a half-erased, rubbed-over, re-transcribed piece of territory in which a jigsaw of the past comes gradually and only partially to life.

The Urr, of course, is a salmon river, and downstream of the motte are many salmon pools. The returning fish, with the scents of the river of its birth encoded in its memory will struggle its way by Step End pool, Cauls, the Battery and Red Braes, and all the various other upstream pools, past the rapids till it reaches its spawning ground on the headwaters up above Drumwhirn – assuming, of course, that it has not been outwitted by the local anglers. There is money in salmon, and there is money in stone. Just beyond Buittle is the steep hillside leading up to Craignair, the home of the granite quarries of Dalbeattie. From the 1850s, the quarries exported this fine-grained stone in setts, founds and blocks to half the world – to the Liverpool docks, the Eddystone Lighthouse, the London embankment, to Valletta and to New York. Fifty thousand tons were exported in 1901. It is difficult now to picture the bustle of a harbour next to Dalbeattie, since little of it remains, beyond a stretch of revetment and one or two bollards. Yet a photograph from 1897 shows fourteen sailing ships at anchor. Imagine the incoming barques, and the indignity of these great sailing ships being dismasted and towed four miles upstream by horses all the way to the port, the Dub o' Hass, discharging fertiliser and lime, which was carted out to make the acid soil fitter for growing rye and wheat.

*

If you have ever driven west to Wigtown and the Machars, or on to catch the ferry at Stranraer, you will have crossed, and possibly glimpsed, the Urr below, at the Ramshill Brig, about a mile from Castle Douglas where it is sign-posted. You are far likelier to have blinked and missed it, unless perhaps you are a fisher, with all that that implies as to a gleam of water and idle speculation. Worlds like these can find themselves at risk if left to their obscurity. Just so now, the region of the river's head-waters, to the north and east of the loch, finds itself in the sights of an energy company. They see it merely as ideal territory for a large-scale windfarm. To err is human. It is an all-too-common story in rural and wilderness Scotland these days.

To help raise awareness of the place, in all its historical and cultural dimensions, we have begun working on a cycle of poetry and song – *Facail aig an Oir*: Words at the Edge – set within a soundscape spoken by the people who live and work by the river. Meanwhile it seems vital to provide a brief cultural geography of the river and its environs, so that all who go hurrying over Ramshill Brig (windfarmers, please note) have no excuse any more but to give pause to thought as they go, and perhaps to turn off the treadmill, tunnel-vision track to follow the twists and turns of the north–south B-road (B794) that runs the length of the Urr Valley. Let them slow down. Let them know that to Urr is rewardingly human and that, in the words of that great mapmaker and makar Tim Robinson: 'Without the occasional renewal of memory and regular rehearsal of meaning, place itself founders into shapelessness, and time, the great amnesiac, forgets all.'

Our goal has been to bring to greater awareness the history and culture of the river valley, and to bring alive its many strata, both natural and human. It is not to inhabit a romantic, idealised view of the past, with some formulaic idea of 'wilderness' or what constitutes beauty in the landscape. To research such terrain is after all to be alert to the acoustic memories and visual eruptions of the everyday as well as having an eye for past history. A cursory scan of the river's history highlights the sheer impermanence of things, and this transience has to be acknowledged: one needs to cultivate something of that Japanese aesthetic ideal (*mūjo)* that values change and perishability above all else, when dealing with landscape.

Kathleen Jamie (NINE)

Well Doubtful

At the close of a recent winter afternoon I was walking across the sparsely wooded bank of a small loch in the hills near my home. On the hill crest westward, some tall larches stood silhouetted against a ruby sky. Nearer, each at a discrete distance from the next, were rowans and hawthorns, now without leaves. Suddenly a roe deer broke cover from a thicket and bounded down the bank toward the water's edge. It was visible only as a density, a shadow leaping, before it was reabsorbed into the twilight.

That seemed the signal for dark. An owl called from the trees, and it was night. Wild, short midwinter dusks. The old year sent on its way.

I'd been out of kilter with things for a while, edgy and listless at once, my thinking lazy and fragmented. The world bored me. Language bored me: its sensuousness and resonance had leached away, words seemed just a means by which people told each other things they thought each other ought to know.

For a year or so, this had gone on. These phases happen. Just before the deer suffered its moment of insecurity, and startled me, I'd been reminding myself of what everyone said, that patience is the best prescription. So it is. We seem to undergo phases of awareness, then unawareness, estrangement then reconnection. Between times it's as though something has to be replenished.

Despite that, I was hoping not to carry this frame of mind into another year. You can't make demands, I was telling myself, but maybe sometimes you can be a bit more pro-active, take steps to re-calibrate yourself.

The track ahead was quite dark now. The deer and darkness, the owl and the trees, the water holding the very last of the light.

Go somewhere, I told myself. A big trip. Get away from the familiar. By now I'd gained the road, it was a short mile-and-a-half walk downhill and home. The yellow lights of the town shone below, I could hear the rush-hour traffic. My children were down there, still quite young. I'd make a big trip one day, a good long one, god willing, but it would have to wait a few years yet.

Closer to home then. Just choose something. No, three things.

Why three?

It's the magic number. Also, it spreads the weight, like a milking stool. No one would be too … significant.

What things?

You know. Simple things. And nearby. Three things, near at hand.

And then what? I've done that kind of stuff before, visiting things.

Well, do it again. Be like a pianist, going through her scales. You never know.

I came back in through the kitchen door and the kids were home, the TV blaring, unwashed dishes were piled in the sink. 'Three things near at hand,' I told myself, but the idea just sounded lame.

*

The road I'd come down, a single-track byway, is called the Sweerie, *sweir* or *sweer* being an old Scots word for reluctant. It's an understandable name, because the road climbs six hundred feet in about a mile towards a hill pass which has been in use since ancient times. A week went by, a week deeper into winter. The little project, the 'three things' forgotten, I again went out a walk, taking the same route. The sky, a cold blue, faded to ashy white round the sun, which lay low in the sky. At the brow of the hill thirty-odd linnets were sitting on a wire, backlit by the sun, but they flew, like crumbs shaken from a tablecloth, and the wire was bare. The loch where the deer had startled lay calm. At its west end, the larches last seen infused with such dark ruby passion, intense and aware, were now a benign copse.

I passed the loch, then on a whim, at a junction of two forestry tracks, turned north through an anonymous stretch of brashy plateau, which ends in a steep slope down to the Firth of Tay 600 feet below. Pylons crest the hill here. Having crossed the river below, they mount the slope and stride on southward. I stood under a pylon, looked at the river widening below, and at the lattice vortex above me. In some lights, pylons have an almost supernatural capacity for invisibility, like animals do – but not for silence, in any wind they become audible, emitting low fluty drones.

There were deer droppings under the pylon among the scruffy vegetation. Maybe the deer I'd seen the other evening had been here. Or its kin.

Two or three of them together. The warm deer, in an open cage.

The electric cables cross the river at much the same point as where the Romans laid their pontoon bridges 1,800 years ago but that's hardly surprising. The topography hasn't changed. Both sets of surveyors must have looked at the river, perhaps from this very vantage point, and come to similar conclusions. There was a Roman military encampment at the riverside; they were pushing north, but this is about as far as they got. The end of empire. You can see why: from here the view north, the direction of their ambition, was only hills receding into snow and pointlessness. The same cold wind funneled down the river-valley; they had the eyes of Pictish tribes on them from the hills around. You wonder if, as they stood here, doubt was already creeping in.

At home the lights were on, the TV too. My husband was in his workshop but when I put my head round the door the living room was empty. There was the red sofa, cushions dented, training shoes and schoolbags strewn on the floor, but *Hollyoaks* played to an empty room.

'Power from the Glens' – that's what they'd called the heroic drive to build dams and turbines to bring to everyone the white light of modernity.

I turned off the telly, and in the kitchen switched on the kettle, and drank a mug of tea leaning my back against the sink, because that way I didn't have to look at it, mysteriously replenished with unwashed plates.

*

Christmas passed. The last days of the old year. It would be some weeks yet before the first brisk true splash of light reached us here on the north side of the hill. If you want sunshine, you best take the Sweerie road.

The kids were back at school. Again with no particular destination in mind, one afternoon I took the dog and went up the hill, this time keeping south of the hillcrest, pines on my right, a flow of farmland leftward. The sun caught a party of siskins in a tree-top, all golden opulence, and a red squirrel, clamped to a pine-trunk, gave me one appraising look then scuttered away up among the branches.

I followed the track through the wood till I came across a path I'd never taken before; a green lace leading off between close-planted trees.

It wound on, turning and definitely, almost playfully *going somewhere*. At length it delivered me out of the wood, to the edge of a sloping field, which I crossed, and at the bottom of the field there was a well. Not much of a well, but a well nonetheless. The lintel stone, four foot long or so, had been dressed, and some boulders piled on it, but aside from that, aside from spangles of light reflected on the lintel's underside, there was nought to announce the place but an enamel sink dug into the ground to receive the run of water. It was full of rotting oak leaves. A sink in a field, and from it, a constant, modest flow.

I took the notion to drink some. It was fine and fresh, but in truth I preferred hot coffee from my flask, so sat in the sun with my back to a beech tree. The M90, maybe three miles as the crow flies, was a faint roar.

I went home by the same route. Already the light was fading. Dusk would come suddenly again, the deer seek shelter, the electric lights be switched on.

*

That night, when we'd eaten and the dishes were done, I spread out the map on the kitchen table, the larger-scale map, the map of the near at hand. I was interested in the well I'd found. There was the river, just where it begins widening into a firth, sand-banked, ambiguous. There were the hills, marked 'fort' and the thin barbed line denoting pylons and cables, strung over the river and the land. Tucked between hills was the loch, and threads feeding it, with sprightly blue words 'spring' 'spring'. There was a landscape the map couldn't give – those underground, geological movements of strata and water. The dowser's land. The well was given at the very edge of the map. Just a blue dot and a curious name.

*

In 1883 an architect called J. Russell Walker wrote an essay on Holy Wells in Scotland and published it in the *Proceedings of the Society of Antiquarians.* There used to be many holy and healing wells; the insane were led to St Fillans, the blind to St Severan's, the Straid well at Stirling was good for whooping cough.

A Walker by name and by nature, our man must have covered the miles. He made up an alphabetical list of saints' wells from St Abbs to St Wynnin and provided some nice architectural drawings of wellhouses. The days of well-visiting were coming to an end; modern medicine and plumbing, more than the wrath of the church, were putting paid to it. Most wells were no longer visited at all, but before they were all forgotten, Mr Walker appealed for information. After the long list of wells with saints' names, the 'titular wells', he closed his essay with another list of wells about which he had no information, and which he had not been able to visit. These he called the 'wells doubtful'. Doubtful whether they were ever regarded as holy. He listed the Cheeze Well, the Galstack Well, the Blints Well and the Dockan Well, the Dubs Pot, the Rottenrow, the Fairy Well and the Marriage Well, the Well of Corhint and Katie Thirsty Well, Willie's Well and Skellie Well – all these and many more. Could anyone tell him whether these wells were ever considered sacred, or renowned for curative powers?

Katie Thirsty was my well. A 'well doubtful', and all unwitting I had drunk of her; a Katie of a sort, with a drouth on me.

*

Maybe it was just the turning of the year, but I found myself engaging with the world again. Caught myself thinking: about the ambivalence and caution of animals, like that deer, who have managed to sustain in the land despite all. About power and inconstancy, and the transience of empires. About the small solemn journeys we no longer make. To healing wells, for example. Even to libraries or postboxes. I thought about the old metaphor of the source, and the ever-replenishing kitchen sink, to which we resort five hundred times a day. Of startled deer, and growing children. They would be gone soon enough: training shoes, schoolbags, *Hollyoaks* and all.

Language began to thaw. I'd enjoyed Mr Walker's litany of wells – merely to read it aloud would surely cure *something*: Arms Well on the Green, Robach, Beardy, Millinmonie's well. What pleasure there is in the flow and play of language, its fluency, its short-circuits and eddies, and its lovely pathetic fallacies, so called, how a hill can be sweer and a well doubtful.

Or thirsty. A well called Katie Thirsty! Some hiccough in the language over the centuries had confused the drinking of water with the issuing of it; or so you'd think, but an expert on local place names told me that Katie probably did derive from St Catherine. Thirsty, on the other hand, may have come from Durst, a Pictish king, once a power in the land and now utterly forgot. To think whole languages, kingdoms, cultures can be lost, except for old names which cling to their places like sheep's wool to a wire.

'After the commanded journey, what? / Nothing magnificent, nothing unknown.'

Better. No longer out of kilter. Thinking again, but to no great conclusion. But then, I'm not sure if conclusions and judgments are the proper end of thought. Maybe a constant deer-like uncertainty carries the day. Better a well doubtful, than a striding emperor.

'Three things near at hand,' I'd told myself, but they'd snuck up on me of their own: a deer, a pylon and a well. Ach. These phases have their own energies, their own hidden geologies, coursing through our lives. And what is 'kilter' anyway? The proper way or knack of doing something. Good spirits or fettle. A slope for the run-off of the rain.

James Macdonald Lockhart
(FOUR)

Raptor

On my desk I have a buzzard's feather I found in a field near my home. It is a wing flight feather with a narrow leading edge. If I hold it close to my eye I can follow the course the air took over it, its subtle contours, the rising lip of its trailing edge. Gull white and downy at the base, the white pales through shades and browns. It is banded by waves of darker brown that run across the vane like a cardiogram report.

I place the feather over a map of the Hebrides and it fits the Isle of Jura like a jigsaw piece; the quill slots into Islay as if it were an inkpot. Along the trailing edge the barbs have split to form a wide V which cuts in as far as the rachis. Beneath this split I can see Loch Tarbert almost cutting Jura in two.

Jura is known as 'the island of deer', from the Norse dyr-ey (deer island). But for me it is also an island of raptors. On my first visit, six years ago, I remember walking down a glen to the north-west coast and being amazed by the number of hen harriers and short-eared owls I saw hunting low over the moor. It was an evening in late May and their long wings worked the deer-grass like scythes.

I packed the buzzard's feather, map and binoculars and travelled back to Jura early in August this year. Waiting in the passing places along the single-track road, I smelt the deep bracken which clots the island's drier ground in summer. In the village a door to the distillery had been left open and I saw the casks waiting in the cool gloom. A smell of cave and malt slipped out through the door. The warehouse reminded me of a ship's deep hull, the cask barrels its cargo. I thought of the merlin that came aboard the weather ship *India* five hundred miles west of Cape Wrath. The crew reported that it spent a week with them, chasing small migrant birds all over the ship. Merlins hunt low over the ground and once they flush their prey – mostly small moorland birds like pipits, stonechats and larks – they harry it relentlessly, twisting and turning, like a shadow, matching its every move, sometimes stalling from the limits of the sky in the wake of a plummeting lark, until the merlin finally kills or abandons the pursuit. They have been known to follow their prey into buildings and I imagined one hurtling down from the moor above the village pursuing its quarry into the distillery warehouse.

If a merlin were to give chase around the whisky casks and shoot out again through the closing door, then swing north and follow the island's only road along its east coast, it would cut across Corran Sands where emigrants gathered from the eighteenth century and throughout the nineteenth to embark on ships waiting in the bay's deep water for settlements in North Carolina. And if the island's smallest raptor were to turn west when it reached the Corran river, it would come to a hillock above the road named after a raptor with a wingspan seven times the merlin's: *Cnoc na h-Iolaire* (the hill of the eagle).

Leaving the imagined merlin at the foot of the hill, I climbed *Cnoc na h-Iolaire* soon after I arrived. Jura is a large island, thirty miles long and in places eight miles wide. I needed a starting point, a place to take my bearings and think about where to look for the island's birds of prey. I didn't expect to see an eagle on *Cnoc na h-Iolaire* but the hill seemed like an opening, a doorway into the island's vastness and the raptors that had drawn me back there. On the summit a red deer and her calf stood below me beneath the quartzite brow of the hill. Her coat was kestrel red. Her undertow, the long throat and chest, was grey like the colour of the quartzite where lichen had darkened it. The hind moved off, coughing a low, guttural bark of alarm, almost like a raven's call, deep and phlegmy. Below me the squat islands of Small Isles Bay peered just above the water. To the west the Paps smoked in cloud, their great slopes of scree like stubble shadow down their chins.

There are two things you should bring with you when you climb *Cnoc na h-Iolaire*. The first is a spade, the second a blue pocket handkerchief. Reading Peter Youngson's history, *Jura: Island of Deer*, I came across a story Youngson had collected when he was minister on the island. The story goes that a robber called McLever buried his treasure at the top of *Cnoc na h-Iolaire*. The finding of this treasure is apparently an easy matter. Once you have climbed to the top of the hill you fix your eye on Lowlandman's Bay to the east. Then you move around until you can see just enough of the bay to cover a blue pocket handkerchief. At that point you start to dig and there is your treasure!

I took out my blue handkerchief and, in the absence of a spade, a trowel. Next I shuffled around the hill-top with the handkerchief flapping in the wind. It kept lifting and billowing like a slack sail and it was difficult to line it up over the bay. Eventually I settled on a spot and started to dig.

A buzzard was calling in the conifer plantation below the hill: *kee-yup, kee-yup*. Through the binoculars I could see some of the shades in its plumage: drenched, weary cornfield, silver birch, the pink-brown gills of field mushrooms. People I spoke to on the island noted that the buzzard population had increased over the last few years and there was now probably a pair attached to every piece of woodland.

I watched the buzzard lift from its perch and glide along the purlieu of the wood. When it reached the end of the plantation it angled its wings back so the carpal joints were pronounced and flew fast into the head wind.

The ground squelched and my trowel sweated against the heather and grass roots. Only an inch down and water was running off the trowel's blade each time I pulled it up. Start digging almost anywhere on Jura and you will first hit a layer of peat. Beneath that the island's backbone is fine-grained metamorphic quartzite, the most extensive tract of this poor, hard rock in the Highlands. Only a narrow strip on the island's east coast escapes it. Here there are seams of hornblende, phyllitic and mica schists and graphitic schist and slate. It is this skeleton which has shaped human settlement on the island. Crofting and all the island's housing is confined to the narrow east-coast schists. Outside the schistose strip, as W.H. Murray observed, 'all is moor, peat bog and mountain'.

I thought back to my buzzard's feather, how its shape also matched Jura's geology: the narrow leading edge an echo of the thin schistose strip along the east coast, the wide trailing edge that great expanse of quartzite. Even the feather's bands of brown waves matched the movement of the ice sheets across Jura from east to west.

Walking back down from *Cnoc na h-Iolaire* I watched a man in a white shirt dig and stack peats on the opposite bank, the white moving amongst the dark sods, a spill of colour against the greens of the moor. It looked like someone picking up the last white chocolate from an assortment box and letting it hover amongst the remaining dark chocolates, as if hesitating over their choice. A few yards on and another chequered pattern: an adder just over a foot long crossed the path in front of me, black wedge shapes running down the seam of its back. Beneath these black zigzags its skin was the colour of dead bracken.

I wanted to get a better sense of the numbers of raptors on Jura. So I arranged to meet Malcolm Ogilvie. He has studied raptors on Islay for many years and also has a good knowledge of Jura's birds of prey.

*

I sat talking to Malcolm in the bar of the hotel in Port Charlotte. Shelves of whisky bottles peered down at us like guillemots on a cliff. We talked about how Jura's raptors have not been persecuted as they have elsewhere. The absence of commercial game bird management on the island has ensured this protection. But I also found on Jura a culture of acceptance towards the raptors. One farm on the island reared a small number of pheasants but always put down an excess of poults to allow for those that were taken by buzzards. I also heard that some years ago one of the estates used to release mountain hares for the eagles. I learnt from Malcolm that there were about ten pairs of golden eagles on Jura and a pair of white-tailed eagles had bred successfully over the last two years. He also stressed that nobody has ever studied the raptors properly on the island. Malcolm was able to give me his estimates for the number of breeding pairs but I had a sense that Jura held some of its birds of prey back in its hinterland, in the difficult terrain, its long trailing edge of bogs, deep tussocks and trackless acres.

Speaking to Malcolm made me eager to head out into that hinterland and explore it more fully. So I planned a series of walks throughout the length of Jura: one in the south, one in the middle around Loch Tarbert and one in the far north. My idea was that each walk would follow the direction of those dark bands that ran across the buzzard's feather, starting from the road on the east coast and heading out towards the west in an arc that would loop back to my starting point.

I began in the south following the coast north to Inver. Within a few yards a kestrel took off from a cliff in front of me and, as if presaging the shape of the walks I'd planned, it flew out high over the Sound of Islay and arced back over the shore and into the woods above Inver house. Malcolm had told me that the south was a good place to see hen harriers and I kept pausing to scan the moor with my binoculars, hoping also to catch sight of a merlin darting over the heather. I walked through low cloud that bloomed and waned as if a shoal was shape-shifting around me. Small bands of hooded crows huffed over the moor. When they launched themselves they looked like a jangle of marionette limbs being hoicked sloppily upwards. I watched a black-backed gull cruise low over the moor to my right. Meadow pipits sprang up out of the grass, as if the black-back was letting off small explosions beneath it.

I reached Inver and walked through one of the few remnants of native woodland on the quartzite backbone of the island. I followed the path through oak, rowan and birch and the occasional holly. Leaving the wood, I crossed the moor and followed a track that ran past a mature conifer plantation, the trees on my left, heather and bracken to my right. It felt like I was walking through a parting between two worlds, the dark tree realm of the sparrowhawk and the open moor of the merlin. My eyes quivered either side of me hoping to glimpse the blaze of these birds.

Malcolm had observed that sparrowhawks on Jura had increased as the forestry plantations had matured. But he had estimated no more than five pairs of merlins. It was possible that peregrines were one reason why merlin numbers were so low, and Malcolm told me he had once seen a male merlin arrive at its nest with prey when suddenly a peregrine stooped down on it. The merlin dropped like a stone into the heather and, the next instant, the larger female merlin came screaming towards the peregrine, chasing it away from the nest.

Further along the coast I reached Cnocbreac and sat down on the hill scanning the heather below me. To the north Colonsay drifted alongside the great length of Jura like a whale's calf. To the north-east Jura's coast curves around into the jaws of Loch Tarbert almost as far as the east coast, before heading west again and on to the tapered northern end of the island. Over thirty miles of coast, of peregrines and golden eagles. It must be one of the great tracts of wilderness in the archipelago. Dotted with caves, whose floors are softened with goat and deer droppings, the coast is lined with some of the best examples of raised beaches in the world. A mile to the north of me the longest medial moraine in Scotland, Sgriob na Caillich (the old woman's slide) slips down the shoulder of Beinn an Oir towards the sea.

I was sitting on the hill where the Welsh naturalist Thomas Pennant had landed in 1772. When Pennant arrived at Cnocbreac he encountered a number of shielings which he describes vividly in *A Tour of Scotland and Voyage to the Hebrides*:

> Land on a bank covered with sheelins, the habitations of some peasants who attend the herds of milch cows. These formed a grotesque group. Some were oblong, many conic, and so low that entrance is forbidden

> without creeping through the little opening, which has no other door than a faggot of birch twigs, placed there occasionally. They are contructed of branches of trees, covered with sods. The furniture is a bed of heath, placed on a bank of sod; two blankets and a rug; some dairy vessels, and above, certain pendant shelves made of basket work, to hold the cheese, the produce of the Summer. In one of the little conic huts I spied a little infant asleep under the protection of a faithful dog.

The only trace of the shielings now are the green patches of fertile ground where their cattle grazed; the moor's long memory of them. Rain began to itch its way over my face and blotched the ink on my notebook. Behind me the clouds had sunk and were rolling over the ground as if the heather was burning. I stood up and headed east, deeper into the moor.

At Loch Tarbert, in the middle of the island, I started out from the burial ground that surrounds a ruined chapel. Sixty-four years after Pennant visited Jura, Lord Teignmouth published his *Sketches of the Coasts and Islands of Scotland*. Coming ashore at the head of Loch Tarbert in wind and rain, Teignmouth describes approaching the cemetery and seeing what first appeared to be 'a collection of crows or corbies' huddled round the carcass of an animal. It wasn't until he drew closer that he realised the 'crows' were a band of mourners at a funeral. I retraced in reverse Teignmouth's route up Loch Tarbert, following its north shore out to the west. I thought about his 'crows' and how they morphed into something else. I would often see hooded crows before I saw raptors. The crows would draw my eye and then I would see the buzzard or eagle they were mobbing. Or sometimes I would hear the corvids first, cawking furiously and look up to see them in pursuit of a buzzard lumbering through their territory.

Near the shore at the head of the loch I paused to fish my binoculars from my bag and immediately saw a movement to my right. A short-eared owl was quartering the ground about sixty feet away. I watched it pause momentarily then drop into a patch of purple moor-grass. It quickly rose again, brushed into the air as if a breeze had found and lifted it.

Malcolm had explained that short-eared owls arrive on Jura late in March or early April and make a very quick assessment of the vole population. They do this by using ultraviolet sight to pick up traces of the voles' urine. If the vole numbers are low that year the owls will move on to find somewhere else to breed. I watched the owl's graceful, twisting flight. The tips of its long wings almost brushed the tops of the bracken. Its pale wings were the colour of murky, unpolished silver. At one point I raised my binoculars and noticed it flinch as if this was the first time it had seen me. Instead of flying off it drew closer and landed on the ground twenty feet away. Its face seemed to become rounder when it perched and I could clearly see its dark-yellow irises and the black band of feathers that framed them.

On my way to the far north of the island I stopped in to talk to Ewen who has been the head stalker on one of the estates for twenty years. Sitting in his kitchen drinking tea, Ewen talked about the eagles and harriers he often saw and how young white-tailed eagles were seen in the winter more frequently. One point Ewen raised was his concern for the lack of suitable live prey for the eagles. Deer carrion was abundant but there were very few hares and grouse now on the island. Ewen said he often saw eagles lift adders and watched them wriggling in their talons as the eagles took off. He knew that the eagles also took young kids in February from the large feral goat population. That concern about the eagles' diet is something Roy Dennis has voiced in his work on golden eagles. For Dennis, the most critical issue for eagles is the degradation of their upland environment, in particular the marked decline in heather. Over-grazing by sheep and deer and the subsequent loss of habitat for grouse and hares affects eagles' breeding success, because there's very little live prey for the healthy development and growth of chicks.

*

Leaving Ewen I headed out into the far north of the island and walked into a land of exiles. George Orwell purged himself of London and came to live here in a 'very un-get-at-able' farmhouse where he wrote

Nineteen Eighty-Four. North of Orwell's old home, across the Gulf of Corryvreckan, looms the island of Scarba with its great cliffs and caves like huge eye sockets. Here the Gaelic poet Mary MacLeod (*c.* 1616–*c.* 1706) was exiled having offended her employer, one of the chiefs at Dunvegan in Skye. On Scarba, before she moved to further exile on Mull, she wrote *Tuireadh*, a poem of longing for her homeland which begins:

Is muladach mì, hì ó	It's me who is blue
Hóireann ó hi bhì ó	Hóireann ó hi bhì ó
O cheann seachdain, hì ó	For a week now,
Ro hóireann ó o hao o	Ro hóireann ó o hao o
Is mi an eilean gun	Dumped on this island
Fhiar gun fhasgadh.	Stripped of grass and shelter.

I looked across to Scarba from the watershed above *Gleann nan Muc*. I could see the dead winter grass pressed beneath the new growth. It offered a glimpse of what the island would become in just a few months and I thought of something Ewen said when he asked me if I had been here in the winter. All that grass turns white, he said, it's more like a desert here.

A raven rowed itself around my head as if describing my own halo. Higher up a pair of goosanders circled as if they were sketching the raven's path around me. It was a pattern that repeated itself later in the day. I was watching a young buzzard mewing above a wood when the view through my binoculars was suddenly flooded with wings. I flinched as if something was bearing down on me. I had swung my binoculars to the north and picked up a golden eagle hunting low over the hill behind the wood. For a while the eagle hung behind the buzzard, like some huge projection of it. At one point the eagle flapped its wings clumsily above its head, almost in the same way that a kestrel pulls up when it checks its stoop a few feet above the ground. But the eagle didn't drop and instead started to gain height very quickly. I watched it straighten its long tail into the shape of an oar's blade and disappear over a ridge to the north.

The eagle had flown off towards Scarba, the reverse journey of another eagle that the artist William Daniell was told about when he visited Jura in the second decade of the nineteenth century. Daniell recounts a man on Jura telling him 'as a well known fact' that 'an eagle once took up a child which its mother had wrapped in a piece of flannel and laid down by a stack of oats (it being harvest season) and flew with it from Scarba to Jura. Some of the people of Jura, observing the eagle descend, with what they supposed to be a lamb in its talons, hastened to the place where he alighted, and, to their surprise, found the infant unhurt'.

Late in the day I paused above a cliff and watched tourist boats swing round close to the shore. All eyes aboard were looking up through binoculars to the white-tailed eagles somewhere beneath me. I could not see the birds, but I sat watching the passengers watching them.

Seton Gordon's book, *Hill Birds of Scotland*, published in 1915, was probably the last bird book to include the white-tailed eagle, before the remaining solitary erne, as they used to be called, was killed in these islands. Gordon recounts a custom in Orkney that anyone killing a white-tailed eagle was entitled to a hen from every house situated in the parish in which the bird was killed. In remote cliff-side eyries burning peats would sometimes be lowered down to set fire to the nests. There followed a long exile for white-tailed eagles from the archipelago and in 1985, after a programme of reintroduction, the first pair bred successfully. Since then, Europe's largest eagle has slowly increased its numbers, spreading along Scotland's west coast.

It is likely that *Cnoc na h-Iolaire* was named after the once more common white-tailed eagle. Should one of these great birds rise again on a thermal above the hill, it would look down on the shallow dent my trowel made, filled with peaty water, gazing back at the eagle like an eye.

Mick Imlah (ONE)

Muck

(AD)

Hey, we were only semi-literate
ourselves: we meant to head for *Mull*, not
where the blessed Kevin miscarried us,
a rank bad place with no words at all.

It was about the year dot – before
MacBrayne and the broken ice; before
Colum and Camelot, whose annals skate
over our failed attempt at Muck –

when the call came (I didn't hear it)
to rid ourselves of the Ulster roof-
and-cake mentality, and work abroad.
So we did go, in wash-tub coracles,

and hauled ashore for an hour or so, on a
black upturned platter of rock, stained
with sea-lichen and scummy pools
of barge flies and crab water.

No trees, then. No welcoming men
or women either. But out on a spur's end
we spotted a sham temple – being a few
upright poles fashioned from driftwood, which

when we straggled over to them, seemed
without a text or rune to vent their purpose
to have their say in fish. ('That's one
of our symbols,' said Kevin, slowly.)

The first was crude, like holy rood,
a shark hung where the Christ might be.
The crossbeam of the second, wavy,
queasy, white, was split three times

by dolphins' leaps and falls; while each
of the mounting horizontals of the third,
carved with a rogue's dash or abandon,
was a fish-beam; the worst given the arc

of a catfish – though closer to, we saw
how this was worked from a lower jaw,
the bass jaw of an ox. Such things might be
the artwork of a class of kids; except

for the cunning that had placed the group
of crosses, if we call them crosses,
in silhouette, against the setting sun,
her *lux in embro*; or the paler moon.

The fourth was set apart. It wore
The red back half of a toy tractor, fixed
to the neck of a pole; and strapped to the spine,
a thermos, meant to last the afternoon.

– the cairn beneath it had been plugged, once,
with a plastic helmet, that was bleached by now
from orange to lime or yellow; and over the whole
was thrown a mongrel dress of fishnets and floats.

K saw a fifth with his second sight
And wasn't telling. Only, 'Back to the boats! –
It's no good, we brought the word of God
to these in their hiding-place, and they don't want it!'

(So we sounded in reply the child's note
of feigned frustration, masking the relief
our code forbids us to have felt, or
having felt, express.) Till as we sucked

our wicker boats and heels clear of their shingle,
he struck up from the front, as if it were his,
Our Founder's lesson, 'Study the Mountains'
(strange how it made him a bully, the borrowed prose) –

'*Study the mountains; then when you fancy
you know the mountains, you can learn the stars.*'
(Just then, Kevin, none of us rowing could
see past the grimed horizon of your neck;

and as the squall got up, you couldn't hear
half that we aimed in reply; until with the double
beating of salt and rain on our hands and face
we crouched back in a bee-shape; kept at the oars.

But we will expect something to sustain us,
soon, beyond the Plough and the Sperrins.
In the meantime, here's to the gay goddess
Astarté – mother of false starts!)

Mark Cocker (TEN)

Maxwell at a Venture

At about midday on Thursday, 19 May 1946, off the Hebridean island of Skye, a young skipper stood at the tiller of his lobster fishing boat, the *Gannet*. Except for the distinctive, finely proportioned profile – high forehead, strong aquiline nose, delicate mouth and firm oval chin – there was little to indicate this 31-year-old's aristocratic background. Coarse trousers were stuffed into knee-length military boots. Just below his ribcage a broad leather belt embraced a tatty polo-neck. Superficially he looked for all the world like the rugged, west-coast fishermen who crewed with him.

All week they had pursued their quarry, the basking shark, one of the largest fishes in the world, without success. Every time the boat closed on the migrating sharks the fishermen's equipment malfunctioned. The worst offender was a muzzle-loaded harpoon. Gunpowder was poured down the long barrel, followed by two wads of felt pushed down with a ramrod. A metal-tipped stick was then introduced to the barrel, and, when one end rested on the powder, the other end, exposed at the muzzle, was fitted with the harpoon head. For some reason, this system had failed repeatedly in the previous four days.

But as the skipper eased the *Gannet* towards a large female shark, they were about to try again. At only a metre's distance from her back just beneath the water, the harpoon struck home into her side. It was the first success of the crew's second season of fishing. For the briefly jubilant skipper, however, this was only the start of a fortnight's problems.

Wary that too much weight on the rope might tear the harpoon from the fish's body, the team took hours to haul it to the surface. Then a further six hours were spent towing the prize back to their factory on the island of Soay. Unfortunately, by the time of their arrival the tide was too low for them to reach the factory's slipway. When they started again the next day the intention was to place the carcase on a bogie-cart which ran into the water on rails. Unfortunately, they found that these rails did not extend far enough. Following several hours' work, after they had managed to balance the shark precariously on the truck, a winch was hauling the load up the slipway, when the cart overturned and tipped its contents back into the sea.

Unwilling to wait for a high tide so that they might attempt the procedure again, they decided to hack the carcase up where it lay. By the time they'd taken a break the tide was up to their waists. When the day's labours finally ended, at well after midnight, the skipper 'had had no food for more than thirty hours, and having struggled all day in that mountain of soft cold flesh and entrails', hoped never to touch it again. The following morning – a Saturday – he started at five-thirty, by which time a second shark had been caught. However, the strict observance of the Sabbath, so important to the deeply religious communities of north-west Scotland, decreed that all work must cease by midday.

By the following Monday morning affairs at the shark-processing factory were, if anything, even worse. When the skipper returned with the timber and equipment to modify the slipway, he found that efforts to haul the second fish up to the factory had incurred the same problems as the first. An over-burdened cart had derailed, throwing its catch back into the water. All this time, nobody had bothered to clear away the heaps of carrion left from the first, which had become a battleground for a great flock of ravening gulls.

Taking their cue from the avian squabble, the factory staff rebelled. Some of them argued that they had only been employed to cut up the sharks, while a joiner, going to fetch tools from the mainland, failed to return. A recent arrival, an expert, contracted to produce samples of glue from the shark's cartilage, complained that he was there merely to advise, not to skivvy. If the skipper wanted the experiments completed, he would have to have the staff currently reconstructing the slipway working for him. He himself would be a labourer for no man; besides he had a bad back.

Exasperated by this final defiance, and barely able to keep himself from hitting the expert, the young skipper replied that 'it wasn't my crew's job to haul wood and build slips, nor mine, but no one made a fuss; all were, on the contrary, anxious to help; that I had synovitis of the right ankle, a duodenal ulcer and an enlarged heart, and that he was likely to survive me'. These were not the typical physical attributes of the man of action, a man who had chosen as his profession to hunt one of the largest fish in the world. But then Gavin Maxwell, the skipper's name, was not a typical man of action.

Maxwell told the story of his shark-fishing enterprise in his first book *Harpoon at a Venture* (1952) a work that seems to become ever more difficult and unpalatable over the passing years. In many ways it measures the cultural legacy of environmentalism upon our modern British sensibilities. How could a so-called naturalist like Maxwell inflict so much slaughter on one of the nation's most impressive animals? Whatever its failings, *Harpoon at a Venture* is still vital for our understanding of Maxwell the man and writer.

*

Maxwell was born into an aristocratic family in 1914 and brought up at Elrig, near Wigtown, in Galloway, in south-west Scotland. He was educated in England, at Stowe and at Oxford, where he reluctantly studied estate management. During the Second World War he was stationed as a Special Forces officer in the Scottish Highlands and there developed a deep and determining passion for the region.

Following a visit to the small Inner Hebridean island of Soay off the southern shore of Skye, he fell in love with the place, and decided to buy it. There he developed the idea of a fishing business, based on the commercial exploitation of basking sharks, for the large quantities of oil in their livers. From the average individual he was able to extract eight hundredweights of the liquid, the value of which had almost tripled to £130 per ton (the equivalent of about £4,800 today), in the course of his four-year operations. Though Maxwell's enterprise recovered a little from the deeply inauspicious start described above, his income was insufficient to keep the business afloat. Only five months after they had caught that first sizeable female on 19 May 1946, he had been forced to sell the island, boats and gear and become managing director of someone else's company. Within two years he resigned even this post and the business finally wound up after another unsuccessful season.

If Maxwell had not become the lone wolf explorer who wrote up his exotic journeys of foreign travel, as he had once wished during his days at Oxford, then by hunting one of the largest fish in the world he had at least faced a dangerous challenge of a kind. His home country had provided him with the adventures of a foreign land. It would also provide him with the appropriate environment and the inspiration to write.

Impoverished after the collapse of the Island of Soay Shark Fisheries, Maxwell had retained a foothold on the west coast, when one of his Oxford contemporaries offered him use of a small cottage overlooking the Sound of Sleat, the narrow channel separating Skye from the Scottish mainland. It was here, several years later, as he combed the beach for a suitable piece of wood from which to make a breadboard, that he came upon:

> a small barrel-top, white, smooth, and sea-worn – exactly the object I required. I pulled it from the shingle in which it was imbedded, and there across the centre of it were the still legible letters ISSF – Island of Soay Shark Fisheries. It had all the nostalgia of a *carnet de bal* tied with faded ribbon; it brought back so many half-forgotten scenes so vividly to my mind that I began this book the next day.

The result was *Harpoon at a Venture.* Whatever else it sought to portray, the book was inevitably about failure. Yet through its portrait of Ulyssean endeavours, through measured, precise and luminous prose and the revelation of error with painful honesty, it gave this failure a certain dignity. In fact, as a focus for literary enterprise, shark-fishing became a considerable success. The book was reviewed and sold well and led Maxwell on to foreign travels that were the background, in turn, for *God Protect Me from My Friends* (1956), *A Reed Shaken by the Wind* (1957) and *The Ten Pains of Death* (1959). Yet it was Maxwell's record of life at his lighthouse-keeper's cottage at Sandaig, given the fictional name of Camusfeàrna in his famous otter trilogy, that made him a household name. The first, *Ring of Bright Water* (1960), has sold millions worldwide.

*

Electricity only arrived in the area during Maxwell's tenancy of Camusfeàrna. Prior to that the homes had been lit by paraffin lamps. When he wrote *Ring of Bright Water* Maxwell's place was still not on the national grid. For years he obtained water by bucket from a stream. His house had no lavatory or bath. It could be reached neither by telephone nor road and to get there initially involved a good deal of walking. His nearest sizeable towns, Inverness and Fort William, were both about a hundred miles away. When he first moved there the nearest port from which he could have furniture shipped to Camusfeàrna was a little more than fifteen miles by sea; by road the same village was over a hundred and twenty.

The region's indigenous community is portrayed as enjoying a deeply intimate relationship with the landscape. The Highlanders are ancient, Celtic and Norse stock whose element-bound, tradition-dominated lives are simple and spartan. In *Ring of Bright Water*, Maxwell describes human types long extinct elsewhere in the British Isles, like the itinerant peddlers who lived in a cave close to Camusfeàrna. In *Harpoon at a Venture*, he wrote of the island inhabitants in Scalpay as:

> a small pastoral community, every visible phase of whose life had a minute and individual beauty, whose every activity enhanced rather than detracted from the wider beauty of their surroundings. Much that the cynical might dismiss as having primarily the shallow appeal of the 'picturesque' is recognisable as something deeper by an eye already long accustomed to these archaic forms of architecture, dress, and speech.

Maxwell's choice of imagery reinforced a sense of organic unity between the Scalpay people and their island. For an intellectually gifted and emotionally complex individual like Maxwell there would be, almost inevitably, aspects of this deep-rooted society that he found less attractive. According to his biographer Richard Frere, they smirked and gossiped about the constant presence of young male companions and found a perverse satisfaction in the collapse of his fishery. In *Harpoon at a Venture* the author spoke with some resentment of the Soay people, whom he had employed in the shark-processing factory, almost as if their unregenerate insularity had been at the heart of his commercial failure. In the opening pages he wrote of the island's 'troubles, internecine feuds, frustrations, and problems', and – on the final page of the saga – the 'civil wars and demands ... of its tiny population'.

Nonetheless, it was the rugged wholeness of north-west Scotland and its rural population which served Maxwell as a standard to which he himself could aspire. And it was that coarse, unpopulated, rock-bound environment that operated as a material correlative for his rejection of the modern world. In the opening of *Harpoon at a Venture* he suggested that his purchase of Soay and the whole shark-fishing adventure were born out of the squalor and brutality of modern warfare. 'If I'm alive when the war's over,' he claimed to have said in 1940, 'I'm going to buy an island in the Hebrides and retire there for life, no aeroplanes, no bombs, no Commanding Officers, no rusty dannert wire.'

In the opening chapter of *Ring of Bright Water*, he wrote:

> Even at a distance Camusfeàrna house wore that strange look that comes to dwellings after long disuse. It is indefinable, and it is not produced by obvious signs of neglect; Camusfeàrna had a few slates missing from the roof and the windows were all intact, but the house wore that secretive expression that is in some way akin to a young girl's face during her first pregnancy.

In both books north-west Scotland was a final sanctuary, or as Maxwell himself wrote, 'to me it was Xanadu', 'my Island Valley of Avalon' and 'remote Elysium': an Eden-like locality that permitted a rebirth of innocence. In the recurrent images in Maxwell's Scottish memoirs of a world before the fall, a world free 'from the prison of over-dense communities' and the 'incarceration of office walls and hours', and in his desire to return to pre-modern simplicity, one can detect a relationship between his books and those of contemporary travel writers like Wilfred Thesiger or Laurens van der Post, whose works celebrated a connection to tribal primitivism.

Harpoon at a Venture fully expresses Maxwell's instinct for the deeper resonances latent in his personal tale. Within a simple story of economic gamble and failure on Scotland's west coast he developed an array of richly suggestive images: the courageous, dignified fisherman, the subtle unseen powers of his quarry and the unfathomable depths upon which their struggle was enacted. It is interesting that in the same year that *Harpoon at a Venture* was published another adventurer-writer, Ernest Hemingway, also produced a tale of conflict between a man and an immense fish. Need one assume that only one of these writers was alive to the much more enduring human drama inherent in the fibre of his narrative?

There is little question that the shark-fishing business did involve a degree of physical risk. John Hillaby, accompanying Maxwell as a journalist with the *Picture Post*, described what he saw as 'almost undiluted derring-do'. Equally the perils of trying to catch the sharks from a relatively small vessel were well illustrated in Robert Flaherty's classic 1934 movie *Man of Aran*. Yet Maxwell cherished and worked hard at his self-portrait as intrepid frontiersman engaging the unknown. When providing the emotional and geographical setting for the fishing business he describes his home on the west coast as a place 'of a different sort of romance: of herring scales and a million gulls, of energy and squalor and opportunity, of feud and fortune, the "end of steel" – the railhead – beyond which all is gamble'.

Similarly important to Maxwell's self-image as fearless man of action is his misrepresentation of the main quarry. Although he explained that seven out of every eight basking sharks they caught were females, he always referred to them in the book as 'he'. A male adversary presumably better suited his heroic sense of the project. The author did acknowledge that basking sharks were plankton-eaters but what he did little to emphasise was the creature's essentially bovine character. If the species has ever caused loss of life, this was certainly inadvertent and contingent upon the risks of sea swell, the sheer strength of so large a creature and the force behind its threshing tail when fighting for its life.

Yet this was not quite how Maxwell wanted his readers to understand the matter. 'I see it now as I saw it at first,' he wrote in the book: 'an ivory-hunter in the deep Congo jungle, standing by the mountainous carcase from which he has cut the tons of flesh, the hide, the bones – all the apparent and gigantic waste … I know now that the shark's liver is the elephant's ivory.' Elsewhere he describes the shark as 'gigantic', 'ponderous', a 'creature from a prehistoric world', a 'dinosaur', an 'iguanodon', a giant with gaping jaws and a body covered 'with irregular python markings', 'dark viscous slime' and 'studded with … spines'. Most interesting of all are the associations he invoked when confronted with a factory pickle-tank of improperly preserved shark flesh that had been infested with fly larvae. Looking at the rotted heap of carrion and maggots, he imagined that 'beneath the surface layer of putrescence were the struggling bodies of all the wounded, but resurrected dragons that we had attacked and that escaped us'. The final chapter of the book is also entitled 'Here Be Dragons'.

The dramatisation of the shark as a mythological monster and himself, by implication, as a dragon-slayer is part of a revealing series of images in the book that hold associations with medieval conflict and the age of chivalry. Maxwell called his west-coast home 'my Island Avalon'. Later, when describing the poor quality of the employees brought in to the Soay factory from Skye, he wrote that this labour merely 'swelled the numbers as dummy figures upon castle battlements did in the Middle Ages'. Expressing his feelings for Harry, the 'strange, contradictory, unclassifiable' captain who sank the company's boat, the *Nancy Clen*, Maxwell thought of him, 'as Prince Hal of Falstaff, "I could well have spared a better man"'.

There were, of course, elements in the author's background which made these historical allusions appropriate. It is surely indicative of his urge to be seen in a noble guise, that he could later write of the shark-fishing gamble:

> I tried to found a new industry for the tiny and discontented population of the island ... by catching and processing for oil the great basking sharks that appear in Hebridean waters during the summer months. I built a factory, bought boats and equipped them with harpoon guns, and became a harpoon gunner myself. For five years I worked in this landscape.

Here we have the valiant and socially minded aristocrat braving the deep and tilting with dragons, not for the £130 per ton of liver-oil, but in the service of his vassal tenants.

Towards the close of his time as a fisherman he could catch fifty sharks in eighteen days, and believed he might easily have tripled the tally had he had the facilities. It was when he tried to combine hunting and fishing with being a captain of industry, a man of board meetings, of research and development, that Maxwell came up against the chief obstacle to success: simple practical reality. When his noble hopes of revival for Soay and its inhabitants were finally dashed, the real villains in his self drama were the small, trivial inconveniences of life: the opposing rhythms of the tide, the malfunction of an engine part, the poor construction of a slipway, the cold, grey and pin-striped rules of commerce, the petty red-tape of an expert in fish glue.

Here in his first published work are the very themes that were to be explored again and again across Gavin Maxwell's seemingly heterogeneous *oeuvre*. The noble, sensitive but anachronistic or, at least, anti-modern central figure, the spell of temporary success, the promise of happiness, then betrayal and fall – these are fundamental elements in almost all his books, whose principal subject, of course, is the life and times of the author himself.

Raasay
Elgol
Soay
Sandaig

Angela Leighton (SEVEN)

Bog Asphodel

Once, by Elgol,
under ikat sunsets, driving affluent rain,
    my two-ply tongue,
tongue-tied for weeks, word-stuck in kind, recognised:
    bog asphodel.

To a cold, conditioning ground, unpastured space,
    its Delphic heavenly
ring brought sandalled toes, Elysian meadows,
    Athens, Rome –
gilding the peat bog, winning a pot of gold.

    Asphodel –
soft echo. Here on the bare, bone-breaking heath
    my tongue's bell,
bi-lingual, local, levies a name from elsewhere
    and finds its place.

Seamus Heaney (SEVEN)

from the Gaelic of Sorley MacLean

Hallaig

'Time, the deer, is in Hallaig Wood'

There's a board nailed across the window
I looked through to see the west
And my love is a birch forever
By Hallaig Stream, at her tryst

Between Inver and Milk Hollow,
Somewhere around Baile-chuirn,
A flickering birch, a hazel,
A trim, straight sapling rowan.

In Screapadal, where my people
Hail from, the seed and breed
Of Norman and Big Hector
By the banks of the stream are a wood.

To-night the pine-cocks crow
And preen on Knockraa, on the heights,
Tall-shouldered there in the moonlight –
They are not the wood in my heart.

I will wait for the birches to move,
For the wood to come up past Cairn
Until it has veiled the mountain
As far as Ben Lack in shade.

If it doesn't, I'll go to Hallaig,
To the sabbath of the dead,
Down to where each departed
Generation has gathered.

Hallaig is where they survive,
All the MacLeans and MacLeods
Who were there in the time of MacCallum:
The dead have been seen alive.

The men at their length on the grass
At the gable of every house,
The girls a wood of birch trees,
Tall-shouldered, arching their necks.

Between Ben Lack and Fearns
The road is plush with moss
And the girls in a noiseless procession
Going to Clachan as always

And coming back from Clachan
And Suisnish, their land of the living,
Still lightsome and unheartbroken,
Their stories only beginning.

Hallaig

From Fearns Burn to the raised beach
In the open secret hills
There are only girls congregating,
Endlessly walking along

Back through the gloaming to Hallaig
Through the vivid speechless air,
Pouring down the steep slopes,
Their laughter misting my ear

And their beauty a glaze on my heart.
Then as the kyles go dim
And the sun sets behind Dun Cana
Love's loaded gun will take aim.

It will bring down the lightheaded deer
As he sniffs the grass round the wallsteads
And his eye will freeze: while I live,
His blood won't be traced in the woods.

Roger Hutchinson (SEVEN)

The Other Side of Sorrow

On a June afternoon in 2004 a small group of people stood on what is now one of the loneliest coastlines in western Europe and heard a poem read aloud, firstly in its original Gaelic and then in English. The English version was delivered in an educated Irish accent. 'There was a tremendous, dignified sense of occasion,' said its reader, Seamus Heaney, afterwards. 'A sense of a circle being completed.' Many circles, circles within circles, were completed that day at Hallaig on the deserted eastern coast of the Hebridean island of Raasay. It was the one hundred and fiftieth anniversary of the forced clearance of the township and the fiftieth anniversary of the Raasay poet Sorley MacLean's astonishing elegy to the ghosts of his forebears. It was the first time that Heaney had visited the place.

These days Hallaig frequently echoes to the sound of living rather than sepulchral voices, of pilgrims drawn there by the great art which has been done in its name. In June 2004 Heaney and men and women from Raasay and its larger neighbour Skye joined company to hear Sorley MacLean's verse evoke once more the mystery of Hallaig Wood. Heaney first heard those words almost forty years ago, in the unforgettably sonorous tones of MacLean himself, at a reading in Dublin's Abbey Theatre. 'MacLean's voice,' he recalled, 'had a certain bardic weirdness that sounded both stricken and enraptured. Whether you were listening to him or reading him on the page, you were led into an uncanny zone, somewhere between the land of heart's desire and a waste land created by history ...'

The lifetime's work of Sorley MacLean created that zone in a variety of places, from the desert war in North Africa to the Cuillins of Skye. Inevitably, for this was the pre-eminent Highland writer of the twentieth century, it reached its most compelling pitch when dealing with the island that he left as a young man. After departing for Edinburgh University at the end of the 1920s, Sorley MacLean never again lived in Raasay. His profession as a teacher and headmaster took him all across the shrinking Scottish Gàidhealtachd. After retiring from the rectorship of Plockton High School in the early 1970s he moved to live with his wife in the township of Peighinn a' Chorrain in the parish of Braes, where he stayed until his death in 1996.

Peighinn a' Chorrain sits by a raised beach on the east coast of Skye. In almost all weathers it looks over to Raasay, virtually within shouting distance but separated by two stern miles of sea. In Peighinn a' Chorrain Sorley MacLean had his back to the Cuillins, rising steeply behind him 'on the other side of sorrow', and his face to the woods of Raasay. Even in childhood he had never experienced Hallaig as a living village. The settlement was largely emptied by the landowner George Rainy on 5 June 1854. It was the morning of the Monday after their last Sabbath, perhaps Sorley MacLean's 'Sabbath of the dead'. On the following day thirty-seven of its people were shipped via Liverpool to Australia.

Thereafter Rainy and his successors used the place as a sheep run. In the 1920s, while Sorley MacLean was at high school in Skye, a series of desperate land raids obliged the Board of Agriculture to buy back much of Raasay for such people as had remained: the restless descendants of the clearances. It suggested the completion of another circle that Heaney was shown around the island on that Saturday in 2004 by a Raasay crofter known as Bradan, whose secured grazings included the high pastures above Hallaig. (Bradan is a cognomen that Sorley MacLean would have recognised with a smile. Raasay men are traditionally nicknamed after species of fish, and 'bradan' is Gaelic for salmon.)

But the village itself was never repopulated.

So we, as much as Sorley MacLean, have been left only to imagine Hallaig as a place of people. A visitor early in the nineteenth century described 'the green and cultivated land ... on the tops of the high eastern cliffs, which are everywhere covered with farms, that form a striking contrast to the solitary brown waste of the western coast.'

In 1833 the people of Hallaig petitioned the Gaelic Schools Society for some educational provision, insisting that 'no less than 60 Scholars could be got to attend School'. Then came the eviction notices and the emigrant ship. By 1861 this busy place had been reduced to a shepherd and a labourer. By the time of the National Census for 1891 the returns from Hallaig in Raasay amounted to one eloquent word: 'Nil.' Its place-name did not even survive in everyday use for long enough to be mauled into phonetic English on Inverness Council's road-signs – Hallaig remains Hallaig, in both languages. And 'Hallaig – Nil' it would remain.

*

Sorley MacLean was born in 1911 at Oscaig on the 'solitary brown waste' of the western littoral of Raasay, into a family with typically long and vivid Highland memories. He must have heard of Hallaig, the Hallaig of 'Macleans and MacLeods, all who were there in the time of Mac Chille Chaluim' before he ever saw the place. When he did see it, his imagination repopulated Hallaig despite itself. It is among the most spectacular of sites. Hallaig looks over the wide sea-plain of the Inner Sound of Raasay towards Applecross. The brooding Skye coastline fills the southern horizon, and all around the high cliffs, waterfalls, woods, burns and hollows of eastern Raasay fall towards the stony shore. But among the ruined buildings Hallaig, like other Highland desuetudes, can become insular and enclosed. When the mists come down and Applecross is reduced to an occasional blur, and the sea smears over and voices echo around the hill, Hallaig is a private place.

Alexander Moffat, Sorley MacLean

Two people had a job to do on that Saturday in June 2004, in the drizzle among the hungry June midges on the green cliff-top overlooking the Inner Sound of Raasay. The poet and novelist Angus Peter Campbell read the fourteen stanzas of 'Hallaig' in its, his and Sorley MacLean's native Gaelic. Then Seamus Heaney opened his paperback of MacLean's collected work and presented the poet's own 'scriptural' English rendering. 'Tha tim, am fiadh, an coille Hallaig … Time, the deer, is in the wood of Hallaig.'

As moved as any deracinated Gael by the sound of his estranged language, Heaney described Angus Peter Campbell's as a 'tremendous reading'. 'I was thinking,' he said later, 'that poetry takes you into once-upon-a-time without betraying your own time – it moves you into two dimensions, and that is what it was like today. There was something about that gathering, something of total dignity without any hint of overstatement, which made it a once-in-a-lifetime experience.'

Heaney was brought up as a monoglot English speaker in County Derry. Sorley MacLean's work in general, and 'Hallaig' in particular, embraced him like a lost relative. Here was a Scottish Gael expressing in Scottish Gaelic the great symbols of dispossessed rural Gaelic Ireland. 'As a youngster I grew up among lonely wallsteadings, empty houses, boarded windows. So knowing the poem, I felt entirely at home here. But the placenames, the Raasay placenames had extra resonance …'

The poem 'Hallaig' deals, of course, not only with its eponymous township. It translates the rest of the small island of Raasay into a mythical universe. Locations such as Inver, Screapadal, Baile-chuirn, Fearns, Clachan and Suisnish – some still inhabited, some now as lonely as the night – and emblematic vistas like Dun Cana, the volcanic plug which looks over Raasay like a watch-tower, are sewn into the tapestry of the narrative.

Before that Saturday those placenames existed to Heaney only in one of his two dimensions. But then he walked to Hallaig from Fearns. Bradan, the Raasay crofter who guided and hosted Heaney that day, drove him to Sorley MacLean's birthplace: a small white cottage by the sea at Oscaig. On returning to catch the ferry back to Skye, Bradan and Heaney went through the white houses of Suisnish, now as in the poem, 'Suisnish and the land of the living'. Most of those places, populated and alive to this day, are on what was the 'solitary brown waste' of western Raasay rather than the 'green and cultivated land' of Hallaig and the east. The poem 'Hallaig' and the place Hallaig summon in all their shared dimensions what Heaney calls 'the great absence that the Highland clearances represent in Scots Gaelic consciousness'.

Before presenting his new translation of 'Hallaig' at the Edinburgh Festival in 2002, Heaney described it as 'at once historical and hallucinatory, a poem in which the deserted homesteads of a little settlement on the island of Raasay are repopulated by a vision of "a fair field full of folk". It arises out of Maclean's sense of belonging to a culture that is doomed but that he will never deny'.

It is a final irony, a final closing circle of 'Hallaig' that the verses written half a century ago to lament and reinvoke a lost – or at least a losing, a doomed – civilisation, have helped to enhance and extend its life. Among the ruins of Hallaig that day in 2004, Heaney was in the company of many Gaels speaking Gaelic: Gillieses, Campbells and MacKays, MacDonalds and MacLeans whose language, if it did not entirely revive, was given new vision, form, purpose, strength and ultimately new life on that day in 1954 when Sorley MacLean sat down to write:

> Tha buird is tairnean air an uinneig
> traobh 'm faca mi an Aird an Iar …
>
> The window is nailed and boarded
> through which I saw the West …

*

In 2006 Bradan was gathering sheep in the desolate far north of the island with his two brothers, Cuddy and Emby. They routinely started the gather at Umachan, another abandoned hamlet on the east coast shore.

'A shower came on or something,' said Emby, 'and we sheltered in a house there. I don't know how it happened, but while we were waiting Cuddy must have spotted something above the fireplace, up the chimney. He put his hand up and brought down a white plastic bag with a collection of CDs inside it. They were by "The Clash". I knew about "The Clash", of course, and Joe Strummer, but I'm not sure we knew of any Raasay connection. Bradan, Cuddy and myself put the CDs back up the chimney and went on with the gather.'

Chrissie Nicolson died at the age of ninety-four in 2009. Chrissie was born in 1915 on a tiny tidal islet called Eilean Tigh. Eilean Tigh is just two miles from Umachan, where 'The Clash' CDs had been found up a cold chimney by those crofting brothers. In her native language the name of Chrissie's birthplace is instructive. It means Island of the Single House. 'Tigh' is one of the essential root words which crop up in all of the detached Celtic languages. In Irish the word for a house is 'teach'; in Manx it is 'thie'; in Welsh, Cornish and Breton it is 'ty'. They are pronounced similarly. When you get your eye in, you find they are everywhere. Avon is another one. The River Avon translates as River River in two languages, the words *abhainn* and *afon* meaning 'river' in Gaelic and Welsh. The great romantic waterway of west-central England carries the DNA of Celtic Britain. From Naseby to the Severn it was once just the Afon – the River.

Eilean Tigh is, then, too small to sustain more than one house and its family, and Chrissie Nicolson was born and brought up in that house speaking nothing but Gaelic. That fact alone told her exactly where she lived. To her north was the barren island of Rona, which she knew as Eilean Ronaidh, the rough island. To her south was the large, green, wooded and altogether more promising island of Raasay, Eilean Ratharsair, the island of roe deer. To her east was tiny Eilean an Fraoich, the island that was home only to heather. To her west was An t-Eilean Sgiathanach, the great winged island of Skye. Her language interpreted and illuminated her environment.

At Torran School in the north of Raasay in the 1920s, Chrissie Nicolson and her contemporaries were supposed to be educated out of

Gaelic into English. Their schoolteacher, a former Customs and Excise officer from Skye, gave up trying. James 'Seumas Ruadh' MacKinnon was, even for his time, an idiosyncratic dominie. He was crippled as the result of a childhood accident and could get about only with the help of a walking stick. He was not a strict disciplinarian. In the words of another of his students, 'He must truly have been the forerunner of liberal studies. The children certainly had the benefit of an unfettered outdoor life, and when the older boys felt that there was a tighting up of school discipline, for some mysterious reason the chimney began to have "blowdowns", and this always heralded the end of another school day.' The 'blowdowns' were caused, naturally, not by a swirling and unpredictable wind, but by the artful placing by one of Seumas Ruadh's pupils of a turf on the Torran School chimney pot.

'Mr MacKinnon ran the Post Office as well,' said another pupil. 'It was in the residents' part of the school. When the postman went past the school window with the day's delivery for him to sort, there was great hilarity – with everybody shouting "post", and Mr MacKinnon went off then to do the post, and of course that's when everybody went haywire – [writing] slates and pencils and everything went flying all over the place.' The Torran School tawse, that painful leather enforcer of Scottish schoolteachers' authority, was on such occasions tossed up into the building's roof ventilator.

Whether or not Seumas Ruadh MacKinnon was a pioneer of liberal studies, he was certainly a rare early-twentieth-century practitioner of Gaelic Medium Education. Chrissie Nicolson received most of her schooling in her native language. '"Ginger James" … taught his pupils in Gaelic and had little time for English!' said one of Chrissie's contemporaries. MacKinnon's successor, another missionary to Raasay from Skye named Miss Rita Campbell, discovered upon arriving when young Chrissie was thirteen years old that 'children at the age of ten and over … had the barest knowledge of the English language'. So Chrissie Nicolson's first language, for much of her life her only language and for all of her life her preferred language, was Gaelic. She became fluent in English as a young woman, while working as a housemaid in Glasgow, but Gaelic remained what philologists call her default language. In the absence of pressure to do otherwise, she defaulted to Gaelic. She was born with Gaelic and she died with Gaelic.

As the decades of the twentieth century came and went, Chrissie knew progressively fewer and fewer people with whom to converse in Gaelic. They died, or they went away and never returned. She continued speaking Gaelic to animals. Her son, who like many of his generation was sceptical about the old language, refused to let her spend much time with his working dogs in case she accidentally trained them to lose their ear for English instructions and they became monoglot Gaelic collies.

But the people, they left, and they took the language with them, if only for a generation.

Chrissie Nicolson's mother's maiden name was Mary Gillies. Before marrying and moving to Eilean Tigh in the 1890s, Mary was brought up in a large family two miles away at Umachan. One of her sisters, Jane Gillies, married a man named MacKenzie and moved away from Raasay to live in Bonar Bridge in the eastern Scottish Highlands, on the border of the Gàidhealtachd with English-speaking Scotland. That sister – Chrissie Nicolson's aunt Jane – gave birth in Bonar Bridge to a daughter named Anna. As a young woman during the Second World War, Anna MacKenzie travelled to London from Bonar Bridge to work. She met and married a young Foreign Office diplomat called Ron Mellor. Their son, John Graham Mellor, was consequently born in Ankara, the capital of Turkey, in 1952.

Gaelic probably did not leave the Gillies/MacKenzie/Mellor family until John Graham Mellor himself in the 1950s. Early in the twentieth century half of the small population of Bonar Bridge still spoke the language. Jane Gillies from Raasay certainly spoke it, so too in all likelihood did her MacKenzie husband, and they are likely to have passed it on as a cradle language to their daughter Anna. If so, the first generation of their family not to speak Gaelic was the generation of Anna's son John Graham Mellor, who was born in a British residency in Turkey with a Gaelic and English-speaking mother but a father who spoke English and no Gaelic. That last eventuality alone precluded the use of Gaelic in John Graham Mellor's childhood home.

In his twenties, back in London in the 1970s, John Mellor formed a cult band called 'The 101ers' and changed his name to Joe Strummer. In 1976 he became the co-founder, lyricist, rhythm guitarist and lead singer of 'The Clash'. That is why Joe Strummer was neither a Gaelic speaker nor a Gaelic bard, and why he was not named after a fish. It was a close call. Strummer knew about his Highland family background, of course. He put seed money into the Future Forests plantation at Orbost in Skye, which has since been named Rebel Wood in his honour.

At the beginning of December 2002 he attended a wedding at Bonar Bridge, and told one of his Gillies cousins there: 'I've been a terrible Scotsman, but I'm going to be better.' Strummer pencilled a visit to the island of Raasay – his first visit to Raasay – into his diary for the summer of 2003. If he had made it he would not only have met his second cousin Chrissie Nicolson; he would have been surrounded by relatives. It is difficult to throw a stone in modern Raasay without hitting a descendant of the Gillieses of Umachan.

But he did not make it. Three weeks after that Bonar Bridge wedding, on 22 December 2002, Joe Strummer died suddenly of an undiagnosed congenital heart defect. He was fifty years old. In Raasay his cousin Chrissie Nicolson heard of his death and felt sorrow. She was eighty-seven and had seven more busy, constructive years of life ahead of her.

The village of Umachan was deserted in the 1910s, not long after Chrissie Nicolson's mother and Joe Strummer's grandmother left the place. In 2006 Strummer's bassist with 'The Clash', Paul Simonon, and the music writer and biographer of Strummer, Chris Salewicz, themselves visited the remnants of the small Raasay hamlet where it had all begun. Simonon, who is now an established artist, took along his canvas, easel and brushes. In the pouring rain at Umachan he made a portrait of the roofless old home of Jane and Mary Gillies. Salewicz watched astonished as Simonon strapped his canvas to the easel in the billowing wind and painted, standing upright, with rainwater running through the colours.

When he had finished, Joe Strummer's former bandmate put a set of CDs of 'The Clash' performing in New York into the chimney place. He then wrote on the blank reverse of the painted canvas: 'I'll be back. Paul.' put the portrait in beside the CDs, and set off along the thin, stony track to southern Raasay and the ferry to Skye.

*

In the 1840s, before the clearances of Hallaig and other townships, the population of Raasay was almost 700. In 1911, the year of Sorley MacLean's birth, 114 people still lived in the island. In 2012 there are fewer than 140 inhabitants. Only three of them live in the north, and nobody lives among the ruins on the high green pasturelands of the east.

> Tha buird is tairnean air an uinneig
> traobh 'm faca mi an Aird an Iar …
>
> The window is nailed and boarded
> through which I saw the West …

John Purser (TWELVE)

Freaghairt bho Iain gu Rody Gorman

Mèirleachd mhath dhut
Iòn-dubh a'goid
guthan eun eile.

Chan eil breug nad bheul
ach maise cainnte
ceilear is seinn
òrain an t-saoghail

Reply from John to Rody Gorman

Good thieving to you,
blackbird that steals
the songs of other birds.

It is no lie in your mouth,
but the beauty of the language,
birdsong and singing
songs of the world.

James Macdonald Lockhart
(TWELVE)

On the Machair

Recently I've become interested in a habitat unique to the north-west coasts of Scotland and Ireland. 'Machair' is a Gaelic word which means a low-lying plain and there are 'machair' place-names dotted across Scotland, from The Machars of Galloway to Machrihanish in Kintyre. In the 1920s the word was adopted by naturalists as a term to describe the cultivated dune grasslands found along the northern and western coasts of the British Isles, the most extensive tract of which lies along the west coast of the Outer Hebrides, particularly in North and South Uist, Benbecula and Barra.

The sand in the machair holds a high shell content, anywhere between 20 per cent to as much as 80 per cent, and this is what distinguishes machair from, for example, the 'links' habitats found along the east coast of Scotland whose sand, composed chiefly of silica, holds a higher mineral content. Machair is created and maintained by the impact of calcareous sand being blown by wind across the land. Climate is also critical in the maintenance of machair. It requires a damp, cool oceanic climate so that the balance between erosion and deposition of sand can be maintained. Strong oceanic winds to dry then blow the sand, sufficient moisture to bind the sand and hold it in place. The presence of grazing livestock (particularly cattle) alongside some cultivation of the land is another important element in defining machair. Machair is a worked landscape, maintained by human interference. Where grazing of cattle, for example, has declined in recent years on machair habitats, the machair itself has deteriorated. Cattle help to maintain a wide variety of plant species on the machair by cropping the coarser vegetation and averting what would swiftly become a monoculture of red fescue. The presence of cattle on the machair also helps to break up the ground, creating tussocks (which attract invertebrates) and hoof cups which provide shelter and nest sites for the machair's ground-nesting birds.

Machair can also be applied more broadly to describe not just the dune pasture but the whole coastal system of which the pasture is one element. Naturalists including John A. Love and, the great authority on machair, Stewart Angus have made the case for viewing machair as less a single habitat, rather an ecosystem made up of a mosaic of habitats including saltmarsh, grassland, strandline, brackish and freshwater lochs. The machair system, then, is made up of a series of bands across the landscape, each of which is impacted, to varying degrees, by the effects of blown sand. Starting with the beach, through to the dunes, then dropping down to the plain which holds pasture and cultivated land as well as numerous lochs and marshes. The gradient of the machair plain often tends towards a slight downwards slope inland as the quantity of blown sand diminishes with distance from the shore. This is significant because it is the reverse of what land usually does. Most land rises upwards away from a shore. Machair behaves differently and this topographical quirk accounts for the large number of lochs and marshes, as well as the extensive winter flooding, which occurs on the machair. From the plain, the final band in the machair system is the 'blackland' where the sand has been blown, often some distance inland, to merge with the underlying peat.

There is a sense of the machair acting as a transformative presence on the wider landscape. Whatever comes into contact with the machair is altered by it. Where blown sand, for example, reaches the 'blackland' it neutralises the acidic peat to form a type of sandy loam. Water which enters the machair from the surrounding peatlands leaves it changed. It can enter the machair system with a pH as low as 4.5 and, neutralised by the highly calcareous nature of the machair, leave it with a pH as high as 8.1.

Another important characteristic of machair and, perhaps the one it is best known for, is the display of flowering plants which grow across its sandy grasslands. Though the variety of plants on the machair is in fact quite small compared to some mainland dune habitats, the machair in flower is spectacular and there is a density of colour which you don't see in many other habitats. Where the dunes tip down towards the machair plain, marram grass starts to give way to plants such as red fescue, lady's bedstraw, white clover, bird's-foot trefoil, buttercup and daisy, all plants which can withstand being periodically covered by sand. During spring and summer, the machair grasslands move through different colour phases, from predominantly white in early spring with daisies, eyebright and wild carrot dominant, through to the yellow buttercups of June and the purples of clover and ragged robin of late summer.

Though the machair has this tremendous pull on me, I find it a difficult place to visit, to adjust to, because it accentuates so sharply what has been lost elsewhere in the British Isles. The machair, though it is not without its threats and problems (erosion caused by increasingly destructive storms being a major one) remains a habitat of low-intensity agriculture which supports an extraordinary rich and abundant bird life. Cultivation methods in the Outer Hebrides lend themselves to the birds. Sowing and harrowing, for example, must be completed in time so as not to interfere with nesting. Cultivated ground is usually left fallow for at least two years before it is used again. This rotational policy produces a patchwork of small areas of differing vegetation, often rich in invertebrates, providing ideal feeding and nesting habitats for birds. The sandy soils mean that artificial fertilisers and herbicides wash out easily so traditional cereal crops like rye and small oats are left to grow alongside the wildflowers, then cropped in the autumn as cattle fodder. Seaweed does a better job of fertilising the land here (and conserving moisture) than chemical fertilisers. Many of the bird species found in such high densities on the machair – oystercatcher, lapwing, snipe, redshank – have dwindled or disappeared elsewhere. The absence of these beautiful birds from large swathes of their historic range is one of the most conspicuous tragedies we have inflicted on our environment in the last few decades. The machair is a fine example, perhaps the best example in the country, where cultivation and wildlife are compatible.

I don't know of anywhere else where there is such a sensory rush of birds as you experience on the machair. It is exhilarating how the birds assert the place as their own. The oystercatchers run lassoes of noise around you, the terns fix you with their bright red bills and, with a high-pitched drilling call, make a beeline for your head. To be upright on the machair, to encroach on these birds' territories, is to invite pandemonium, to trigger a furious alarm of heckles, shrieks and yells.

The loudest, most conspicuous bird on the machair is the oystercatcher. It is a bird I have come to love very much. Their dark-red eyes, the bright orange bill, their shallow, rapid wing beats. The way they tilt in flight, tipping their wings to reveal chinks of white. Brightness and speed. When they are out, perched or feeding, on the wet sand that brightness is even sharper. I think I love them most, though, when the oystercatchers flock together in the air. There's a brief moment which I look for inside the flock. I don't always catch it, but when it occurs it is always memorable. A flock will be flying quickly over the dunes and then suddenly there is this pause, a collective mid-air hesitation. Their wings stop and lift above their heads. The flock stalls and hangs there as if it is holding its breath. Then exhales, a flash of white, and the birds flick back into flight.

The machair is a wonderful stage to observe these colourful, noisy waders. You can go, with just a twist of the head, from watching oystercatchers feeding along the shore to defending their breeding territories behind the dunes. The oystercatchers serve as an early-warning system to all the other birds of the machair. They are the most readily alarmed by your presence, the first to object, the first to spread the word across the machair you are coming. Often they will be perched on fence posts, gaining that extra height to keep watch over the vast flat terrain. Lapwings can react to an oystercatcher's alarm with such rapidity it's as if the two species are joined by circuitry. On South Uist I watched a flock of a hundred lapwings shaken into flight by an oystercatcher's alarm. The lapwings rose so lightly they looked like leaves being lifted by a breeze. The flock hung floating above a loch. Then, after a few restless minutes, they began to descend in drops of nervousness. The lapwings lowered themselves so tentatively – flickering, feinting – it was as if they could no longer trust the ground to touch.

There is a sense of a mutually supportive dynamic at work between the nesting species on the machair. I've seen redshanks nesting very close to common terns, clearly benefitting from the terns' relentless harrying of any potential predator. Even cattle lumbering past the tern colony will get the dive-bombing tern treatment. On one occasion an oystercatcher alerted me to the presence of a merlin. The oystercatcher was calling loudly, swirling around the merlin to drive it away. There were large flocks of starlings in the vicinity and the oystercatcher's alarm immediately grounded the flocks. I watched the merlin rush low over the dunes towards the starlings. It flung itself at one of the flocks and the starlings puffed apart like smoke. But the birds kept very low and landed almost as soon as they had risen, not giving the merlin the space or time to pursue them through the air. One flock of starlings landed in amongst a herd of cattle, huddling close to the herd for protection. Some of the starlings took up position directly beneath a cow, shuffling along to keep in step with the animal as it grazed. The cow's belly was like a roof above the birds, and it looked as if the starlings were sheltering inside the open door of a huge barn. I watched the merlin trying to nudge the starlings out from beneath the herd, but the flock would not budge. Eventually the merlin huffed away to a rock where it perched, glaring out over the meadow.

Thanks to the oystercatcher's alarm the starlings saw the merlin approaching from a long way off. I've seen oystercatchers perform a similar role when a larger predator – the hen harrier – shows up over the machair. All hell breaks loose at the harrier's presence and the oystercatchers inevitably lead the alarm. It is fascinating to see the reaction of large numbers of wading birds to a predator and the effectiveness with which the waders deter the bird of prey. The odds seem greatly stacked against the predatory bird. On one occasion I watched a male hen harrier hunting dunlin over the wrack line on a beach. The harrier was engulfed by furious oystercatchers who quickly hustled the harrier away.

The ways the different bird species interact with each other is one of the great synergies of the machair. Waves of warning and agitation can surge across the plain for half a mile. A tern's scratchy grinding call says a raven has appeared and the ripple of alarm is felt by starlings, way over on the distant dunes. I'm especially drawn to the ways the birds' voices interact with one another. There is a beautiful acoustic layering of their respective calls. The ringed plover's call is lower and slower than the redshank's, and when the two species are calling together it can sound like the plover is keeping time beneath the redshank's peeping. Lapwing calls dip and tremble, a rising raspy note, then a flurry of electric bubbling. When the oystercatchers are in full voice, they dominate the soundscape of the machair. The calls of other birds, like lapwing, carry beneath the oystercatchers like an undertow.

Another sphere of interaction between the birds on the machair occurs in the way they feed. Each species of wader has evolved to exploit its own cross section of silt or sand or mud. Depending on the size and shape of the bird's bill there is a clear demarcation of foraging zones along the shoreline. I've watched flocks of bar-tailed godwits, knots and oystercatchers feeding together. The birds worked quickly, jabbing, probing at the wet sand, moving along the water's edge as they fed. The godwits, with their long, slightly up-curved bills, probed deep into the sand. The knots, with their shorter bills, worked much closer to the surface, with the oystercatchers operating somewhere in between.

Foraging is frantic, a fast-paced, constant sifting through the sand. Total absorption in the task. A larger wave than usual is the only thing that momentarily distracts the oystercatcher from its feeding. A quick readjustment, it scurries away from the wave, then head down and the bird is feeding again. Sometimes their bills probe the sand deeply, almost the whole length of the bill is inserted. Other times just a fraction of the bill goes in. Probe, shake, swallow – stab. The bill is constantly working. The oystercatcher is moving all the time. Two steps – probe, two steps – probe. As the long bill works the sand, it is slightly parted, flexing like a pair of tight chopsticks. I am amazed at how often the oystercatcher's probing is successful. It appears to secure prey almost every other probe. Through my scope I sometimes catch a glimpse of thin, small worms the oystercatchers are lifting from just beneath the surface of the sand. The birds always seem to know where to stab. They can detect the position of the worms from cues – feeding marks and faeces casts – left on the surface by the invertebrates. It's as if the oystercatchers read the beach like braille. Any surface anomaly will be pecked at, investigated, and every type of surface is worked over by the oystercatchers. They will feed in water a few inches deep, over wet and dry sand, over rocks and seaweed. Oystercatchers are one of the few wader species to feed their young. In the majority of waders the young feed independently as soon as they hatch. So you will see these satellite birds, almost fully grown juvenile oystercatchers, following a parent around, snatching food from the adult bird's bill. These juvenile birds don't yet possess the adult's bright colours. They have greyish legs and a pale orange bill with a smudged black tip. Their eyes are dark-brown and their backs are a dusky brown colour.

One of my favourite spots on the machair is a fence post on the dunes where I can sit and look out across a huge flat plain. The expanse of the machair here gives it a prairie-like feel. The cattle are pinpricks in the distance. Sometimes, in the haze, all I can make out of the cattle are the small explosions of sand they trigger as they move over the drier ground. In the foreground there are many hundreds of oystercatchers. There is one flock of twenty-five birds in front of me about a hundred feet away. Some of the birds are resting with their bills tucked under their wings. Others are alert, pacing about. There is a strange tension about the flock. Every so often a troupe of four birds break off to perform a tense, shuffling dance. Beaks open, pointed downwards, the birds start up a crescendo of trilling, turning around each other in tight synchrony. They remind me of dodgem cars in the stiff, jerky movements the birds make to avoid colliding with each other. Those oystercatchers not taking part in the ceremony appear indifferent to the dance. But whenever one of the hunchbacked dancers sways into a non-dancer, the spectating bird is forced to do a leap-frog to avoid a collision. Sometimes, too, a pair of dancing birds collide and usually a leap-frog by one of the birds – a fan of white tail feathers, outstretched wings – allows the dance to continue. Though one collision I saw erupted into several minutes of scuffling between the birds, a roiling ball of black and white and orange as the oystercatchers jabbed and folded over each other in dispute. Fights like this are rare, though, and the purpose of these strange, beautiful dances, known as 'piping parties' seems to be more about trying to diffuse tension, whether that tension has arisen from a sexual, hierarchical or territorial dispute. The fact that their sharp, powerful bills are pointed downwards, rather than at each other, suggests that the birds wish to avoid injury during these disputes. They are hypnotic to watch, these piping displays. The noise the birds make when they are dancing, a fast-paced trilling, is very loud and the way it erupts so suddenly, it's as if a car alarm has gone off on the machair.

The machair is often described as a dynamic habitat. It changes, moves and adapts as the sands shift and water floods and drains from the land. Its dynamism is also reflected in the noise and movement of its birds. From the swirling flocks of starlings, to lapwings in their hundreds drifting over the dunes, to the mesmerising oystercatcher piping dances, the presence of these birds is a pulse which gives the machair a dynamism I have not encountered elsewhere. It has always been an exceptional habitat in this respect. Though in recent years wader numbers have declined on the machair (the introduction of mammalian predators including hedgehogs and ferrets have contributed to these declines), it remains a habitat of global importance for birds. Already one of the last refuges in this country for a once widespread species, the corncrake, the machair increasingly looks like becoming the last refuge too for many species of wading birds. This unique, rare habitat may be all these birds have left.

Alan Riach (SIX)

Returning to Assynt

It was odd but necessary to be reading John MacAskill's book, *We Have Won the Land*, the story of the purchase by the resident crofters of the Lochinver Estate in the far north-west of Scotland, in Cornwall in July 2011. It was likewise odd but equally essential to reread Milton's *Comus* there as well. The two works, and the two locations, connected, moved something on into new possibility, balanced on certain prehistoric facts, as Bate's Creed has it: 'prospect is to geography as retrospect is to time' (p. 344 below).

I've travelled to Lochinver in Assynt two times, once in the 1970s, once in 2010. In the second half of the twentieth century, the area for me was entirely the territory of Norman MacCaig. I'd read his poems since childhood, and later got to know him and met him, from time to time, in Edinburgh. The first time I went there I was a boy, my parents were driving, we were on holiday, roaming, stopping for bed-and-breakfasts here and there around Scotland. We travelled up the east coast, to Dingwall where my father was born and his parents are buried, north to Caithness and Strathnaver, west towards Assynt and along the one-track roads winding through a landscape that shifted every three hundred yards. Mountains changed their locations, slopes their incline, rivers and burns their direction, speed and width, with every turn of the path. The car moved at what seemed walking speed. It was sunny and the windows were down. Later I discovered that MacCaig was probably there in that landscape, that summer, while we were driving through, maybe up in the hills, fishing, maybe in the village, having a drink with friends.

In November 2010 I drove back there to take part in the hundredth anniversary of his birth, delivering a lecture with the artist Alexander Moffat on poetry and landscape. It took us two days to get there, through blizzards on day one and into bright sunshine on day two. The terrain became familiar as we neared the village and we saw the mountain, Suilven, its huge crest rising on the horizon, a dark, massive thing heaving itself upwards in its grandness and weight, shaped like Brazil's Sugar Loaf. You think of a mountain as its shape at first, its surface, paths and areas, its terrain, but then consider its magnitude of solid rock, its sheer compressing density, its deeply earthed interior, its geological history and presence. In the sunlight, in its own domain, the mountain rose above its landscape and the shapeliness of everything seemed arranged and attuned to it. Wallace Stevens placed a jar in Tennessee and the wilderness that had been slovenly suddenly seemed located in an order and sequence around it, attentive to human decision and the act of its creation. But here there is a different order, a different relation between the human and inhuman world.

Alexander Moffat, Lochinver

This is at the heart of all MacCaig's poems. They are familiar as portraits of animals, birds, trees, things, but their subject is equally the inefficencies, the inexactnesses, of language. A thorn bush is 'an encyclopedia of angles' and a sheepdog goes through a fence 'like a piece of black wind' – very precise indeed. But the human mind plays tricks. If we can imagine water and a wall, we can imagine a wall of water. Midnight is always happening somewhere and in every skull but in that darkness, magic happens too, the jewel in the toad's head is the imagination happening in human language. He shows us how to see with his words. The last time I was with him, he urged and implored me to go to Lochinver, to visit this place he was too old to return to. It was, he said, his most favourite place in the whole world: 'It's the place I think of every night when my head hits the pillow.' He told me that once he had seen a couple of tourists, visiting the area. He saw them over a couple of days but then spotted them packing their car, about to leave. Did they not like the place? he asked. No, they said. 'We can't see the landscape for the mountains. They keep getting in the way.' He shook his head sadly and we shared a smile.

The difference is real, though. There is a familiar stance, an address to the landscape that Rilke, in the eighth of the *Duino Elegies*, describes:

> Who's turned us round like this, so that we always,
> Do what we may, retain the attitude
> Of someone who's departing? Just as he,
> On the last hill, that shows him all his valley
> For the last time, will turn and stop and linger,
> We live our lives, for ever taking leave.

If the prototype of the great Romantic sinners, from Byron's Don Juan to Melville's Ahab, is Milton's Satan, perhaps the prototype for this retrospective glance is that of Adam and Eve, at the end of *Paradise Lost*, looking back at what they must depart from. As Jonathan Bate puts it, 'the point about Eden is that those who write about it have been expelled from it'. Of course, to any student of Scottish literature, the quotation from Rilke will be immediately suggestive of the opening sentence of Stevenson's *Kidnapped.* But if David Balfour's departure, taking the key for the last time out of the door of his father's house, marks a similarly reflective moment of leave-taking, the whole circular trajectory of that novel brings him back, by a commodious circulation, to reclaim his inheritance.

And MacCaig's returning again and again, summer after summer, to Assynt, brought him back to be inside this landscape, in contact with its permanent residents, friends and companions. 'Why would anyone in their right mind want to be in Edinburgh at the time of the Festival?' he asked me once, 'when they could be there …'

Alexander Moffat, Lochinver

After the lecture, Sandy and I returned to Glencanisp Lodge, by Lochinver. Through the late afternoon, as daylight faded, the range of mountains looming on the horizon, with Suilven shouldering indifferently above them all, had merged into the darkness and could still be sensed out there. The company poured drams and the conversation began to flow. Glencanisp Lodge was a writers' retreat and we commented on the value of such a place. And then the question came: 'But you do know what this building used to be, don't you?'

We waited for the answer.

The Lodge belonged to the previous owners. The property was theirs, before the buy-out by the local crofters. The grandness of the building, the room we were sitting in, the view from the great wall-window through the day, all had been occupied by the landowners, and the story of how the local people had been able to acquire the land was told to us then, a large Ordnance-Survey map laid out on the floor so we could trace the extent of the property, the shapes of the landscape, the location of the nearest shops, mountains, streams and rivers, the tracks and places MacCaig had walked and visited, the lochs and lochans he had fished, the names I had read in his poems.

In the longest poem he ever wrote, 'A Man in Assynt' from the book *A Man in My Position* (1969), he describes the area and asks the central questions:

> Who owns this landscape?
> The millionaire who bought it or
> the poacher staggering downhill in the early morning
> with a deer on his back?

Is it the property of the man who, by right of deed of purchase on a noted piece of paper, 'possesses' it, or the poet himself, who is 'possessed' by it? That question is about the authority of the imagination and the physical experience of being in a place, but it also opens another question about other people and history. Where have they gone, MacCaig asks, the people who once lived here? At the end of the poem he uses his imagination in a different way, thinking not of the reasons for an elegiac sense of the past but rather of the possible future that might be configured by an act of will and hope, that the tide of the 'sad withdrawal of people' may one day turn, and that 'the bays and sheltered glens' may someday be flooded by a return of people, new generations 'replenishing the land' and 'coming, at last, / into their own again'.

When I first read that I thought it was extremely wilful, an assertion of possibility that had almost no chance of materialising. And yet the story we were told that night at Glencanisp Lodge revealed that in fact the unthinkable had happened. The land had been reclaimed and the possibility of new generations living there in a working economy once again had become a reality. This is not to idealise. John MacAskill's account gives details of how much work, how much good fortune and collaborative support had been required in the economic and legal process of acquiring ownership, and what that would mean for future owner-occupation.

The wilderness stays wild – a permanent symbol of what is beyond us – Gerard Manley Hopkins's vision of Inversnaid in perpetuity – but at the same time, it is occupied by the sympathetic human imagination in a new way, or in a return to other ways. And MacCaig's poem acquires a new meaning. He told me once he did not rate it very highly as a poem: he thought it was too long, had too many longueurs and sagging passages in the narrative, was insufficiently varied in tone, was maybe too schematic: evocation, elegy, description, rhetorical flourish and bordered on being embarrassingly direct in its political statement. Yet it seems now justified, both as a poem written from a particular moment in the history of land ownership in Scotland and the literary imagining of landscape generally. Its conclusion is beginning to be in the wrong tense. It is not that people might one day return, but now rather that they are returning.

*

Reading John MacAskill's account of the crofters' purchase of the Lochinver while I was in Cornwall and thinking back over Norman MacCaig's poems and the distinction of participation they enact, I was also thinking about the connection between where I was in the far south-west of the British mainland and the far north-west, MacCaig's territory. Cornwall has its artists and writers, of course, not least MacCaig's Scottish contemporary W.S. Graham, who lived there and occupied the landscape in a similar but different way. Cornwall is like Sutherlandshire in this respect: for Graham as for MacCaig, you are in the landscape and at the same time utterly outwith its inhuman, elemental fact. That balance is liminal, bordering, dependent on perspective and particpation. Things look different from where you stand: Lochinver is in Sutherland, so named to mean 'land of the South', from the perspective of people who arrived from further North, while Cornwall is visible by virtue of what lies underneath, a sense of prehistoric presence. We were staying in the fishing village of Newlyn, where the fishermen live and work even now, and live in houses on a steep hill overlooking the bay, over to Penzance and St Michael's Mount, across depths of water beneath which, some say, unknowable remnants lie: Lyonnesse, the land undersea. The bells of Ys, imagined sounds beyond the gulls' cries in the watercolour paint of dawn. The ends of the earth all claim us, the depth of ocean and the fossil in the pine, the precellular rock beneath it.

But it would be wrong to leave it like that, for the balance and commerce between the ideal stillness of dawn and the effort and acts of the day regenerate themselves, prospect and retrospect both. And that's why the other book I was reading in Cornwall was so necessary. Milton's *Comus* is from the heartland of Puritan England, a masque first presented at Ludlow Castle in 1634 in honour of chastity, to celebrate the appointment of John Egerton, the first Earl of Bridgewater's new post as Lord President of Wales. Comus is the tempter, trying to bring corruption to the virtuous Lady. She defends her temperance and chastity, but even after the Attendant Spirit helps her brothers defeat the beguiling Comus, she still remains bound to her chair, until finally the Spirit sings and, by virtue of music, conjures the water nymph Sabrina, who frees the Lady. Celebration follows. Heaven will be there for wayfaring souls, winning through various trials, the impositions of evil or the beguilements of temptation.

It would be easy to read this simply as allegory, legitimising England's rule over the Welsh marches. But it goes much deeper than that. Sabrina is the Roman name for the River Severn, the longest river in mainland Britain, that takes its circling route from the Cambrian mountains in Wales through the English counties of Shropshire, Worcestershire and Gloucestershire. The name of the river in Welsh is 'Hafren', meaning 'boundary'. It forms a boundary and crosses a border, it runs through places and across histories, its story is of depth and at the estuary, of tidal change, and the role Sabrina plays in *Comus* is to free us in the balance of corruption and chastity, the world in which we live. All things come into her song because transition is her life, practice and blessing. What has changed in Assynt, since I was driven through it by my parents maybe forty years ago, is not only its ownership but also the very meaning of ownership, from that of the absentee landlord to that of permanent residents. The wilderness remains but is not merely scenery. Seen in this way, through participation, it cannot remain merely property. Wayfarers may get lost, but to find the way once again requires the song of the river, Sabrina. The landscape is a permanent defence.

Michael Longley (THREE)

On the Shetlands

On the Shetlands we don't know anyone,
So we gossip about the animals
Or we contact home on the mobile.
As we wait at Toft for the Yell ferry
You walk up and down the little beach
Too deep in conversation and sad news
To notice an otter's kelp-flashes. Look!
I'm trying not to frighten him away.

You climb alone to where witches burned
And disturb a white hare. Albino
Or snowy-coated still? I've no idea.
Shy behind his streaming forelock, he
Approaches us, one dishevelled pony,
A grandchild's mount. Shall I comb his mane?
His hoof-prints fill with rain and inspire me,
My hobbling, diminutive Pegasus.

Shetland Mouse-Ear

We got as far as Unst,
No nearer, as if the idea
Of Shetland mouse-ear's white
Petals, hairy leaves, roots
In debris, growing nowhere else
In the world was enough.

Whalsay

He fitted all of the island
Inside a fisherman's float – his
Cosmology of sea breezes
Cooling the seabirds' eggs
Or filling otter prints with sand:

For such phenomena, for
Sea lavender and spindrift, he –
Ravenous, insomniac – beach-
Combed the exact dialect words
Under a sky of green glass.

Alan Riach (EIGHT)

Infinite Whalsay

The island itself, five miles long, two miles wide, is gentle to look at, bare of trees but benign and shapely, covered in summer in pink flowers, thrift and campion, the blue spring squill, the rare sea aster. Other islands are threaded and studded in the waters around it, and inlets and voes run in. Streams run over it, a maze of waters and landforms, layered in archaeological depths of human habitation across millennia, and active with seabirds, gulls, duck, waders, red-throated divers on the inland lochs, migrating birds from Scandinavia by the high cliffs on the east side. The rocks are schist and the fragments of the original are xenoliths still visible, present in the granitic gneiss, with crystalline limestone on the north-east coast. In May 1933, when MacDiarmid stepped off the boat here, the days were long and lengthening, the sunlight opening further horizons and subtleties of terrain and colour on all sides.

Everything was new to him. He had gone from the metropolitan centre to the furthest peripheral edge, from constant dynamism to utmost isolation. He was forty-one years old and everything was left behind – or so it seemed.

*

There are many strands of stories to be told about this time in MacDiarmid's life. There is the love story: MacDiarmid's broken marriage and the conflict of longing for his first wife and children, while Valda, his second wife, grew more deeply into his affection and love for her and their young son developed. There is the story of his health, the severe physical and nervous breakdown in 1935, mental stress and physical debilities, rendering him hospitalised in Perth from 17 August to 3 October. When he returned to Shetland, he was a wreck. Emaciated, traumatised in mind and spirit, and materially destitute. He was in the most isolated place, personally, profoundly uncertain in his own psychological and physiological identity. He looked at the future and the immediate palpable barrenness of the island with a fearful sense of his own deep, helpless, vulnerable weakness, his life and hopes hanging by threads. In the following year, there is the story of the eruption of his anger at Edwin Muir's declaration that Scottish writers must henceforth write in English exclusively. This MacDiarmid saw as betrayal of his commitment to a plural, multi-lingual Scotland, in which Gaelic, Scots and English could flourish.

There is the story of his excursions from Shetland, to the cities, Glasgow, Edinburgh, London, to make broadcasts and seek publishers' contracts, and then the story of his reading and writing practices, endless hours of gathering information from journals and books sent on loan by post, longhand work on large sheets of paper, chaotic accumulation, careful ordering and editing for publication of masses of material seemingly otherwise utterly inchoate. There is the story of new friends, new generations of poets visiting him in Shetland, foremost among them Sorley MacLean. In 1938, a young man named Grant Taylor arrived to work for no payment as MacDiarmid's secretary, typing increasingly long manuscripts. MacDiarmid was working on 'A History of Scottish Doctors' and 'Red Scotland': or, 'What Lenin Has Meant to Scotland', Taylor typed them and posted them by steamer to the mainland. Neither was ever published.

When I met Grant Taylor in 1992 in his retirement in Melrose, in the Scottish Borders, looked after by his family, a paraplegic then but a man who had clearly been handsome, lean and strong, he was tired and nodded at times, then would bring his head back up and recollect things with startling precision. From his wheelchair, in his living room, he talked quietly to me. He remembered translating articles from foreign journals with MacDiarmid beside him, using a small pocket German dictionary to get the meanings of words in an article on Rilke. He would be turning the pages but MacDiarmid would intuitively have guessed ahead of him, again and again, the accurate meanings of words. He recalled the all-night sessions of MacDiarmid writing and himself typing, once to meet the deadline of the morning ferry, finishing the work with his head heavily drooping on the typewriter, falling asleep, and being woken up by the ferry's blast booming over from the harbour. He told me he raced to parcel up the typescript in brown paper and string, sprinted over the fields and down to the harbour and got there just in time. When he told me he had never seen the typescript again and never knew what had become of it, I informed him that I had read them both, 'Scottish Doctors' and 'Red Scotland', or what remains of the typescripts, in the National Library of Scotland. They might not have been published but they were there, in the archives still. The smile that came to him then was beatific.

*

But I want to concentrate here on only two stories: the story of MacDiarmid's personal engagement with Shetland and what emerged from it, and the story of the way in which that led him to a wider exploration of the islands of Scotland and a deeper sense of the multiplicity of the whole coherent nation.

How far do you have to go, how much do you have to surmount, to arrive at the perspective that allows you to see the whole world as islands in their archipelagos of connection? MacDiarmid once said that by going to Shetland he was trying to understand if the utmost diversity of Scotland could form a coherence, and that he discovered there that this was true. The images are metaphors, there in the poems, again and again, in 'Harry Semen', the multitude of islands 'each inhabited by a single man' in the arbitrary splash of sperm from which he came; in 'The Terrible Crystal', where in the 'diamond body' achieved in a cave by the sea, the slow perception dawns that the sea itself stays still, but the earth itself is moving as the tides change, and what are individuals but porous parcels of water, stranded on the earth? In 'Scotland Small?' where the question mark refutes the narrowing of nationality by opening out in microscopic, precise historical detail the variety of the country, the potential of regeneration.

In his first year in Shetland, biographies, letters, accounts made by others, all tell of his eager exploration of the archipelago, the travelling by sea that connected the islands and immersed him in the working economy of the people around him. He went aboard a haddock boat to the Out Skerries, five miles north-east of Whalsay, with Thomas Robertson, H.M. Survey Geologist, with whom he formed a friendship and learned the words for the stones. He went as an observer on the square-sail drifter herring boat the *Valkyrie* into Yell Sound, sailing into the deep waters north of Shetland with the herring fishers in June 1936, writing on board, lying in his bunk, paper pressed to the boards of the bunk above. Listening to the fishermen's words, scribbling them down. When they saw him noting their words, quick wits, they started to make things up, one said later. MacDiarmid asked for the meaning, wrote more notes. But writing has its revenge. The words go into the poems, and have their effect as well as their explanation. In 'Off the Coast of Fiedeland' he describes his voyage, the poem dedicated to Skipper John Irvine, of Saltness, Whalsay:

> Twenty miles out to the main deep
> Due west o' the Ramna Stacks
> And sou-west o' the Flugga Light
> I ha'e a' that my pleasure lacks.

They navigate the 'tricky tideways o' Yell Soond, fu' / O' sunshine noo – on white horses!' – and head home:

Three reefs and nae comfort up or doon
Where I'm still thinkin', my love, o' you
While play Lant in an air smoke, steam,
And sweaty socks mak' like an Irish stew.

Lant is glossed as an old and complicated card game favoured by Shetland fishermen. The poems carry their own value but following MacDiarmid through his correspondence gives an immediate biographical sense of the exhilaration he felt so intensely. The same voyage is recorded in a letter to Valda of 2 June 1936:

> Went to sea yesterday in hailstorm at Symbister. Very cold up Yell Sound but turned splendid night. Shot nets about 10 to 11 pm about 20 miles beyond Ramna Stacks and Muckle Flugga lighthouse and drew up again about 4 am – light fishing; about 8 crabs. All boats had small catches.
>
> Wednesday night
> Out again 20 miles S.W. of the Flugga light and about 10 due West of the Ramna Stacks, and just about to shoot our nets. Big fleet all about us – fifty or sixty sail-boats, motor boats, drifters, etc. Hope we get a big shot tonight. Wrote two good lyrics today, lying up on the deck on the herring-nets in the sun. But it's dashed cold now. However we will be getting our supper-time porridge soon.
>
> Thursday morning
> Colla Firth
> No luck again last night – fewer herring than we could eat ourselves.
>
> In sight of Foula
> Thursday night
> Casting our nets again under a perfect weatherhead. Hope for better luck tonight.
>
> Friday 4 am
> Hauling our nets since 1 am. Nearly finished now. Much better catch. Deck littered with fish. Was helping to haul myself for a while. Lovely

red sunrise. Soon the cabin will be a snug little place with a fine smell of smoke, steam, cooking and sweaty socks. No doubt I'd prefer to be with you in our own little house, but this suits me A1 to go on with.

Friday night
Colla Firth
Very high wind-storm, and dense small rain. Conditions quite impossible on the West Side grounds especially for sailing boats. The motor-boats and drifters even tried to go out but had to come back. So we'll lie here tonight and go home to Whalsay tomorrow if conditions permit.

Saturday morning
That is to say – to Whalsay, *if* we can win. It is blowing a furious gale up here at the top of Colla Firth, but the wind and tide may suit us once we get into Yell Sound ...
Came down with sails three-reefed. A most exciting experience – but not for any except good sailors.
Landed at Whalsay in fury of wind & water.

He visited the Faroes on the steamer *Tjaldur*, saw 'the monstrous shapes of Litla Dimun and Stora Dimun ... pyramids rising to needle-points, sheer walls of basalt, fantastic ridges with razor edges'. He attended the Faroe festival of St Olaf and praised the Faroese, returning to reappraise Shetland as geologically deep, culturally negligible. This won him no friends in Shetland but it prompted his most necessary poem of the 1930s, 'On a Raised Beach'.

The first draft was written in 1933, sent to the composer, MacDiarmid's boyhood teacher, F.G. Scott, then revised accordingly, in a musical structure of immensely challenging, complex coherence. This is one of the greatest poems in world literature. Its premise is Miltonic, but materialist: How can you believe in human value, in the scale of geological time? How can you affirm it? Does it truly exist? In politics and culture, mankind in totality and any single life, what is all the struggle worth? What is here at stake? What is the cost? It brings us back to the earth, indeed, with greater difficulty and ultimately more certainty than T.S. Eliot, firmly in MacDiarmid's sights, could envision or subscribe to. 'On a Raised Beach' evokes *The Waste Land* only to reject it: this is not a heap of broken images, MacDiarmid tells us, but: 'All human culture is a Goliath to fall / To the least of these pebbles withal.' It is the central poem in the book called *Stony Limits*, published in London by Victor Gollancz in 1935.

For MacDiarmid in the 1930s, Shetland was the desert he sailed into, like his favoured English poet Charles Doughty, walking into desert Arabia, to learn what human value is. He saw it and wrote it as fascism and communism were growing their perversions throughout Europe, both from socialist ideals – in 1917 Russia and in post-war Germany and Italy. Stalin had begun his Terror in earnest after Lenin's death in 1924, and what had seemed to some like Mussolini's bright beginning in the early 1920s was caught and turned in Hitler's rising tide. By the 1930s, Spain was already fascism's target. MacDiarmid was aware of most, not all, of this.

The radio was there, but not in every house. People would gather together to listen to the news reports, as the decade gathered its storms.

Such things as war impinged as they would, but it was the life of the islands that mattered in the end. MacDiarmid praised the Shetland people as frank and kindly, but, he said, 'They are a secret people, not by active concealment, but because they are so natural and unselfconscious in their unobtrusive but very real differences that these habitually escape the observation of the impatient and uninstructed.' Away from the centre of Lerwick, 'one of the signs of this different life and attitude to life is to be seen in the fact that the cottages, instead of being grouped into little villages or clachans, stand separately, each on its own croft. This does not mean that the people are unsociable – they are far from that – but simply that they are independent and self-reliant'. Visitors from the South may think their lives hard, but 'to go into these seemingly poor cottages is to appreciate at once that, despite appearances, there is a "routh of gear", an unexpected degree of comfort, a rich family and social life. So it is with all the outward appearances in the Shetlands: a very vivid and generous life lies behind them – a different tradition of existence'. This is what he called 'Halophilous living by these cold northern seas' – a halophile being an animal that requires the salt in the air.

MacDiarmid catches this perfectly in a sketch, 'Old Eric's Hobby', where he describes the septuagenarian's speech as 'an endless outpouring of broken phrases, unfinished sentences, a most disconcerting scrappiness, with lapses into the ancient Island language, insinuations and innuendos, a general taking for granted that you are far more familiar with the background than you can possibly be which makes him obscurely allusive and maddeningly elliptical, and these fragments of speech are eked out with a range of inflectons to the significance of which you have no clue, queer little giggles, sly looks, nudgings, and gestures of all sorts'. While his wife looks after their shop, Old Eric 'diddles back and forward, making faces and mumbling away to himself; but he always carries his gun'. His hobby, it appears, is murdering the green cormorants, shooting numbers of them every year and leaving their 'shattered corpses to float about, bloodying the diamond-like transparency of the waters of the voe'. Yet he justifies himself as the protector of the sillocks, the young saithe, swarming in the shallows and the main food source for the vast masses of cormorants standing like battalions on parade. Eric, MacDiarmid concludes, is a cormorant himself, eating the sillocks with equally eager appetite and relish, and yet, neither fish, birds nor man seem cut off from each other in the miracle light reveals of all created things and their unfathomable motivations. We become intensely 'aware of the idea of countless kinds of invisible light and of the existence of innumerable colours we can neither see nor imagine – given as we are but one octave out of some sixty octaves of ether wavelengths already explorable by the methods of physics, a gamut reaching from great radio waves at one end to the inconceivably minute waves of X-rays, and cosmic rays bombarding our planet from outer space, at the other end'. In such a world, 'the scandalous figure of Old Eric shuffles into sight' and is welcome, for, with the repeated *crack!* of his rifle shots, he riddles 'the whole illusion of the sun, here where the mind goes out, not in serene reception, but in abstract speculation, disdaining earth'.

The sketch is an astonishing transformation of what at first appears a naturalistic description of a local character, repulsive, compelling, eccentric, into a provocative essay on the inter-relation of life forms in a universe that can only ever be partially explained. Naturalism, here, is not enough.

Yet this is no excuse to retreat from material reality and political purpose. In 1939, MacDiarmid gave practical help to a group of Whalsay cottars, opposing the County Assessor's raising of rates. At their request, MacDiarmid argued forcefully for them, in meetings and in letters, pointing out that they shouldn't be charged any rates, as they had no public amenities at all. The Assessor, Thomas Johnston, wrote to the Laird, William Bruce, MacDiarmid's erstwhile bridge-partner in Symbister House, who agreed that the poet was 'an infernal nuisance. He is being well-watched here I can tell you, and will be reported if there is any sedition'. MacDiarmid secured Sir Alexander MacEwan, a solicitor in Inverness and SNP man, to act as the cottars' legal representative but it was impossible for him to get to Shetland in time. When the appeals were dismissed, the Assessor wrote a letter to the Lerwick paper to justify himself, and MacDiarmid replied, noting of Johnston and the 'reactionary Council' who supported him: 'I repudiate all the "conventional lies" which are used to dignify Mr Johnston's business – and mask his personal responsibility for what he does. I am simply and solely concerned with the ultimate fact that on no matter what specious pretexts in the home country of the wealthiest empire in the world, and at a time when national service is being appealed for on all hands or made compulsory, the administrative system finds it necessary to "put the screw" on the poorest of the poor and wring a few more shillings out of people below the subsistence level. That is what it all boils down to, and I have no hesitation in stigmatising it as a shameful and intolerable state of affairs and condemning lock, stock and barrel the system under which it takes place and the officials who work that system.'

In his autobiography *Lucky Poet*, MacDiarmid pictures himself in his croft, 'a nice commodious four-roomed cottage standing on a hillside and looking out over a tangled pattern of complicated tideways, voes, and islands with snaggled coasts to the North Shetland mainland and the Atlantic'. The human scale is suggested again when he says, four hundred pages later, 'These are the thoughts with which I sit by my Shetland window completing the writing of this book …' So when we consider the matters of MacDiarmid's day-to-day business, domestic work, local conditions, contexts of social inequality and political injustice, and see them measured in his imagination and literary production, there seems no discrepancy between the daily work, the material facts, storms, opposition and darkness, and the love of islands, the returning tides, the value of the lives of the people around him and what his best art might deliver. What mattered for MacDiarmid is not what the artist has to teach in any condescending way but rather what the artist has to learn from the lives of the people he lives among, forms of attention, knowledge, experience, action and articulation. In the last chapter of *Lucky Poet*, he describes a ship's captain on the bridge in a storm, the waves crashing over him: 'Being covered and lost under water meant nothing to him. But the blow of the water – that was something! The deck had been boarded by a moving mountain – "He'll be drowned!" – "No more than a fish!" – The mountain had slid off.'

The same thing is there in the poetry, magnified and even more sharply focused, as in 'The Wreck of the *Swan*':

> No dreamers these but hard-bitten men
> Used to all the tortures of Old Feathery legs
> – The black villain who rides every crested wave
> North of 65 degrees – he and his accursed legions,
> The fog, the blizzard, the black-squall and the hurricane.
>
> Up to their waists in water on the foredeck …
>
> A wave as high as the mast-heads crashing on deck
> And sweeping all hands in a heap on the lee-scuppers,
> Their arms and hands clawing up through the boiling surf
> Still grasping wriggling fish and gutting knives.

The poem has its documentary imperative: 'Time the public knew what these men have to face.' There were then, MacDiarmid tells us, nearly 100,000 of them at sea, and if you consider the fishing industry to include shipbuilders, rope, net and box manufacturers, fish-friers, buyers, retailers, salesmen, railways and road transport, coal, salt and ice industries, you might say that around three million folk depended on the trawlermen for a living.

Again, the specific working economics connect to literary perception and social vision. Making these connections allowed MacDiarmid access to the world beyond Shetland in precisely this way. Towards the end of *Stony Limits* is the poem 'Lament for the Great Music', which takes us from Shetland south and west to mainland Scotland, out from the pre-eminently Norse influences and into the Gaelic and Celtic worlds of Scotland, connecting them deliberately, beginning to encompass and envision a plural nationality, and to go beyond that by connecting all this, in the opening lines of the poem, with the archipelago of ancient Greece. As Greece once was, so Scotland's archipelagos and Highlands are now, a singular 'fold of value in the world'.

This is the meaning of the questions that open the poem, 'Scotland Small?': 'Our multiform, infinite Scotland, *small?*' The multiplicity of meanings and identities uncovered in this poem, of flowers and insect life, are tied to the specific post-Clearances history of the landscape in view, with its peat-hags 'not worked / Within living memory' (because the crofters have gone) and where 'the little Blackface sheep' that have replaced them, are found grazing. The result is a poem that famously evokes the intrinsic potential of Scotland yet also connects that unsentimentally to its specific history.

MacDiarmid was the first poet of the last century to work like this so comprehensively and deeply, the process extending from Shetland to the western archipelagos of Scotland. In September 1937, he made an extensive tour of the Western Isles. His letters allow us to track his journey through the Hebrides, visiting Skye, Raasay, South Uist, Canna, Eigg, Barra, and Tobermory on Mull, and on. In 1939, he published *The Islands of Scotland*, the first book of its kind to shift the focus decisively away from the Hebrides. Up till then, they were the islands romanticised to the point of cliché and associated most in the popular imagination with the nostalgic and ill-fated destiny of Bonnie Prince Charlie and related legends. MacDiarmid devotes fifty pages to Shetland, twenty to Orkney and twenty-five to all the Hebrides – vastly disproportionate, you might argue, but also, perhaps, a necessary counterbalance, emphasising contemporary living conditions as well as lasting qualities of social life and spiritual identity to be found nowhere else in the world. This is anti-romantic, in one sense, but realism is not its only strength.

The major result of MacDiarmid's multi-faceted understanding of Scotland's plural identity was his editing *The Golden Treasury of Scottish Poetry*, published in 1940. In this, poems in English and Scots appear alongside translations from Latin and Gaelic, the latter made with the help of Sorley MacLean, including major poems by Duncan Ban MacIntyre and Alasdair MacMhaighstir Alasdair. MacDiarmid was introduced to MacLean on a visit to Edinburgh in 1934, and the Gaelic poet visited him on Whalsay in 1935, before going to war. MacDiarmid tells us that his own poem, 'In Talk with Duncan Ban MacIntyre', was written after making the translation of 'Praise of Ben Dorain', which dates it to 1939. He praises Duncan Ban by saying that only in his poetry can we feel that we stand in the woods by a river as three hinds and a stag approach, rise on their hind legs and browse on the twigs above us, close enough to touch as their breath comes into our faces. Then he continues:

> We have the feeling of having reached that state
> All watchers of animals desire
> Of having dispensed with our physical presence.
> Or is that it? Is not really the bottom of our desire
> Not to be ignored but to be accepted?

MacDiarmid's entire understanding of identity had been fashioned anew from his experience of the archipelagos of Shetland, then Orkney and the Western Isles, and then as this applied to Scotland as a whole,

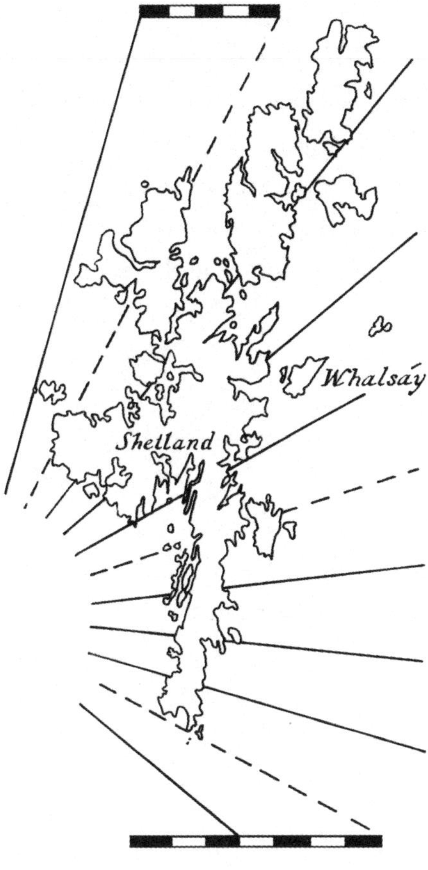
Whalsay
Shetland

and beyond that to all the world, through all time. In the same years as he was working on *The Golden Treasury*, he was putting together the pieces and passages that would ultimately form what he hoped would be the biggest poem in history, comprehensive yet open. He sent the typescript of an early version of what was to become *In Memoriam James Joyce* to T.S. Eliot in 1938, from Shetland, when he was forty-six years old, though it was not to be published till 1955, when MacDiarmid was sixty-three, and he had been working on it right up to its publication. Parts of *The Kind of Poetry I Want* appeared in *Lucky Poet* in 1943, the book of that title in 1963, and further passages have appeared since, but all of this magnum opus, what he called a 'vision of world language' (not a single language for all people but a multiplicity of forms of expression changing through time across all nations and localities), had begun to come together in Shetland.

Tim Dee (THREE)

Darkless Night

I will sing of the white birds
In the blue waters of heaven,
The clouds that are spray to its sea.

EZRA POUND, *CINO*

It is hard to sleep under a northern summer night. At midsummer in Shetland rain galloped on the roof. Outside, arctic terns and blackbirds kept up their noises through the darkless hours, a troubling mix of scream and serenade, harangue and consolation. I half-woke again and again to a pared-back version of light – like a prisoner's memory of daylight – and my broken sleep was crowded with a trapped dream of an impossible project.

I had the task of launching into the sky all the seabirds from all the cliffs of Shetland: the shags and razorbills from the boulders at the sea edge, the guillemots and kittiwakes from the open faces of rock, the gannets from their shanty towns along ridge-backs and fault-lines, the fulmars from the tussocked *neuks* below the cliff-lip, and the puffins from their burrows in the turf on the top. It was hopeless: no sooner had I flushed one wheel of puffins out over the edge than a gannet banked close to its nest and landed; kittiwakes dusted off in a cloud of bleached white, but guillemots flickered back, chocolate and cream; razorbills came, shags went.

To lie awake on the grass at a Shetland cliff top and watch a seabird colony is not so different from my Shetland dream except the birds resolve what my sleep couldn't. To get to the cliff edge at Hermaness or the Noup of Noss and look down and out is to find yourself dizzyingly, exhilaratingly, in the middle of a performance. Through every summer and for as long as the devastated seas can feed them, the wheels and flights of birds from their cliff places out over the sea and back again will continue. You will never have got there before it starts, and you will always leave before it ends.

Without colliding, without even appearing to have to adjust their flying to avoid one another, thousands of birds are perpetually in flight. There are clouds of birds, there are wheels of birds, birds alone joining groups, other bird parties breaking up, birds landing, birds taking off, a line of shags heading out to sea, a line of guillemots rising to a cliff ledge, a carousel of puffins that collects and deposits participants on each, always anti-clockwise, rotation, gannets singly and in tiers, beating away from the cliff, fulmars spreadeagled on landing attempts and forced back into the air by irate neighbours. My eyes cannot stay on any one bird for more than a second or two, always another has come between me and the bird I was watching, always another flies behind it. I reach for words: it is a city, a metropolis, a theatre, a cloud of gnats, Brownian motion, heaven, hell, space dust, bright stars in a floodlit universe – but nothing but what it is will do to describe the colony. A true account of it would have to be it itself. And it would have to include time, space and sound. The colony is above me, below me, perched and in flight, far out, close to, huddled and singular, in burrows and beneath the waves. It begins with noise and smell and ends with light and quiet.

I heard, and gagged on, the gannets at Hermaness before I could see them. Low cloud smeared the rocks at Muckle Flugga and the nearer stacks. The thousands of nesting birds on them were hidden, but the rain from the north brought in their shy whiff in gobbets of stink along with their homely rubbery conversation. Shafts of sunlight broke up the rain for moments and I could see patches of open sea beyond the shrouded stacks. In every patch at every moment there was a gannet dive. I have watched them plunge into the sea thousands of times before. Over and over they do the same thing to catch their food, but each dive shines with the specifics of its moment. Nature's repetitions are never boring. Every time it is like witnessing a fresh marvel in a new world: their visible-decision making, with its corrective twisting and corkscrewing, the rapid origami of themselves, and then their brilliant white match strikes, fizzing into the water (at 60mph) to leave puffs of lit sea spray. It is hard not to blink and hold your breath as they go in. The birds were far out of earshot and against the hubbub of wind and rain and puffin coo and gannet vibrato it would be impossible to hear them break through the sea, but the splash they made looked exactly like a sound and I found myself adding it to the ruckus.

From the cliff top I could see how the bubbling blue turbulence made by the thrown-down brilliance of their dives traps the shape the gannet forms under water. The diver pulls away and surfaces with or without a fish, but the cast of its plunge seethes like a tight net of ice just below the point where the bird went in. It is rare for a bird to leave evidence, even fleetingly, of how it has moved through the world. It reminded me of the dusted imprint a collared dove left on a window at my home in Bristol. A bird misjudged its flight from the bird table and briefly crashed into the glass. A ghost trace of the dove's raised wings was printed onto the pane by the oil and dust of its feathers. It looked religious and medical at once: an annunciation and the scan of a single flap. The dove continued to come to the bird table, and for weeks it and its flight print could be seen together, one through the other. The ghost lasted all summer, visible only when the sun was low, uncollectable, not even photographable, and I was sorry when the first heavy rain of autumn washed it away.

The rain at Hermaness had thinned. I could see more. The gannets pull up to the surface of the sea after their dives with a bucking torpedo energy. Every one I watched had to break out of a caul of water that their dive had thrown around them. They were hatching from the sea. I followed one bird dive and surface and take off, galloping along the sea to get airborne. I tried to track it back to the stacks but lost it in the mind-wiping swirl of birds. To see vast numbers of birds in silent movement is beautifully strange. In this crowd of so many moving things your eyes leap constantly from individuals to the whole event. These are not flocks but countless single birds caught in a life-storm. Individuals fly fast but the ensemble seems to be moving at dream-speed. The rush of the single bird somehow slows in the crowd. I cannot focus for long on a puffin with its hurrying wings in the wheeling cloud, instead I see a tumbleweed of birds rolling out from their grassed lawns and terraces over the gulf of air, a slow-motion collective rotation. Its drift reminds me of the paper mobiles that hung over my infant children's beds that were blown above them through the night by their sleeping breath.

Andrew McNeillie, Gannet

The noise of the cliff and the sea's moan down below is also silenced by these flights. On the ledges, through my binoculars, I can see the auks jabbering and the gannets at their pother. Nearer to me, fulmars *ack ack* and puffins are busy with their matronly growls. But the flying wheels and lines of birds move with a filtered quiet. The birds are silent in flight. I can hear the whicker of the close puffins' wings but that is all.

The gannet at sea and the gannet on its nest are hard to grasp as the same bird. In the air they move like great white flying planks. They never touch one another. But they must pair and breed and live within a beak-jab of others in a teeming midden glued to a dripping rock. They squabble and moan. Their nests are heaped bleached thatches built up over years, each merging into another, all held together with string and other irresistible rubbish the birds have collected at sea. They look like the nest of a sea-stork; guillemots, like house sparrows sheltering beneath storks' nests in Spain, breed underneath the gannet's eaves. Who would call the gannet the scrap merchant of the ocean or its bin man? But it is. A shag's nest for all its putrid reek is a far more organic affair. One gannet's nest has a blue plastic carrier bag carefully woven into its seaweed heart; another has a length of blue marine rope hanging down like a bell pull, and gannet neighbours occasionally lean over and tug it, as part of the continuing neighbourhood battles over space and furniture.

The sharp angles of the gannets' wings and beaks do half their territorial fighting. Their non-song does the rest. At sea, singing, talking, arguing, speaking of any kind has very little place in bird life. A gannet's face is silent. But on its nest it finds some half-aggressive half-soothing noise in its throat. This does for love song and battle hymn. It is an elasticated gurgle, and oddly domestic. Bonxies or great skuas, which breed over the moor behind the cliffs at Hermaness and on Noss, have an even more comically bathetic voice. 'Bunksie' means thickset in Norse and perfectly suggests – their business is the piratical harrying of other birds – and the heft of the meaty ballast they seem to carry. They are dog-food brown and chunky. In the air they are heavyweight bullies who behave like doormen to their own club, but on the ground they are lumpen and look dim and there is something of a leftover dodo about them. Some call with a baby gargle *gu gu gu gu gu gu gu gu*; others manage a cave-man *ug ug ug ug ug ug ug*. I spotted three bonxies coming in off the sea at Hermaness. As they reached the beginnings of their breeding moor of blanket bog, they raised their wings simultaneously into deep Vs and held them hieratically for a few seconds in a tough-guy balletic harmony. Then they came closer and they let off an *ug ug*, and I thought of the sea-world they had come from and the land-world they had returned to.

We want birds to be wild and free, but we bring our ideas of them indoors – into our houses or into our minds – and we domesticate them there. I was doing it by defining the skua calls as baby-talk and seeing their wings as heraldic. Neither really would suffice. I thought of my grandmother's house in Keynsham near Bristol where three ceramic drake mallards lived in permanent flight up the wall of the front room. Their raised wings reminded me of the bonxies. But what could be less wild than those china ducks? A gannet stealing string from a neighbour, or a bonxie clucking at its babies? To see the seasonally grounded lives of these great maritime heroes, to know that they must land and coddle their eggs and sweet talk their young ought to stretch our perception. The bonxie isn't only the oceanic corsair, the gannet not only the fisher king. 'Wild,' as we have it, does not say nearly enough about the lives of these or any bird. Their domestic arrangements seem cute or comic and we think we can relate to them, but these are as 'wild', if we must, as their gobbling of kittiwake puke or their four months alone each year far out in the Atlantic.

Puffins do this too. They come up stooping out of their burrows like badgers and they stroll at a post-prandial pace through the shivering pink flowering thrift of their front gardens. On the cliff top they seem at a kind of leisure. For a few sun-driven days of the year they are happy to walk with grass stems in their rainbow beaks. They dig tunnels, garden their lawns, take up flower arranging and live like northern bowerbirds. They dance and croon and preen and kiss their lovers. They gurn at their rivals and joust with their multicoloured bills. It is hard not to laugh.

Then the puffins fly out over the cliff edge, joining a rippling flex of themselves, and are taken utterly from the world we think we share with them. At every moment some slip from the turf and are shaken out over the sea into the air, forming and yet always joining a spiral of puffins that rolls along the cliff. Sometimes a bonxie or a great black-backed gull has drifted close to their burrows and a mass panic ensues; at other times, as some puffins land, new birds simply go. Their launches are briefly clumsy: a miniature badger is taking off. But once they are taken up into their tensile spiral, their flight is superb. There are maybe four hundred birds all rotating in the same direction. On any one wheel, all the available puffins are lifted and spun centrifugally in a continuous circuit three hundred feet across and a hundred feet deep. What function these spirals have is hard to know – the strategic befuddlement of predators perhaps, but it could just as well be a way of reducing collisions on departure, or practice for their whirring parrot-flight, or – dare we say it – simply fun.

I sat on the cliff top at Noss watching the endless and soothing helix of puffins. By turn I resisted and succumbed to mapping the birds' world onto mine. The puffin on the grass at its nest is where we live; the puffin in the air is where we dream. We see the standing bird as substantial; it has two feet like us on the ground. The flying bird by contrast is transitory and adventuring. Flight thrills us because it suggests the weightlessness we cannot achieve but also the freedom of mind that we can. I was scribbling this in my notebook until a splash of egg-yolk yellow puffin shit from a passing wheel-rider put a dribbling full-stop to my thoughts. It is still there now, like the Shetland sun pressed into my page.

Norman Ackroyd (NINE)

The Broch of Mousa; The Noup of Noss

Sally Huband (TWELVE)

Black Stane

At the point where the voe turns outwards and into the ocean, there is a narrow cleft in the rock that brings the sea inland. And here there is a storm beach, a beach that sits well beyond the usual reach of the high tide. It is formed from dark, shattered rock. The spaces between the shards of rock are infilled with white fragments which at first I mistake for plastic or polystyrene but then see that they are shell, the broken remains of dog whelks. There are a few painted top shells too, completely stripped of their pink and pearlescence by the sea. It is a threshold, this place, between shelter and exposure. I startle a redshank and the redshank in turn startles me and leaves the beach through the narrow passage of the cleft, its alarm call amplified by the rock walls.

The first time that I came here, a year ago almost to the day, I did not know the story of the Black Stane. I had been surveying this shoreline for purple sandpipers, small wading birds that winter in Shetland after breeding in the Arctic. Their name in Latin, *Calidris maritima*, means grey waterside bird of the sea. They hold to the hard coastlines of Shetland and their winter plumage is dark and tinged with mauve, a colouration that seems to capture the process of darkening at twilight. But Shetland is south yet and we have light enough in winter. Along the shores of Finnmark, in Arctic Norway, over-wintering purple sandpipers feed in darkness, for two months.

There will be six hours of light even on this mid-winter's day, time enough to linger if I can withstand the cold. Fulmars are looping around the ragged cliff face watched by ledge-bound mates and now that the redshank has fled with its noise, I am glad of their company. I sit on a ledge too, though much less precipitous, and let my legs hang over the drop. From this perspective the Black Stane is low-lying and wedge-shaped, though its exact form is always changing with the passing of the swell. It is an isolate and not quite in-shore, not quite off-shore. On this day and nearing high tide, each wave washes part way up the rock but never covers it entirely. It is gentler in form than the spiny, needled skerries that lie close in below the cliff face and its looping watchful fulmars. Even so, it is hard to see how someone could be landed there, on the Black Stane, especially against their will.

The noise of the waves breaking on the rocks below my feet excludes all other sound and I feel the need to glance over my shoulder to check that I am still alone before resuming my watch of the Black Stane. At the edge of my field of view a small fin emerges from the surface of the sea, a porpoise and then more, at least seven, one with a small calf hugging its side. They are heading north but inshore of the Black Stane, and then they turn east and into the voe. They move slowly, coming to the surface to breathe, one at a time, before diving again, spines bent so tightly that their backs form a perfect curve. The noise of the crashing sea below my feet intensifies and draws my attention away from the porpoises. Large waves are mostly submerging the Black Stane and as each passes the rock is riddled with the off-pouring of white water. It becomes possible to visualise the image of a woman being swept to her death on repeat and synched to the timing of the swell.

*

It was a neighbour that first told me the story. He had pointed to a tiny speck on the map, a sea-bound rock that that the mapmakers had deemed worthy of naming while others remain, on paper at least, anonymous. A woman, thought to have been a witch, was left on the Black Stane, he explained. If she was found alive in the morning it would be proof of her guilt. He moved his finger across the pale blue ink of the map's sea to a beach on a nearby island. This, he said, is where her body is supposed to have come ashore.

I've only seen the beach from afar. It is formed from stone that is as pale as the Black Stane is dark. The island is uninhabited. The compulsion to go to the beach is strong but the difficulty of getting to the island gives me a welcome excuse not to visit. The thought of walking there, on the beach, on my own, scares me. I have a notion that I might be trespassing in this story. It is already enough to sit where I am, beyond the cleft and its storm beach, in the low light of January, watching the waves pour over the Black Stane.

I search for a written trace of the story but find nothing. An archivist at the Shetland Museum helps me but it seems that there is no mention in the court records nor in the main texts on the folklore of Shetland. It is still possible that there is a grain of truth in the story, he counsels, and judgments did sometimes take place outside of the law in areas distant from administrative centres. He urges me to keep asking locally and directs me to the work of a Norwegian historian, Liv Helene Willumsen, and her book, *Witches of the North: Scotland and Finnmark*.

I find nothing of the Black Stane in this book but I become absorbed by Willumsen's analysis of the trial of a Shetland woman, Marion Pardoun. At the time of her trial, Marion was thirty-nine and married and had 'a reputation of knowing sorcery and healing'. On 15 March 1644, the moderator and the other brethren of the Shetland presbytery signed an indictment that listed fifteen accusations, all of which relate to spell-casting to cause illness to people, and illness and death to livestock. Marion was not, at this point, accused of causing death to any human. But then she was tortured, deprived of sleep until she was 'clearly out of her mind'. She, the scribe wrote, clothed her spirit with the whale, a porpoise to be exact. And, so transformed, she capsized a boat and four men drowned. The boat is reported to have been close to shore, away from any hazards and the weather had been fair. Whatever the actual cause, cetacean or not, the boat's tragedy became Marion's and she was executed. Marion was strangled and her body was then burnt.

Willumsen's analysis of Marion's trial is compelling:

> The voice of the scribe is heard particularly through the text's repetitive demonological phases. An understanding of Marion Pardoun's sorcery activity in relation to the Devil, thus leaving her God and Christian faith, is superimposed on her by male questioners, and this becomes very distinct in the document. The whole rhetorical apparatus of condemning a fallen woman because she is an enemy of God and has given herself to the Devil is used repeatedly, almost like an exorcism. The arguments for condemning her come from the witch-hunters. They interpret her deeds in the same way as if she had confessed to a demonic pact – and judge accordingly. This demonic aspect of the text is taken good care of by the scribe, hammering and hammering on the same expressions, an indication that the text itself reveals important ideological attitudes on the part of the interrogators.

It is clear that Marion never stood a chance.

In Shetland 74 per cent of those accused in witchcraft trials were women. In Finnmark, this figure rises to 82 per cent, although it is important to note that Sámi men were accused more often than Sámi women; the missionaries, as men, had less access to the women of this community. But in Finnmark there is, at least, the Steilneset Memorial. It can be found in the small island of Vardø, where most of the executions in this region took place. Vardø is noted, in *Birding Varanger*, as a good place to see purple sandpipers. I hope to visit the memorial one day, maybe in winter and perhaps these birds would be resting at high tide, motionless and dark against the white of ice.

Willumsen lists the Shetland women for whom there is a known sentence and date of execution. In 1616, Jonet Dynneis, Barbara Scord and Katherine Jonesdochter. In 1644, Juenit Fraser and Marion Pardoun and in 1675, Helen Stewart. A detail in the court records of Katherine Jonesdochter's trial makes me double back and read the section again. Katherine had a sea bean, the one thing that I hope to find, more than anything else, when I beachcomb. A sea bean, of the kind that I seek at least, is the drift-seed of a tropical *Entada gigas* vine. When the seeds fall from their pod, some are washed into streams and rivers and then the sea to be swept all the way to Shetland on a relay of ocean currents. It is rare to find them and so it is lucky to find them. But such a find on a northern shore at the time when Katherine lived, would have meant much more. Sea beans were used as good luck charms when death was more likely, during childbirth and when travelling by sea.

I wonder about her sea bean, what it meant to her and did she herself find it and where, which shore? Or was it passed down to her by generations of women? And what became of this sea bean, was it burnt with her body? I wish to ask Katherine so many questions. Her story was not told, her voice was silenced and all we have left are the court records, according to which the sea bean she possessed was given to her by the Devil the last time that she 'lay' with him, the time that he marked her 'on the privie membris'. And so it is documented, and there for me to read, four hundred years later, that she was humiliated so, subjected to a physical examination of her vagina, as I think this phrase must mean.

Katherine was specifically accused of casting the illness of her husband onto another man who subsequently died. The sea bean seems incidental to this accusation but her use of it as a charm is reason enough for the accusers to elaborate and falsify its story, to introduce a demonological origin, to justify their examination of her genitalia, to paint her as a fallen woman. We are sometimes urged to go easy on the past, to apply a kind of temporal cultural relativism. But I find this not so easy to do, when the poison trickles on still, from that past and into this present.

*

The woman of the Black Stane remains unnamed. And the absence of her name and my inability to find a written record of her death, of her story, makes me question whether her drowning ever took place, though I know that not all stories are transcribed, and even when they are it pays to be questioning of the scribe. But I keep asking. Some have never heard of the story, others nod but tell a different version, of straightforward murder, that a woman was simply left on the rock to die. I hear too that the Black Stane is reputed to glow when there is a full moon and wonder if I am being gently teased, but anyway I don't have the courage to walk the shore to the cleft and its storm beach in the dark.

But I do visit the beach where the woman's body is supposed to have washed ashore. I hitch a lift to the island in the boat of the farm manager who knows nothing of the story. It is June, not quite mid-summer, and the day is overcast and cold and I feel daunted by the distances that I must walk and the disturbance that I must inflict on the tirricks, the Arctic terns. I am here to count them, four colonies in total, and the method I am to use is flushing. I have to make them rise from their warm eggs. When this is all done, I am glad to walk into peace and away from the tirricks and their screeching. There are no ravens in Corbie Geo but I stand and watch a pair of rock doves sitting so tight together in the gloom that they seem one bird and it is good to listen to their shadowy cooing. The clouds part and the sea glints but the geo stays dark enough to hide the sea that slops around the confines of its walls.

I reach the pale beach from above, from the height of the cliffs. There are bodies strewn across the fine sand of the lower beach, ten common seals. Two face the sea, heads held aloft like the prows of hauled-up boats. The rest are scattered at angles like the driftwood that lies at the back of the beach. The pebbles are tinged pink and the parallel strandlines of desiccated kelp are dark but run through with the bright colours of plastic. The seals are motionless and the place seems exceptionally quiet. There are no oystercatchers or ringed plovers on nests and no meadow pipits or wheatears flitting about the grassy slope behind the beach. I'm glad that there are no oystercatchers, they would have seen me by now and alerted the seals to my presence. I can sit for a while and watch.

Outside the shelter of the rocks, there are small waves and beyond them the island of Gruna is busy with nesting common gulls, and the green of its name is intense but softened by the pink of thrift and the white of cotton grass. Beyond Gruna, the Black Stane sits apart. Fulmars are still looping round the cliff face, but the purple sandpipers are now further north, perhaps some are still waiting for snow to melt so that they can form a hollow in the lichen and moss and line this with willow leaves. And there they will sit, perfectly camouflaged, their bright summer plumage merging with the colours of the tundra.

I rise to my feet and in an instant the seals see me and make for the sea. Once in the water, they turn abruptly to watch as I make my way down the steep slope. I wish for an oystercatcher now, to break the silence. The sun is behind them and their eyes are in shadow, deep black sockets. On the beach we look at each other for a while. They stare, and it is difficult to turn my back on them, and, when I move to do so, quick as a flash they leap and slap through the surface of the sea in perfect synchronicity.

There is not much litter compared to the other beaches of the island, but it has gathered enough. There are ten plastic bottles, several strips of foam pockmarked where the hooks used for longline fishing would once have been stowed. Two fat rolls of sticky tape, an onion and a yellow tin of Swedish Vaseline decorated with a green trefoil. A small, round fishing float is covered in tacky patches of oil and there is a Nescafé capsule, opened and empty. I experience a flicker of hope, that I may find a sea bean but settle for two lobster pot tags, one from Newfoundland dated 1989, and one from Maine, the date too faded to be read. I'm soon so absorbed in the familiarity of the finds that I momentarily forget the Black Stane and its story.

There is the body of a gannet, mostly intact, and a dead guillemot, the thick skin of its neck pulled tightly back over its head. Its chest cavity is exposed, the wish bone is still attached to the keel, and all this is held taught by a thin translucent sheet of connective tissue. I imagine for a moment a woman's body lying on the beach, but the image is too contrived and the sun is warm and the beach is saturated in light. I feel no sense that the story was anything other than just that.

*

Two days later, I experience the second of two exceptionally vivid dreams. The first occurred when I was away from home and staying in an island that lies out beyond the Black Stane. I was alone and the door of the damp and dark house did not lock and I knew that I would not sleep well. But when I did fall asleep, I dreamt of the room in which I lay and of a man stood behind me, his hands tightly gripped my neck and I knew that he intended to strangle me. The fear of this dream does not fade, even in the almost all light of mid-summer. The second dream felt as real as the first but I felt no fear, none. I was sinking into sleep in my bed in my home, and in the dream I was watching my sleeping self in the same room. A woman stands behind me. I cannot see her face. She reaches down to touch my spine, slips her fingers through my skin and pulls apart the flesh of my back and climbs inside.

The next morning, I think that my subconscious is suggesting to me that I should maybe leave the Black Stane and its story alone, avoid walking to the cleft and its storm beach, to not walk again on the beach where the woman's body is said to have washed ashore. But I cannot. The woman, those women, are known to me now. And the Black Stane sits apart and will always draw my gaze.

Peter Davidson (EIGHT)

The Latitudes of Twilight

We move towards high summer, and the twilight shadows us. In a month, even here, the prodigal evening light will already be dwindling: in the words of the resplendently miserable A.E. Housman,

> The dark
> Has passed its nadir and begun to climb.

I would like to think for a moment of my own country, northern Scotland, at this time of year, the season of the white nights. We would go out in mid-evening at this time as the sun begins at last to go down. Out into the cooling air and the level light, and we would walk away from the garden and into the wood behind our house.

This is the time of the June night loved by the northern Romantic painters of the early nineteenth century, this peaceful evening offering its glimpse of the otherworld, the physical landscape under the twilight opening out into spiritual territories of the imagination. As the English painter Samuel Palmer wrote in his 1824 notebook, these things 'shed a mild, a grateful, an unearthly lustre into the inmost spirits, and seem the interchanging twilight of that peaceful country, where there is no sorrow and no night. Every light eternally on the change: yet no light finally extinguished'. The sun is setting now behind the trunks of the trees to the north: gold and vermilion float and dissolve in the blue air. It is almost exactly the light of Caspar David Friedrich's painting *Evening* in the museum at Hanover, and we might almost be standing amongst the ferns and flowers in his foreground, where he places his two figures. But the light is so faint under his trees that the figures are themselves little more than grey shadows amongst shadowed and overshadowed green.

Or we could be in another northern wood with a belated glimmer of midsummer sky: in John Sell Cotman's *Duncombe Park* in Tate Britain, one of the sequence of experimental wilderness paintings which he made on his tour of the north of England in 1805. Both Friedrich and Cotman delighted in painting obscure places, retired places, even disappointing places, and transforming them by their concentration on what the light reveals or conceals. After the turmoil of wars and revolutions which brought the noontide certainties of the eighteenth century to an end, all the arts in northern Europe seem to have turned together to the celebration of twilight – think of the 1780s draft of a twilight poem by the very young Wordsworth:

> What is it tells my soul the sun is setting?
> For not a straggling ray tells her he is in the
> East or west[;] 'tis the brown mist which
> descends slowly into the valley to shed
> that burden of ghosts? See where a
> son of other worlds is sailing slowly on the
> lake – no! 'tis the taper that twinkling in the
> cottage casts a long wan shadow over the lake?

All Romantic artists shared, to some extent, their epoch's intensity of feeling about light and landscape: engaging in a passionate colloquy with place, as though it could answer them, respond to them, instruct them. But how different Friedrich's woodland sunset is from Cotman's. Friedrich's bears a precise weight of religious allegory, where Cotman's invests personal, Wordsworthian, emotion in the memory of his solitary walk amongst the trees under the fading sky. For Friedrich, sunset is the paradise to which the shadowed walkers are travelling. The fence of tree-trunks and the rising powder-blue mists from the valley beyond are the barrier of years and their illusions which stand in the way of the couple's journey together to the paradises of the evening sky.

This is another essential distinction of north and south: southern artists can make their paradise-gardens on earth, lit by the lamps of the orange-trees, Virgilian sunsets. For northern artists, paradise is removed to the clouds or composed in the distant mountains by the evening light. (The implications of this for the religious sensibilities of north and south would reward investigation.) This kind of allegorical landscape comes to Friedrich and other painters of the north so naturally that it is as if their painting is simply giving form to the shared feelings of a generation and a region.

Looking north from the high-summer twilight of the 57th parallel, just short of the magical 60 degrees, where it is truly twilight all night long, the sky is still a pale blue from horizon to zenith – the fullest expansion of that brilliant line of light which is scored along the northern horizon for a month either side of midsummer night. Tree branches and hills stand out in clear silhouette against it. And, at this height of the summer, there is a glimmer of amber above the horizon, a diffused red along the profile of the hills.

It is the distant reflection of the sun at midnight, the bright sky over Shetland, the absolute north of the absolute light and dark, the shadowless night of the Scandinavian north. 60 degrees is the meridian of the north: I think of a friend's house on the mainland of Shetland, a long, whitewashed house near the sea. The light will be bright enough there to read outside at midnight. Treeless slopes, scattered houses, stone beaches, the wind never quite sleeping. The true north defined by the light in the sky above, reddened by the sun just below the horizon, what is called there *the simmer dim*, itself a reflection of the sun of the far north riding clear of the summer sea.

*

We could multiply relative frontiers of the north, but one apprehension of north is defined by the fall of the light and the presence and absence of light in the round of the year. The long midsummer evenings of this time of year are uniquely of the north, as are those midwinter days which you get, even as far south as London, when the sky never seems to have been switched on properly.

If one explores this idea of the north as defined by light, the 60th parallel takes on an importance as lying more or less at the midpoint of those latitudes which experience what I feel to be a distinctly northern pattern of light. Ten degrees either side of the 60th parallel, to a greater or lesser degree, experience those contrasts of light and dark and, crucially, those twilights which shape and define the north. So the 60th parallel is the meridian of the half-lights, the long evenings, the protracted melancholy sunsets (northern winter days ending in damp and frozen air) which stretch from about 50 degrees to 70 degrees.

At 70 degrees and beyond the north is the frontline of the battle of the light and the dark. Thinking about the arts of the north, the 60th parallel is nearly a centre-line, from 50 to 74 might be said to encompass the inhabited north, all places where awareness of light is not only essential and formative, but the foundation of modes of feeling which find expression in all the arts, but most especially literature and the visual arts.

These are *the latitudes of the twilight*: all these territories have some degree of twilight rather than darkness all through the night at midsummer. North from the regions of *the white nights*, far beyond the reflected *simmer dim* of the Shetlands and the Faeroes, are the shadowless, lucid midnights of this arctic place and their dark corollary in the mirk-tide of midwinter. Absolute north is defined in absolutes of light and dark.

South of the 50th parallel are the territories of full darkness at midsummer, the year-round equipoise of night and day, curt purple twilights, the noonday demon of the August sun. Heat and light can be the enemy here, the hours of darkness – *la madrugada* – the time of release and pleasure. 'No twilight,' wrote Coleridge, 'in the courts of the sun.'

*

The definitions of the science of twilight are memorable ones:

> When the sun has just dipped below the horizon, up to six degrees below, and when the first stars are just visible, is *civil twilight*, the blue hour beloved of nineteenth century French writers and painters. This is the time when the white flowers in a summer garden jump forward to the eye, when a whitewashed house on a winter hill shines out of the dimness.
>
> When the sun is six to twelve degrees below the horizon, it is *nautical twilight*, darkening cobalt on a clear night, at the end of which the horizon line is no longer defined by visible brightness.
>
> From twelve to eighteen degrees below the horizon, it is *astronomical twlight*, apparently dark to the casual observer, to whose eye the constellations are as bright as they would be in full darkness.

The defining twilights of the north manifest themselves not only as long evenings, absence of complete darkness at night, but also as states of light which can last for days and weeks. May I attempt a summary of this geography of twilight?

Twilight lasts the longer the further north (or of course south) you are. Polar twilight can last for a fortnight, coming in and out of the darkness of midwinter. In the territories 10 degrees either side of the 60th parallel the twilights of midsummer and midwinter are the longest, emphasising thereby the emotional and psychological effects of the unignorable change of the seasons.

In the regions of the deep north, midsummer is light. *Civil twilight* lasts all night at midsummer at 60 degrees – that glimmer of redness in the northern sky seen from the north of Scotland. Nautical twilight lasts through the midsummer night at 54 degrees north, astronomical twilight at 48 degrees. Civil twilight over Shetland; nautical twilight over Newcastle and the Scottish Border; when the sky grows dark on midsummer night over London, it is actually astronomical twilight.

The dark shadows the light: Sara Maitland points out that Norse mythology is the exception amongst European mythologies. In pre-Christian Scandinavia the victory of the light at the last day is not assumed. It remains wholly possible in minds used to the black trough of the dead year for a fortnight and more either side of the winter solstice, that the dark will win the last battle.

> Norse mythology is the only theistic theology I know of where the issue remains in serious peril. The gods will go out to fight at Ragnarok. They will do their best for themselves, for humans, and for the light; but Baldur the Beautiful is dead and we do not know if they or the forces of the dark will triumph.

Grim hints in the Poetic Eddas suggest that both the sun and the father of the gods will be devoured by the Fenris wolf, at the last battle. It has been suggested that the mitigating prophecy that Odin will be avenged and the sun may have a daughter to shine on the unimaginable world of the future are retrospective interpolations by a Christian editor of pre-Christian material. What this mediaeval editor, Snorri Sturlusson, is doing is trying to show that his own northern people were natural Christians, whose chthonic mythology held seeds of the truth, and thus he makes of their pagan last battle something of a parallel to the sun darkened at the Crucifixion, darkness as prologue to triumphal light.

It is possible that this parallelism of the last battle of dark and light in Norse mythology with the Crucifixion and Resurrection form the subject of what I like to think of as the seminal work of northern English art (although it would perhaps be more accurate to describe it historically as southern Scandinavian): the relief-sculptured cross, dating from about 940 still in the churchyard at Gosforth in north-western England. This work inevitably concerns itself with the light and the dark. The Gosforth cross is one of those absolutely compelling works of hybrid art which can embody two sets of meanings, two world-views, at the same time, and interpretation depends entirely on the mental positioning of the beholder.

At Gosforth there is a battle, with one warrior, as it might be 'the champion Christ' menaced by the jaws of Hell-mouth or fighting the Fenris Wolf who will devour Odin himself and consume the sun. There is also a carving of a radiant young man with outstretched arms who is Baldur reborn or Christ resurrected. Perhaps it is more accurate to say that he is both Baldur reborn and Christ resurrected.

The shadows of the relief carving on the Gosforth Cross have grown shallower with a millenium of the wind and rain and pollution, but it remains today a work about the light and the dark, about the battle of the unconquered sun with the winter, even if we know (in this instance) better than Wagner that Ragnarök means the *judgment* or *ordeal* rather than the *twilight* of the gods.

*

Let us return to the romantic era where we began, when the painting of twilight became an apprehension of spiritualised landscape as well as an attempt to glimpse a metaphysical territory lying beyond the northern evening, the allegorical landscape lying just below the visible landscape, the paradise which is located (like Wordsworth's cloud-heaven in *The Excursion*) in the territories of the sunset.

> Glory beyond all glory ever seen
> By waking sense or by the dreaming soul …

I was talking to the Scottish landscape painter James Morrison about Caspar David Friedrich last summer and he said that he thought that Friedrich's evening skies, like the skies in his own paintings, are to some extent less a likeness of one moment than a record of the changes of light over the span of time that it took to make the initial notations for the painting.

*

Evening melancholy is a characteristic of the northern zone of the long twilights, as in the work of the mid-Victorian Scottish painter Alexander Dyce, whose transformation of the sparse woodlands of a Scottish castle in the after-light of an early summer evening into the *Garden of Gethsemane* is achieved by the addition of the bowed figure of Christ. And Dyce's *Pegwell Bay* is a wholly familiar image of the end of a holiday day, the figures rather detached from each other, the light beginning to go, happiness suddenly seeming fugitive and circumscribed with the chill falling on the seashore. This is the whole world of late-summer sadness of Lewis Carroll, the tense and melancholy seashore of the Gryphon and the Mock Turtle and their Lobster Quadrille, as much as it is the memory of evenings on the coast of Northern England which haunt Tennyson's poems of departure and farewell, which shape the warm, menaced stillness of the opening chapter of Wilkie Collins's *The Moonstone.*

Or the other sadness of autumnal England, the urban melancholy of the Victorian north. Winter skies of ivory and umber, streetlamps and bare trees, city sunsets of smoke in frozen air. Our response to these images is a kind of recognition, even resignation. The northern English painter Atkinson Grimshaw's familiar, aching images of lighted windows and the early dark are a haunting not yet exorcised. Grimshaw finds echoes in so much writing and feeling about the north: the aching response to city twilight in Angela Carter's *Black Venus*: 'Sad; so sad those smoky-rose, smoky-mauve evenings of late autumn, sad enough to pierce the heart … a nostalgia for things we never knew, anguish of the turn of the year, the time of impotent yearning, the inconsolable season,' and Eliot's sombre tracing of the fall of the light,

> Afternoon grey and smoky, evening yellow and rose.

*

The urban evenings of the nineteenth century can show a kind of gallantry or elegance as with Whistler's cobalt London night and the fall of the rocket from the other shore of the river. Robert Louis Stevenson's *New Arabian Nights* is one literary equivalence for this image, the twilight fables of Chesterton or Conan Doyle another.

One of the most persuasive images of the monochrome of winter London was painted in the early years of the twentieth century by the Danish painter Vilhelm Hammershøi, considering the railings of the British Museum on a lightless midwinter day: the absolute restraint of his palette here evokes the anti-light, that northern light which is a negative, a lack. And it invokes too the wonderful sculptural quality of the great iron railings and the cold in the air. It is one of the most intense paintings of London, the visual rhyme to T.S. Eliot's misted, evening city,

> With the smoke coming down above the housetops ...
>
> The burnt-out ends of smoky days ...
> And then the lighting of the lamps.

Hammershøi is most celebrated as a master of the fading light in his depictions of the interiors of the Copenhagen flats in which he and his family lived. Occasionally these show a bright morning throwing sunlight across Biedermeyer furniture and grey-painted panelling. But usually these are evening pictures, some of the most haunting depictions of the northern light and its fall. They are often extraordinary experiments with the very last of the light, the ebbing of definition from grey things, the catching of a sliver of belated reflection on the moulding of a panel or along the bevel of a mirror. Sometimes in his paintings it has grown so late that the only light in the room comes from the streetlight outside. Again we are reminded of Eliot's 'smoke and fog of a December afternoon', of his

> The October night comes down; returning as before
> Except for a slight sensation of being ill at ease ...

And, almost always, in Hammershøi's paintings the figure of his wife has her back to us, like the figures in Friedrich's metaphysical landscapes of the evening. Melancholy, silence, dusk. The last of the autumn light over the quay and the inlets of the Baltic, with the Greenland icebreakers lying at anchor almost under the windows.

*

How acutely the writers of the north trace the death of the summer in ebbing light, in lengthening twilight. Tove Jansson's *Summer Book* moves to its end at the point in the northern August when it is no longer possible to pretend that summer will last, when the first intimations of winter are beginning to appear:

> Every year, the bright Scandinavian summer nights fade away without anyone's noticing. One evening in August you have an errand outdoors, and all of a sudden it's pitch black … It is still summer, but the summer is no longer alive. It has come to a standstill; nothing withers, and the autumn is not ready to begin … The can of kerosene is brought up from the cellar and left in the hall, and the lamp is hung up on its peg by the door.
>
> Not right away, but little by little and incidentally. Things begin to shift position in order to follow the progress of the seasons. Day by day, everything moves closer to the house.

In another key, Tove Jansson also catches the precise moment of the turn of summer in her children's book *Moominpappa at Sea.* When Moominmamma brings the lamp onto the verandah, the summer is over. The end of August is the season of shortening evenings, bad temper, forest fires. Although this is a book for children, the tension and the melancholy which attend the change of season are neither softened nor explained away.

> Moominpappa said: 'you've put an end to the summer. No lamps should be lit until summer is really over.'
>
> 'Well, it'll have to be autumn then,' said Moominmamma in her quiet way.

> The lamp sizzled as it burned. It made everything seem close and safe, a little family circle they all knew and trusted. Outside this circle lay everything that was strange and frightening, and the darkness seemed to reach higher and higher and further and further away, right to the end of the world.
>
> 'In some families, it's the father who decides when it's time to light the lamp,' muttered Moominpappa into his tea.

The father in Emma Tennant's magical Scottish novel *Wild Nights* does precisely that: 'He had had to put on the light, and by doing so he had ended the summer. He had bundled the long days, the dog days when the grass begins to show yellow and the haystacks slip over to one side, into one of the drawers of his enormous desk.' It is only in the northern countries, that literature and the visual arts are so acutely aware of this progress of the twilight at the turn of the year. So much so that this very concern with light becomes a defining factor of the literature of the northern countries, of *the Latitudes of the Twilight*.

*

But I would like to end with the delusive repose of high summer, returning to the contemplation of the northern summer evening, back to Samuel Palmer's notebook of 1824, where we learn how such things 'shed a mild, a grateful, an unearthly lustre into the inmost spirits, and seem the interchanging twilight of that peaceful country, where there is no sorrow and no night. Every light eternally on the change: yet no light finally extinguished.' This is as calm, as unchangingly changing as the midsummer sea seen from the windows of the northbound evening train out of Edinburgh: streaks of colour on the waters that are almost monochromes, shifting and passing in layers of stillness as far as the horizon. It is like the moment of evening quiet at the end of the life of the Victorian sage John Ruskin, his projects in ruins, his selfhood shattered by mental illness, following a bird's cry to the otherworld through the fields above Brantwood:

> The hayfield … where the grass in spring still grew fresh and deep. There used always to be a corncrake or two in it. Twilight after twilight I have hunted that bird, and never once got glimpse of it: the voice was always at the other side of the field, or in the inscrutable air or earth.

So let us rest for a moment on this image of the northern summer light. Let us reflect on it here, where we are, in the north. In absolute quiet and absolute distance, under the midnight dawn.

Douglas Dunn (EIGHT)

A Basket of Apples

(in memory of Barbara Murray)

I see them still as a painting by Peploe
Or even a lesser colourist on a good day,
These fruits of early autumn's visible taste.
A memory, but it's not one of sorrow.
Offered to all – 'Don't let them go to waste' –
Outside your office door, as if you'd said
'It's not all work, you know. Take a good bite.
Relish slowly.' That was your gift to us,
An annual present, freely given away,
Out of consideration, out of kindness.
Your country apples savoured of East Neuk light!
Apples, teaching, scholarship, and care –
Commonplace fruits, except you placed them there,
Their green, their gold, their yellow, bronze and red.

OTHER WORLDS

'From where will a renewal come to us, to us who have devastated the whole earthly globe?'

SIMONE WEIL (ONE)

Tim Dee (NINE)

Atlantic Seaboard

And lodgings. This year now and its incidents. Words after the facts.

Gros Islet, St Lucia: Green steam from the forest. A sign: Ferry Boat For Sale. The boat grown over. Hot rain. Green figs and saltfish for lunch on the beach. That night, a sweat-dream sticky with half a memory and itched with mosquito-music: women in China wearing silkworms in a papoose-belt around their stomachs to keep them warm and generative. The tropics: this feculent helix to the world. A stuck season with a desultory tide. I overslept and woke late. Too much pink rum from a plastic cup on a catamaran under the *whump* of sun and then my first flying fish, conjured by its own silver skitter out of the black sea, and right above my head, at the same moment, a magnificent frigatebird, two dagger tails hanging from an old black dinner suit, cut into Creole by the ship's crew as *ciseau la mer*. Blades to travel by.

Go north. Go south.

A chaffinch the last bird noted at the slip-road to the airport in London. A chaffinch the first bird heard on getting out of the car from the airport in Cape Town. A new hemisphere. The same species. Twelve hours in the air and one season exchanged for its opposite. Midwinter made midsummer. And back again with birds looping between. North of Cape Town, through the Swartland, the steppe buzzards began, every other telephone post held one, clenched like a fist. In the northern autumn they had come out of Asia to lay down the playing cards of themselves (Jacks, always Jacks), one after the other, south and then further south, through Africa. Nearby, six European bee-eaters in the crown of a burnt cedar like grave-goods unearthed, jewels around a skull. Amongst them, through the wires and the branches, European swallows cut and stitched. Home and away.

South – the north in the mirror? Negatives in the darkroom. Reach back to those first European eyes computing black swans, black oystercatchers and black skins. And now: an upside-down, blindfolded rhinoceros tied at its four feet, one rope to each, and lifted by helicopter from its dangerous home. And, the man who fell, frozen or not, when the wheelhouse was lowered at dawn, to land dead in Surrey.

Newlands, Cape Town, South Africa. In the zipped dark of my holdall four frozen blind golden moles stowed for take-off. To earth over London and, there, be opened with a scalpel. Their golden fleeces, dead or alive, are not built from pigment but are fashioned by the bending of light as it reflects through their fur. The moles are blind and live underground and they have no use for gold. It does not, in any case, exist.

Unst, Shetland. Unzip the midsummer night light. White over a black sea. Arctic terns between my eyes. The yawing snap of bright tail pennants. Prick-songs scratched from bloody pliers. Oystercatchers, like tiny cows, walking the fields. Later, at Skaw, sitting in the car in rain. A cold drumming on the roof. Through the wipers, a sea bird and a land bird new in from over the waves. A summer visitor, dark-phase, arctic skua preened on the beach, turning its head over its back and reaching down to its oil-gland between its folded wings, seeking its lanolin, a lubricant to baffle the sea. Adjusting its dress before leaving. The rain eased. On a farm fence behind the beach a migrant spotted flycatcher shook rain-water droplets from the cape of its wings. Flies appeared for it to catch.

The same sea working at all these shores. Listen, then, to its light.

Mousa, Shetland. At midsummer midnight, black storm petrels came in moth-stutter about the black broch. As filings to their magnet, dusk wings brought to a dark house, a black bobbin wound with black threads. Black bees to their skep. The birds waiting release on their nests in the rocks sang, the purr of the play-out groove, after all the music has gone, the sound of the old raw materials, of cooling stone. At one in the morning the light thinned overhead, a lower wattage, grandparental, but stayed on. Were the gannets of Unst asleep now? What berth could keep them at sea? What hammock?

False Bay, Cape Town, South Africa. False – either because it tricked mariners into thinking it offered good anchorage or was thought not a cul-de-sac but the way around. At midsummer first light, from a shallow cave in the cliffs above Muizenberg, black men in black suits stand and shout the gospel. Below them, at sea, white men surf in black suits. There are ways and ways of walking on the water. From a boat, a little further out, I saw the baby-pink grin from the saw-pit mouth of a great white shark. A toothed O. As it broke open the sea, coming into unwanted air, the fish's dark eye and still-darker pupil scrolled forward, taking in me and the other dry goods put before its aqueous humor – Cape gannets, a Subantarctic skua, a southern giant petrel, and the unfiltered sun. Horizons. Orisons. O-zones. A cage was offered. My wife accepted, I declined.

Unst, Shetland: Island talk. Arguments about what makes a place ordinary and of the mainland. Mainstream. Neither special nor remote. How then to write up an ordinary day at Muckle Flugga? Record the chocolate bars eaten. The subfusc sky. Make light of it. To try, without looking away, to see the scene as not special. Might that deliver us to its truth?

Once on Noss in Shetland a fledgling wren ended its first ever flight by landing on my shoulder and did so as I was watching a family group of killer whales swimming a mile offshore. Careless all. And the bliss came to me of watching things not care for me. On Unst there was an otter eating a crab at the flat surface of the black sea in the purple midsummer dawn, salt-water beads rolled from its whiskers to dimple the water. They caught the light that lay above the sea and made ripples that were paler than the water they disturbed. On Noss, the killer whales' black and white skin dried even in the single second of its rolling exposure to the upper air. They bowled under and went down more matt and less shiny than they came up. And their breaths, silent and odourless at one mile, made wind-dogs or rainbow-spars that hung above the black sea as long as the whales' blow, their out-breaths, lasted.

Zennor, Cornwall: Spring seeking, walking south-west, under D.H. Lawrence's 'incoming' and 'uncreated' days, towards the tilted places of Alfred Wallis, Peter Lanyon and W.S. Graham. Gannets showed the muscle of the air. The sea boiled on the rocks below me as it kettled itself into the gouges it had cut into the granite. Each bird, with its white planks for wings, looked as if it was carrying its own crosses. Wind blew off the sea into my head, then out and on again, an earshot, its pipe-cleaner flossing the U-bends and down-pipes of the brain. My hair, after forty-eight hours, was blown like a cliff-top thorn tree; my right leg stretched with an extra fall at every stride, my left an inch retracted every time. Afterwards: a dream of turning about at Land's End to leg-correct and undo my hair.

*

Ocean seeking, driving west out of the desert, Namibia. In the museum at the land's edge at Swakopmund, the old German seaside town, two sperm whale's eyes, loosed cannonballs, petrified over time, and staring blindly from a cabinet of whale curios. For a few decades in the last one hundred the coastal waters offshore were colonial whaling grounds. Whale-fish were landed at Walvis. Guano platforms were raised at sea too, to farm nitrogen-rich seabird droppings. Everything that could be wrung from ocean desert-edge was taken. Humpbacks and others were fished to the brink. 'Today they are practically extinct in our waters,' the sign says in the museum. Our whales, our waters. Sitting beneath a palm on the sea-front, Himba women, migrants from the north, chasing tourist money, drank cola and passed bank notes between them. They laughed as they reddened their skins and hair with *otjize*, a butter paste mixed with ochre or, it seemed here, shoe polish. This makes them look more like themselves.

Látrabjarg, north-west Iceland: A midsummer day on the high cliff edge, westering, up and down its dells and headlands. An arctic fox working the auk ledges, like a feather duster hurried along a mantelpiece, beat me by ten yards to be the westernmost land mammal in Europe. White light above the black sea. A raven stole a fulmar's cream egg from the cliff below me and flew inland with it wedged in its beak; ten minutes later a glaucous gull stole another and did the same. A day of black and white: twenty feet from me, the ledges near the cliff-top had Brunnich's guillemots breeding on them. They bent to the single egg cradled at their feet and nuzzled it with their beak. A mile offshore, killer whales came, encore, through openings they cut in the sea's dark cloth. Measure the spaces in a guillemot's life and a whale's: the inch of ledge and the ocean, the second with the sun on your back and the years beneath the waves.

From Greenland came high shifts of thin white cloud pluming overhead to mares'-tails, the shape of the drifting wind itself, ice falling through the sky's blow, the way things were, the weathered past decaying as it signed itself into the sky. The air was cold even on this sun-stuffed summer day. It felt like the old cold of rock. A cold sea or cold wind is nothing but seasonal to the long dying of the rock. After the cliffs, I flushed an eider from her nest on the shore. As she left, she shat onto her eggs, and spattered her down. I felt around her clutch of four and put my hand into the springy grey muff. It seemed a kind of world-felt. A soft fence against everything.

Kirstenbosch, Table Mountain, Cape Town: A midsummer walk along the line held, still to this day, by the first hedge made by a white man in Africa south of the Sahara. Cape white-eyes singing and a black sparrowhawk overhead. By 1659 Dutch hostility towards their Khoikhoi neighbours forced the colonial administration at the Cape to undertake a number of defensive measures in order to plant itself more fixedly. Under Governor van Riebeeck, it determined to define a boundary to the settlement by ploughing up a strip of land twelve feet wide and 'to plant and sow bitter almonds and all kinds of quick-growing thorn bushes in the form of a land barrier so thickly that no cattle or sheep will be able to be driven through it'. Something closed across the whole continent at the moment this hedge was made. Part of it was declared a national monument in 1936. As I walked, European swallows zipped over the hedge to feed on the flies in its lee.

Fair Isle, Shetland: For six days there was no tree taller than my ear. And every bird that wanted a tree was shown to me. The spring migrants had no place to hide. The island is unhedged, its one plantation has five stunted trees and they are dead. The wind comes from all quarters. I saw a frog orchid so blown that its flower couldn't leave the shelter of the soil. I heard a marsh warbler sing from a dead Christmas tree, plaiting its tune with the voices of those birds it had lived amongst before it blew in to the island: blue tits and robins in Sweden on its summer grounds, scrub-robins and weavers in Zambia in its winter. At Shirva, Stewart Thomson, in his tenth decade, sat outside his house on a painted blue pew spinning brown wool from the island's fleeces. In his garden roses was a western subalpine warbler, less than a year old, just in off the sea and two thousand miles out. One in the roses and how many more on the seabed? Passages and crossings. At home and gone wrong.

Lerwick, Shetland: Three objects catch me out in the museum: *Klo*, black potato-sized stones from Unst, fashioned between 1750 and 1800, and used to prevent cows from bolting on unfenced ground. The stones were tied between the animals' horns and knocked at their heads if they tossed too much in their excited nomadism and sent them running for home. Nearby, two Stone Age ploughshares from Tingwall looking like the ruddy teeth of a whale, and inflating the old truism that, while Orkney was the place where crofters kept a boat, Shetland was an archipelago of fishermen who also had a field. And, next-door, in a cabinet of odd scrimshaw, a sperm whale's ear-bone, painted by a Shetland whaler in South Georgia in the 1940s, as a human head in profile and the spitting image of Adolf Hitler. Afterwards: fish and chips near Sullom Voe where they told us that *Prolific*, LK986, had caught our haddock. And the story of the man who set out to visit all the islands of the British Isles: he did well in the south, Wight, Bryher, Sheppey, Canvey, Steepholm, Flatholm; progressed on through Wales and up the coasts, Holy, Anglesey, Walney, Hilbre, Coquet; and then went mad in Scotland.

Olifantsbos, Cape Peninsula, South Africa: Common terns fretted at the sea edge. The last elephants were known here in 1620 before Europeans settled at the Cape. The name of the place, the forest of elephants, comes perhaps from the shapes of some rocks. Offshore, the reef's undertow is a claw hammer for the unwary: the *Holland* 1786, *Napoleon* 1805, *L'Alouette* 1817, *Thomas T. Tucker* 1942. On the Atlantic shore near the wrecking grounds, a white tower, like a blind lighthouse, was raised in honour of Vasco da Gama who in 1497 disembarked on the peninsula for a while, stepped onto its shoulder, until, following a misunderstanding with the people on the land, a Khoikhoi spear grazed his thigh and he hurried back onboard.

Another white obelisk, not far away in Cape Town, marks the site of John Herschel's telescope, which allowed him in the early 1800s to be the first European to map the stars of the southern hemisphere. Herschel's lenses were a mile or two from van Riebeeck's hedge and within its kraal. The obelisk has been a national monument since 1934. More recently a ditch at its base was stocked with goldfish. Twenty-five years ago my wife ate her school-time sandwiches eyeing the fish. *The rain's thing* some Khoikhoi called Eland because they appeared when it was wet. There are weathers and weeks.

The Cape of Good Hope was known first to Europeans as the Cape of Storms. The story of the ghost ship, the *Flying Dutchman*, was made from the mixing waters offshore at the Cape. A *looming* allowed the ghostly form of a ship to appear above the sea's horizon. The bending of light across different refractive indices is to blame so that objects that are just beyond the horizon are hoist above it. Herman Melville liked the word.

Látrabjarg, north-west Iceland: In December 1947, the *Dhoon* trawler, out from Fleetwood, was flung in terrible weather onto the rocks at the foot of the high cliffs. From the top, I couldn't hear the sea, but in winter the sound of a south-west storm meeting the rock-face can be heard thirteen-and-a-half miles away in the farmhouses on the far side of the peninsula. Their landward windows frost with salt spray on those days. Wind comes around and goes around. Men from the farms, who were also whalers and fishermen and eider-keepers, went to help the *Dhoon*. The boat had been launched in 1915 as the *Armageddon*; was requisitioned and served in the First World War as a minesweeper; was renamed and resumed fishing afterwards. In 1935, fifty miles west of St Kilda, she lost her wheelhouse, part of her funnel, and her lifeboat.

Once more, she felt the tug of war and assisted at the Dunkirk evacuation, before being refitted as a minesweeper for a second time. She returned to fishing in 1945 and worked the Icelandic grounds. She left Fleetwood for them once more on 6 December 1947. FD54 was painted on her bow. On 13 December 1947 farmers from Hvallátur (named for its whales) and neighbouring farms descended the cliffs eight hundred and fifty feet down to an outcrop called Flaugarnef, still two hundred feet above the sea. A party of four was lowered to the beach at low water and walked five hundred and fifty yards to the wreck of the *Dhoon*. The skipper, the mate and a deckhand had already been lost to the sea – Fred Kirby, Harry Ellison and Fred Wolfenden. A line was shot and twelve survivors were helped ashore. Not all could be hoisted to safety up the cliffs before the tide returned and an overnight bivouac was found on an icy ledge for seven crewmen. They were brought up the following day and taken inland.

*

The blows, the Atlantic. Air taken below, used and returned to its place. The sound of five members of a family of killer whales exhaling as they came to the surface of the South Harbour on Fair Isle as I was watching a lanceolated warbler walking like a mouse through a stand of oats behind the beach. The sound and smell of a minke whale's blow, its benthic musk, as it surfaced next to the little rowing boat I was in between the islands of the Shiants in the Hebrides. The sound and sight of a fin whale's blow as it surfaced alongside the car-ferry crossing the Bay of Biscay, a sound that seemed to me, as I craned towards it, louder then than the ship's roar and made by an animal that seemed bigger. The sound of a humpback's blow syncopated with the retching of my neighbour on a tourist boat out from Provincetown in New England. The sound of three right whales, surfacing and blowing, in accidental concert, off Fish Hoek, Cape Town. Air taken below, used and returned to its place: pneumatic ghosts of the animals' sometime land life blown from their warm bodies as brilliant, gathered steam.

*

Off Cape Point, South Africa: You are at sea. Even on the calmest days it breathes. Its lips are at the shore, where the saltwater thins to the land, with lifts and drops, eddies and runs, puckers and shouts in endless argument, hurt obliterated then hurt reiterated. The animal lies on its back, the open sea is its chest: a great streaming blackness, running with the heave and lean of falling yards, plastering cliffs and walls, spillways and trenches. The world's animated skin worked with such diligence. Ten miles out on a little boat we motored from one trawler to another and waited for them to haul their nets. The great continent of land sunk out of knowledge. With it went the space-time continuum. My compass drowned. The black sea slapped at the white sky. The sky pushed back. And birds came between the two. That was all I knew. The trawlers wanted hake; we wanted albatrosses, shearwaters, and petrels. Thousands came to the chumming wakes. Once or twice they squawked but otherwise the great parade was made and remade in silence, the birds describing their endless entry into the yards of salty air behind the nets, over and over again. I heard their wings creak as they came past, I heard the splashing patter of their feet on the sea as they landed and left, and I heard their shit hit the water. I felt I might live by what I saw. I write their names here but the swirl was all and the bonanza and the refulgence of life at home where I would not last thirty seconds beneath the sooty shearwaters, the shy, black-browed and yellow-nosed albatrosses, the Wilson's, white-chinned, pintado and southern and northern giant petrels.

Hermaness, Unst, Shetland: Signs warn against the wearing of slippery over-trousers near the cliff edge. Lambs bleated on the moor and the breeding bonxies *ugg*ed in a similar fashion: here was the nervous and foolish inland world. At the teeming edge it was otherwise, sounds became smell and light and all became blow. A gannet wind. Cullen skink. Vulcanised sea. The cooking rubber of ten thousand breeding birds' songs joined the gag of their guano and the fish stink of their homes, the rain of shit they launched on arriving and leaving and the vegetative rot of the seaweed they clung to, and it all became the breath of the place. The cliffs of nesting gannets were strung with blue marine rope and salvaged fishing nets that the nesters had collected.

Sometimes the net had trapped the rag-and-bone bird and the loot had killed the looter. A gannet hung newly dead from some webbing. Another older corpse made a nest for a living bird, the dead legs and feet and neck and beak twisted into foundations, its salt-sealed body serving as an eggcup. At Sandwick, around the coast of Unst, there was a gannet alive but downed on the beach, with a strangling necklace of green fishing line that had also earlier gathered a guillemot, later dead, which had perhaps lured the gannet into a foolhardy dive. Other albatrosses are available. The guillemot's body was like a dirty medal pinned to the gannet's breast. I threw my black windcheater over the gannet's white bulk but still it jabbed at me, so keen to live even in its agony, its blue-rimmed eyes directing its furious beak towards my face with hiss and judder.

Goethe Street in Usakos, Namibia: A man with home-cut hair and cornflower-blue eyes walked his two daschunds past a shop called 'Bernard Christ Fruit, Veg & Butchery'. Other old white men sat outside their dried-fruit stalls with dusty knees and fried arms, their toenails like gravel chips, their eyes like snakes'. Old black men sat alongside them.

On the shelves of a shop were cardboard boxes of haberdashery, labelled 'Kortbroeke' and 'Kopdoeke', shorts and headscarves, a uniform for the past. One truck had two cows in the back. There were fifteen sheep in another. A black teenage girl read to herself as she walked home from school, as she passed I could see her book cover: 'Love is a Challenge'.

Ísafjarðardjúp, north-west Iceland: A message from the radio of the Hull trawler *Ross Cleveland* on 4 February 1968: 'We are going over.' Pause. A few seconds later. 'We are going over. I am going. Give my love and the crew's love to our wives and families.' This text etched on a monument in the yard of a local museum. Next door, the redundant steam trawler 'Mummi' and, next-door-but-one, a pair of redwings carrying food at midnight to their nest in the opened head of the ruined cockpit of a stranded United States Navy plane. The female had a beak crammed with craneflies, the male sang from his perch above the sockets of the plane's eyes: *dee dee dee day* and then a swirl of chewed notes.

Scarborough, Cape Peninsula, South Africa: Seen from our back garden: a shy albatross a mile out at sea and a malachite sunbird ten feet away on the telephone wire are both bent as one under the same determining north-west wind.

Gros Islet, Saint Lucia: 'Is there anything you need, my friend?' Dope for sale on the beach, where there was also a stalled northbound turnstone with only one leg. As I walked the seashore it was the last of the little flock to fly and the first to land. It was going to stay there, in the middle, half-way until the end. In the beach-bar a resident bananaquit, a tiny yellow bird built like the waxy bloom of a tropical orchid, came proprietarily to my beer and drank. It returned several times and was never the worse for wear. Drunkenness is unknown in bananaquits.

Lerwick, Shetland: I crossed the path of the little boy of the house who was coming up the steps from his garden. He was talking to what I took to be a toy mobile phone that he had held to his cheek. As he passed me he stopped talking, lowered his hand and opened his palm, and showed me the hen's egg he held there, new fetched from a straw nest in the little coop to the side of the garden. Its warmth had warmed the boy's cheek and he was talking to it before his mother scrambled it with others and we shared it for our breakfast.

Tim Robinson (TEN)

The Centre of Gravity: Two Incidents Joined by a Note

Something was wrong; I knew it as soon as I woke. I was where I was supposed to be – in one of the beds of a six-bed dormitory on an RAF station in the Far East – but of the clothing I had worn the previous evening, and which normally would be strewn on the foot of the bed or hung over the back of a chair beside it, not an item was to be seen. For a few minutes I could not make sense of this situation. But then a blissful memory gradually condensed, purely tactile at first, in my skin rather than in my mind: the touch of cool air on my naked body as I strolled by moonlight among soaring palm trees. But where had I shed my status in the world of the dressed, my externalised social centre of gravity? I wrapped a towel around me and, as if following the spoor of a dream, retraced the hundred yards or so from the cluster of dormitories to the washroom block. There I found my clothes, neatly piled in the corner of a shower cubicle.

My room-mates had long been trying to persuade me to join them on one of their forays to Pleasure Island, a short ferry ride from a little jetty a mile or two from the station. What mattered to me of this island were the butterfly-haunted walks on the flanks of its central, jungle-clad hill, and the meditative calm of the Million Buddhas Precious Pagoda in the garden of its chief temple. I knew its port town only as a few streets of little open-fronted shops exhibiting gorgeous drifts of shapes and colours. Behind these shops I knew was another realm, a seething complexity of dwellings, bars, sweatshops churning out that avalanche of forms for sale, temples of at least four faiths, and brothels of none. Along the shoreline and encroaching on tidal flats were the poorest houses, ragged birds' nests tottering on stilts over black mud. The Military Police made occasional sweeps through this agglomeration of humanity, parts of which were out of bounds to us because of the activities of Chinese Triad gangs and of communist terrorists. Nevertheless one of our number was reputed to know this labyrinth intimately and was well enough received there to be let dodge from house to house and so evade the MPs. He was in thrall to one of the lovely girls with whom this human coral reef was bejewelled; she was an immigrant from Siam, and was feared as a witch by her Chinese neighbours. Also she was said to be a prostitute, as some of his unfeeling mates liked to remind him; but he never accepted this.

Although I was fascinated by the thought of this secretive quarter and aching with adolescent desire for its exotic girls, my entrenched inhibitions, shyness and cowardice had so far kept me out of it. But it seemed unjust to me, who regarded myself as the artist, the bohemian, the adventurer and romantic of the radar workshops, that one of my comrades, and he the most prosaic and unimaginative of us all, was having a passionate love affair with a Siamese witch while I was spending lonely hours in the camp's sterile cafeteria. And so, the evening before the awakening described above, I had let myself be carried along with the gang, whose prescription for my troubles was drink, drink, drink.

There are a few narrow windows in the wall of forgetfulness surrounding that night. Since I disliked beer and whisky I probably drank a lot of sticky-sweet liqueurs. I remember swaying as if my centre of gravity was orbiting like a moth around a light, while I raised a glass in a bar, empty but for one of my comrades who had stayed to watch over me when the others had disappeared into the unknown, and three Chinese barmen observing me with deferential smiles. And then I was on the phone to the station guardhouse, swearing that I was someone else and another someone else was doing my guard duty for me that night, until my mate poured a drink into the telephone and I was cut off. Finally a glass of brandy knocked me stony sober in a dancehall called the City Lights, leaving me on a gloomy island in a sea of hilarity, so that I saw what a horrible place it was, like a huge dark derelict railway station with vaguely indecent paintings on the walls and a raucous band far away, a dense throng of Chinese, Malays, Indians and whites dancing, and a few servicemen propped semiconscious on the tables. Then I was marshalling a group of my friends into trishaws, dissuading them from visiting the brothels and racing through the silent streets to catch the last ferry, at half past one, to the mainland.

Something rather incomprehensible happened on that ferry. I was slumped on a bench on deck, half asleep and trying to remain unconscious of the reeling rout packing the deck around me, when I became aware of a persistent annoyance: a face thrust near mine and bellowing at me. It was that of a loutish fellow from the camp who spent his days insulting all who came near him. When I think of him now I realise that he must have been mentally disturbed, but I did not understand this at the time; in fact I had already made up my mind that I was going to challenge and fight him the very next time our paths crossed. This rather public-schoolboy determination is so far from my nature that I am sure I would have somehow evaded my commitment; however, as it happened (and I do not know how it happened), the occasion never arose. As the irritating growling and yelping continued I slid down on my bench, brought one knee up to my chest, planted my foot against my tormentor's pulpy ton-weight centre of gravity, and, without troubling to wake up any further, vigorously straightened my leg. The ugly face was withdrawn and disappeared with satisfying finality.

It is surely a mere coincidence that I never saw the man again. We were a shifting, rootless, society; people were posted to other camps for no known reason, repatriated for discharge, or sent off to a hill station for rest and recuperation, sometimes at very short notice. I never enquired after him. I like to think he is in orbit still.

*

Associated with any object having weight is a point, called its centre of gravity, such that the object responds to any external force as if all its weight were concentrated at that point. (I glide over technical distinctions between weight and mass, centre of mass and centre of gravity, as they are irrelevant to considerations of bodies – such as ours – in the almost uniform gravitational field obtaining near and on the earth's surface.) Thus my own centre of gravity can be seen as the nexus between my materiality and that of the rest of the universe, the umbilicus of my gravitational being. Body parts that have achieved iconic status include the brow (the Enlightenment thinker lets his head fall forward as if weighted down by its contents, and buttresses his forehead with his knuckles), the heart (in the days of sensibility orators would signal their sincerity by clapping right hand to left chest), the loins as the ageless seat of desire (rock-star sex-deities propose the groin for ritualised lust). Today a purely conceptual point should be added to the list, the centre of gravity, the bearer of the truth that we are wholly and without surplus parts of the material world.

I say 'purely conceptual' because an object's centre of gravity does not always lie within the substance of the object. For instance the centre of gravity of a bowl is in its hollow, while that of a double star is somewhere between its two components, and nearer to the heavier; both revolve about it, but it may not lie within either. The centre of gravity of a high-jumper's body follows a trajectory determined by its weight and the force imparted by the legs at take-off, which the jumper tries to maximise – and then by arching the body like a horseshoe he or she can get each part of it in turn over the bar while the centre of gravity passes beneath it, thus stealing another couple of inches of height above what seems possible. In fact any mobile human body's centre of gravity is in perpetual negotiation with the external world; it is a coin spent and recuperated, the price and profit of passage through space.

Can one ever lose one's centre of gravity? In metaphor, perhaps; in the fantasy of the spiritual, of being rid of the ball-and-chain of embodiment. Not in dreams though, if mine are anything to go by, being all too often of precarious flight over horrid depths or slipping and overbalancing on the verge of precipices. And certainly not in reality, not even in the experience of weightlessness, in which one's physical response to non-gravitational forces is still ordered by the centre of gravity. However, there is a slight incident that in long-distance memory feels like an instance of loss of the centre of gravity. Like the episode described above, it answers to the recall of my youthful oriental sojourn.

*

Left to my own purposes in the camp I soon discovered a little theatrical society that spanned the straits between service personnel and the intellectual elite of Pleasure Island. This sybaritic group never got around to putting on a performance, but in the processes of choosing a play, designing the setting, reading and rehearsing, it provided amusement to its members. That at least is how it seemed to me, ignorant of the secretive politics that agitated one or two radical young Chinese members of the society and were perhaps discussed only in private by their seniors. Our mentor was a cultivated expatriate school headmaster who, with his wife, entertained us bountifully on their airy, shaded, verandas. Two or three technicians of the same lowly status as myself, undergoing National Service before entering university; Mike, an anarchical intelligence officer who abused his rank to liberate me from the tedium of the radar workshop by sending for me to undertake urgent missions, such as translating some bit of French pornography I found as baffling as he did; a rubber planter deeply versed in Britishness; the beautiful Bee, an oriental Audrey Hepburn; Mavis, of some lovely concoction of races but convicted of irremediable seriousness, having been caught reading a British Council pamphlet on Milton during a picnic … such were my new soul companions.

Picnics were the essence of our lifestyle. Shaded by the coconut palms that leaned protectively out over the broiling beaches and womb-warm coastal waters, we lolled and laughed; I probably held forth, more than was appropriate for one so inexperienced, on the tumult of ideas fermenting in my head. I had a theory of God as a construction out of the immediate data of mystical experience, which lost us many a half hour; also a demolition of the concept of free will, which one day we decided to put to the test by making no decisions at all. Mike and I were swimming when this experiment was to begin; we soon found ourselves adrift in a gentle longshore current, which seemed perfectly apropos. We had perhaps taken a glass of wine. As the dark-green wall of close-packed vegetation behind the beach glided effortlessly by we intoned a favourite poem of our sect, Thomas Love Peacock's grown-up rendering of the old nursery rhyme about going to sea in a bowl:

> Fear ye not the waves that roll?
> No, in charmèd bowl we swim.
> What the charm that floats the bowl?
> Water may not pass the brim.
> The bowl goes trim. The moon doth shine,
> And our ballast is old wine.

… and we droned and drew out the refrain in hollow tones, again and again: 'And our ballast is old wine …'

Nothing went wrong; we were not swept out to sea and thrown ashore on a desert island, or snapped up by sharks. Simply, we remembered that the distance we had travelled was real, and that we would have to walk back – that is, our centres of gravity, our wills and weights, had been shipped along with us in the bowl of tipsiness. So we struck out for the land, abandoning the search for an experimental proof of my theory of free will, whatever it was.

John Elder (SIX)

Catchments

Rain is general all over Connemara. In every month of the year and for parts, at least, of two days out of three, it swirls in over Roundstone Bog then drums down onto Errisbeg. Some of these spatters will wash due south, over the two-lobed peninsula of Goirtín and out to the sea, without relying on a fixed channel. Others, relinquishing their individual surface-tension after being hung up in the sphagnum, will pool eastward over the sheep tracks that edge the bog, eventually arriving at the newly paved roads and driveways of an uninhabited housing estate; now they can hasten onward, past the studio of Folding Landscapes and into Roundstone Bay. But the drops trickling north and east from Errisbeg will gather into rivulets that trace a network of softly inscribed glens. These will become the tributaries for dozens of irregular lochs strewn across the bog's interior like puzzle-pieces scattered on a table. Visible streams connect some of these bodies of water to one another, while arteries under the peat link the whole system into one soggy pulsation.

'Catchment' is the word by which Tim Robinson designates a unit of the Earth's surface bounded by higher edges and within which springs, rainfall and smaller tributaries converge, in most cases flowing onward to an outlet that joins it to a more broadly encompassing drainage. Every point on the Earth's surface is mapped in such a way by elevation and the movement of water. In *Listening to the Wind*, the first volume of his *Connemara* trilogy, Robinson further characterises a catchment as 'an open, self-renewing system, supporting and supported by a vast number of life-forms and all their interrelations. Even its basic topography, the most skeletal and reductive representation of its geometry, is profoundly suggestive of a way of looking at the world and caring for it'. Across the seasons and over the decades, Robinson has walked the catchments near his home in Connemara. Not only has he come to know them in intimate detail, but he has also tracked their confluence with the geology, language and history of western Ireland.

Since moving to Ireland almost four decades ago, Tim Robinson has produced maps and gazetteers of the Aran Islands, the Burren's limestone labyrinth and Connemara. In 1986 and 1995, he published *Pilgrimage* and *Labyrinth*, respectively, the two parts of a project called *Stones of Aran* that has been widely acknowledged as a masterpiece. In 2011 he saw into print the third volume of his equally impressive and absorbing *Connemara*. Though Robinson is British (half Scottish, half English) by birth, his writing has long since been recognised as a treasure of contemporary Irish literature because of the questing intellect manifest within it, the vividness of his prose and the dignified, authentic and respectful manner in which he engages with the stories and landscape of his adopted home.

Beyond Robinson's specifically Irish impact, however, his extraordinarily localised work also holds great meaning for the inhabitants of other rural areas who are striving to discern and to convey the significance of their own home-landscapes. He both perpetuates and enlivens a tradition of Romantic revolt against centralised, mechanised and hierarchical views of humanity and the land. In an essay from *The Spirit of the Age*, William Hazlitt identified the genius of Wordsworth's early poetry as 'a proud humility', taking 'the commonest events and objects, as a test to prove that nature is always interesting from its inherent truth and beauty ...'. In the rapt attention Robinson brings to 'the thousands of tiny trickles' in a catchment, he similarly asserts the significance of a boggy region located far from any capital, and at the extreme western edge not only of Ireland but also of Europe.

As a fellow denizen of the hinterlands, though living far from Ireland, I feel personally grateful for Tim Robinson's example of dogged and eccentric excellence at this ancient edge. By focusing on what Gary Snyder would call the lineaments of the land, rather than on political boundaries, Robinson invites his readers to contribute to a collective effort of re-mapping and re-storying our homes on earth. The best way I can find to express my appreciation for Robinson's achievements is through a dialogue between my own landscape in the Green Mountains of Vermont and his in western Ireland. Specifically, I want to concentrate on the part of his Connemara map that depicts Roundstone Bog and on the corresponding portion of *Listening to the Wind*, relating them both to a landform near my home that is called the Hogback Ridge.

*

My US Geological Survey map of the Bristol Quadrangle is heavily seamed from so often being folded into backpacks or jacket pockets; its formerly white margin is soiled and splotched, its corners dogeared. The street-grid of Bristol is shown in the south-eastern corner of the map. But its central feature is a dramatic and heavily forested upland called the Hogback Ridge running north–south and rising over a thousand feet above our village. Hogback is a finger of quartzite about ten miles long and between two and three miles across. Glaciation and erosion have stripped away the softer dolostones that once enclosed it within a higher plateau, sloughing them down to enrich the heavy clays to our west in the Champlain Valley. Hogback thus constitutes a resistant limb of bedrock and, although logged off several times over the past two centuries, has never been cultivated or settled. Our house on North Street stands less than a quarter-mile from this roadless area that enlivens the village with its wildness.

In walking out our backdoor to an outlook called the Ledges, from which I can look straight down at our house as well as clear across Addison County to Lake Champlain, I pass under a band of broad-branched, open-grown trees where wild turkeys often roost. They venture out to glean on nearby farms in the months between harvest and the coming of the snow. In continuing my uphill hike, I enter thickening woods where evergreens are more prevalent. Deer trace their daily circuits here, bedding down under the hemlocks at night, while moose pass through on their way from the heights to the wetlands at the western edge of town. Farther up the slope comes a broken, rocky scramble of land where bobcats and black bears den.

Along with the various discolourations on its margin from tea and peanut-butter sandwiches held by fingers numb from the cold, there are three lines drawn onto my map in pencil. One of these traces the ridge of Hogback from the north to its southern terminus at a rugged cliff called Deer Leap, then angles sharply west through the village. All of the land east and south of this line drains into the New Haven River as it runs through Bristol towards its meeting with the northward flow of Otter Creek and its ultimate destination in Lake Champlain. Much of the water washing down to the north and west of the ridge will end up in Lewis Creek, travelling north through Hinesburg after its detour through Bristol Pond. On a cold afternoon in February, two and a half years ago, my neighbour David Brynn and I hiked up onto Hogback to figure out where the *rest* of the precipitation on the ridge ends up. We hoped to confirm that there is a fan-shaped wedge of land on Hogback's western slope that intervenes between the New Haven and Lewis Creek drainages, ultimately conveying water due west along Plank Road into a tributary of the Little Otter Creek.

We climbed up onto Hogback from Mountain Street, passing through a tattery piece of wooded ground just to the south. Map in hand, we wanted to locate a particular little knoll we believed might be just above us to the east. While far short of the height of country, it seemed from the map to be a possible location for the headwater of the Little Otter. We had little success at first, since most of the surface water was frozen into taut skins of ice the size of drumheads, silent and motionless now until we crunched through them in our boots. At one point, though, as we stopped to listen to the world beyond our own motion we heard a bubbling. A patch of cobbles lay with the looseness of talus just below the place marked by an X on our map. In our part of Vermont, the temperature of groundwater holds at around 46 degrees Fahrenheit, so that springs can be discovered running in all seasons. This one spilled down into a descending seam of land, establishing a watercourse that did indeed run directly west.

Above that point of origin and division was a rugged granite erratic carpeted with common polypody, a robust and abundant fern in the Green Mountains. Kernels of snow from a recent storm nestled among its shriveled but still green fronds. Just up-slope from this landmark crossed an icy, treacherous road left over from a recent A. Johnson Company logging operation that had also left a hedge of slash along its track. The boulder we were concentrating on was about ten feet high and with steep sides. But we managed to scramble atop it. We'd tossed up a few rocks before making our grand ascent so that we could erect a commemorative cairn on a bare, level area of that ferny roof. Three large flat stones established a statuary base of narrowing circumference, on which I set a rounder and more massive rock. Then we saw that a long tooth of ledge was already waiting for us on the erratic. One side of this triangular piece was cut away in a curve that let it tuck up smoothly beside and over the top of that round stone. It held steady there, a slender tip flickering above the cairn like a gray candle-flame.

After we had marvelled at this providential balancing-act, we got out a jar of maple syrup we'd brought with us and dripped some of its dark viscous contents down the sides of that crowning flame. It collected onto the stones below but also clung to and ambered the grainy surfaces of the vertical piece. We hoped that some rodent might happen upon this trove of calories and win the chance to survive for one more Vermont winter.

My Folding Landscapes map of Connemara, too, is far from pristine. Flecks of dried sphagnum tell the story of an outing I took into the Roundstone Bog when visiting Ireland last May. I wanted to pursue the topic of catchments through a comparison between Hogback and Roundstone Bog because these two largely roadless areas are similar in size as well as each being immediately adjacent to the center of a village. One heavily forested, the other nearly treeless, they are alike in being easily explorable by classes from the local schools, by tourists who decide to set out for an afternoon hike after a slice of pizza at Cubber's in Bristol or a glass of cider and a crab sandwich at Roundstone House, or by writers coming back day after day in search of the big picture. One place has been preserved from development through its steepness and rockiness, the other through its standing water and mire, but both offer portals into the processes of self-renewal through which the meaning and potential of these rural communities too have evolved.

I intended to identify the catchments circulating through Roundstone Bog, just as David and I had done when climbing up the eastern side of Hogback. What I found, however, was that so much open water, surrounded by immense stretches of saturated sphagnum, kept me from discerning any clear sequence of watersheds comparable to that three-part scheme of division in Vermont. At one point I attempted to find my bearings by reconnoitring away from the sheeptrail I was following. Plunging up to my waist in the mire, I feared I'd meet the Tollund Man's Irish cousin face to face before finally managing to wallow back to firm ground. Though I reached no clarity about catchments that day, it was still a lovely outing, with harriers gliding overhead, the northern horizon crenellated by the range called the Twelve Pins, and graduated terraces cut into the trail-side peat where turfs had been dug out in a way reminiscent of the staircase walls of Vermont's marble and granite quarries.

After many hours of poring over his map upon returning to Vermont, I finally resorted to emailing Tim Robinson to ask what *his* analysis of the Roundstone catchments was. He responded that 'Most of the area you mention drains through the Ballinaboy river to the NW, another good proportion of it through the Doohulla river to the SW, a marginal basin to the E is drained by a stream called Kelly's River (not named on the map) … Since the relief is so subdued over most of this area the margins of the catchments must be very vague; there are indeed substantial surface streams linking long series of lakes, but there are level boggy patches in which the direction of flow could be determined by tiny accidents and interventions, mere oozings, droolings and snivelings marshaled one way or the other by a cow's hoofmark or a snipe's egg.' This message was a useful reminder not to give way to droolings and snivelings myself the next time I ventured, map in hand, into bogland.

*

In comparison with a USGS topo map, Robinson's cartography has a strikingly open quality. There's no colour scheme of white for low ground, green for mountainous terrain and blue for water. And instead of the dark-brown contour lines that swirl and gather when elevations quickly rise in the Green Mountains, Robinson indicates contours with fine broken lines. Rather than overlaying schematic information onto the landscape, his intention is to scour off the blurry surface of the Connemara palimpsest. He wants to rake away the topographic gravel deposited over the past century and a half so that the springs may run clear again and the holy wells may be revealed. One of the ways he manages this, having started out with the Ordnance Survey maps of Ireland, is to dispense with as many of the superimposed English placenames as possible – substituting the Irish names which he has painstakingly recovered through a combination of bibliographic research and conversations with elderly, Gaelic-speaking neighbours. Names and stories, not simply rainfall, bring exactness to the map of Connemara's catchments.

A reader who unfolds a copy of Robinson's map while standing atop Errisbeg, the 917-foot-high promontory that presides over the southeastern edge of Roundstone Bog, will note that the map's primary identification for that peak is the much older name *Iorras Beag*, meaning 'small peninsula' in Irish. Such a return to the earlier name both establishes its historical primacy and suggests a characteristic and indigenous way of responding to the land. Mountains are not separate from and exalted over low places. They are instead simply the most visible manifestations of a larger area from which they derive a meaning and identity much more significant than the mere fact of elevation. Both the mountain and its southern skirts have been named, it seems, for the Goirtín Peninsula, which lies due south of Iorras Beag and southeast along the coast from Roundstone Bay.

In the *Gazetteer* Tim Robinson published to accompany his map, he elaborates on the peninsula's name, '*Goirtín/*small plot. A fine tombolo or neck of foraminiferous sand links this islet to the mainland; the deposits of seashells and the darker levels of soil visible in the faces of the eroded dunes here and on the tombolo represent ancient (perhaps Neolithic) settlement levels.' For both the native Connemaran and the visitor just being introduced to Ireland and its ancient placenames, the deeply historical character of Robinson's etymology has a strong appeal. As the dunes of imperial history erode, they also disclose. A midden of language is exposed beneath the sandy years, allowing a hiker who carries this map to imagine centuries of forerunners in the misty, windswept vastness of the bog, including some who made it their home long before all recorded histories of this turbulent place.

The Ordnance Maps with which Tim Robinson began were highly accurate with respect to the scalloped indentation of coast-lines, or to the location of towns and mountains. As Brian Friel's play *Translations* reveals, however, the creation of these maps in the early part of the nineteenth century saw the introduction of many misleading placenames. Surveying parties were sent out under the leadership of officers in the Royal Engineers, to take stock of the Empire's Hibernian real-estate. But many of the names they came up with were either inept attempts to translate the Irish names' meanings or transliterations of their sound into English orthography – as understood by cartographers who generally knew no Gaelic. The overall effect was one of effacement, since the long-established Irish names had often carried with them mythical, historical and familial narratives that spun and wove a living web of stories in the land. In *Listening to the Wind*, Robinson never loses sight of the damage caused when such deep cultural continuity with the land is lost. As he says at one point, 'Irish placenames dry out when anglicised, like twigs snapped off from a tree.' A place may become more vulnerable to exploitation when bereft of a deeply rooted name that pointed to its natural characteristics and recalled its history. Ecological and social withering can follow from linguistic desiccation.

Robinson's insistence on indigenous placenames, in his writing and on his maps alike, has sent me back to the topo map for the Bristol Quadrangle with new eyes. There are in fact almost no placenames of any kind associated with Hogback itself and its catchments. English names from the nearby towns of Bristol, Starksboro, Hinesburg and Monkton nibble around its edges, while the New Haven River is prominently labelled as it wraps around Deer Leap. But with the other exceptions of the Ledges and the tributaries flowing down into the Champlain Valley, the many plateaus, cliffs, boulder fields and vernal pools that are landmarks for hikers within Hogback's dramatically contorted terrain go nameless on the map.

Residents in this part of Vermont who are of European descent are impoverished by a general oblivion to the names and stories woven into the land over many centuries by the Western Abenaki, just as the original people's descendants here are disenfranchised by that ignorance. In contrast to other parts of North American where Indian names are prevalent and large local tribes persist, many Abenaki withdrew into Québec because of the frequent armed conflicts in the region during the latter part of the eighteenth century. Those who did remain, after European settlers arrived here around the beginning of the nineteenth century, encountered prejudice and hostility that often led them to disguise their identity.

I would not propose a complete parallel between the histories of indigenous naming in Vermont and Connemara, since the Irish have reclaimed control over their land and language while the Abenaki remain a politically marginalised group struggling for official recognition as a tribe by the state of Vermont. Still, Robinson's dedication to helping recover the earlier placenames of Connemara convinces me that a deeper experience of affiliation with this north-eastern corner of Addison County will require learning as much as possible about the original Abenaki names for this landscape. A good place to start might be with the catchments on the slope above Bristol. In the work of an ethnographer named Gordon Day, I have recently discovered that Otter Creek was called *Pecunktuk*, or the Crooked River, in Abenaki; that the Little Otter was known as *Wonakakituk*, or the River of Otters; and that Lewis Creek was *Sungahnetuk*, the Fishing Place – or perhaps the River of Fish Weirs, with reference to stones placed there for use in such weirs. The name of Alaska's Mt McKinley, the highest peak in North America, has already reverted to its Native name of Denali, thus scraping away the detritus of a third-rate President's surname and restoring the grandeur of its original Koyukon title, the High One. But Tim Robinson's example suggests the necessity for a sustained process of recovery extending even to more modest locales like Hogback – carried out with the patience required for tracing the thousands of rivulets in a catchment.

Such an effort of attentiveness to the testimony of elderly residents in suppressed communities, while essential to both greater groundedness and greater fairness, inevitably sounds an elegiac note. 'In noting such almost obliterated communal memories,' Robinson writes, 'I sometimes feel like a priest bending his ear to the mouth of a dying man to capture the profound and determinative sense of his last breath.' The solemnity of this sentence is all the more striking coming from a writer who has, from as early on as his 1986 book *Pilgrimage*, asserted his identity as an atheist. As the self-comparison to a priest reveals, however, reverence is at the heart of Robinson's view of history and the land. Not reverence for a transcendental truth, but rather a compassionate and deeply respectful concern for how people worked and carried on in the face of a resistant environment and under the heel of rapacious invaders. When elegy reaches deep enough to touch the bedrock of history, it arrives at a tragic perspective on survival in the land and it comes to seem, in Robinson's words, 'wrong to treat the Famine as just a period. It was in fact the keystone in a triumphal arch of suffering … There has never been a year in which it would have been appropriate to celebrate the end of the famine; instead, it has been forgotten while the ragged edges of its shadow still lie around our feet'. History, in a wounded landscape, can feel like a haunting – the embedded persistence of so much that has been lost.

*

The mapping of catchments and the tracking of tectonic plates as they drift across the mantle with their cargo of continents both require attention to the rocky surface of the earth. Despite their striking differences of spatial and temporal scale, these are both physical phenomena whose evidence and effects are apparent everywhere. Tim Robinson's knowledge of geology not only infuses his readings of the surface and history of our planet with drama but also provides a model for understanding shifts and continuities in the realms of ecology and culture, as well as in the pilgrimage he and his wife Máiréad have undertaken to Europe's ultimate headlands. While a number of environmental writers have integrated current geological models into their work, none, in my opinion, has done so more compellingly than Robinson. Here he is in a late chapter of *Listening to the Wind* entitled 'Walking the Skyline', as he describes a band of rocks near the Twelve Pins:

> These rocks are of schist and marble; that is, they are of clayey and limey materials originally deposited in layers on an ocean floor and later metamorphosed and upended by geological forces. The Dalradian ocean in which they were born once stretched from what is now the Shetlands to the west of Ireland, and it lay within a vast supercontinent that comprised most of the Earth's present land masses, for this was long before the Atlantic came into existence … Eventually the stretching and rifting of the continental plate culminated in the birth of the Iapetus Ocean, the predecessor of the Atlantic, which lasted for some 100 million years and began to close up again around 510 million years ago. The Dalradian sedimentary rocks were caught up in the reunion of the continents; they

> were crumpled and torn, pushed down into the hot depths of the Earth and thrust up into mountain chains of Himalayan proportions.

Just as every point on the surface of the Earth is situated within a specific local catchment, so too all parts of the landscape are borne along on tectonic plates that collide from epoch to epoch, raising new mountain ranges from deposits on the continental shelves that are collected, compressed and lifted up as one edge rises over another. In this connection, I was fascinated to discover another concrete connection between Ireland and Vermont when I set aside my Bristol topo and the Folding Landscapes 'Connemara' in order to lay two bedrock maps of the regions side by side. They had been made up for me by Ray Coish, who teaches Geology at Middlebury College. I took the rubber bands off the long, rolled-up maps and anchored them on my study-floor with books at the corners so that I could stand above them and take a long view.

These maps revealed a remarkable correlation between the bedrocks of Connemara and the Green Mountains. The intricate mix of rocks in the Dalradian Schist Robinson describes is closely replicated in the composition of schists in the mountains of Vermont. Such a similarity is neither a simple coincidence nor a common sort of parallel. Instead, it reflects a shared geological origin. Just to the east of present-day Lake Champlain (which defines the western boundary of Vermont for about half of our state's 159-mile length) there once lay a continental shelf. When the Iapetus Ocean began to close as Robinson describes, it folded together and compressed the sediments on that shelf, raising them into mountains that were in fact the much higher ancestors of our present-day Green Mountains and the Appalachian chain to which they belong. They rose near the middle of the great super-continent called Pangaea.

When Pangaea began to break up and the Atlantic Ocean to open, approximately 130 million years ago, the new line of separation lay to the east of the earlier shore. The Appalachians were pulled apart, with one remaining ridge running from Newfoundland through New England and the Carolinas to Georgia. Other parts of the range migrated eastward with the European Plate. Millions of years of erosion, including major episodes of glaciation, have effaced much of the mountain chain in Europe, while also lowering it significantly in North America. But the remaining bedrock shows remarkable similarities between Connemara and the Green Mountains, both in overall composition and in the specific, intricate sequence of mineralogical bands that organises the two landscapes.

Just before Pangaea began disassembling itself into separate continents and drifting apart, Newfoundland and Ireland were directly attached to one another. Their bedrock maps are thus absolutely identical. But the geological parallels between Vermont and Connemara also remain quite striking, except in one regard. On the geological map of Ireland, the Dalradian schist in the center of Connemara is composed of east–west bands of the various Dalradian Appin and Argyll Groups, as well as of the Killary-Joyces Succession; these are represented on my map by a bracing shuffle of emerald, fuchsia, pink, brown and violet. But the bands in Vermont, which exactly align with the north–south orientation of the Green Mountains, appear as north–south on the map. When the Iapetus was closing to form the Appalachians, the coastline of the North American, or Laurentian, plate curved dramatically, which led to a similar change of orientation in the mountain chain formed along its shelf. Thus, today's Appalachian bedrock, after heading north and then north-east through New England and Newfoundland, turns almost due east in parts of Ireland, Wales and England, before resuming a north-eastern course into Scotland and Norway. Portions of the original mountain system also ended up in the Netherlands, coastal France and north-western Spain.

One reason for my fascination with this family resemblance, geologically speaking, is a growing interest in Irish music over the past decade. My life, from birth in Kentucky to adulthood in Vermont, has involved a progression up the Appalachian spine. The fretless banjo eventually gave way for me to playing Irish flute. Even before observing those colourful Appalachian bedrocks splashed into the maps of Ireland and Vermont, I was struck by the strong continuities between Celtic musical traditions and those of the southern Appalachians and New England. (The subject has of course been much written about.) Tunes like 'Blackberry Blossom' and 'Langstrom's Pony' have been played on both sides of the Atlantic since the middle of the eighteenth century. In another intriguing connection to their identical bedrock, Newfoundland is often described as the most Irish place outside of Ireland, as well as being the only one with its own name in Irish – *Talamh an Éisc*. When I asked Ray Coish, a native Newfie, if there was much Irish music played where his family came from he said, 'Well, we call it Newfoundland music.'

It's intriguing to contemplate such musical continuity within a tradition that, while not confined to any one country, is strongly associated with certain rocky landscapes that resist easy cultivation. A haunting heritage is transmitted through modal structures that can madden amiable guitar players who try to join in with their standard chord progressions. Right up through such Celtic offspring as bluegrass, there's a keening quality in the music, as melodies break across ancient droning shores. For the growing number of Celtic music's devotees who live far from the Appalachian arch, including many in eastern Europe, Russia and Japan, it also seems to express a longing for values too often neglected in the modern conversation of nations. Though no one would settle in the rocky, depopulated reaches of Connemara or the Green Mountains out of a desire to get rich, many who have been 'in populous city pent' long for the strategic retreat to rootedness and away from consumerism that such places seem to represent. For them, tunes that don't fit meekly into a standard key, instead waywardly toggling between C-natural and C-sharp, offered a liberating contrast. The bedrocks of the Champlain Valley Belt, Green Mountain Belt and Rowe-Hawley Belt that flow from the chambered heart of Connemara down the length of Vermont have no causal relation to the fiddle, flute, banjo, concertina and pipe music connecting our two regions. But the similar tunes played in both are nonetheless tokens of something more essential to our sense of place than the products lining the shelves of big-box stores and the sizzling urgency of news flashes on the television or the computer.

In chasing this musical rabbit, I've once more veered off the page of Tim Robinson's majestic and highly localised precision. Despite the melodic cadences and fricative rhythms that bring such music to his prose, there's no getting around this warning lodged near the beginning of the Preface: 'History has rhythms, tunes and even harmonies; but the sound of the past is an agonistic multiplicity. Sometimes, rarely, a scrap of a voice can be caught from the universal damage, but it may only be an artefact of the imagination, a confection of rumours.' How easily can a reflection puff up into a confection. Indeed, my earlier remark that Robinson's writing invites inhabitants of other hinterlands to lay their maps edge to edge with his was not quite right either. The vitality of his book is like that of a catchment. It is a system to be observed, walked around and returned to; neither a doorway nor a staircase that might lead away from Connemara. Yet for all that, his fierce attention to overlooked places that have temporarily lost their names remains 'profoundly suggestive of a way of looking at the world and caring for it'. Time to brush last spring's sphagnum off the map and climb back up Errisbeg.

Sinéad Morrissey (EIGHT)

Jigsaw

The Royal children have been sent a gift –
A map of Europe from 1766
Complete with longitude, painted onto wood,
Like any other map in brown and green and red,
But then disfigured: cut up into parts,
A disassembly of tiny courts
Strewn across the table. There is a key
To help the children slot, country by country,
The known traversable world in place:
Little Tartary, Swedish Lapland, France,
The Government of Archangel. The sea
Has been divided into squares, crudely,
As though the cast-iron sides of nations
Still applied (but with more attention
To geometry) while the engraver's signature
– A circle, his name, a folded flower –
Has been deftly sawn in half. If successful,
The three young princes and the oldest girl

(This is not, after all, a lesson in diplomacy
So she can play too) will, ironically,
Undo the puzzle's title and its claim:
Europe Divided in its Kingdoms
Shall be Europe reconfigured, whole.
They start in the top left corner with the scale
Then fill the other corners in: 'Part of Africa',
A scroll, the blank of simply 'Asia'
Rolling off to hoards and steppes and snow
Beyond the boundary. Outlines follow,
Aided by exquisite lettering:
'The Frozen Ocean' solidifies across the map's ceiling.
And so the Royal children spend an hour
Staring and exclaiming, clicking together
(What joy!) the angled buttress of a continent –
Their own unlikely island on a slant
By its farthest edge, and in their trance ignore
What will no longer fit: Aortearoa, America.

Andrew McNeillie (ELEVEN)

The Minotaur and the White Cow

Mallorca

Luis the boatman thinks of himself as a 'Mediterranean man' – next an islander from the Balearic archipelago, and then a Mallorcan. His mother was a monoglot Mallorquin speaker. He is at least trilingual (Mallorquin, Spanish and English). But Mallorquin is his first language – his mother tongue. He will not hear a word that classes it as a mere dialect of Catalan ... What do I know about it, except what I read? He has nothing against Catalonia and approves its separatist ambition. Separatism is in the air, everywhere, I tell him, thinking of the English referendum campaign then cooking. He has nothing against Spain – except the bitter memory of Franco and what the General's regime visited on his parents' and grandparents' generations. At my mention of the man, he holds his hand in the shape of a pistol. Then he fires a few shots across the waves, making the kind of noise – *pee-you pee-you* – a boy might playing war. That was Franco's way with the folk of Catalonia and Mallorca, speakers of Catalan and of Mallorquin.

Not long ago Luis won a sailing race from Barcelona to Puerto Rica, and did so short-handed, having lost one of his crew of three to illness at Cape Verde. He is a man of the sea. He knows how to steer by the stars and, as all skippers must, how to use a sextant. 'There are places out in the Atlantic where GPS won't help,' he said, 'where you are out on your own.'

We were on a more modest little voyage from Puerto Pollenca towards Cap Formentor. The vessel was an elegant creature, a local fishing boat or *llaüt*, converted for sight-seeing. A *llaüt* has an elaborate rig that needs several practised hands to get her under sail. So we were propelled along by engine. Think of it perhaps as being aboard a Galway hooker powered by an Ailsa Craig. Or as I recall from my youth, the North Welsh equivalent known as a 'Nobby Cutter'. For some years Luis worked on container ships. But it was no life. It was monotonous and dull in every way. He pined for his family and the islands, for the Mediterranean itself, as for his life-blood.

A short, wiry man, perhaps in his early forties, Luis stood at the stern to steer, astride the low-slung tiller, correcting it between his legs, not much above his ankles, with deft footwork. I thought as I watched him of a cathedral organist, but one with the sea for music – and volume undreamt of even by Bach. We are the music-makers, we are the dreamers of dreams ... As I sat astern on the port side, it was easy for us to talk together as we ran along. He felt sure we'd met before. Why does this happen to me? Does it ever happen to you? There was something familiar about me, he thought. But I doubt he was more than a small boy when I was last in Mallorca. And I was a far cry then from what age has done to me since. I wouldn't know myself across all that time in any direction. Perhaps we archipelagians have a tell-tale air in common – a keenness to come aboard, a preoccupied look, an eye for the horizon, for seabirds and fish. I've certainly met the like of Luis in many places. And no doubt he's met my kind even more often.

*

It was not quite a millpond day. The sea shimmered and shimmied in a fair breeze but nothing to rock the boat or send it soaring and plunging on its way. Which was all to the good. 'What's the worst injury you've seen?' 'Death,' said the trawlerman with a baleful look, 'Death.' The sea has many voices, as the poet of 'Dry Salvages' said. Today it spoke with mirth, a kind of chatter, joppling in the sunshine, dazzlingly bright, in the cool breeze. You could see the heat among the high limestone-and-sandstone cliffs and in the trees – the pines and tamarinds – ratcheting up beyond midday, tinder dry. Were it not for the sound of the sea, you would hear it, the creaking and crackling of pine-cones opening, the light rattle of them falling to the steep wood floor. The rocks glared. The trees stood as if stunned. High above we saw eagles riding the thermals, so high they were all but out of sight. But no question about it, they were eagles. Peregrines plummeted. We kept an eye out for ospreys but they weren't to be seen today. Nor did the dolphins escort us on our way as they had yesterday and might tomorrow.

The sense of unaccommodating wildness there in the north of the island was stark and stirring. Luis took keen pleasure in all this and in the complex and highly sensitive environmental issues involved in its preservation, from mountain peak to sea floor. We passed or took detours into bays and then moored in a narrow inlet. It is forbidden to drop anchor in areas of seaweed. So Luis manoeuvred expertly, with little spurts of power and fallings-off, until, above a narrow run of sand, the brightest sand, the clearest turquoise water, between wine-dark seas where the weed grew, he sprang forward and dropped anchor. There we rode. The waves lapped.

After a little while some walkers descended to the shore, as if from nowhere, and sat among the rocks, to set their backpacks down and rest, to get the benefit of the cool sea-breeze. We could see them but not hear their voices for the waves. They were following the old mule track that runs the many miles to the point of the cape and the lighthouse at its end. Mallorcan mules are held in high regard the world over for their hardiness. They were used to carry oil to fuel the light in former times.

A gull with a red beak flew down to lollop on the waves, paddling a couple of yards from us, beady-eyed for the main chance, yet wild and wary. Not a scrap did it get from our picnic or the heavens would have descended with its sisters and brothers. It seemed to my beady eye to be of a sturdier type than our own black-headed gulls, more the size of a herring-gull, but that might have been an effect of the light. Luis called it the Mediterranean Gull.

Just as the sky above darted with peregrines, so the sea here darted and glinted with fish. There is good fishing in these parts, bass and grey mullet, and across on the other side from Puerto Pollenca, John Dory. Whatever depletions the larger Mediterranean has suffered, fish in these waters just offshore appear to hold their own, though perhaps not as well as once they did.

As we came on our way, Luis had pointed out under a wall of cliff something that has haunted me since, all the way and back on a subsequent journey, ten days later, to Inishbofin – off the coast of Co. Galway, just out from the little port of Cleggan. Many will associate that name, as I do, with the poet Richard Murphy and his pioneeringly archipelagic book *Sailing to an Island* (1963). Some will recall the poem in that volume called 'The Netting' with its reference to Phaestos, the Cretan city, associated with Europa. It's a poem that always holds me fast in its finely made mesh.

What Luis showed me were a series of buoys, plain black buoys. They marked the location of an *almadraba*, an ancient labyrinthine system of fishing for tuna, consisting of a submarine maze of nets, chambers of nets into which the tuna are steered, with no turning back, rather as customers are led to the checkout at Ikea, but fatally, in this case, ending ultimately in a bloodbath worthy of Odysseus at Ithaca. It is an ancient method said to have been used by the Phoenicians in the days when they ruled the Mediterranean, *c.* 1200–330 BC. There is an especially red-blooded, ritualised, example of its use in Sicilian waters. It is famously associated with the eponymous village of Zahara de los

Atunes, in the Spanish province of Cadiz, on the Atlantic coast. And, as I discovered, it is used in Mallorca. Far fewer tuna are caught by this method than by the commercial vessels that roam the seas, purse-seining and long-lining, endangering the species. It is a seasonal and sustainable way of fishing and is allowed a quota, though a relatively small one.

Cleggan

It was Mallorcan weather in Ireland. I'd flown from Birmingham, where it rained like November in Connemara, to Ireland West Airport (brainchild of 'The Visionary Monsignor James Horan') in Mayo. Here the day was paradisal. It was the first of June.

Whichever route you go, it's a circuitous maze of a trip to Cleggan from the airport. Travelling through such country in such weather fills the eye with pleasure. Today the Holy Mountain of Croagh Patrick soared into the blue, as if on its way somewhere. I nearly drove off the road from looking at it. Its barefoot pilgrim track shone like a bright coppery seam up its side, a lightning conductor, a Jacob's Ladder. As the roads wound their way, growing narrower and narrower towards the sea, I dwelt on names that have one way and another put on resonance in my lexicon with gathering intensity: Castlebar, Westport, Leenaun, Letterfrack ... Cleggan itself, which called to mind Rossadillask, Claddaghduff, Omey, Clifden – all part of Richard Murphy's lore.

For a miracle I didn't take a wrong turn all the way. Murphy's Law itself seemed to have been rewritten for the day: anything that can go right, will go right. So I turned right at last, off the back road from Moyard, round the bay and into Cleggan.

*

'Your heart beats when you hear my name,' she laughs and tells it him again. 'Joe, Joe ... your heart beats when you hear my name.' She calls in mirth, the landlady of Oliver's Seafood Bar. Is it from a tale or song of along ago? I cannot see her or tell who Joe is. They're round the corner of the L-shaped bar. And what are you doing at the festival, she had asked me. 'Just a little dancing and some strip-tease,' I said. 'Oh,' she exclaimed, 'I didn't know it was *that* kind of an affair.' 'Think what you're missing,' I said. Then I confessed I lied about the dancing. But reading your poems to an audience is very like taking your clothes off in public. Only in much poorer taste, as Michael Longley commented when he heard my story.

I like to travel with at least a day in hand when sailing to an island, ever mindful of the watchwords 'weather permitting'. So I stayed the night at Oliver's with two days up my sleeve ahead of when I was due, at the latest, on Inishbofin – the Island of the White Cow. To say the weather permitted would be a gross understatement. The sea stood still in its tracks, at a sudden halt by the shore, as if startled by something it had never encountered before and had no idea what to do next.

'What time were you up?' someone asks an aging fisherman, perched on a high stool, propped up by the bar. 'Five ... o ... five ...' he says, with a yawn, and to make sure you feel the weary weight of it, he says it again, with the same deliberate emphasis: 'Five ... o ... five ...'

Now the morning filled with folk keen not to miss the first boat, at 11.30. I sat in the bar, eavesdropping, making note. A group – three men and a woman, older people – came in and the men spoke Gaelic with a little code-switching, I think for the benefit of the lady. They would board the ferry too. Whenever I eavesdrop on Gaelic of course I remember J.M. Synge's broken window-panes and floorboards through which he eavesdropped on Inis Mór. What was the conversation? Two or three times one of the men said 'British Army'. So I could hazard a guess and take another, pensive, measure of the world about me. I thought of Murphy's poems in *The Battle of Aughrim* (1968). It's a book for me with a prophetic feel, an intimation of resurgent violence round the corner, music of old scores, conflict with seigneurial rights – allowing as I do that prophecy is always just hindsight with a future.

At my back in a frame on the wall was a copy of a newspaper spread (from the *Daily Mirror*) recording, with photographs, the exodus in October 1960, from Inishark, Inishbofin's next-door neighbour. 'I'll not be grieving for it,' Thomas Lacey (73) was reported to have said. 'It gave me only poverty and it took two of my sons ... drowned eleven years ago.' What's the worst injury you've seen? The government resettled the six families in new bungalows at Cleggan, by the sea, with eight acres of land, a share in grazing rights on a mountain, and turf rights on a nearby stretch of bog. It was, the *Mirror* said, 'cheaper ... to do this than to sink many thousands of pounds into a new harbour for Shark'. That might not have been the way in later times, in the era of the Celtic Tiger. But so it was in 1960 and a story ended. We've seen it end before, on the Blaskets, on St Kilda. But not all islands and islanders want their stories to end, as you will see.

Inishbofin

Imagine you are at the bottom of the sea. Only there's noise in that silent world, booming loud, almost deafening, as in a cinema when the titles start to roll. You begin to surface. You come eye to eye with a salmon. You meet a jellyfish. Then suddenly you surge to the surface, and are standing in the prow of a fishing boat – I think it's the *Silver Rose* – looking seaward, as if, symbolically, aboard the doomed *Titanic* perhaps, but not with arms outspread. The noise now is of the fathoming engine and the shouted calls of fishermen at work on the high seas, hauling a drift net, landing salmon. We are bound for Inishbofin, a smaller Inishbofin, an even smaller community, to the north, off the coast of Donegal, all seated on a Saturday afternoon, in the Community Hall at Richard Murphy's Inishbofin. And we're aboard Loïc Jourdain's documentary *A Turning Tide in the Life of Man*.

The film tells the story of John O'Brien's eight-year struggle to take on the Minotaur. It isn't remotely patronising to call John O'Brien an ordinary fisherman. He's a small-boat fisherman, an Irish-speaking fisherman (a version of Mallorquin-speaking Luis), from a small community whose future survival has been put at hazard by the Minotaur, the monster at the heart of the Brussels labyrinth, and one as demanding of human sacrifice as its equivalent in myth.

As you will remember from the labyrinths of Greek mythology itself, the Minotaur was fathered by a white bull on Pasiphaë, wife of King Minos of Crete. A kind of white Trojan cow was devised for her, to trick the bull into mating with her. There is some confusion as to the identity of this bull but in the version of the story that suits my purposes, it is the same bull that bore Europa to Crete. It is essential here for our little parable that we get Europa (mother of Minos) roundly in the picture too, of course. Let us free-associate. Let us make our own labyrinth. Robert Graves would approve. No one shows better than Graves, in such books as *The White Goddess* (1948, 1952) and *The Greek Myths* (1955, 1960), the porous nature, the borderless, shape-shifting interrelatedness of European myth and myth-telling.

Something should be said here of the Irish 'cow' tradition too, but it's a vast literature, of cows of various shades from white, to dun, to rose, to green and so on, associated with various adventures, rites and rituals, and the phases of the moon. I must not lose my way here. Perhaps I have already. Where is my thread? Are you still there? (I wake in the night hearing W.S. Graham's telephone ringing at the bottom of a crevasse, or is it at the heart of the labyrinth?) I do not know what cow legend stands behind the naming of the two Bofins. But my favourite in the genre is from Lady Gregory's folktales. It is the story of a Mac Kineely (O near namesake), one of three Tory Island brothers.

'Tory is at the heart of our mythology ...' says someone in the film, as John O'Brien joins forces with the people of that island and of Árainn Mór ... 'There used to be a hundred boats going there, in and out – now only one,' the voice continues ... 'The EU brought disaster ...' another voice. All at least as I recall.

The Mac Kineely in Tory myth owns a coveted cow called Glas Gaivlen which he loses to Balor, a monster with one eye in the front and another at the back of his head. Not only does Mac Kineely lose his cow, in the end he loses his life to Balor too.

John O'Brien's story has a happier, Herculean outcome. But it is no small wonder he didn't lose his life, or his sanity, dealing with the politicians, the bureaucrats and other interested parties in the labyrinth of what he calls 'the high corridors' of Europe, between the rock and the hard place of Dublin and Brussels, Dublin proving as stubborn as Brussels.

There is no doubt in his mind, and the minds of others like him, that before Ireland joined the EU, the islanders fished sustainably, rotating round the season, following the species: herring, salmon, mackerel, whitefish, with lobster and crab as options too. Now even to bait their pots they are bound by regulation to buy frozen fish from the foreign trawlers, trawlers licensed to fish in Irish waters that are forbidden to Irish fishermen. Now they can only fish for crab and lobster. Salmon are prohibited, preserved for wealthier upstream interests, while the issue of the damage to salmon stocks caused by river pollution goes neglected too, in the interests of farming. I call to mind those lines by Auden in his poem 'Islands' – 'They go, she goes, thou goest, I go / To a mainland livelihood: / Farmer and fisherman complain / The other has it good.'

'Have things become so bad that we have to fish illegally?' asks O'Brien at a hearing in Gweedore, Co. Donegal, up for catching salmon. 'You should read nature,' urges a man with no hope of being heard, either by the politicians or the environmentalists. All the big trawlers are fishing in the NW Box, wrecking it, at Europe's say-so. While 80 per cent of fishermen are permitted only to fish 10 per cent of the stock.

The political process is often an ugly, strident business. It makes unattractive reading in pages like these, and makes depressing viewing too. The film redresses this with poignant scenes of communal island life. There is music. There are festive bonfires. There are children in the beauty of their childhood, still holding out hope to the shrinking population. Father John-Joe Duffy ministers to the islanders, backs them every inch. John O'Brien goes not to sea, as he would prefer, and as his sons now must, but here and there, haunted by fears that his sons might come to grief, while he's away, without him to watch over them. What's the worst injury you've seen? He travels by Skype to talk with Scandinavian islanders. We see him most movingly in Alaccio on the island of Corsica joining in a festive ceremony, taking his turn to bear a corner of a palanquin, as it emerges from a church and onto the street, mixing with his Mediterranean fellow fishermen. At last, we see him forge an alliance with environmentalists – said to be the only campaigning fisherman ever to do so. Usually fishermen give that lobby a wide berth. We see him meet the controversial Fisheries Minister Maria Damanaki.

'Who is actually pulling the strings behind the scenes?' wonders O'Brien, now away from home again, missing his daughter Aobhinn's birthday again (her seventh) to fight his people's cause. It is the big commercial interests that dominate the lobby and broker the deals in favour of the industrial-scale trawlers. 'This is my main signal. If we want to keep fishing, we need change. We don't have enough fish to give the licence to everybody,' Damanaki pronounces.

In the end John O'Brien addresses the European Parliament itself, this heroic man, whose life and way of life has hardly prepared him for such a task. He calls on them to turn the tide, to save the most important species of all: the human beings who make up our coastal communities. Then it is in the laps of the gods. We see the gods. How grey and commonplace they look. It is hard not to remember old scenes from Moscow and the hollow procedures of the Politburo. It is hard not to think of a Bingo parlour or an online casino as the politicians sit round in their tiered ranks at their Euro Lottery hit-or-miss, to vote, at the press of a button, with seconds only to spare, on some 2,300 proposed policy amendments, of which John O'Brien's is 14A. Surely it would be wrong to suggest the politicians aren't diligent and considered in their decisions. But what are their concerns and interests? With whom are they in league? Where do the votes of land-bound member countries go and why, or the votes of those fishing states with other agendas? For what trade-off? What horse-trading behind the scenes? Who is voting for whom and for what pay-off? Watching the spectacle, it is indeed hard not to think you're witnessing democracy at the limits of credibility, representation sacrificed to the Minotaur at the heart of the labyrinth.

Almost beyond belief, as it seems, John O'Brien wins his day. Now it is up to the individual States to implement the changes or not, and with irony, enough to lacerate anyone's breast with savage indignation, it emerges that the real culprit in all this all along is the Irish government. In their eagerness to please Brussels they imposed restrictions and blanket bans they need not have introduced at all. Only now do they admit past mistakes. It is the bigger scandal. They lift the ban on small-boat fishing in the cod fishing area. The island communities breathe again. The seasons restart their round after years on hold.

'The sea is showing good signs of fish,' says an islander, an Inishbofin salmon fisher, contemplating 'an bradan' – the salmon. 'We feel it in our bones.'

Small-boat fishing is returned to its old ways. Sanity is restored too, as to fishing, anyway. But then in these island communities there are other rules to contend with, more rules devised by the Laputan projectors of Brussels. Natura 2000 ... is to John O'Brien another EU policy that legislates against the human, restricting house building on the islands, in the interests of conservation, and admitting no middle way. Here is a new movie in the making. Look out for 'Minotaur II'. Where are the next generation to live? What might entice them to stay? But he hasn't the energy to rejoin the fray. He is a fisherman, an ordinary, indigenous Irish-speaking fisherman, a rare species, one Europa herself purports to want to protect, for a host of reasons.

Norman Ackroyd, 'Cromwell's Castle, Inisbofin'

Coda

'"And what about our friend? How does he make out?" "Ach," the answer came, "he spends his days just walking round the island, working the head."' Those lines are from 'Our Mystery', a prose poem by Seamus Heaney first published in *Archipelago* Issue 1. I had not been on Inishbofin more than three or four hours before a man I hadn't met before came up to me and referred to it. That kind of thing is music to an editor's ears. James Harrold of Galway knew who the man was. It was the Scots-Irish poet and dramatist Sydney Bernard Smith (1936–2008), a rather brilliant but famously irascible man. I remembered asking Heaney who it was. He didn't want to say. If you look out Issue 1 you'll maybe see why. Smith's best known play was called *How to Cook a Strasbourg Goose*, a European satire, not entirely out of context here.

I had been until then walking the island myself, working my head, to the west and round to the northeast. There across the bog I saw two men cutting turf against a far backdrop of Sléibhte Chnoc Maol Réidh – the Mweelrea Mountains – and a nearer one of white dwellings, walls and gable ends. It was like a twenty-first century take on a painting by Paul Henry, a moment of simple continuity, a hazy dream, life at the peat-face of old. The men had a sheepdog tethered to their truck. It barked at me as I passed. The nearer of the men called to it to be quiet and waved at me as he did. I went on round the island, working my head, thinking about them, labouring there at their walls of glinting, black-brown peat, excavated from time immemorial, fuel for the winter, its smoke a soporific drug, dream-inducing at the hearth and in memory.

*

We are the dreamers of dreams. In dreams begin responsibilities. As Yeats knew. As Shakespeare knew and shows us in *The Tempest.*

The corncrake went at it hammer and tongs in the evening grass, as I walked the road with Bernard O'Donoghue, as I walked the road with Antony Farrell, as I sat with Theo Dorgan and Michael and Edna Longley. *Crex crex* its music carried us away. Was it playing too on Inish Shark, out there across the narrow strait, with no human to hear it, among the roofless houses in their sea-haunted ruin? *Crex crex crex crex crex crex …*

What is it we want? Not to turn the clock back. Leave that to the corncrake. He has the way of it by first nature. We want things to go on as we know and love them. We want others to drive down the island in low gear, dabbing brakes, their tail-lights glowing into the dark, and the sea whelming, and the fishermen asleep to wake at Five-o-Five in the morning to catch the turning tide. It is not sentimental. Nothing is and nothing can afford to be in island life. It is communal and responsible. *The Tempest* immortalises nothing less. What's the worst injury you've seen? We want good things to go on as they are and not the bad. It is as simple as that. And who could not know it, this side of the labyrinth, on the island of the White Cow?

Norman Ackroyd (ELEVEN)

Croagh Patrick from Inisturk

Andrew McNeillie

The Corncrake Timer

crex crex crex crex crex crex crex crex crex crex crex crex crex crex crex
crex crex crex crex crex crex crex crex crex crex crex crex crex crex
crex crex crex crex crex crex crex crex crex crex crex crex crex
crex crex crex crex crex crex crex crex crex crex crex crex
crex crex crex crex crex crex crex crex crex crex crex
crex crex crex crex crex crex crex crex crex crex
crex crex crex crex crex crex crex crex crex
crex crex crex crex crex crex crex crex
crex crex crex crex crex crex crex
crex crex crex crex crex crex
crex crex crex crex crex
crex crex crex crex
crex crex crex
crex crex
crex
cre
x
c r
x e
c r
e
r x
c
r
e e
x c
x c r
r e
c x e
r x
x c x e
c r e r e x c re x crex

Michael Longley (TWELVE)

Wild Orchids

In my synapses early purples persevering
As in a muddy tractor track across the duach;
Close to the old well and the skylarks' nest, briefly
Marsh helleborines surviving the cattle's hooves,
Then re-emerging at the waterlily lake
Between the drystone wall and otter corridors;
A stone's throw from the Carrigskeewaun cottage
Two introverted frog orchids; in the distance
A hummock covered with autumn lady's tresses,
Ivory spirals that vanish for a decade;
On the higher bank of the Owenadornaun
Above the sandmartins' nesting holes, butterfly
Orchids like ballerinas; at Kilnaboy
Bee orchids under the sheela-na-gig's display;
Dowdy *neotinea maculata* at my feet
Where the turlough below Mullaghmore disappears
Underground; against limestone grey at Black Head
Red helleborines igniting; the lesser twayblade

With its flower spike like a darning needle, tiny
And hidden away beneath a heather stand;
On the Tyrrells' Kildalkey farm, pink pyramids;

Along the path to the waterfall at Cardoso,
Near Elvira's overgrown olive grove, tongue
Orchids folded like napkins; lizard orchids
In the Mugello, shaggy, thigh-high; on Paros
Bee orchids (again) beside the marble pavement,
A blackcap singing (in Greece or Ireland?); just one
Bedraggled fly orchid in a forgotten field,
Its petals cobalt, chestnut-brown, as I recall.

Gail McNeillie (FOUR)

Spring Flowers

Douglas Dunn (EIGHT)

Botanics

Multicoloured clothespegs on the line
Are tiny tropical birds hanging upside down.
Their songs are all imaginary.
The tree peony's a candelabrum,
Botanical flame-holder. Maples speak
Native American languages, a eucalypt
Aboriginal Australian, Pieris
A secret tongue of the forest. Magnolia –
Which I don't have although a neighbour does –
Discusses Missisippi in a Dixie drawl.
Ranks of *en garde* gladioli speak
Byzantine Greek, roses Babylonish
And other floral tongues, while quince
Talks Arabic, and an azalea is
A chatterbox in Hindi and Chinese.
Lilies whisper across continents
In secret, erotic dialects
That baffle botanical philologists.

Crab-apple – good for jelly – it speaks
Weathered and salty Atlantic lingos,
Survivors' syntax. Spare a thought
For currants, strawberry, raspberry, gooseberry,
Indigenous desserts, mother-made jam,
For lilacs, elder, and the evergreens,
For the big library of tree-poetry
In botany's symphonic chorus.

Mick Imlah (TWO)

Wallflower

... the name
Of Wallace to be found, like a wild flower,
All over his dear Country ...
(Wordsworth)

'In Vogue', but also in my garden:
    The scent of homegrown champion
Was out, between our moonlit beds
    And the rubble of white campion

(*silene alba*; hairy perennial;
    Native wherever a cause is found;
Flowers from May to October;
    Favours disturbed ground).

We know how certain nights they cruise
    The length of the city wall, on foot,
In the Scotland strip, to court abuse
    Or pose for a photo-shoot;

But doubly strange, for me: to find
        The Wallace, first – then have to depict him,
Not as a freedom fighter, mind,
        But as a fashion victim!

For here, he was sporting a hose and sark
        In the 'Fairways' sett, of browns and mauves:
Not women's, but beyond the mark
        Where a man's clothing becomes clothes,

The country, town; with an overskin
        Of velvet, parted into four
Like the hockey shirt of the Harlequin:
        Azure and sable, gules and or

(A quarter gold, a quarter black,
        A quarter red, and a quarter blue),
And each with its buttoned hole in the back
        To tug one of his organs through,

The heart, the liver, lungs and spleen:
        Those relics to be borne away
To Haddington, and Aberdeen,
        To Galloway and Stornoway.

It seemed a rum choice of jacket
        For quite so fine a fugitive:
Chalked up, for anyone to hack at,
        Like the trace-coat of a Smithfield beef!

(I ought to add, that in a sling
        Bearing a bent spike for a bonnet,
He twirled his head, like a precious thing
        With the price still on it.)

Yet then he seemed to shudder, as all
        My eye was taken with his gear,
And in a grating whisper, told me
        News which even now I fear …

This done, the moon went overhead;
        The bell of Mary Magdalen
Struck one; and smartly off he sped
        In several directions.

John Kerrigan (FIVE)

Archipelagic Oz

'It's the Wild West out here', says Eco, as we drive into the Darling Ranges out of Perth heading for the Wheatbelt. 'There's something going on,' he adds, as two dirty white farm trucks start to shift across their lanes. Mmm, right: melodrama for the visitor. This is the poet who likes to declare 'I'm paranoid' in his lectures. But now I'm starting to wonder. There's a worrying jangle from a chain that hangs loose from the second utility vehicle, rattling along the road. The sun is going down over ratty-looking bush, strips hanging from the paperbarks. The shifting of the trucks seems more intent. A whiff of testosterone. One ute gets behind the other, front bumper to back, and starts nuzzling and jolting it up and down. Weaving and skidding they go. We roll past as quickly as we can, though at this speed it feels like slow motion, Eco's hands tight on the wheel. Looking back in the mirrors we see the trucks pulling to the side. 'Hope they aren't armed,' says I. 'They will be,' Eco assures.

It's my first encounter with the macho, pig-headed streak in the psyche of Western Australia – this vast, damaged region of wheat, sheep and cattle farms, bush dying into desert, open-cast mines and heavily logged timber. With its soaring plate-glass structures and confusing loops of highway, wealthy, downtown Perth had presented a different face. We have only driven a few miles out, along a road slashed and lifted on ferrous sand and gravel, as though to defend it from the bush, and already we're into arduous territory. Stretches of pink, saline waste land. Dead trees surrounded by hard, thick grass-clumps, thin black pools and mud. At its worst it's like a view from the trenches. Other times, it has a bare, stripped beauty. Nature cut back to the bone.

Swinging into York brings relief from the ribbon of road, and an abrupt introduction to history. The town feels washed up here, as though at a tidal limit of nineteenth-century settlement – though plenty of places in the outback are a lot more precariously established. There is a façade of civic order: gaol and courthouse, post office, town hall, a couple of hotels. A few balconies and terraces, a fringe of Sydney lace. There's an old Catholic church and seminary, the beginnings of a street-plan, but it breaks up into patchy bungalows with corrugated iron roofs and sheets of brick-red dust-soil. Dirt roads contest the surface with swatches of spring-issue grass that is almost lividly green, as though getting its growth in quickly before it is burned off in the summer heat.

We head for the Anglican church, as in the other York you would for the Minster. It's away from the centre, though, and to get there we must cross a river that has been poisoned by salt and amoebic bugs. As we stride over the chain-and-board bridge, we are shaken about by a gang of bikers. They brag about ripping through the bush, probably to wind up Eco, who has tried in the past to convince them that they're spreading dieback spores on their tyres – destroying root systems and killing trees from the top. These youngsters in their heavy-metal tee-shirts are the next settler generation, getting ready to play mad games on the roads and take chainsaws to the forest. The colonial spirit frustrated.

What follows makes it easier to believe that history is replicating itself. 'That's been cleared since I was last here,' says Eco, as we get across the river. Where flooded gums used to grow along the bank is a raw expanse of sand. Someone hated the trees, or hated something else so took it out on the trees. With a folk memory of endless timber, people feel they can do this. Clear-felling means progress, destruction masked as a virtue. But the remnants of forest and mountain are visibly now just fragments, and with every sweep of the bulldozer the ecosystem gets more fragile. Messing with a riverbank is particularly short-sighted, given the unpredictability of water. Anyone could have done it. Put in a sewer pipe, take out an acre. Maybe Eco is right, not just indulging his anarchist politics, when he points at the local big-wigs, and says that they didn't like cockatoos in the trees crapping on their bowling green.

So I have to look more than once at the interior of the Victorian church, which turns out to be lined with gorgeous, red-brown jarrah wood, like the polished hull of an upturned boat. As we step into the lustrous gloom, there is an organist playing Bach. Betjeman would love this outpost of Anglicanism, and you can't deny its magnificence, a display of craft and devotion. It shows a civilisation better skilled than our own transferring itself all the way around the globe before the age of steam was properly under way. Yet the church sits in rough ground, behind its little gate, a seed of the vision that York has never become. And the beauty of the wrap-around woodwork is caught up in the church's assertion of man's dominion over nature. One day, this place will stir guilt, like an elaborately worked piece of ivory.

Eco drives me to Wallaby Hills, where you get a sense of what the country must have looked like before the British and the Irish pushed the indigenous off the land. We pass undulating '28' parrots, flights of pink and grey galahs. Not a wallaby in sight, and worse, no kangaroos, though with light now hanging and fading, this is when they should appear. I am impatient to see my first. Frilled lichen and spiders. Termite mounds among the blackboys – better call them xanthorroea. I look at the plants with the clarity of ignorance, fluffy blossoms, tufts and spikes, then watch them shrink into order when Eco tells me their names. Sun orchids with pointy petals. Sprigs of bottle brush. But around them, as in East Anglia, fields of oilseed rape. Western Australia was settled by people who cleared and ploughed it in the image of the archipelago they came from. Perth, York, Shannon, Ludlow. The outline of our itinerary. But the ground was too exposed, the climate too extreme. Soil blew away, salinity came to the surface. On the way back from Wallaby Hills we pass levelled copses and corners where trees have been pushed over and left to die. Illicit, stubborn damage. What remained to protect the land resented and claimed as a profit margin.

The house is at the edge of York, at the foot of Walwalinj or 'the hill that cries', sacred to the Ballordong Nyungar. To call it Mount Bakewell, like the English settlers, would be an insult. Makes it sound like a cake, when it has a mysterious, palpable presence, folded into its own shadows. As though to spike its power, a wireless mast has been stuck on top, but it looks like a diminutive toy. The bobbled green of the bush sweeps up and over, unbroken. In the paddocks around the house are York gums and jam trees; at the top of Walwalinj, some of the rarest plants in Australia. Why does the mountain cry? Across the wide, flat valley of the Avon we can see a second hill, Wongborel, almost equally sacred. According to indigenous legend, one of the hill Nyungars eloped with a woman from the valley, despite the warnings of the elders that their relationship was taboo. There was fighting on the hillside and the couple died under a curse. Now their spirits are separated, until Walwalinj and Wongborel come together.

Next morning, the heat is already pent-up in the sky. You can feel the 45 degrees it's going to be in the summer. We clamber into the car with a box of vegan treats, and head into our road movie. Driving fast, south through the farm towns, we go at it hammer and tongs. A messy, tangential conversation. Poetics, politics, pacifism. Olive-farming and aquifers. Going off-line to save the planet. Eco need not be abstract. The Wheatbelt has its disasters, wreckage already or impending. Huge combines, silos, chemical dumps. War declared on the land. At the side of the road, scraps of pink ribbon hang from branches or sticks, marking areas to be felled. There is a logic to veganism here. This country produces meat with the same brutal primacy as it extracts mineral sands from protected forests and grain from depleted soils. The stock in the fields are up against men in machines. There are no ties of co-habitation, no sense of shared needs and mortality. The price of meat is physical suffering and industrialisation of the animal.

We go down through Wagin, where I'm photographed next to a giant, fibreglass ram. Totem of White Australia. This isn't ironic, it's moronic. Red pom-poms on the trees. A yellow, diamond road-sign with a tortoise crossing the road. 'Where are the Nyungar?' I ask. Hunted down by the hard men of the Swan River Colony (1829), and scattered to Geraldton, Esperance and Perth. Language loss, alcohol, abuse, though their culture persists and resists. And so out of the Wheatbelt heading east into the outback. The towns get smaller and less solid. Where there is aspiration it's to the American mall and diner. We are heading for the Stirling Range, through expanses of jarrah forest. The granite foundations of the country are exposed and eroded into domes, baked and split into big round boulders, then exfoliated into sand. The mountains swell out of the plain like a sea monster coming to the surface.

We march up the slope together, buoyed by the belting sun. Into drier air but more exposed. By now we're onto Prynne, Keston Sutherland and Wilko. Technique or mystique. The pace is so relentless that I'm forced to stare down at the track, the miles of bush around us more felt than seen. Flicker of a marsupial, slipping back into darkness. We're higher than I thought, and Bluff Knoll further on looks like more of the same. Not something that Eco is ever keen to put up with. So we turn and take in the view, or let it pull us to the distance. It's a thick carpet of foliage, crumpled like drying pond weed. There is rain down to the south, where the weather is always cooler, distant curtains of grey. So much wood you can't see the trees – I must be turning into an Australian – only the fire tracks distinct within it, unless, as now, fatigue helps, and eyes rest on the immediate. Up close this trunk is a maze, layered with browns and creams against the threat of fire. Thin skins to shed, tough to resist the heat. The xanthorroea is astonishing; its hard black coat is a tesselation of plasticky squares and triangles.

Now for the really big timber. After another sweep of road, we're into great stands of karri trees, barkless, mother of pearl, soaring up to the canopy. Every one a glorious creature. We walk through silence and bird song. Crunch of boots in the grit. I'm wearing thick-soled lace-ups in case we run into snakes, but no snakes will be stirring in this temperate, solemn air. I take a couple of photos but only fractions can go into the frame. Too many of the roots are exposed; this hollow path we're treading will break the big trees' grip. Downhill we see right to the sky. There was a raging fire last year – probably arsonists doing what bulldozers can't – and a lot of large trees came down, or were stripped of their branches. Uphill the canopy looks thicker. But again there's damage to be reckoned with, chemicals in the air. There is no virgin forest. My old-world eye is attracted to purple curls of wisteria, an import that garlands the paths.

And so down to Albany, next stop Antarctica. Huge stacked clouds, big pillars carried up on heat. Endless reaches of road, first swathes cut into timber. The roads are older than the fields. The roads are primary incisions, the spurs and tracks going off them are routes the pollution takes. We are burning carbon ourselves, in Eco's eco car. The problem trails behind us in a plume of invisible smoke. Am I offsetting the carbon now by turning it into prose? On the contrary, if this ink is mineral and brought to you on wood-chip paper. It is something we'll argue about over vegan pasties in our motel, but first we put everything in perspective by heading to The Gap. This is a mighty cleft in the ocean cliffs looking south. A shadowy, mellow orange spreads across ripples of eroded granite. It ought to be place for reflection.

But the gap in the cliff is terrifying, as befits a suicide spot. It's an edge opened up, sheer and abrupt. Stacks of tilting rock pile up to left and right, lashed by milky waves that seethe over depths of green and blue, laced with layers of froth. They crunch into the cleft with the weight of the ocean behind them and spout up like champagne. Eco tells me about a friend who threw herself in, doped and desperate, then changed her mind in the ice-cold jacuzzi. By a miracle she was picked up by a fishing boat, way out from the shore. She lived to die again, in a coma in Peru, her organs harvested for sale. Bits of her maybe still live to die again. Nothing terminates at this edge. The peninsula reaches out to islands, the Recherche Archipelago beyond. The wind along the cliffs is a constant, gusty turbulence. You feel on your cheek the cold of the ice blocks that have split off the Antarctic shelf and drift beyond the horizon. Everything is in movement, even the tough, barky, furze-like plants that wriggle away at ground level, like a forest turned on its side.

We stop at a whaling station, out of use but only just. The whaler is beached beyond the pier. Neat, snub-nosed and brightly painted, she should be floating in a bath tub. But there's enough rust around the rivets to suggest a working vessel. Eco's grandfather used to fly out in the spotter plane for this ship. Picking out the prey, when spouts or fins broke the waves. Beside the pier there are still-shiny storage tanks, like miniature gasometers. There the oil from the whales would be stored. Industrialisation again. Harvested body parts. An hors d'oeuvre to our pasties, as we settle down at the motel table. Porky chunks of peanut-derived protein, mixed in with the vegetables. Soy cheese with vegan spread, yellow like fat butter. Lincolnshire sausage made from tasty, grizzled tofu. This diet still revolves for me around the meat that's being avoided. I seem to have lost my bearings on the spectrum of consumption. All eating is voracity, omniphagous excess. I elbow Eco with the thought that veganism is denial, a desire for invisibility.

He would rather chew over Alice Oswald's latest, which I'm carrying in my bag. Is she succumbing to the whimsical? Saved by a meticulous ear, I'd say, and an eye for the quirky. So much for *Weeds and Wildflowers*. But what she says in an older pamphlet, *A Green Thought in a Green Shade*, provokes the activist in Eco. The title misappropriates Marvell to reflective, romantic ends. But Oswald probably didn't choose it, and her angle is her own. She wants poetry to reconnect with digging, raking and the sounds made by places. Yet her ideas about 'putting texts back into landscape' are strangely artificial. She wants to make a mobile out of sculpted metal words that will chime in the wind. She writes about a ballad recorded and played down a well in a field – wires trailing underground. Conceits of disconnection. As she says later in her essay, 'The trouble with putting poems back into the landscape is that landscapes don't behave like words.'

That begs questions too, but for Eco this whole approach is a distraction from responsibility to nature. It makes yet more of the world revolve around the human. Gardening as control. Verse can scan forests and wetlands, as it can bricks and mortar, all spondees and pyrrhics, but mimetic correspondence is not enough. There has to be integrity of practice from using recycled paper to making time for protest and getting polemic and critique into verse. A profligate impurity of means, poetry not as an end. And involving self-denial. Knowing when not to inscribe a line of verse on stone and drop it into a river (another Oswald installation) because it won't be good for the river. Especially if people come looking for it in their 4x4s and hiking boots. Eco has made himself unpopular by pulling out of a scheme to install poetry and sculpture along a trail into unspoilt forest at Northcliffe.

He won't hear of trade-offs, the notion that damage to the forest would be worth it if 'putting poems back into the landscape' educated people in ecology. It's the leading edge of consumption. Just as 'sustainability' is a cover for corporate exploitation. The fashionable, green arts industry has its own complicities, but domination of the environment is already so advanced that I wonder whether it wouldn't be better to let poetry into the forest and harness its power to preserve what is left. Eco is worried about the spores of dieback that cling to the feet of poetry thanks to the feet of its readers. It would destroy the integrity of his poetics if verse put into the landscape drew in lines of pathogens. But wouldn't it be better for Western Australia to start thinking about itself as a garden? It's an old-world view that takes a knock when we drive past the new visitor-centre and car-park at Northcliffe. A degradation of the edge, which has been cut into to make room for the facilities.

We dash along open roads, passing timber lorries. Fish-tail skid-marks on the tarmac. More loops of pink ribbon. Where are those kangaroos? I'm nearly at the end of my trip and the only ones I've seen have been scrunched up dead on the road. I get a message back from Cambridge. 'Text finished at "southern tip of aus". I hope u didnt fall off! That wd be an unarchipelagic moment.' We talk about the English and Irish settlers, moving in from the coast a century and a half ago, shedding Gaelic and some of their antipathies. United to dispossess the Aborigines. The archipelago had enlarged as we drove from Albany through Denmark. Indigenous place names flash by on the road signs: Dombakup, Manjimup, Nannup. Transliterated but not translated, *dindsenchas* that we drive through or pass.

One more nature walk. We drive to the Valley of the Giants, to see the enormous tingle trees. It's an island of unique habitat that has become a drop-in attraction for tourists. Park your car, pay at the booth. They have tried to rise above dieback by installing a huge steel walkway which sweeps up into the foliage so that you are walking as though through shrubs with a hundred-foot drop underneath. The canopy is restful despite the clanging sway of the gantry. The older trees are open at the base like eighteenth-century garden temples, complete with Gothic portals. They are blackened inside by fire, like chimneys sitting in compost. I mix with Japanese visitors and click away with my camera. Then the sociable, slightly aimless quiet is cut into by a screaming chainsaw that Eco must have sponsored to underline his message. When we get back to the car park, they are clambering up trees with ropes and helmets, lopping the branches to stop twigs falling down on the coaches. Men and their kit, happy as Larry. Walkie-talkies, hard-hats, clamps.

Busselton is a dull place. Not a ton of bustle. Long pier, over the last few months half-broken at the end. The ocean is fighting back, the fish no longer viewable from the submerged chamber at the foot of the pier. So we head back to the settlers' graveyard. English, Scottish and Irish names. Now it would be Italian and Greek, Chinese and even Iraqi. We look for Eco's ancestors. Most of the graveyard (the early part) has been covered by a caravan and chalet park. Headstones shattered, neglected. At least the town is consistent in the way it mistreats the ancestors, European as well as indigenous. It's not sentimental about its past, which may point to not much of a future. Like most towns on the coast Busselton has a T-shaped plan. The cross-bar along the shoreline is a road linking shops and bungalows. The vertical stroke runs inland to the farms, the mines and the forests. What we desire is where we go.

Driving out of Busselton on our way through Ludlow to Bunbury, we pass a long stretch of wetland being divided into blocks and built on. This area is supposed to be under international protection for its sea eagles, pelicans and egrets. Not to mention the sacred ibises. All of which we see, hard up against the zones being raised and levelled by bulldozers. Local politicking has got round the grandiosely named Ramsar Convention, which is now being cited in adverts as a badge of environmental quality to attract buyers to the houses and the Enterprise Park that are colonising the area. One problem with the fashion for green living is that it turns once-marginal sites into magnets for development. Tribunals and boards of enquiry mull over the issues while damage is made irreversible on the ground. So our drive into Ludlow is blighted. As we get there I see a farm worker in the long grass spraying pink-dyed Round-up. Lovely in the sunlight, toxic and drifting.

My first live kangaroo. A hunched emblem, or space invader, hominid, sentinel presence, between two stands of tuart trees, apparently alone, although we'll soon find a whole family group. He waits to be photographed, then lopes uneasily away on his big springs, designed for much more. There's something going on. We find out what when we advance along the walkway, brushing away mosquitoes, to the hide for viewing black swans. I see a piece of wildlife waving up a fence, awkwardly flexible, like one of the big brown snakes I'd been worried about coming across. When Eco starts to run I guess we've seen something rare. All too common, rather. A young doe kangaroo caught in the wire, her right leg twisted and twitching. Short of food, the roos push through fences to eat new planting and get stuck.

Eco pulls at the wire around the trapped, slender paw. The doe is hanging like a haunch of venison. I take a couple of photos – as witness, use or intrusion. The shock of her trauma makes her a photograph for a moment anyway. You get out of yourself to look. The dirty velvet fur like felt, stripped back from the injured paw. A vivid trail and splash of blood. We are programmed to notice the hurt. Since kangaroos are essentially nocturnal, she must have been here for hours. I come in closer to help, pulling up the loop of wire while Eco twists out the limb.

The doe falls free but lies there. Long, spiky claws at the front, like a young woman with manicured nails, dark nails glued on. A Japanese comb, a little black rake. Leathery tail and pads. She lies on her back, immobile, her injured leg held vertically as though still tangled in the fence. Eyes soft and unreacting. Slender, delicate features. I would not call it anthropomorphism, this sense of another animal's difficulty. Little anus wincing tight. Big ears flat and open like an alien.

Mosquitoes settle at leisure. Flimsy wobbling helicopters, choosing where to insert their needles. I brush one away from her leg with a twig, a futile gesture. These are nasty beasts, swaying like loaded drones. The signs are up about Ross River virus. A single infected mosquito bite can drain your energy for years. Higher, against the blue, a wedge-tailed eagle is circling. The doe's chances are not good, unless she gets up and hobbles away soon. We can best help her by leaving her alone. Walking back to the car, we spot the family group, a dozen under peppermint and tuart trees, loyally waiting for the doe or just resting up for the day. Some lying, others crouched, a joey following its mother.

Eco goes through the options. The local farmer with his Round-up would dispose of the problem by shooting. We decide to return to Busselton and visit the local vets. No point in going to the city hall, they're trigger-happy to a man. We drive back past the bulldozed wetlands. The first place is unsympathetic. The hard-faced receptionist 'can't drop everything to deal with a roo'. At Vet 2 the girl has a few piercings, which naturally encourages Eco. She tries quite hard on the phone. Passed around the agencies, she speaks to a ranger who is driving down from Bunbury. He promises Eco, not very convincingly, that he'll check up on the doe later. Her best hope is to get out of shock and lope away before anyone with a gun finds her.

Bunbury is near the end of our own journey. It turns out, with apologies to Oscar, that there's not much joy in Bunburying. There are hardly any books in the bookshop, and the town is strips of concrete around Pioneer Park, Anzac Park and Prince Philip Park. A history of modern Australia. At least the shopping mall sells vegan bread rolls. We dip into a tub of margarine and cover our jeans with crumbs. One last breaking of the bread before we barrel up the road to Perth. Settler farms to left and right. Thin screens of trees. The cars now come in waves, unleashed by traffic lights. When I leave, a few hours later, the last thing I see at the airport is a hoarding which reads 'Development Land for Sale'.

Les Murray (THREE)

Lunar Eclipse

Many birds were making outcry
at the rotting Satsuma-plum moon
rising above the ocean cliffs
stacked high as a British address.
Moon was queer, too, a burnt-sugar
apparition with clouds of its own
darkening its face above the city
but then two Tongan bouncers
from the club found the word:
foi'atelolo, a baked pig's liver
fat with oil, a chief's portion
or praise-name for a pretty woman –
At that, the round man of the sky
began to reveal his gold edge.

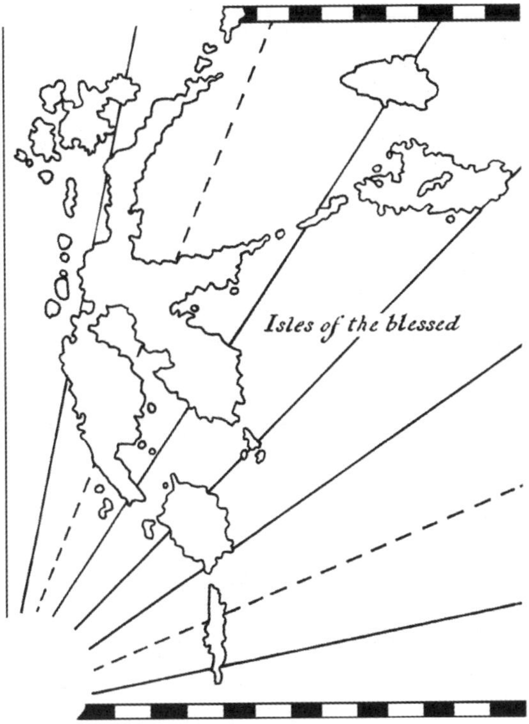
Isles of the blessed

Andrew McNeillie (ONE)

Ghosts: Ian Niall (1916–2002)

Ian Niall belonged to a time when nature was abundant in its presences, in places that seemed to haunt the limits of time, at the edge of loneliness, where ordinary folk led hard, unromantic lives, yet filled with spirit and vivacity. Their spoken word, song and dance, belonging to an earlier era, just hanging on, unwittingly gave the lie to the march of time. Culture was still oral and practically minded, yet it loved the spirit of the letter, where it heard it, as in the living poetry of Burns and the ballad tradition, or, in Wales, in the singing of hymns, ancient rather than modern. As well as the great ruralists of the English language prose and verse traditions, Ian Niall loved Turgenev. He spoke of peasant life, as proud to have belonged in it, almost as if he was a Russian. Nature for him was red in tooth and claw, and an unsqueamish humanity a part of it, acquainted with necessity, at first hand.

Ian Niall, as young as nineteen or twenty, wrote in wonder at the way 'the poor folk of the earth, living on the meanest of life's requirements, seem to thrive and reproduce, coming up again in the next generation stronger than ever before'. But he knew what their hardship was and could not sentimentalise it. He wrote an influential novel about Traveller people that spawned a classic Irish movie directed by Paul Rotha. He wrote of rural rogues, of poachers and of fishing and shooting, in over forty books in which his eye for natural observation found expression in sentences of an unaffected lyric plainness, delightful to ear and eye, in simple narratives that charm as they compel. His witness in the wilderness places of our archipelago demands remembrance.

He had been in his day a wild man, by his own assertion. He had killed more creatures than liberal conscience could nowadays turn a blind eye to, or the environment happily sustain. At the heart of such killing, as a poet like Ted Hughes knew and many common folk, native at the margins of the archipelago, still understand, is an engagement with nature that also keeps us honest, and makes naturalists of us too. Which is to say: it is life, as the majority of people on earth, the wretched of the earth, still know, endure and celebrate it.

Today Ian Niall's writings should all perhaps be prefaced by the following fatalistic passage, an account of 'what living has made of me', from an autobiographical essay published in 1971:

> I have changed and not entirely in my old age. I was once a wild man in some respects. I valued my own life but I am afraid I had little respect for the life of other creatures. Now I see the only hope for man lying in respect for all other forms of life, understanding that he doesn't own the world, or have some priority in the business of living, but simply shares existence with other livings things. He dies and the worms eat him. His death may be brought about by the living things for which he has no regard, or by their death. This is not an original view, I know. It doesn't matter what philosophy takes my way of thinking and puts a name to it. I don't care whether I am branded a sentimentalist or not. I don't deny that I have been a barbarian. I am not repenting before I go to heaven. Heaven is here and life is integral, everlasting and, I think, in some form or other, quite indestructible.

Barbara Greg (NINE)

Woodcut

Andrew McNeillie (THREE)

i.m.lah

There is no darker hour and you've fled North,
I like to think, haunting where I'd love to stay.
But my train speeds south, in the wake of storm.
So in the wake of you, my heart careers
to think how in the midst of death, I am in life,
witness to your obsequies, come Wednesday.
No one can stay and leave. But as you know
it works the other way. The image in the jimmy-mirror,
with just a wipe of the hanky stays
eye-bright for eternity … Just so your poems run,
like the river at my window, and can't be late, or early,
however fast or slow they make their journey.
But always and forever now, they go, and stay,
strong in themselves, as you were at leave-taking …

And would you put that one in your drawer?
Then pluck it out for print, months later,
to surprise me when a column fallen short,
at the hour's last ditch, needs filling at its foot,
with an inch or two pitched against purity,
not far from the fount of our shared grief
… Choose life? O Flying Scotsman!
The lesson of poem-spotting jumps all points
and *caesurae* like the purest drug or drink
ever distilled to the page. What else? Please ask
when next you see them: Dunbar and Burns,
Hogg, Scott … MacLean and Hay, MacDiarmid …
what other route you might have taken
out of this earthly station and still been here in time?

Douglas Dunn (ELEVEN)

Dairsie War Memorial

Was it your wish – or is it our wish –
That you who died so very far away
Died to perpetuate your placid parish
Or the memory of a sunny harvest day?

Seamus Heaney (ONE)

Fragment: 'Nairn in Darkness and in Light'

One summer night in Nairn, when the Moray Firth
Was a gull-backed, gull-breasted afterglow
We stood out on the pier with other watchers

Sharing their low-voiced, self-contained excitements
As an intermittent silkshine furled and roiled
In the half-light. Then somebody said 'Dolphins!'

Dolphins for certain, though none there could agree
Which shift or gleam contained them
Out at the earth's rim and rondure:

We just kept standing, as if in our twos and threes
We'd gathered providentially
And they'd appeared. I thought of David Thomson's

Unfaulting, damaged eyes that saw waves
And waterfalls in young girl's hair, of sex in Eden,
Sweet-flexed, given, low-voiced, quickening, starry

One summer night in Nairn.

Andrew McNeillie

Lunch with Seamus

I saw him hurry by a hotel window where I sat
Killing time over a steadying glass
Before I went along to keep our assignation
At Doyle's, a few yards away. Bloomsbury
Seemed to suit him, and I thought as I thought
Of MacNeice in October and said to myself
This is the life. Not our first time
But first time *tête à tête* and both of us I think
Uncertain how lunch might pass *Chez Gerrard*,
The occasion to mark his pamphlet *A Shiver.*

I'll tell you now, we got on like a house on fire.
A turf fire too, burning underground,
Through worlds in common, though mine
Much second-hand from my father's time,
With North Clutag steading called to mind,
The Hill Head, the smithy, the far moss ...
A common universe slowly synchronising
Helped by a bottle he paused to praise.
Reckless now I asked would he read
A new poem I'd done set by the Súile.

'Slower,' he smiled when slowly he'd finished,
'A slow air.' Now animated, he leaned
Closer and said, intimately, as if in confession:
'*This* is what I like. This is how it used to be.
Usually now if I go to lunch like this they sit
Silent, waiting for the oracle to speak.'
I reined myself in, now he had his head.
'I got the Nobel Prize too soon,' he said.
'It nearly did for me, you know, the fame.
It stops the clock and steals your time.
Shall I say, it made the electric light flicker ...?'

As if on cue, a young man with a piece of paper
Rose from a table nearby, to beg an autograph.
I watched him sign. His hand at once caught my eye,
I mean the hand itself, a small hand,
For a big mind, born for the pen,
Unbruised by past spade-work or other labour.
By now it was fast approaching four
And with the bit between my teeth I offered
To take him fishing. He looked at me, as if in pity:
'You know, I never did it, but only saw it done.'

Eye to eye we met and his canny look
Made me think again the nature of the man.
I felt as if sobered into reality, by the redress
Of poetry, what might be done by merely
Seeing things, if you are Seamus Heaney.
But now the place was empty but for us
And the waiters wanted us gone.
We parted and I watched him disappear
As if I'd dreamt the whole affair
But knowing I hadn't. I'd seen the man.

Seamus Heaney (TWO)

The Fields of Light

Aeneid VI, 638–78

They emerged into happy vistas and the green welcome
Of the Groves of the Fortunate Ones who dwell in joy.
Here a more spacious air sheds crystalline light
Upon the land, they enjoy their own sun here
And their own stars – some at their exercises
On the grass, some competing in earnest, wrestling
On the tawny sand; others are dancing dances
And lilting tunes, Orpheus among them
In his long musician's robe, keeping time,
Plucking his seven notes from the seven-stringed lyre
Now with his fingers, now with an ivory plectrum.
Here too were members of Teucer's ancient stock,
That noblest of families, magnificent heroes
Born in better days – Illus and Assaracus
And Dardanus who founded Troy. Aeneas gazed
In wonder at their armour and the chariots beside them

Standing idle, their spears stuck upright in the ground
And the horses loosed out, free to graze the plain
Anywhere they liked. The pride they took in armour
And chariots when alive, the attention they paid
To their glossy well-kempt horses, it is still the same
Now they have gone away under the earth. Others too
He sees on every side, feasting in lush meadows
Or singing songs together to Apollo
Deep in a laurel grove, where the Eridanus
Courses through on its way to the earth above.

Here was a band of those who suffered wounds
Fighting for their country; those who lived the pure life
Of the priest; those who were dedicated poets
And satisfied the god by worthwhile work; others still
Whose discoveries improved our arts or ease, and those
Remembered for a life spent serving others –
All of them with headbands white as snow
Tied round their brows. These the Sibyl now addressed
As they bustled close around her, Musaeus
In particular, outstanding at the centre of the crowd,
Looked up to, towering head and shoulders
Over them. 'Tell us, happy spirits,' she began,
'And you, the best of the poets, tell us
Where does Anchises dwell, what is his district?
For his sake we have crossed the mighty waterways
And are here.' Her question the great hero answered
Briefly: 'None of us has one definite home place.
We live in the shade of woods, bed down on riverbanks
And on meadowland in earshot of running streams.
But you, if heart is set upon it, ascend this ridge
And I'll direct you soon on an easy path.' He spoke,
Walked on ahead and opened his arms wide
Above the fields of light.

ENGLAND

'Even while we watch the boatman mending the sail, the petroleum is hurting the sea'

DAVID JONES (ONE)

Ivor Gurney (THREE)

Prose & Poetry

On Sailing a Boat on Severn

When the great tides change a channel twice a week one needs a rough-and-tumble affair, no expensive toy, to get fun out of Severn. If there are shallows on the left hand, stones and stakes on the right and a sand-bank somewhere, one's pleasure is spiced, and always a furious gust may come down from the left of Barrow Hill.

But there are orchards and spits of pasture, far Cotswold with white scars to look at, the best clouds in England, and a chance of elver fishing at the Equinoxes; to say nothing of eeling in summer.

If one lays lines one may catch flounders also, and mullet, having been trapped by receding water, are also known to have tasted well in that one happy village. The best game, however, is to have gone up river on half-tide as far as impetus went, or on the stillness even of meeting tide and current, and then to return in comparative certainty, with above-Newnham in sight and a headwind of which the return of water makes no account. This is, indeed, worth doing, though the baler be more in use than the rudder almost.

Since there are three or four public-houses within four miles of the river there is no danger of any common thirst being made to suffer, and certainly there are two bakers.

The chief trouble is that this side of the river there are many stones, on the other smooth sand enough, but one does not wish to be ferried across to one's boat – the thing seems absurd – and in big tides the anchor drags; but there is no non-chargeable way of managing the affair. Making friends is not always a cheap arrangement, and beer is a most dangerous equivalent for favours. Cheaper often to purchase an empty barrel and float out to the boat in that.

River-dangers are not serious. River worries not too many to prevent pleasure. Almost always one can sail, save in sultry summer, and the sight of bank objects always delighted myself. One likes to see Wick Farm draw itself out of line of the landing stage. Food and drink are easy to obtain. One can never be becalmed, and there are explorations on the hither shore that one does not get at proper sailing.

[*c.* 1920–22]

Praise of Britons

I think this land so well set and square framed
Was not redeemed by Rome as some think; the Land
Trains so and makes so, Britain the yet unashamed
Accepted Rome's rule and managed to that command
Leavings of Severn flood, or crumblings of upland
Brought down by silver runnels of spring flood
Rome's form, Rome's strength, Rome not fulfilled or made good ...
Save by the good will of the tillers of the old soil,
Who by mere tending and day-by-day just toil
Guarded the nourishing of the outbringing-mood.
Not painted savages to be well reclaimed
By letters and mild arts, but masters of the tamed
Serviceable earth, to one generation at least good ...
Covering itself with increase, a tender green hood,
Yet wild as a girl's thought in May's Atlantic quick mood

It is not to be thought that this valley needed foreign
Guiding to bring out increase, stone, wood and iron,
The long allies of Britain; nor men were brought
On Gaulish tides with new significance fraught
Rome not all learning or goodness, came over Channel carrying.
[1922; rev. 1924]

Crickley Height

The Dane there, high up above the world, but below crest
Of Crickley, sheltering from chill spring blasts, cold airs,
Musing on fiord huts of home, and considering breast
Of Chosen, through thought; and comparing those here-and-theres.

Now on Rome turning his thought; seeing round him the curving
Camp-slopes eternal fixed in green masterly swerving,
'Now we who found Iceland and further land-shape,
Galleys cleaving deep water in homeland escape –
Endured yet loved; leave never on any land
The sure unmistook sign of our Northern hand.'

'Nor to Norway's self bring love to command
Axes shape huts; we bring tools; and our ships are a tale,
Sword-work, gold twists, helmets and thrice-tempered mail … .
Yet Rome's roads lead folk to market, towns set as they set,
A thousand signs of Britain not yet to forget.
Love of the conquerors stays; the beaten race loves;
Still stay the Southern trees, the circle of shade of the groves.
And Danes will pass as the birch passes, not be remembered
Save as the sea-kings, roughly named, harshly thundered;
Terror and spoil of making in the rich farms;
The weak good work swallowed up by masterful arms.

Rome stays yet, Rome stays. The Vikings must sail west again
To set permanence against these hill-shapers, these fen-

And forest masters, these persuaders, these drawers of faith.'
Crickley laughed high out in the chilly, sunned breath
Of Spring's midday, there was clearness but no true peace
Anywhere on the valley face, and no colour had release.

[1922; rev. 1924]

Crickley Cliffs

Crickley cliffs blared a trumpet ever, ever golden,
A flourish of trumpets against the late afternoon light.
Rome spoke out intangibly yet matchlessly,
And defied Land and high air with boy-soldiers might.
Such huge tramplings of brass sound about
Cliffs of white stone … … the kite floated there, and also there
Rabbits run clumsily about the warrens unnumbered there.
To have a mind of music, a body of delight,
And Crickley cliffs to stare at before returning,
Is at least a touch of glory – and for man to be right.
But when later all Wales was set on burning,
One trembled and shrank, one was hurt and refused the sight.

[June 1925]

First Framilode

When I saw Framilode first she was a blowy
Severn tided place under azure sky
Able to take care of Herself, less girl than boy.
But since that time passed, many times the extreme
Of mystery of beauty and last possibility
Of colour, sea breathed romance far past any may dream.
With 'Treasure Island', 'Leaves of Grass' and Shakespeare all there,
Adventure stirring the blood like threat of thunder,
With the never forgotten soft beauty of the Frome,
One evening when elver-lights made the river like a stall-road to see.

[June 1925]

Philip Lancaster (THREE)

Ivor Gurney

Within a marshy pool high in the Cambrian Mountains it emerges, tumbling through the Hafren forest and onwards, steering northeast into England and thence southward, bounded within an age-old rift which, had it broken fully, may have found the Welsh country in the Americas. In its long passage southwards it is reinforced by the waters of the Teme and Avon, advancing across the rift's plain in its journey to Atlantic waters. At the southernmost, pre-modern crossing point of the river there grew a town: Roman Glevum; Gloucester. This river, the Severn, the meadows of its plain, the Cotswold hills to the east and Forest of Dean and Welsh border to the west, became the heartland of the poet and composer Ivor Gurney, born in Gloucester in August 1890.

Gurney's view of his Gloucestershire home found voice in his poetry of the First World War, written whilst serving in the trenches of France. The war brought his poetry, which Gurney regarded to be his second art, to its first fluency, and in November 1917, two months after he was invalided home, having been gassed, his first collection, *Severn & Somme*, was published. Six months after the end of the war, in May 1919, a second collection was issued: *War's Embers.* The last two poems of this volume to be written, 'Old Martinmas Eve' and 'Passionate Earth', date from November 1918, and for Gurney's friend and fellow Gloucester poet, John Haines, they seemed to mark a new departure for Gurney's poetry. One might argue that they mark the beginning of his maturity as a poet, although, ironically, the first mature collection offered to his conservative publisher, in 1922, was rejected, and only a small number of further poems were to appear during his lifetime, published in periodicals.

On his return from the war in September 1917, Gurney had been admitted to hospital in Edinburgh before being posted on a signalling course in Northumberland in November. In late February 1918 he was admitted to hospital suffering from the 'effects of gas', but it becomes clear that he was suffering from a mental breakdown. In June, having been moved to hospital in Warrington, he attempted to commit suicide, but was unable to go through with it. Gurney's mental problems, although perhaps not helped by his being gassed, had been diagnosed in 1913, when he had had to take some time out from his studies at the Royal College of Music in London. He joined up partly with the idea that the physical work and routine of life as a soldier would help to keep his mind in order – a notion that was to persist throughout his years of freedom. His breakdown in 1918 was apparently, at least partially, brought about by the breaking off of his engagement to a nurse whom he had met whilst in hospital in Edinburgh, Annie Nelson Drummond.

Discharged from the army in October 1918, Gurney returned to Gloucester where his family and friends became concerned at his erratic behaviour. He made several attempts to go to sea – a lifelong desire that was born of the tales he had heard from the sailors at Gloucester docks, where Gurney briefly held the post of organist at the Mariners' chapel, and also from Gurney's own experience of sailing on the river Severn in the *Dorothy*, a small boat bought before the war by Gurney and his friend, the poet F.W. Harvey. The lessons learned from the latter are contained in the practical essay 'On Sailing a Boat on Severn', written in around 1920–22.

Gurney's favourite place on the river was Framilode, a village within a kink in the river south of Gloucester renowned for its elver fishing, the Severn elvers being a particular delicacy once supplied to the royal household. The village was one of the places foremost in his mind while in the trenches, having come to know it particularly well during 1913 when he stayed at the Lock Keeper's Cottage, recovering from his first breakdown. As he declares in 'The Fire Kindled' (*Severn & Somme*), apparently written at Merville, west of Laventie, in October 1916, 'God, that I might see Framilode once again!'

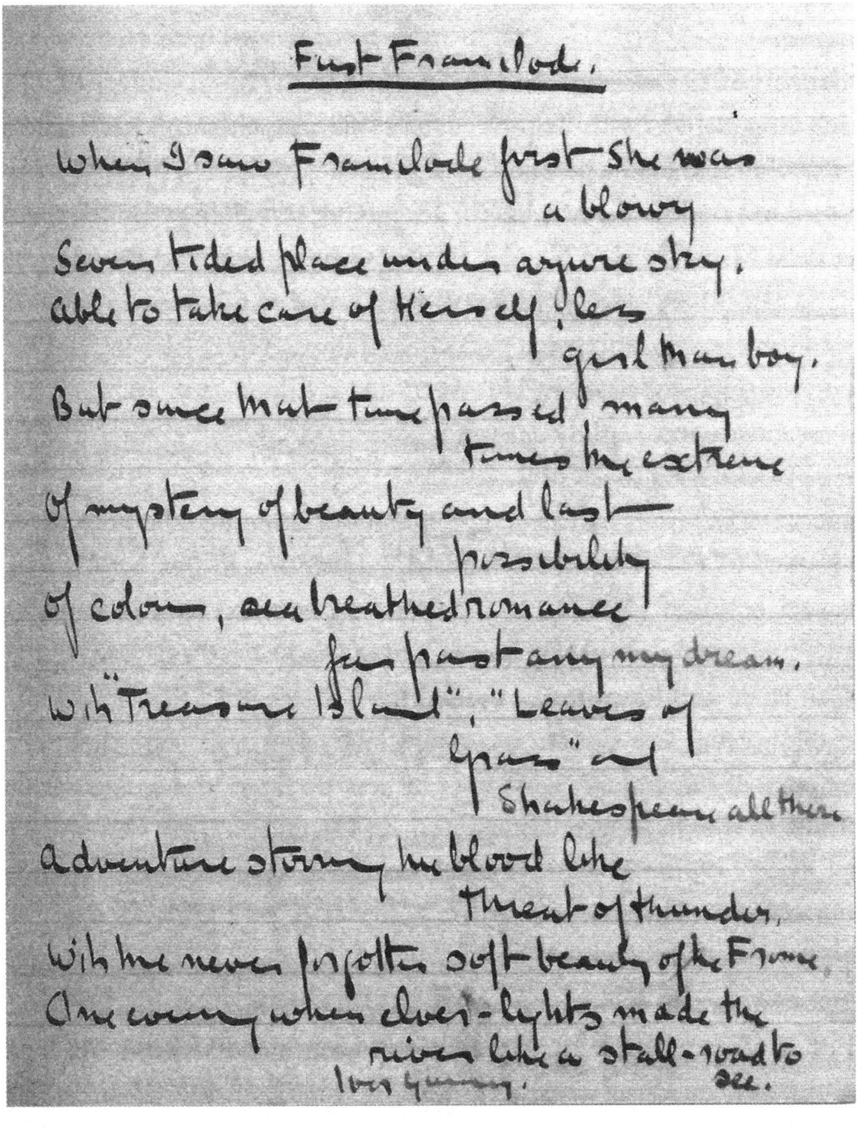

First Framilode.

When I saw Framilode first she was a blowy
Severn tided place under azure sky.
Able to take care of Herself ! less girl than boy.
But since that time passed many times the extreme
Of mystery of beauty and last possibility
Of colour, sea breathed romance far past any my dream.
With "Treasure Island", "Leaves of Grass" and Shakespeare all there
adventure stirring the blood like threat of thunder,
With the never forgotten soft beauty of the Frome
One evening when elver-lights made the river like a stall-road to see.
Ivor Gurney.

In January 1919 Gurney was ready to return to the Royal College of Music, studying composition with Ralph Vaughan Williams, although his attendance was fitful. He also held a position as organist at a church in High Wycombe. His return to London was notable for acceptance into literary circles, including Walter de la Mare, Edward Shanks, Wilfrid Gibson, Edmund Blunden, John Masefield and others. However, he often returned to Gloucester, sometimes on foot from London, and spent periods working as a farm labourer at Dryhill Farm on the slopes of Crickley Hill, overlooking Gloucester. In May 1920 he found an abandoned, slightly derelict cottage at Cold Slad, close to the farm, where he briefly tried to set up home.

By July 1921 Gurney had given up pretence of attending the Royal College and returned to the village of Longford, Gloucester, to live with his Aunt. He moved between Gloucester and London, working as a labourer, and either side of new year 1921–22, holding two short-lived posts as a cinema pianist in Bude and Plumstead. During the twelve weeks that he held a job in the Gloucester Tax Office, from July 1922, Gurney's state deteriorated further until, at the end of September, he was declared insane and admitted to Barnwood House asylum, Gloucester. In December 1922, he was moved to the City of London Mental Hospital, Dartford, where he was to spend the last fifteen years of his life.

Through all the erraticism of 1919–1922, Gurney had been working at an extraordinary rate, producing poetry and an enormous amount of music, much of it of remarkable quality and increasing individualism. As he had before the war, he spent many days walking, mostly in the Gloucestershire countryside, often with a book in his hand (perhaps declaiming passages from Shakespeare or Ben Jonson to some unsuspecting cow) and a notebook in his pocket. This walking brought both relief from the concerns of his mind and stimuli for his writings. Gurney's relationship with the Gloucestershire countryside was arguably more intimate than that of most other natives. He had walked widely across the county, through both day and night (referring to himself as 'nightwalker' in some letters and poems) and sailed its river.

He had dug its earth and slept in its hedgerows. The open air of the county was certainly more his home than any house was to be.

As Thomas Hardy observes in *The Woodlanders*, the local inhabitants of an area know 'those invisible ones of days gone by, whose feet have traversed these sods'. Jonathan Bate, in *The Song of the Earth*, writes that 'those who truly dwell in a place are attuned to collective memory'; 'the presence of memory means that the country is inhabited rather than viewed aesthetically'.

Earthworks or stone remains of previous generations – scars in the Gloucestershire landscape – are the most obvious memorial evidence, and likewise the buried items that occasionally emerge from under the plough. One of Gurney's poems, 'The Brooch' (*The Book of Five Makings*, 1925) recounts an occasion when the farmer at Dryhill showed him a 'metal strange thing' found while ploughing and described it as being a Roman 'chieftain's brooch once and held his cloak'. On recalling the situation, Gurney exclaims, 'And how the centuries in my blood shouted and woke!' Place names offer further clues, supplemented with whatever local folklore there may be relating to people or places.

Gurney saw himself and his poetry as being an important part of this continuous heritage. In August 1918, prompted by Edward Thomas's 'Lob', Gurney wrote to John Haines, 'Praise God for Poetry – it is a good thing and fills up spaces in landscape and life with human interest and memory.' Haines, who came to know Thomas during the last few years of his life, introduced Gurney to Thomas's poetry shortly after Gurney's return from France. As with the poetry of John Clare, to whose work he was to be introduced by Blunden in 1922, Gurney found an immediate affinity in what Haines told him of the man. Their association with the English landscape was not superficial or trivial, but displayed a deeper, more fundamental awareness of place that captured 'the breath of her earth'; her seasons and cycles of renewal.

Thomas became an important model in the development of Gurney's maturity as a poet, in voice and in matter. In 'The Stone Breaker' (*War's Embers*), 'Lob' himself seems to make an appearance when, greeted by the countryman, Gurney observes, 'the earth spoke / From his mouth, as if the eld dark red / On our right hand had greeted me / With words, that grew tall grain instead.' In his poetry, the history of England is often seen through the eyes of Gloucestershire: the Roman, Danish and, to a far lesser extent, Norman occupations (although, as we find in 'In Praise of Britons' the Romans only succeeded with the help and knowledge of the locals who were already the masters of the earth they tended). In one poem Gloucestershire's trees are being taken to build ships to fight the Spanish Armada. It is perhaps due to the echoes of the Roman occupation that Gurney views parts of the Gloucestershire landscape in a regal manner, as in 'Crickley Cliffs'. In both this poetry and the music of his most important extant orchestral work, *A Gloucestershire Rhapsody* (1919–21), the landscape is ablaze with fanfares and is depicted with a quasi-martial nobility.

After Gurney had been in the asylum for a few years, where he wrote prodigiously, he became increasingly interested in literary sagas. In 1926 he was reading northern sagas, such as the *Kalevala*, and finding that they strongly evoked the landscape. Unable to envision the histories within the physical landscape as in Gloucestershire in his freedom, it seems that Gurney was endeavouring to discover the landscapes within the histories. However, as he appears to have become resigned to his fate, and having been for so long separated from the landscape that inspired so much of his creativity, in around 1928 Gurney appears to have stopped writing both music and poetry. He finally returned to his beloved Gloucestershire to be buried following his death on Boxing Day 1937.

Believed to be The Dorothy *in full sail on the Severn, with supposedly Ivor Gurney at the helm*

Jem Poster (TWO)

Ghosts: Edward Thomas and Richard Jefferies

> Tumulus. Gloucester. The bones reared against the wall of colossal stone within – As if I could look back and feel *then*; the sunshine of *then*, and their life.
>
> (Richard Jefferies, notebook entry, 1887)

> Perhaps ... we are aware of the passing of time in ways too difficult and strange for the explanation of historian and zoologist and philosopher.
>
> (Edward Thomas, *The South Country*, 1909)

In the stories we tell to keep ourselves awake at nights, ghosts tend to visit unbidden, intruders from an alien world forcing a way into their victims' lives. In reality, we often summon our ghosts or deliberately seek out the haunted places, actively searching for connections, for evidence that the world of the living and the world of the dead are one and the same.

August 1971, and I'm on my knees in the south-east quadrant of a half-excavated Bronze Age barrow. We're taking down the compacted earth of the mound layer by layer, our progress slowed by the unusually high concentration of funerary urns we're discovering. One of these is embedded in the baulk that runs north–south across the site: a brown earthenware vessel, its collar neatly incised with a herringbone pattern. I'm drawing the section, measuring and plotting the sloping tiplines of dumped soil, the little pocket of sandier material where the urn was inserted, the angular profile of the vessel itself. Around me, the heath is hazed with light and dense with sound – the background hum of insect life, an overlay of birdsong.

It was a scientific project I was engaged in – the careful sifting and recording of evidence, the conservation of threatened artefacts – but I don't think my reasons for being there had much to do with science. Whatever I was looking for, it wasn't the analysable data of the material world. Gazing back now across almost forty years at the hunched, intent figure of my younger self, I interpret his kneeling before the dark text of the past as an act of homage, and his quiet absorption as a form of communion.

And this, so recent as to seem qualitatively different from the earlier memory, though it's intimately connected with it. Gathering material for the article I'm writing now, I find on the shelves of my university's library a copy of Edward Thomas's *Rose Acre Papers*. It's the first edition, a tiny, slender volume bound in buckram and faded marbled paper, and I'm struck, even as it's issued to me, by the thought that it shouldn't be on general loan.

I arrive home late. Walking up the stairs with the book in my hand, I turn back the issue-slip – which shows no borrowing but my own – and come to a sudden stop. Beneath the slip, on the browned flyleaf, I see in Thomas's neat script: 'James Guthrie / from Edward Thomas / 1907.'

It's a small thing, as small as the discovery of a fire-blackened potsherd or a worked flake of flint – and as momentous. I'm holding a book which, exactly a century ago, rested in Thomas's hands – the 'large and powerful' hands whose strength and tenderness his wife, Helen, remembered above all else when she thought of him after his death. I feel those hands ghosting mine as I close the book, and the years between us fold and blur.

Thomas was himself deeply responsive to the presence of the past. His reading of landscape was in part an archaeological exercise, an examination of the layers laid down by successive generations as they patterned out their everyday lives or were caught up in the larger progress of their nation's history. 'It is a battlefield,' he wrote in *The South Country*, 'and the earth shows the scars of its old wounds; or a castle or cathedral of distinct renown rises among the oaks; or a manor house or cottage, or tomb or woodland walk that speaks of a dead poet or soldier.' Thomas sifts the land with an archaeologist's eye for meaningful detail, offering the earth's hoarded relics – 'skull and weapon and shroudpin and coin and carven stone' – as objects for fruitful contemplation. Landscape is explicitly presented as an endlessly rich, if largely arcane, text: 'If we but knew or cared,' he observes, 'every swelling of the grass, every wavering line of hedge or path or road were an inscription, brief as an epitaph, in many languages and characters.'

As the phrasing of these passages suggests, Thomas's archaeologies, like mine, had a dimension beyond the narrowly analytical. He insisted, first of all, on the value of the artistic imagination, on the need for our histories to grow out of a creative sympathy with the past: the interpreter of a parish's history, he argued, should ideally possess the qualities of a great novelist. And since, for Thomas, the truly artistic imagination was also a visionary one, it's not surprising that his account of our relationship with the past should sometimes assume mystical overtones: 'We, too, like Taliesin, have borne a banner before Alexander, have been with our Lord in the manger of the ass, have been in India, and with "the remnant of Troia", and with Noah in the Ark.' It's a vision of continuous time and space, of fused identities; and in calling up, via the pages of the Mabinogion, these spirits from a distant (as conventionally measured) historical and legendary past, Thomas is also tacitly invoking a more recent ghost, that of Richard Jefferies.

It's possible to overstate Jefferies's influence on the evolution of the mystical aspects of Thomas's reflections on time: both men were, after all, treading ground mapped out over many centuries by visionaries from a range of different cultures, and both seem also to have had relevant personal experience to draw upon. Even so, the impact of Jefferies's writings on Thomas's imaginative development was, by Thomas's own account, extraordinary, and it's not difficult to trace the connections between the two writers, or to recognise in those connections something more profound than a merely literary affinity.

Jefferies's 'mystic consciousness' – that's the phrase used by Thomas in his 1909 biography of the writer – found its fullest expression in *The Story of My Heart*, the passionate spiritual autobiography which Thomas regarded as the culmination and validation of his predecessor's work. For Jefferies, conventional chronologies seem always to have been alien: 'Existence is continuous and knows no break,' he wrote in a posthumously published autobiographical fragment, 'and what is meant by dates I could never grasp.' In *The Story of My Heart* he refines and elaborates the idea of temporal continuity, feeling his way back into the life of the occupant of the prehistoric tumulus he habitually visits, and letting that life infuse his own: 'As my thought could slip back the twenty centuries in a moment to the forest-days when he hurled the spear, or shot with the bow, hunting the deer, and could return again as swiftly to this moment, so his spirit could endure from then till now, and the time was nothing.' In such a universe, the ghosts are numberless and omnipresent: 'Now is eternity, now I am in the midst of immortality; now the supernatural crowds around me.'

In that continuous corridor of time, with its endless two-way flow, how can we distinguish the haunter from the haunted? The spirit of Jefferies is certainly abroad in Thomas's 'February Afternoon', but knowledge of the poem also shadows and complicates our reading of Jefferies's meditations on time, inviting us to think in terms rather of sympathetic resonance than of sound and echo. Written in February 1916, the poem acknowledges the war for which Thomas had already enlisted and in which, a little over a year later, he would be killed, but its hints of present disruption are subsumed in a broader vision of continuity:

Men heard this roar of parleying starlings, saw,
A thousand years ago even as now,
Black rooks with white gulls following the plough
So that the first are last until a caw
Commands that last are first again, – a law
Which was of old when one, like me, dreamed how
A thousand years might dust lie on his brow
Yet thus would birds do between hedge and shaw.

At the risk of betraying the poem's syntactical and imagistic subtleties, it's worth trying to plot its fluid chronology: from his twentieth-century vantage point, the observer looks back across a thousand years to examine the temporal space occupied by a shadowy predecessor who is himself dreaming of a future a thousand years after his own death; more than this, the dreamer is recognised as witness to a law already ancient in his own lifetime. And the vision is further complicated by intimations of a future lying as far beyond the observer's immediate vantage point as the poem's present moment lies beyond the dreamer's: that deftly inserted 'like me' opens up a prospect as dizzying as the more explicitly defined retrospect.

Whatever it shares with Jefferies's work in conceptual terms, the poem has a stylistic poise which was, I think, beyond Jefferies: the fluidity of Thomas's subject finds its perfect correlative and expression in a complex syntax which draws together past, present and future in a single sinuous sentence. It's a recurrent feature of Thomas's poetry – evident, for example, in the finely balanced opening lines of 'Rain':

Rain, midnight rain, nothing but the wild rain
On this bleak hut, and solitude, and me
Remembering again that I shall die
And neither hear the rain nor give it thanks
For washing me cleaner than I have been
Since I was born into this solitude.

Again, there's that vertiginous sense of temporal slippage as, in this case, the thinker arrives at the moment of his birth by means of a meditation on a time beyond his death: the passage's subtle conceptual and syntactical turns are neatly encapsulated in the third line, in which memory and precognition are indissolubly linked.

Nowhere in Thomas's poetry is that linkage more darkly intimated than in 'Old Man'. Contemplating the bitter herb of the poem's title, the thinker threads a frustrating maze of half-definitions before homing in on the image of his daughter plucking the herb's leaves and sniffing her scented fingers. 'Not a word she says,' he continues,

> And I can only wonder how much hereafter
> She will remember, with that bitter scent,
> Of garden rows, and ancient damson-trees
> Topping a hedge, a bent path to a door,
> A low thick bush beside the door, and me
> Forbidding her to pick.

As the lines pattern out a trajectory in which the thinker's present becomes another mind's remembered (or unrememberable) past in an imagined (or unimaginable) future, they amplify the significance of the frustrated quest for meaning, and prepare the way for the poem's disquieting close:

> I have mislaid the key. I sniff the spray
> And think of nothing; I see and I hear nothing;
> Yet seem, too, to be listening, lying in wait
> For what I should, yet never can, remember:
> No garden appears, no path, no hoar-green bush
> Of Lad's-love, or Old Man, no child beside,
> Neither father nor mother, nor any playmate;
> Only an avenue, dark, nameless, without end.

It's not only because of our knowledge of Thomas's life – and his death – that we register, in the thinker's contemplation of that dark vista, a faint premonitory shiver. Although the endless perspective is ostensibly a retrospect, the clues to a more ambiguous reading are there in the poem itself – in the earlier projection of the narrative into a future in which the thinker has become a fragment of his daughter's remembered past, as well as in the obsessive play on other forms of ambiguity. And when we place the poem among others – those discussed above, for example, or 'The New House', in which a house and its occupant are more unambiguously haunted by the future – it becomes still more obvious that its veiled complexities are aspects of Thomas's protracted meditation on time.

If the sympathetic resonances are there in the art, they are also – and perhaps more mysteriously – present in the lives of the two writers. It wasn't knowledge of Jefferies's writings, but a family connection, that brought Thomas, as a child, to within walking distance of Jefferies's boyhood home. Holidaying in his grandmother's house in Swindon and exploring the countryside around, he found early inspiration in the very landscapes that had played such a formative role in his predecessor's intellectual and spiritual development. And there's an odd congruence in the shape of the two lives – not just in their closely matching spans (Thomas's the longer by a bare four months) but also in the creative intensity of their last few years. In his biography of Jefferies, Thomas described the delayed emergence of his subject's visionary genius in these terms:

> For a long time Jefferies must have been imperfectly conscious of the meaning of his mystic communion with Nature. It was as a deep pool that slowly fills with an element so clear that it is unnoticed until it overflows. It overflowed, and Jefferies wrote 'The Story of My Heart' in a passion.

The slow gathering, the late, unprecedented spate as the constraints are breached: as a metaphor for Jefferies's artistic development the image is certainly apt, but few readers familiar with the story of Thomas's life will fail to register its dual significance. In 1909, more than five years before the start of the two-year outpouring of poetry that represents the fulfilment of his creative being, Thomas's excavation and re-articulation of Jefferies's life has revealed the pattern of his own future.

Taking a leaf from Thomas's book (the phrase is peculiarly apposite) I want to slip back through time and my own narrative to re-examine the 1907 presentation of *Rose Acre Papers*, tracing in the volume's dedicatory inscription the shadowy, ineradicable presence of the dedicatee. I invoke him now – James Guthrie, artist, writer and printer – and imagine him reaching out to accept the book, or balancing its small weight lightly in his hands as he reads. Forward again almost a decade, to 1916, and Guthrie is preparing for his own Pear Tree Press, in the cluttered upstairs room which Eleanor Farjeon would later characterise as the spiritual centre of his home, the handful of poems that constitutes Thomas's tentative, pseudonymous poetic debut. The gift and its dedication mark a specific moment in a durable friendship, but they also gesture importantly towards Thomas's literary future and a reputation which is still, of course, evolving as I write.

I've opened that presentation copy of *Rose Acre Papers* again, to find the passage in which Thomas contemplates a vision that might encompass 'the strange, the desirable, the beautiful, of every time and clime, the dreams of a hundred centuries that have passed away and have not perished'. Passed and not perished: the equivocation foreshadows Guthrie's mature assessment of his friend's life and writings. Looking back from the eve of the Second World War, a war which would prove in some respects even more terrible than the one in which Thomas had died, Guthrie wrote mournfully, consolingly: 'These are indeed not times for men like him to be living in. His time has gone along with the sweetness which he drew from it; and in his work we savour it again.'

Jos Smith (ELEVEN)

White Thresholds – Fugitive Space

A man looks down at the page before him, a large page, more like a sheet from an artist's sketchbook than a poet's notepad. There is something coastal about the experience – a mind peering over an edge into another element: 'What one has learned is inadequate against the new silence presented. WOW!' He has soil under his fingernails from digging potatoes and a nicotine stain on the knuckle of his middle finger. But the page itself is clean. It looks back up at him like a space that contains something deeper and more distant than its modest proportions would suggest: a threshold, a white threshold, beyond which there is something abstract, even sublime.

Like the sea where it wells over the rocks not a mile away, the page seems intimate, completely *here*, and yet somehow in touch with everywhere else as well in a way that we, washed up land-lubbers, cannot ever really know. Sharp gusts of wind and rain rock the caravan and the man feels alone, under the heel of his isolated geography, his bounded little coastal periphery, all too *here*. He writes in one of two caravans in a wind-flattened field just outside the village of Germoe, newly arrived in south Cornwall among memories of the north where he is from, of the streets and docks of Greenock on the Firth of Clyde, that other coast for him, many impossible miles away all of a sudden. The page is before him and he peers down into it like a cove receding out towards a difficult horizon. Coasts within coasts; thresholds within thresholds.

Later, this page and perhaps several others too, these large pages, will be in pieces, some arranged on the table, some pinned to the walls of the caravan – a word or a phrase written large in ink here, a line or a stanza nested between sketches there. This cutting up is part of his method. To surround himself, to find a way over that threshold and into the unnerving weather of the page, neither *here* nor elsewhere but both at once, working the landscape of the poem itself.

*

W.S. Graham left Scotland and the Greenock of his childhood in the summer of 1943 for a penniless and precarious lifetime in caravans and cottages around the Cornish coast. He had been teaching at the alternative Kilquhanity free school in Dumfries and Galloway where he had met Mary Harris, a friend of the owners. When Graham's contract was up Harris suggested they move to her family's caravans in Germoe on the south coast which he might use as a base for writing. Harris soon returned to Scotland but Graham would stay on alone through the winter and would live there in this remote field on and off for two years, later with Nessie Dunsmuir, his future wife. Many of the poems for his first collection with Faber and Faber, *The White Threshold* (1949), were written here. It was an insecure existence in so many ways, and especially in winter. They were poor, the caravan leaked and they were both a long, long way from home. 'Already midwinter all over me here and shouting through my letterbox,' he wrote to the painter John Minton in a characteristically flamboyant poem-letter. 'The gales from the sea rock me about and my poor arkvan and flood comes in through the wrenched seams. I'll have to be fixing scuppers round the walls to drain away the waters.'

The caravan-become-ark is a recurrent metaphor in the letters of these early years and suggests a coastal exposure and vulnerability that he found as exhilarating as he did daunting. They lived on wild mushrooms, cabbages and turnips dug from neighbouring fields; Nessie grew violets to sell at the London flower markets, and they worked lifting potatoes on a nearby farm ('Here I am on a hot day lifting 564444 potatoes,' he writes to Sven Berlin); they ate conger eels given to them by local fishermen and Graham went hunting for rabbits at night with a ferret.

Nested above the now popular tourist beach of Praa Sands, Germoe itself is a very small village indeed for such a sociable man who, in Scotland, more often than not, could be found drinking with artists, authors, booksellers and publishers. Its quiet fields and lanes are one gentle slope towards the sea with the sense that if you let go of a marble it would eventually find its way down to the water's edge. Last year a friend and I went in search of 'The Wheelhouse' (Graham's name for the caravans) along with several other places Graham stayed but we only had the name of the lane – 'Pengersick Lane' – and it is a long lane. Otherwise, we were looking for a field and it is all fields.

How might one begin to recognise the heritage of a character who lived so provisionally across Cornwall? The question is a particularly difficult one for a displaced poet like Graham. A blue plaque on a field gate, beyond which, just the lowing of cows today? Charles Causley was a Cornishman through and through. His house in Liskeard has been preserved intact as if he still lived there, his paintings on the wall as they were, record collection in its cabinet, favourite trinkets now arranged in wall-hung perspex boxes, and his threadbare armchairs still bearing the shape of his body. A young woman I know was offered a residency in the Causley house, finding her own way among the flotsam and jetsam of a life long over, sleeping uncertainly in his bed and playing his records in the evening. No such heritage work for the fugitive Graham, home being too difficult and unanswered a question.

We see in the poems of this 'arkvan' period Graham's attention becoming more grounded, bounded by the coast and locked into his self-imposed exile. It is the view of a man for whom the south is the remote extremity of an archipelago, the distant centre of which is in the north:

> Very end then of land. What vast is here?
> The drowning saving while, the threshold sea
> Always is here. You may not move away.
>
> 'The White Threshold'

The south coast, as an extremity and threshold for Graham, begins to take on a fierce significance in the poems he writes here. It becomes imbued with a personal symbolism that must be understood in relation to Greenock in the north rather than – as is too often the case with versions of Cornwall – in relation to London in the east. It is intensely alive with those key tensions that Alan Riach identifies throughout all of Graham's work between 'distance and intimacy', 'loneliness and proximity'.

There is a poem from this period titled 'My Final Bread', a characteristic wordplay which has to it the combined ring of 'my final lot in life' and 'my daily bread' capturing that sense in which exile in the 'arkvan' in Germoe is the poet's comeuppance but also the sustenance for which he must be humbly grateful. It begins:

> The arrival wakes sunstruck from a million men
> Gulled on the waters, wilderness of my beginning
> Part sailored by my own likeness part maintaining
> My continual farewell. I am continual arrival.

These four lines seem to capture the ambiguous geography that would haunt Graham's work for decades, a geography that is lifted by the two magnetic positives of 'continual farewell' and 'continual arrival'. Graham discovers a voice that is balancing (or unbalancing, as he might say) between feelings for Scotland and feelings for Cornwall, unbalancing, 'Gulled' inland, of course, from the dividing and connecting sea below him. As the collection goes on the coast, and visions of an animate, seducing sea in dialogue with the poet, come to dominate *The White Threshold* and give the sea an almost mythic character.

Night's fall unlocks the dirge of the sea
To pour up from the shore and befriending
Gestures of water waving, to find me
Dressed warm in a coat of land in a house
Held off the drowned by my blood's race
'Night's Fall Unlocks the Dirge of the Sea'

The syntax seeps and swells inland as 'befriending / Gestures' lure the poet out. Later, we hear of the 'welcome-roaring threshold', the 'saving seadoors' and the 'hailing / Seabraes', where 'Seabraes' sees a nice compound of Scottish landscape and Cornish sea. Then we have that double meaning in the line: 'Held off the drowned by my blood's race'. Initially we read 'blood's race' as 'blood's movement' or 'blood's rush', an intimate, fragile portrait of the physical body just safe from drowning. But we might also read it with 'blood's race' as the 'Scottish race', an equally intimate and fragile portrait of the Scottish poet in exile far off in the south of the archipelago. As ever, he thrives on the energy sparked between both of these precarious identities at once.

Graham's relationship to the Scotland he left behind is a complex one. He had a lifelong difficulty in conciliating the modernist impulse to experiment with any allegiance to a national community. As he writes to William Montgomerie while living in Germoe: 'I wish we could do something to waken things up and get the National bias down and more poetry in Scotland to be made of words instead of heather and homerule and freedom.' He moved away, critical of the 'National bias' then, but he continued to read Scottish poetry, to correspond with notable poets – Edwin Morgan most famously – and to publish his work in Scottish magazines, including his now well-known thoughts on a method of writing in 'Notes on a Poetry of Release' (1946). In fact, Alan Riach notes that part of what divides Graham from his contemporaries is also just what they have in common. Though it took him in a completely different direction, Riach sees Graham's experimental use of language, pushing and testing its limits, poring over its opacity, as part of a twentieth-century Scottish tradition that includes Sorley MacLean, Norman MacCaig, Edwin Morgan and Hugh MacDiarmid. Language is the theme and the problem for Graham, but it is also the environment. This is language as an anonymous, elemental material, through which the poem passes and out of which the poem constitutes itself; in flight from its anchoring national and cultural contexts, perhaps, though never really escaping them. This is language as a big organic difficulty, bigger than any one speaker, as inviting as it is eventually unwieldy: 'Here I am hiding in / The jungle of mistakes of communication,' confesses the older Graham. 'I know about jungles. I know about unkempt places.'

There is a striking relationship between poem and place in Graham but it is an unexpected one. The poem (and the white space of the page) had qualities of the land and sea for him that they rarely had for other poets of the 1940s and 50s. What gives the poem its qualities of land and sea is not its capacity to describe them but rather the way language might emulate their own materiality – the mute and forceful ease with which they are really present and there for us – with its own distinctive qualities *as language*. He wrote about this in 'Notes on a Poetry of Release', published in *Poetry Scotland* in 1946 (and you might picture him writing it in the leaky arkvan): 'Let the poem be a still thing, a mountain constructed, an addition to the world. It will have its own special function and purpose, to be that certain mountain. And there is the reader going on to it with his never-before exploration after his perfect hunger's daily changing bread.' His ideal reader would take these routes through the geography of the poem, a different route every time in fact, as immersed in the cliff-fall enjambments and the rhythmic shapes – repetitions echoing from one dense stanza to the next – as a walker along the coastline's scattered granite and foam.

The poem becomes a landscape and a place of its own then for Graham. Like Joyce before him (and he was an infatuated reader of Joyce), Graham's mind would continue to occupy the landscapes of his past as an imaginative territory – Greenock, not Cornwall, is the repeatedly named landscape for *The White Threshold*. But he was nonetheless alert to the resource of his immediate environment as well. An ambiguous geography begins to emerge, part Greenock, part Cornwall.

His most famous long poem 'The Nightfishing', written immediately after publication of *The White Threshold*, would explore an ordinary night's voyage out from the land on a fishing trip and the return home with a catch after dawn.

The mythic coast established in *The White Threshold* is crossed in an almost ritualistic fashion that really makes the two works inseparable. Graham began work on 'The Nightfishing' after he had moved from the 'arkvan' in Germoe to a cottage loaned to him and Nessie by the novelist Frank Baker, set back on a lane above the busy harbour in the small town of Mevagissey, also on that southern extremity of the Cornish coast. (We tracked the cottage down when we visited but today it has the empty look of a second home rented out for holiday lets, the telling key safe mounted on the stonework of the front door alcove.)

There was a very welcome social life in the town for Graham after Germoe with numerous artists and writers moving in or visiting, among them George Barker and Derek Savage, Ben Nicholson and Bryan Wynter, the latter of whom would become a good friend of the poet. He was also working irregularly on fishing boats for money so he had immediate source material to draw on here too: the comings and goings of what was a busy harbour in the late 1940s in spite of the war's detrimental impact on the fishing industry; the noise and the nets, the bells and buoys and engines. And yet the few named co-ordinates that find their way into 'The Nightfishing' suggest a distinctively Scottish geography: 'The Black Rosses', as notes in the collected poems now point out, makes use of 'Ross', a common place name component associated with west coast of Scotland (and indeed other coasts in the archipelago), and 'Skeer' is from the Gaelic *sgeir*, an isolated sea rock.

As Matthew Francis has shown, an early draft of the poem shows 'The Skeers' rather than 'Skeer' suggesting that Graham was dabbling with a carefully fabricated coastal seascape. 'The Mor Light' that the boat passes on its way out also seems to be invented. It carries the Scots Gaelic meaning of 'Mor' as big or lofty, but it is also the Cornish word for 'sea'. So where is Graham's sea really? Over what elusive geography does his 'white threshold' look? Cornwall, Greenock and the fabricated space of the poem itself seem to hold the coastal vision of his early poems in a tension that articulates its own gripping space. The ambiguity of Graham's geography, always unbalanced between his two coasts, coupled with the linguistic density of his early voice, gives the poems that rare and remarkable coastal space all of their own. It is a more-than-representational space belonging to the page and the poem that would bring Graham into contact with the abstract painters of the St Ives area in the 1950s and '60s.

*

When we visited the place looking for the coastguard's cottages where he lived at Gurnard's Head, and for Carn Cottage above Zennor, loaned to him by the painter Bryan Wynter, we were at the end of our Graham tour that had taken in Germoe and Mevagissey on the way down. We had quite appropriately struggled to locate the places of this ambiguously placed poet, the fields long-since abandoned and the loaned cottages now empty second homes or holiday lets. The sun was going down and the whole western sky filled up orange as the light was diffused by a thin haze. On the way we had heard a story of Aleister Crowley performing ritual magic in Carn Cottage, leaving behind him a trail of grim stories associated with the place: nearby villagers and subsequent residents falling foul to heart attacks, suicide and insanity; locals who even today wouldn't tell what they knew about its history. Perhaps it is a story that says something about the pull of mystical energies in this extraordinary landscape. Or perhaps, more likely, it says something about the kinds of artists, misfits and bohemians that have been drawn to the area throughout the twentieth century.

Cornwall of the 1940s might have had the allure of wild isolation for some but increasingly poets and artists were moving in, migrating in droves from across the UK. In the early years of the war it had become a retreat of relative safety from the bombing, and a number of European modernists who might otherwise have stayed in their Hampstead studios had moved to the St Ives area in 1939. Most famously, Ben

Nicholson, Barbara Hepworth and Naum Gabo would bring Cubism and Constructivism with them. Michael Bird suggests that they almost convinced Piet Mondrian – who was working in Hampstead at the time – to join them but in the end a distaste for the countryside (and apparently for the colour green) won out. Art critics, poets, editors and translators, among them David Wright, Michael Hamburger and George Barker, would follow – many as penniless as Graham and surviving on the kindness of friends and some light farm labour.

*

For the painter Peter Lanyon, Cornwall's distinctiveness apart from Britain helped in identifying with a wider European community of political rebellion and Modernist experiment. And it was Lanyon more than anyone who managed to bridge – with no apparent contradiction – the new Constructivist tendency towards abstraction and a feeling for the Cornish landscape. Such an independent-minded culture appealed to Graham and no doubt fed his articulations of wilfully precarious identity, the self as in a state of radical flux and change, raised to a point of intensity between arrival and departure, between belonging and exile. 'Romantic Moderns' this group certainly were, to borrow a phrase from Alexandra Harris, but much more radically Romantic and much more radically Modern than their English counterparts over the Tamar.

Perhaps it was something of the region's reputation as an outsiders' retreat that drew Graham to the south-west in the first place, but it seems a remarkable coincidence that he found himself among artists experimenting both with abstraction *and* with landscape at the same time. His explorations of the poem as its own space, its own intimate and isolated world above and beyond its descriptive and representational qualities, meant that he found an immediate kinship with, and was able to relate to the work of, painters like Bryan Wynter, Roger Hilton and Lanyon himself, and long nights were spent in boozy, benzedrine-fuelled discussion. David Whittaker has described the often quite heated meetings between Graham and Hilton, whose work was perhaps the most committedly abstract of these three painters, and he quotes the following passage from a letter Graham sent to the artist after their first meeting; it gives a strong sense of how the poet felt nourished and inspired by those artists around him:

> So, Roger, my love-chasing abstract boy, my hero of the graphic plain, my boy alone and lost in the disguising angers and rudeness and precipitations of catastrophe, my touchy switherer and butter-fingered bearer of your self-esteem, artist of the astringent, the uncharming, the unkitchened, the unpotted and panned regions of the great proportions and intercoursing areas of light trying the eye, hurry up and come down soon ... Shall I compare thee to a day of storms. Batter my Gurnard's Head. The wind roars and the waves rumble in.

For Wynter and Lanyon, however, the way in which their paintings pushed towards abstraction was much more closely engaged in a dialogue with the elements: Wynter most famously with water and Lanyon with air. Both worked their own elemental thresholds and took immersion in them seriously, searching for new ways of seeing and new ways of painting. Wynter would improvise diving equipment from an army surplus store and Lanyon would take to the skies in a glider in his later years (in fact he would eventually die in a gliding accident). Graham and these artists were working in different media but they shared a common experimental and contemporary goal. They endeavoured to generate a quality of immersive and imaginative space that was more than representational, that was elemental in its own way, whether that was on the painted canvas or on the written page. Lasting friendships were struck and Graham would go on to write moving elegies for each of them.

For Graham, the space of the page became increasingly inhabitable. The 'white threshold' remained a threshold but in the later poems we tend to find him on the other side of it.

> Between the typing hammers I spied
> Myself with looking eyes looking
> Down to cover me with words.
>
> 'Untidy Dreadful Table'

> I stand in my vocabulary looking out
> Through my window of fine water ready
> To translate natural occurrences
>
> 'A Note to the Difficult One'

In fact, the wider problem of occupying language as an environment becomes a recurrent motif. But the energy of struggle, working that threshold in all its uncertainty and material difficulty, is much more vibrantly alive in those earlier collections, *The White Threshold* and *The Nightfishing*. In these, the poem as landscape is lit up with a fierce energy that sets it, not apart from, but between the landscapes of Cornwall and Scotland. Graham's is a richly coastal and archipelagic voice, working the littoral edges of identity and place in the spaces *between* islands. The boat of 'The Nightfishing' carries the image of that voice perfectly. It is a journey enacting the very articulation it is searching for, its own balanced or unbalanced survival on the swell of a vast and unstable element. It risks everything for a kind of high-wire act that is a state of constant negotiation with the changing world, a state always of becoming other than itself, free from the overdetermination of the inland world. In this he finds, quite simply, grace.

> At last it's all so still. We hull to the nets,
> And rest back with our shoulders slacked pleasantly.
> And I am illusioned out of this flood as
> Separate and stopped to trace all grace arriving.
> This grace, this movement bled into this place,
> Locks the boat still in the grey of the seized sea.
> ...
> What sudden perfection is this the measurement of?
>
> 'The Nightfishing'

Graham's coastal vision is an attempt to articulate a fugitive space away from the suspect securities of the land and its various biases. It is the vision of a Scottish man living in the extreme south of the archipelago a long way from home; and it is a vision of an international artistic community living on the outside edge of Britain. It is both of these things and the important tension between them. As tradition gave way to experiment, as identity gave way to becoming and as 'movement bled into this place', the poetry began to create the very spiritual home from home that it described. To read the poem aloud today is to take your own route through that seascape and coastal vision and inhabit this home from home for a fleeting and exhilarating moment in one of the most extraordinary poetic geographies of the twentieth century.

Katherine Rundell (FOUR)

Bate's Creed

I never knew Bate, so this essay, which I wrote just after I turned twenty-two, is guesswork and patchwork and hope rather than biography.

I have been warned that the stretch of sea between Padstow and Rock is two times too wide and wild to swim. The warning is inherited from my great-grandfather, whose body understood the sea. He had a face of ripples: pouches below his eyes, swells around his lips, jowls lapping at his neck. His name, Bate, suggested water and flax fishing lines. In common with most of the old men of Padstow and Trebetherick and Polzeath, his mouth was a black cave with an irregular growth of stalactites: he was of that generation before NHS dentistry, which spoke with the susurrations of the sea. He chose to live within wind-distance of water, up by the cliffs of Stepper Point where the view across the Estuary blurs in the breeze and gales reach force 10 on the Beaufort scale. He could bear, he said, a lot of weather.

Though he was no mystic, he believed you went to the edges of the land to see clearly. His son, my grandfather, recited Bate's creed for us: *prospect is to geography as retrospect is to time*: it is at the ends that you begin to understand. Charles Smith's meticulously veined *New Map* of 1806 shows Cornwall as a place rich in such extremities and extremes, with a coastline scribbled and erratic; the promontory of Stepper Point thrusts sharply out into the sepia space signifying water. Bate said, it's not the Ends of the Earth, but it's *an* end of *some* earth. (In a world so multitudinous, it is only the foolish and the myopic who demand the definite article.) I believe my generation has reached an edge – a crisis point my great-grandfather raged against and saw coming, a world too prone to ignore rain and time, cluttering up the space cleared for patience – and I therefore took up the old advice and took a ferry to the Point, where Bate lived the grey-green life of a hermit until he married.

It was a precarious way of existing. When a doctor was needed from across the Estuary, Bate rode without shoes to the edge of the shore, set a branch alight and stood in the water, waving his torch until the boat arrived. If the sea would not carry him, no doctor would come. Today the Black Tor ferry can run through an infinite variety of weather; but even in this, the thickest and coldest and most charred of afternoons, one can see that the Black Tor ferry is not black. What boat is? It is yellow and white, boat coloured, but it is named for a tor of the West Country – a balancing rock formation, shaped by erosion – and so it is of fragile landmasses and precarious equilibriums that the boat speaks. The name, on this day, makes a very particular kind of sense.

The tide was too low and water too sparse to reach Padstow harbour, and the Tor released me (me alone, and only charged three pounds) further north, at a shingle cove blanketed in bladder wrack and egg wrack and the remarkable coppery brown of the tooth wrack. Throughout the last decade of the nineteenth century Bate's mother loaded her donkey with this seaweed here, tied a white string round its muzzle and led it, slick with mucus, back to the land. They made use of what remnants the world provided; farming for that family extended to the very edge of the sea and into it. It was undifferentiated, defiantly unlegislated. Bate had no money, and poverty was as important to him as wealth must be to a wealthy man. His belief arose through chiasmic logic: if money made for impatience – and if impatience made a misery out of fishing – and if fishing made for high pleasure – then, pleasure cannot be made through money. He did not say, *QED*, but he would have spat, which signified the same.

It was two miles to the Point and already the wind was angry and salt-haunted. I ran and climbed at the pace of the weather to stay warm and relished the height. Two hundred and forty-two metres is not the highest point in Cornwall, but here the earth and rock have not been mesmerised by the clumsy need to be the most. Bate, so short and so plain, believed in words with Anglo-Saxon origins: rough, tough, enough. Just before he died, exposed suddenly to the hyperbole of television, he raged – bearded and incongruous and even weeping – against its *never before*s and *most of alls*. (They're not expressions built to last, he said: he was a builder.) It was because of this – the superior value of just-enough – that he loved the shell called Warty Venus. It has concentric edges, like the ripples of a rivermouth, and rough lumps. He told my great-grandmother it was the honest shell: it wasn't perfect, because nothing is. After meeting her he had to come inland, but his choice of professions made sense; he became a stonemason and undertaker, still working with rocks and the unseen. He believed in the land. He believed the world was a fearsome and a hidden place. He would have approved of the etymological hypothesis for Padstow given in Holinshead, 'two rockes, secretlie hidden at full sea, as two pads in the straw, whereof I think it taketh the name'.

I watched the waves for the two rocks as I ran up to the head, but the rain was sweeping in like a lift door and the water was silver and rough and indifferent; it would not stand still for me to look at it. Where the upwards splash of the rain mixes with the sea spray Bate would speak of the *double wet*. Across the bay, a girl was walking in the wind with no shoes.

The underbelly of the cliff below me was black and white, like the gulls, except where the sea rose to cover it; there it compromised, turned grey. It was local wisdom: it might not be the highest, but lose your way at the Point and at the bottom there's eternity. It was *high enough*: and it was turbulent enough and rough enough that day, vertiginous enough, to cut through to the head. I remembered Jonathan Swift's Deathbed poem: 'That old vertigo in his head / will never leave him, till he's dead.' It would not be difficult, here, to die. I was winddriven to the edge of the edge. (That word wind-driven, born in the fourteenth century and popularised by a Captain Wyatt in the sixteenth, 'huge mountains of windedriven sandes': it has been found dispensable and is gone. We are losing our words. I know we must lose things, my generation. But we must lose more carefully.)

And the thunder came, at that moment. Jabs of brass ripped across the sky (the Point is a rough place to be in such rain, without shelter. Being wet, though, is a part of the Point; Bate told my grandfather, water goes deep. It serves to anchor memory.) At the second lightning flash a gull was underlit in a nest of light. The earth felt very old. Larkin's poem made wet and glorious sense:

> If I were called in
> To construct a religion
> I should make use of water.

Water and religion mix well in Cornwall: the waves cut up into inverted *w*s and *v*s, and out over the estuary they were mimicked in the n-shaped tip of St Enodoc's stone spire. Bate favoured St Enodoc above any church in Padstow; it was smallest, plainest, toughest and closest to the sea. Watching it from across the Estuary, it is easy to believe in beauty: its spire twists in compromise with the winddriven world and the tip is humped like one of the tumuli that complicate the grassy surface of Brae Hill to the south. I was glad of the resemblance, where both give shape and meaning to death.

Bate was on first-name terms with the church: to him it was Neddy, Sinking Ned, Sinkininny Church. The name was a relic of the two centuries before Bate's own, when fine sediment flew in from the dunes at Daymer Bay and entered the grave yard. Over a hundred years the sand embraced the stones and mounted the walls, until the church was almost drowned. Half-smothered, the church turned back to the earth; in the nineteenth century the vicar's boy told how it was taken back by mould and worms and became a wet growing thing; the pews put forth green tufts, and bats lived in the belfry. It was used only once a year, when the vicar and parishioners dropped like a calendar of Saint Nicholases through a hole in the transept roof. It would have been dark (and cramped: the nave is as narrow as a ship's corridor. That makes sense for a sea-church; *nave* comes from Latin *navis*, ship, and the vaulting is angled like the keel of a boat) but there would have been the twin shivers of cold and coincidence, then, to the word at half-mark in the Apostles Creed, *buried*. I hope they paused, and smiled, even though in church.

There is nothing now to suggest that it was once all but conquered by that aeolian process. In the nineteenth century St Enodoc was rescued, undug and new-roofed. The pews were made smooth and varnished into steadiness again. The *xanthoria parietina*, a yellow lichen you will find painting sea walls, has covered the church's spire. It resembles snow and it has the same effect: it makes the earth seem fathomable, and still. It is like its own photograph, an image lifted out of time: St Enodoc, with its *xanthoria*, looks as though it has ever been thus. The church, then, tells a dangerous story which I feared from my stand at the dark-aired sea-flashed Point is a lie: that nothing is ever lost beyond recovering.

I shivered, with the cold and the thought and the height. I am not the Padstow mermaid, and it is possible to be too wet. I turned back to the town and the ferry, up along the farmland and the dry stone walls that legislate the fields. I passed between two hedges and saw how they had sagged in the middle, and bent towards the land. Cross-section them, and they would become cursive brackets made of brambles, and I, within them, was parenthetical: which is to say, an irrelevance. There was a liberation in knowing myself small; I was unnoticed even by the white line of gulls chalked across the black sky. By the concrete quay, the gulls will become human. There they rarely fly; they walk with a sailor's leer and visitors give them chips and verbs of human volition. But here they are winged. Their wings curve to mimic the shape of the waves; they and the sea are of a piece. They belong to Archipelagos and edges, but not to us. I stood still to watch them, though the wind blew darkly. A great deal was at stake; Bate taught his four children, it is worth watching the birds. It is to say: the things that do not belong to us will give us most pleasure. I preferred these gulls to their incarnations on the quay. It is freedom that makes the stomach flap and take flight.

A mile on the mud turned into sand; into concrete; took on sign-posts and the paraphernalia of modernity. I passed a stone barn – the first uncompromisingly vertical walls of the day – filled with leaves and cans and the traces of sex not blown away. Defoe wrote of Padstow that it was 'a very good harbour ... the first, and best, if not the only haven on this shore'; and in the eighteenth century it sent out ships freighted with hand-cured pilchards and wheat, oats, barley, minerals and giant purpose. That is over now; for the past decade, the harbour has been filled with tattooed leisure boats waiting to take tourists round to Gull Rock on the loud and italicised *High Speed Trip* advertised on sandwich boards along the quay.

The Padstow I found that day was empty, barring the two old men who sat along the covered harbour edge. They were beerless and without occupation. One of them had a total of six teeth, his lower jaw an uninterrupted horizon of gum, and he spoke, like Bate, with a voice made of waves. I had seen them before, but never in the summer frenzy, when there is no place for them on the bench and the streets are full of aching and exhausted trippers. During those months, there is a mess of chaos and eating; ketchup pools in place of sea anemones, and dog faeces crusting into sandy whiteness. Every summer, the sea is made subordinate to man. It is easy to believe that the world is cheap and ugly.

The town has a careful, shop-front feel to it. Everything is reduced to primary colours; there is only one shade of yellow to serve for spades and awnings and postcards of the sun. The yellow of the grass that sheets the Point, and of the sand by the church, and the *xanthoria* and the yellow of the spleenwort flowers covering the cliff like flicks of paint which together speak of an infinite and unretractable earth: these do not have a place here.

Rick Stein's shop sells household goods in the shapes of the sea. Throughout the town, you could (if you had so odd a wish) buy from eleven different shops a soap in the form of the Warty Venus shell. It is a hybrid; half cosmetic and half nature. It is a monster of therianthropy. Bate believed in doubles – a double fishing rod, doubled ropes and the double wet, above all – but not in halves. Across the road, Padstow's art galleries peddle sentimentality and a past that is atemporal, invented, untrue. They trade less on the sea than on the idealisation of the sea, and to idealise is to disguise: it is a suppressing of fears and doubts about a thing (that is a sentence I inherited from Bate; though he told it about the innocence of children and the softness of women, in neither of which he believed.)

Padstow is no place to be in the rain. I ran past the four Rick Stein restaurants, and away. The graffiti on the wall nearby looked like it was scratched angrily with flint from the beach. It says, *Welcome to PadStein!* Up at the Point the rain muddies the paths and puddles the sand: the earth believes in compromise, in bends and diversions and mixtures. Until we revolt, Padstow must trade in oversimplification: blue sky yellow buckets red ketchup. It cannot bear too much weather.

At the end of a text we hope for redress; the same was true of that dying afternoon. I took myself through the town to Padstow's end and the excellent loneliness of the sea. The tide rose high and the water, colder than winter, had returned. The widest and wildest of pedagogues, it will continue to make its liquid overtures to our solidity. I believe that Bate was right; water is thick and counter and strange. It has a depth that bathymetry cannot measure. Only the beauty of the sea, Bate believed, is past change.

Robert Macfarlane (TEN)

Fold, Twist, Loop, Layer, Slip – Towards a Topology of a Topography

In 1971 Derek Jarman made a ten-minute silent short called *Journey to Avebury*, documenting a summer walk through the chalklands of southern England. The film seems, at first, more pastoral home-movie than avant-garde: sheep graze, footpaths dwindle into the long distance. Gradually, though, an eeriness builds. Where are the people? Who is holding the camera? The landscape feels emptied rather than empty. Clouds glower and loom. A psychic weather communicates itself to the viewer: close, clammy, threatening. Scenes seem to repeat themselves, with inscrutable intent rather than by accident.

Vital to this disturbing atmosphere is the Super-8 film on which Jarman shot the work. Super-8 flickers and blebs. It *bleeds*. Colours lustre and thicken within it. Its scratchy textures suggest another set of frames underneath, showing through here and there; other stories trying to pry their ways out. When the stones of Avebury are at last reached – the upright *sarsens* that form the ceremonial henges of the site – they appear almost animate: dark figures shaken into movement by the unsteady camera-hand of the absent filmmaker, and by the natural agitations of the Super-8 stock.

Early in 2014, I began a collaboration with a talented young filmmaker called Adam Scovell. Inspired in part by Jarman's example – and excited by the possibilities of Super-8 as a medium that was also a form – we set out to make a short film about the sunken lanes in South Dorset that are known as 'holloways'.

I had first become fascinated by these strange folds of land some ten years previously, led into them by Geoffrey Household's compelling eve-of-war novel *Rogue Male* (1939), a rural-pursuit novel in the tradition of *Kidnapped* and *The Thirty-Nine Steps*, in which our nameless narrator-hero is tracked through England by a Nazi assassin disguised as a tweed-clad toff. He eventually takes refuge in a steep-sided lane, harrowed down into the sandstone of the region by the passage of centuries of walkers, carts and water. He hollows himself a cave in the sandstone walls of the lane, and there 'goes to ground', seemingly protected from his German aggressor by the old English nature-fortress to which he has retreated (palisades of brambles, a glacis of stone, a barbican of nettles).

Subsequently, I travelled to the holloways of Dorset on the *Rogue Male* trail with my friend Roger Deakin, and we discovered that Household's was only one of several histories – and fictions – of pursuit, risk and concealment to have occurred in and around the holloways. The Chideock Valley, where these particular holloways ran, had long been a niche of south-coast Catholicism, centred on the Catholic chapel at Chideock Manor. During the recusancy, priests and lay-people had been hunted down in the holloways, arrested and barbarically executed for their faith in nearby Dorchester.

I wrote about that journey in a chapter of a book called *The Wild Places* (2007) and tried there to catch at some of the ways in which history appeared to repeat – re-pleat – itself within and around the holloways. It seemed to me then that the holloways possessed a kind of territorial imperative that expressed itself across centuries in patterns of ply and echo, which in turn had affinities with the sedimentary structures of the sandstone bedrock into which the holloways were grooved.

Twist, loop, layer, fold: I wanted to see if it were possible to render some version of such möbian structures in linear narrative prose. But of course, sentences laid end to end, and tasked also with the jobs of narrative, reference and explanation, are ill-suited to enact a rendering of this sort. The holloway was such a compound-complex place that I keenly felt the limits of conventional non-fiction prose, however much I tried to flex and buckle its surfaces, to represent it.

So in the autumn of 2011 I went back to the holloways, this time in the company of a young writer, Dan Richards, and the artist Stanley Donwood. Stanley is perhaps best-known for his long-term work with Radiohead: he has done all the artwork for their albums and shows since the band's formation. He has also, for a decade now, been the artist behind Glastonbury's iconography. He is a quiet, gentle, rather shy person – who has a global cult following. The Dalai Lama wears his T-shirts. People come up to Stanley in the street and ask him to sign their arms or bare chests with a black marker pen, or to sketch one of his famous toothsome teddy-bears onto a patch of flesh. He stopped doing this when he realised that most of these people were going straight to tattoo-parlours, in order to have the marker-pen trace converted into permanent skinwear.

In the course of our days in Dorset, Stanley, Dan and I began to seek and combine other ways of recording the holloway and catching at the ghosts and repetitions that attended it. Dan took double-exposure photographs on pinhole cameras. Stanley sketched. I jotted image-fragments and isolated details, trying to devolve away from the demands of plot and towards the freedoms of pattern. Later that year, Dan returned to the holloway with a composer and sound artist called James Bulley, to record pure acoustics of its spaces and sounds: what filmmakers call 'wildtrack'. Stanley's notebook sketches unfurled, over the months that followed our visit, into scores of images: magnesium-plate etchings of ink drawings; gold-powder holloways, in which each layer of powder was applied separately and consecutively, with tissue-paper; pencil-works showing webs of branches, requiring tens of thousands of individual interfolded pencil-marks; technicolour acrylic holloways with blazing yellow suns at their ends that were simultaneously nuclear-blasts and dream-visions ...

Eventually, we made a small collaborative book called simply *Holloway*, we founded a small press – Quive-Smith Press – and we published it in an edition of 277 copies, typeset with letters that we had fresh-cast from a lump of lead (such that the medium itself could be said to possess a geology), and finally hand-printed on an old press. Stanley's images were folded into a spare text written by Dan and me. I wrote the first half of the book, Dan the second, though our authorships were not indicated, and by that means tried to bring our writing to move outwards either side of an invisible mirror-line. It was a means of re-plying (from the Latin *re-plicare*, to re-fold) one another's words.

It was a consciously (archly) baroque response to a baroque landscape. The baroque, as Deleuze notes, should be understood not as a movement constrained by period, but rather as an operative function, that function being the fold. The baroque, in Leibniz's phrase, 'endlessly produces folds'. It plies, replies and multiplies. For Leibniz – its first great explicator – the baroque was born of geology and nature: visible in 'the caverns and crannies of porous shapes opened in the twists of limestone', there in the form of waves that 'heave, tumble and atomize when they crack along an unfolding line being traced along the expanse of a shoreline', there in a horse's mane in motion, in clouds, in the curls and wisps of colour that move on the surface and in the recessive depths of marble, and in the whorled strata of buckled sedimentary rocks.

Pleat, curl, crease and twist: these are the baroque's modes; perpendiculars, rectilinears and points its anathema. It turns its folds upon one another – re-plying, multi-plying – proliferating them to infinity at either end of the scale, such that scale itself is extinguished along with any notion of inner or outer, for a fold is always folded within a fold. In its investment in infinitely continuous surface, the baroque challenges the very idea of a subject who might preserve either a point of view or a unitary distinction from the environment it inhabits.

*

Three years after travelling to the holloways with Stanley and Dan, I started work with Adam on our short film. It was my surmise, and Adam's certainty, that Super-8 – Adam's preferred stock from his earlier short films, which included work on Alan Garner and M.R. James – was the ideal substance on which to shoot the holloways, given its palimpsestic surface and its shivery rhythms. I wrote a slender text to be spoken quietly as voiceover, drastically sparser than the *Holloway* text, and several further steps away from the narrative prose with which I had begun. I tried to grain it with doublings and reversals, and to excise conjunctions to the degree that could only really be experienced by the listener as pattern, a series of uncanny doublings, or doublings-back. I handwrote the script on a single sheet of paper, and then overdrew it with what became a twisted network of ink-lines connecting text elements that recurred or echoed.

Adam spent three January days filming in Dorset. He took his 1970s Canon camera, and three 3½-minute rolls of Kodak. That was all. No room for error on a nine-minute film. None of the digital luxuries of firing off test-bursts or letting the camera run. I admired his parsimony and control. He lucked out with the weather: hit winter days of white light, rain, water flooding the bellies of the holloways and sun flaring on the water so that the paths ran with mercury.

After he had filmed, Adam edited. On and off for seven months – approaching a month per minute. I admired his patience and commitment. He layered in wildtrack of the holloways, recorded by the artist and composer James Bulley. He underlaid the Super-8 here and there with Stanley Donwood's artwork: spectral pencil underworld to the celluloid upperworld. He began to experiment with ways of giving the screen a lateral mid-level split, from which top and bottom halves then folded equally outwards. He re-spliced image-fragments so that, in their duplicities, they mapped onto repetitions in the text.

At last there was a near-final version. At that point we approached the remarkable musician, composer and poet Richard Skelton to see if he would score the film. To our good fortune he agreed. He wrote original music for it, structured chiasmically so that it rose over several minutes to a quiet pitch, and then fell away from it. So at last the film found its finish. *Homage* to Jarman and the holloways and the shapes of their histories. A layered film about a layered place; a film of folds about a folded place.

The Super-8 had a last surprise for us, though. When Adam viewed his rushes back, embedded in the footage, were several dark forms, humanish in outline, unidentifiable but unmistakable, visible within the shadows of the holloway's verges as a densening of the darkness, or hovering in the leaves of the bushes near the Chideock Martyrs' Chapel. 'What the *hell* is that thing at 2.02?' I emailed Adam. 'I'm glad you can see it too,' he replied. 'My dad thinks I've gone mad ...' Artefacts of the medium or artefacts of the origin? Unclear, for by that point place had bled into its representations beyond easy unmixing.

Two months before we finished the film, I received an email from a journalist and campaigner in Dorset. It concerned the fate of one of Dorset's largest holloways – Dinah's Hollow at Melbury Abbas, which was almost fifteen metres deep at its lowest point, and through which runs a minor C-road. The council had become anxious at the possibility of a dangerous landslip, though no such slip had occurred in living memory. They had employed consultants to assess the situation: the consultants had recommended the effective destruction of Dinah's Hollow.

The recommendations included denuding the holloway sides of trees and vegetation, scalping its banks of hundreds of tons of earth and then binding those banks in heavy-gauge steel mesh and plates, held in place by 'soil nails' punched into the earth in a regular grid, before armouring the lower slopes in hard casing. All of this – carried out in the name of safety – would, conveniently, permit the eventual widening of the road, such that the C13 could become the A350, thereby allowing quicker car travel between Blandford and Shaftesbury.

A campaign was mounted. More than a thousand names were gathered for a petition. Walkers, conservationists, archaeologists, land-scapists and other lovers of the holloways gathered to lobby the council against going through with the ruin of Dinah's Hollow. Like many others, I wrote letters and gave quotations in support of the campaign, arguing that holloways are time-tunnels; habits of a landscape that keep and shape history in unique ways; landscape archives that take centuries to come into being, but that cannot be 'restored' to their complexities once they have been destroyed.

In the face of the campaign, the council paused. They closed the road. Then they reopened the road, controlling vehicular access by means of traffic lights, and narrowing the thoroughfare to reduce the likelihood of a car being engulfed in the event of a dangerous slip. As I write this in July 2015, it remains unclear whether fold, twist, loop and layer will be erased by slice, flatten, encase and widen.

Alexandra Harris (TWELVE)

Flint

Below the ridge of Cocking Down on Midsummer Day I took a flint in each hand and made a tiny shower of sparks. They were visible for an instant in the shade of the steep-sided track: flakes of hot stone, the merest flecks, cold again before they landed in the powdered-milk ruts and puddles of a path not yet dried out from winter. They may not have been enough to light a scrap of tinder, had I had one, and had I known how to strike the flint so that one grain of fire landed, just so, in a char-cloth. But something caught from this mote of light, the first I'd made knowingly from stone, though I grew up under these hills of chalk and flint where the sharp crack and the sulphur on the air were familiar to men and women of every generation here before me.

I walked all morning as the heat grew, out onto the high open pasture, and along the white highroad of the South Downs Way for a short time before dipping down into the woods on the southern slope towards West Dean. The two farmers mending fences on the ridge were the only people I saw in six or seven hours. Was everyone at a midsummer fiesta I was missing? But the sheep were there on the eternally nibbled turf at the top, and the woods were busy with pheasants flapping out from undergrowth in sudden skirmishes. The traveller's joy was shooting out its arms, two at a time, covering hedges so rapidly with its swags of sappy bunting that, when I stood for ten minutes, I think I caught a tendril moving towards the next supportive branch. So the company was various, and more than ever before I enjoyed the company of flints.

I picked them from their little hollows in the path, and tapped – gently at first, the chink of marbles, pétanque balls sidling into each other, and then with conviction. Here was the chink, tap, crack that made human life possible in the beginning by turning cold to warmth. Here was the original alchemy in my hands, the first philospher's stone. Later there was steel on flint: the sound made by serving-girls in the darkness of damp kitchens and the sound made in the watching hour, unless a candle had been left burning. It was the sound, Thomas Hardy noted, that betrayed conspirators in the quiet of night. All over the world, tinderboxes were brought down from mantelpieces and pulled from coat pockets, little curves of steel struck against shards of dark stone, *der feuerstein* in Germany, *pyrolithos* in Greece.

Surrounded by flint in Sussex, I had never thought much about its fieriness. It was not 'firestone' to me, but the material from which churches and houses were made. Here, flints do not live only in tinder-boxes or stove-lighters or guns. They come loose in the paths and you kick them into the verge, where they lodge in grass splashed grey with chalky water. They lie on the surface of ploughed fields as if there's been a sudden rain of sharp-angled rocks, something between a meteor shower and a hailstorm. Many of the downland villages are made from flints like this, gathered from fields, picked and sorted, bedded in lime mortars derived from the chalk in which they have always belonged. Garden walls, barns, cottages, smart houses: all built with flint, some roughly arranged to do the job, some knapped and tessellated with marquetry precision, or with white-bait shoals of gallets swimming round them, or lacy ruffs of gallets (sometimes 'garrets'), invitingly intricate but razor sharp to the touch.

Paul Nash thought of flints as eggs which one might crack open. 'If I broke all the shells of all my wild stones,' he wrote, 'I should find that precious yolk which is like precious stones, the black core of the flint.' He liked to gather little groups of 'wild stones' and believed that he was solving a kind of equation. The flints lay apart from each other, scattered by plough and erosion; he brought them together, and made a new whole. He was on his way to West Dean, perhaps on the very same path as me. I wrote in the margin of Nash's essay once that every builder who makes a straight wall from a pile of nobbly field flints must solve this equation a thousand times over. But there must be power in what Nash says because his images kept coming back to me on the Down, and not just because.

His mystical way of thinking need not be at odds with practical knowledge, so every so often I cracked another egg to find its gleaming yolk. There's no whisking the 'white' of a flint: the rind looks like chalk but is as tough as the silica within. It's not like any other rinds I know: cheese rinds, fruit rinds. You couldn't grate it or peel it off. Silica is slightly translucent, so you look past the still surface to faults and fractures below. Pooled rock: Nash was right, the yolks looked curiously liquid. But then they seemed wilder and larger than rock pools. There's an Anglo-Saxon riddle in which a storm drives the waves of a 'flintgraeg' sea, which brings back for me all the coldest and darkest waters I've known: sheeny, unforgiving, with a little surface transparency and black depths. The breaking-open is known as 'snapping', though the word suggests a brittle and lightweight material, sticks rather than stones. A builder will snap open flint nodules to produce sheeny planes which will form the surface of a wall. They will glitter, especially after rain, and earn their name of 'Sussex diamonds'.

A single cloud appeared in the midsummer blue over Colworth Farm. Nash painted his 'wild stones' so that they look like megaliths on an open plain and simultaneously like the modest, jagged stones they really are, gathered in a grassy dip. Another picture of his, *Event on the Downs*, includes no flints at all, except that the tree-stump in the foreground is oddly close to being a nodule of stone, and the cloud hovering in a clear sky above might be white-rinded silica, flying for a moment like one of the birds he imagined born from flint eggs, and about to plummet back down. Fantastical, yes, but it is fantastic to think a small cloud might weigh many tons, and that stone might turn to fire.

The cloud made a shadow for a moment at the field edge, just where a tiny bird skull lay among a scattering of bony flints. Flints specialise in boniness. You won't find long ones to make a shin or femur but you'll be over-supplied with ball and socket joints, knees and knuckles, ankles and heels. Teeth are plentiful too: dentists' waiting rooms full of giant molars. Henry Moore found flints so suggestive of human bodies that he arranged examples in his studio. He would set them on plinths as found sculptures, sometimes adding plasticine to round out a shoulder or a hip.

Moore was used to making casts in plaster and bronze; the flints he revered as sculptures were also casts, made when silica filled the jelly moulds beneath prehistoric tropical seas. The calcium ooze which, under the pressure of its own weight, would eventually form chalk, was a malleable seabed into which the marine creatures of that ancient ocean of the South Downs burrowed. They formed networks of caverns and tunnels, not unlike a great aquatic rabbit warren, I thought, as I passed the old West Dean warren, which was continuously burrowed from the sixteenth century to the early nineteenth, edged with a high flint bank to keep the rabbits in. On that other scale of time, when there was no-one here to make rabbit-pie or count the years, when this area was underwater, crustaceans nosed their way through the calcium left by the creatures before them. Calcium fell to the floor over millions of years, burying the bodies of sponges and sea urchins. Infinitely slowly, as they decayed, the skeletons of all these creatures released silica into the water and the water crept deep into the burrows. At depth, and at pressure, chemical changes took place so complex that they are not yet understood. Molecule by molecule, precipitating silica replaced chalk. The liquid flint, the not-yet flint, filled the moulds of the seabed paths, and filled hollows within the round pincushion bodies of dead sea-urchins. Was it like filling in a tooth: dark liquid pooling and hardening in a calcium cave?

Emerging from woods into open sunlight was something like coming up from underwater, though my path was all downhill. The lane zig-zagged on the slope into Warren Hanger. A single house in the crook of the bend was the first building I'd passed since the farm on the ridge, and it was flint of course, with brick quoins. I used to think of flint and chalk as black and white. That's what you see in the iconic cross-section of the Downs at Beachy Head: white cliffs studded with a dark grey that passes, in bright sun, for black; the lumps of coal that are the snowman's eyes. But then, bizarrely late, I realised that flint was all around me and was grey: not just grey but all imaginable greys, and some browns, and whites. It was the library and the church and the wall around the car-park and the terraced houses with gardens I particularly loved. Flint walls have a distinct effect on the colour of hollyhocks, and all the flowers that thrive on chalk. Pinks and blues are lit up against the grey, as in the light before a thunderstorm.

It only takes a morning's looking, on the path from Cocking Hill, to see that black and white is rare. The colour depends partly on the biography of each stone – how often in the ice-ages it was frozen and thawed, whether it's been ploughed and broken. Near the surface, flints lead disrupted lives and are so fractured inside that they break unpredictably and unevenly. You can snap them open to give a gleaming face, but you can't work precisely with them: you can't knap them into a straight-edged square or into the blade of an axe.

For workable flint you have to look deep below ground, and the deeper you go the purer the stone, right down to the lowest band, 'the floor', the most prized flint of all. Neolithic men and women, whose lives depended on the sharpness of the arrows and knives they made, knew this very well, opened the flanks of the hillsides and burrowed in. The Downs are pitted with flint mines which show themselves now, mostly, as sunken thickets. Skirting brambles, you'll realise there are trees among the scrub, and that you're at eye-level with their crowns. Below their roots, shafts reach down through white to seams of black. Far underground there really is a world of nearly-black and nearly-white, though no light of course to see it.

I was in the shade of another woodland path, the last part of the drop towards the village and the River Lavant in the valley. Where sections of the wood had been coppiced, the sun was filtering through onto fleshy young hazel leaves, and the stones were glinting on the path where their facets caught the light. Coming out at the A286, there was the usual staggering, blinking moment of arrival, the steadying of sea-legs which have been used to the dipping, curving, downhill paths, the uncertain throbbing in a body which has got up a swinging momentum of its own. Here was a scrap of pavement and two-way traffic and, next to a smartly gabled estate house with its flint walls shining in the sun, a bus-stop sign tied to a streetlamp, its timetable a beacon to the car-less.

Tap-tap with the flints in my pockets. There it is again: the crack in the night made by an unseen figure with a tinderbox, fumbling with flint and hemp in cold hands. The scratch of my grandmother's lighter kept on the stove-top, followed by the tamed roar of the gas. She lived at the foot of Cissbury, below some of the very oldest mines. She was too old to go up the hill and see them, though I don't think she minded much – flint being less a matter of history than the making of dinner.

Skilled flintworkers assess the quality of nodules by looking, weighing and listening. They tap with hammers, and the sound rings through the stone in ways which form a map of its construction. The purest silica rings like a bell, sound travelling through the dense-packed molecules. A fine flint is a 'ringer'. Where the structure is irregular, the sound is dull and flat, its quality lost in the cracks. Knappers listen for the right place to strike the stone: a hollow ring at the saddle, high and sharp at the dense compression points. Tap-tap and the rapid strike: again and again through all the hours and days for the men who made flintlocks by the thousand, and for those who built in the Downs.

The number 60 took me back to Chichester, winding out from between the hills to the coastal plain, from field-flint villages to the cobble-flint walls that appear more and more as you near the sea. A wall of cobbles laid in random formation is a domestic beach, the shingle hung vertically in front of you. If I could choose, I'd lay my cobbles in courses – not like a beach but with the smiling look of a holiday villa, each row underlined with emphatic bird's-beak pointing. The round stones have a way of sitting in their lines as on a cross-stich sampler, or in a well-tended allotment. The character of beach cobbles and field flints is different altogether: cobbles have been rubbed and rounded by two tides a day. Chatter-marks, their cracks are called. Their bony protrusions have been chipped off and sharp edges smoothed away. The chalk which once held them has fallen, powdered, washed away, leaving the flints to roll over each other, the infinite bag of marbles that chatters on.

Cobbles, or 'pitchers', wear down eventually if they spend their lives this way. But flints and time give each a run for their money. A flint wall may weather, but it's the mortar and not the stone that wears. The city walls I walk beside, to and from my father's house, have been rebuilt many times: the mortars changing, the stones coursed then random then coursed again. But as for this or that flint, I can't tell whether it was worked last year or by a Romano-British builder two millennia ago. Flint knappers who hone their skills by making arrows are asked to store their productions carefully. A well-made modern arrow is indistinguishable from one made when the tumps on Cocking Down were newly raised.

I put two flints from Cocking on my desk, though I can't remember whether they're the ones that made the first spark, or were picked from the maize husks on the ridge, or from the path in the woods or the verge by the bus-stop. They'll be the longest-lasting objects in this house. Like the gold crosses the Anglo-Saxons forcibly bent in half, they might be buried but they'll still be there.

Are there flint people and granite people and gritstone people, their minds and bodies tuned to the kinds of world those materials make? I remember my amazed recognition when I first went to Norfolk and found it was made of flint. I'd like to visit the flint places of the world, and I wonder how far any of them might feel like home. In the deserts of Jordan, where flints lie thickly strewn over the dry ground, the architect Ammar Khammash recorded the sound of his car-tyres crunching over this 'continuous keyboard'. I'd like to hear that: in a place which I imagine to be as foreign to me as anywhere on earth, the familiar sound of flints.

I'm looking now at the shapes made on my geological map of Britain by the Cretaceous bands which indicate areas of chalk and flint. The great sidelong V is marked in green, its upper arm reaching up from the Chilterns to Norfolk, its lower arm the North and South Downs, its middle eroded to the boggy hollow of London Clay. I'll get French and Belgian and German maps to follow where the arms go next. And a Middle Eastern one. I might even cut out the flint places so that I can see the shape of them more clearly. Yes, I like the thought of my flint map, and the archipelago of flint-grey islands it will show.

David Lea (TWELVE)

Marvels of the Night

The Study Site

The Harringay ladder is a grid of 19 Victorian streets, bounded on the south by Finsbury Park, in the east by Green Lanes, in the west by Wightman Road and in the north by Turnpike Lane. Despite these rather bucolic street names, the area is resolutely urban. The ladder's eastern stile, Green Lanes, is characterised by Turkish restaurants and greengrocers, numerous betting shops and hardware stores, one of Britain's first 'drive-thru' McDonald's and a permanent though often gridlocked flow of traffic along what is one of London's principal north–south routes. On the east side of Green Lanes sits the famous Harringay Arena, built as an ice hockey stadium during a short-lived British enthusiasm for the sport, and subsequently a ballroom, concert hall and much else besides, before being demolished to make way for a somewhat uninspiring retail park. In partial contrast, Wightman Road has very few commercial premises, but a number of places of worship: a Greek Orthodox Church, a Mosque, a Roman Catholic Church, an evangelical church and an unpredictable array of house synagogues and casual churches. In effect, it's a Medieval fresco turned on its side: Heaven, or several versions of it sit on the left, and several versions of Hell sit on the right. I've seen the area described in the press as 'unloved', but in fact it inspires in its residents, drawn from every tribe on earth, a deeply tribal loyalty.

Two intriguing features cut through it. The New River, which is neither new nor a river being in fact a seventeenth-century aqueduct dug to provide fresh water to East London, enters at the north-east corner of the ladder, and meanders through the parallel streets under a series of low bridges before exiting into Finsbury Park and the Stoke Newington reservoirs. The pedestrian Harringay Passage runs through the middle of the ladder, and, on school-day mornings, sees a traffic jam of children on bikes and scooters, their parents on foot and bicycle and their younger siblings in buggies making their way to the area's two schools in a sort of benign parody of the motorised jam taking place a few yards to its east. It's not, on the face of it, a promising site for the study of wildlife. But, in a small and somewhat scruffy garden on one of the ladder's rungs, for the last five years I've been collecting moths, or, at least, collecting their names, occasionally their photographs, and even more occasionally drawing or painting them. For these marvels of the night, the urban fringe is pure wilderness, patrolled both day and night by ferocious predators. It's also a land of milk and honey, given the propensity of some residents to fill their gardens with exotic plants from every continent, and the propensity of others to allow their gardens to run riot with vigorous natives.

SOME MARVELS OF THE NIGHT

Gypsy Moth – Welcome Back

A regular visitor to the garden in late July and August, the Gypsy Moth has a distinctive appearance, and an interesting history and ecology. The males are large, dark-brown moths with magnificent feathered antennae. Male Gypsy Moths will fly many hundreds of miles in search of females, using those magnificent antennae to detect the females' pheromones. In contrast, the female, slightly larger than the male, largely white in colour, although resplendently winged and quite capable of flight, seldom moves more than a few metres from the site of her emergence. Until the middle of the nineteenth century there was an apparently stable but geographically constrained breeding population of Gypsy Moth in the fenlands of East Anglia. A combination of habitat destruction and over-collection led to the extinction of this population, and throughout most of the twentieth century the only records of the species in Britain, mainly along the south coast, were of far flying males searching, hopelessly, for their sedentary mates.

Then, towards the end of the last century, a breeding population reappeared, apparently centred on Epping Forest to the north-east of London. No-one knows for certain how they got there. Typically, the species is dispersed, as a tiny caterpillar, by wind, a process that doesn't work well over water due to the lack of thermal currents. It seems likely that they arrived, in egg form, as stowaways, plastered to the undercarriage of a vehicle crossing the English Channel then heading north, or across the North Sea and then heading south. The moth's reappearance initially caused alarm – it is regarded as a significant pest of forestry in continental Europe and in America – but alarm seems to have largely subsided. Whatever the story behind its reappearance, to judge from the regularity and number of male Gypsy Moth in my light trap, the species is now well-established in its new/old home. A handsome, striking and welcome re-addition to England's night skies.

Jersey Tiger – Free at Last

The forewings – pale cream, verging-on-white background with dark-chocolate brown-verging-on-black stripes across it in an asymmetrical, but as far as I've ever seen, invariant pattern. The hindwings – a vivid orange tending towards scarlet, peppered with a few dark spots. When at rest, the Jersey Tiger has a sober, rather austere appearance. When it flies though, and it sometimes does so in daylight, it explodes into colour, and I'm put in mind of a Puritan cleric hoicking up his drab outer-garments to break into a run and revealing surprisingly flamboyant underwear. They're instantly visible against the pale brown walls of the moth trap, sometimes in large numbers, but when they fly from it, usually to a small Silver Birch at the edge of the garden, the effectiveness of stripes as camouflage becomes clear. Although I see exactly where they land, I can hardly ever pick them out among the leaves. They are, I suppose, having their cake and eating it. Their primary strategy is camouflage, remaining invisible to daytime predators, but if that fails, they can become exuberantly colourful, startling the predator for long enough to make their escape.

Across most of Britain, Jersey Tiger is a rare moth. Most records are of vagrants, though there are small breeding populations in the South-West, and as the name suggests it is abundant on the Channel Islands. But in the capital, in the 1980s and initially in South London, Jersey Tigers began appearing with a regularity that suggested a growing breeding population. Where had they come from? How did they get here? As with Gypsy Moth, the story is probably unknowable. It's possible that a vagrant from the continent or an exile from one of the English colonies became a nucleus for a new population in the gardens of suburban London. It seems more likely though that one or several moths escaped or were released from a captive population somewhere to the south of the Thames and have since spread gradually across the city.

Silver Y – A Doomed Invader

Small and dark-complexioned, its forewings marked with a comic sans lower case letter 'y' in shocking white, this doughty flyer of a moth irrupts every summer from its winter quarters in southern Europe and North Africa, travelling through the continent into Britain as far north as the Northern Isles. Doughty flyer though it may be, its constitution and ecology mean that it cannot easily survive the cold winters it finds here. Like its more familiar diurnal second cousin Painted Lady, Silver Y will die, sometimes in large numbers, in the lands it sought to colonise. Whenever I see this lovely and courageous little moth, I can't help thinking about Napoleon's *Grande Armée* in Russia in 1812, or H.G. Wells's Martian invaders in *The War of the Worlds*, and about how the apparently invincible can be brought low by the pure and simple facts of life.

Tree-lichen Beauty – Voortrekker

It is, I think, about ten years since a friend sent me a photograph of a strange moth he'd seen on the window of his sixth-floor North London flat. We concluded that this little geometrid, similar to Garden Beauty but dark-green where it should be white and with a pale-green collar, was Tree-lichen Beauty, at that time a rare vagrant according to the available literature. Ten years later I see them frequently, and it's become clear that what we'd seen was not a vagrant, but an early participant in a thoroughly benign and largely unnoticed colonisation, analogous to the far more noticed range expansions of Collared Dove in the middle of the last century and Little Egret in the early years of this one. The species is now well established throughout the Thames watershed, the river and its banks, having apparently been the Tree-lichen Beauty's chosen point of entry.

Box Tree Moth – Too New for the Book

A fairly large moth, white with a black border interrupted by a scribbled white comma, or all dark, a sort of shimmering deep purple apart from that same scribbled white comma, making it clear that it's the same species (at first I assume I'm looking at sexual dimorphism, but it transpires there are two colour schemes for this moth, which seem to happily coexist). I'm mystified. Such a large, striking and seemingly common insect (there are six of them in the light trap) ought to be in 'The Book', but it isn't. The internet provides the answer, by means of a local residents' chat-site, and my small, occasionally scruffy garden is being sucked into the maelstrom of a moral panic. This is Box Tree Moth, the scourge of topiarists, whose larvae can entirely strip a Box of leaves in a matter of days. A native of East Asia, Box Tree Moth was first recorded in Britain in 2008, but a couple of 'What the Hell Is This?' records (it isn't in 'The Book'!) probably push the date of its arrival back a year at least. It's almost certain that it arrived in Europe an accidental hitchhiker, as egg or caterpillar, on imported Box plants, and then like Rip Van Winkle, Woody Allen's *Sleeper*, the paradigmatic victim of a stag party prank or Superman sent in sudden and unexpected exile from his native Krypton, awoke to find itself in a new continent, a new place, a new world. Its voracious caterpillars are variously unpalatable, toxic and invisible to the impressive array of Europe's moth predators, parasites and parasitoids. It seems a bit unfair to describe the species as invasive, given its complete lack of agency in the matter of its invasion, but many people, not all of them topiarists, have adopted a policy of Search and Destroy. An internet acquaintance of mine, a gardener by trade, adopts a more casual approach – 'Box is boring. Moths are interesting. Get over it.'

Two Harringay Hawks: Heroes Just for One Day

Looking through the window at the moth trap in the just-after-dawn sun I see what at first seems to be a group of small moths, five of them perhaps, at rest on the sidewall in an oddly symmetrical star-like pattern. As I approach more closely, this strange sight becomes a stranger one – a single moth in various shades of grey, white and brown which somehow seems to have its wings attached back to front. This is Poplar Hawkmoth, which, when perched, holds its hindwings so far forward that they stick out in front of it from underneath the forewings. It takes a moment or two, and an exercise in mental topology, to resolve the resulting unmothlike silhouette into something more conventional.

The Hawkmoths specialise in 'weird'. The two Elephants, with their pinks, purples and yellows, seem to have been coloured in by a precocious toddler as an open challenge to those who think of moths as small, brown and boring. In contrast, the Bee Hawkmoths dispense with wing colouration altogether and resemble a child's drawing of a hornet. The huge Death's Head Hawkmoth is decorated with a perfect image of a human skull, embossed in gold, and the Hummingbird Hawkmoth is occasionally mistaken for its avian namesake as it hovers in front of flowers, sipping nectar with its impressively long proboscis.

The other member of the family to visit the garden, in addition to Poplar, is the Lime Hawkmoth, a scale model of a V-wing fighter aircraft painted by a meticulous but imaginative hobbyist in the greens and browns of military camouflage. If this distinctive colouration is camouflage rather than display, (although I guess in fact it's both), then it only needs it for the shortest time. In common with several other Hawks, including the Poplar, the Lime has no functional mouth parts and as an adult imago does not feed. Like many of natural selection's most beautiful and moving works of art these marvels of the night exist for one purpose only: to reproduce.

Gail McNeillie (SIX)

Wake-Up Call

Alice Oswald (SIX)

Two Voices

I own the dawn the cockerel claims. The light
Still loiters with intent to take the night.
Wind steals through woods. The democratic dew
Gives equal weight to everything. A few
Blank seconds and he starts again. He yawns
And voice possesses him. I own all dawns.
I stand on dignity he shouts out, shut
In his dark hovel, stooping on a strut.
More pained impatient crazed each time he crows
He has to wrench his larynx, curl his claws
To let that shout surge through him. Glancing out
I notice nothing answers except light.
Whose answer makes the earth's hairs stand on end
And shadows fall full length without a sound.

Pause

What is the word for wordless, when the ground
Bursts into crickets? There's a cracking sound
Like speaking speeded up. A skeleton
Crawls across leaves, still in its cramped position.
One minute stooping on a bending blade
Rubbing its painful elbows, next minute made
Of pinged elastic, flying hypertense,
Speaking in several languages at once.
Not like a mouth might speak, more like two hands
Make whispered contact through their finger-ends,
Like light itself which absent-mindedly
Brushes the grass and speaks by letting be,
But when you duck down suddenly and stare
Into the startled stems, there's nothing there.

Pause

Mark Cocker (TEN)

Blackwater: Commonplace Things

Bird

There are precious few instances when modern farming seems at peace with nature, but this moment by the beet field under the winter sun was glorious. The constituent parts were entirely prosaic. There was a huge bright-red harvester going back and forth along the beet rows by Blackwater. This machine aligned its operations with a John Deere tractor and trailer that intermittently dumped the beet on an ever-larger sugar mountain by the field edge.

Enveloping all the agricultural action was a ceaseless flow of about five hundred black-headed gulls. Bird for bird, the species is a modest beast. In winter the creature looks glinting white against the dank land, but in detail the pearl-grey wings bear a pale blade on their leading edge and each fan is obliquely angled at its midpoint like a scimitar. In concert these wings create an aura of flashing motion around the bird's pink bill and dangled red legs. In unison a flock of five hundred produced a shining river of movement that washed over and crazed the sculptural outline of man's machines in a steady flow of grey and silver.

Together the birds and humans enfolded their shared action in audible dissonance. The grind of gears and engine noise and then all that vile swede-sour sweetness tumbling heavily onto the steel plate of the trailer floor all cut across the wild music of the birds' rolling 'craa' notes. Yet the entire vision itself seemed nicely unified. There was even a distinct visual rhyme between the perpetual wheel of the birds and the toothed belt that relentlessly dug the beet out the soil, then uplifted the crop to a holding bin on the harvester's back. Adorning the scene were a few filigree details: a scatter of pied wagtails that swirled up and around the larger event in airy lines, a marsh harrier twisting overhead against the burning sun, and then the surrounding stoical, bare, dark oaks that turned this field into a moment of English theatre.

Bush

For several years now in my wooded fen called Blackwater I've been favouring a bramble patch by clipping out all competitors and creating space for the outlying shoots. It has slowly expanded but this spring it has grown with fresh confidence, sending out curving red-taloned arms more than eight feet into the sky. It is fascinating to see how, after a period of strong winds, the patch has become a casualty of its own formidable armoury. Scores of new leaves are covered in self-inflicted tears where they have been battered against the spines on other parts of the bush.

Yet July brambles mingle a pale-pink generosity with all this aggression. The flower season may be past its best and from the middle of each withered old bloom emerges the knobbly green tonsure of a fresh berry, complete with its hair-line of dead stamens, but there is sweetness still in my bramble to satisfy a million insects. In an hour's search I found so many flies I couldn't name I finally understood how, after forty years of observations, I know next to nothing about British nature.

There was consolation in the dazzle of commas or red admirals and in the commuter traffic of vestal cuckoo, garden and common carder bumblebees. Even just the warmth of the leaves seemed a lure for the wonderfully named marmalade hoverflies and a stoop-backed relative with bug eyes called *Volucella bombylans.*

Then my bramble patch repaid my loving care with a rarer gift. The red-tipped clearwing is one of a strange and highly localised group of moths whose appearance mimics various species of stinging insects. I've seen clearwings on just five occasions ever and the hornet clearwing looks so like its namesake it is uncanny. Luxuriating in this perpetual traffic of life, and immersed in the songs of wrens or whitethroats and the base gravel notes of crows, I began to see how this great breast of thorn with its pastel-toned orbit of flower and nectar, is an entire world unto itself – intricate, evolving and beautiful.

Fly

One cannot call it autumn, perhaps, but there is a moment in early August when the year begins its next metamorphosis. Summer seems to sclerotise and in the breeze the leaves begin to sound brittle; you notice that the flowers are steadily more magenta than yellow, and then there are suddenly the dragonflies. This remarkable increase among our largest insects is a definite waymarker of seasonal change. On the approach to Blackwater there are dozens of them, mainly common darters, brown and migrant hawkers, luxuriating in a tunnel of hot air cut through the vegetation by the track.

Yet the highlight was a southern hawker in the wood by the gate. Unlike the other species, this one often cleaves to the edge of woodland. This male hawker patrolled a longitudinal tunnel of shadow above a dyke but he mainly kept to the cave mouth – so to speak – darting from out the gloom into the wider shoals of light, up the bank and across the track where I stood to watch. The lattice pattern of sunshine falling through the poplar leaves overhead meant that the acid-green stripes in his abdomen glowed momentarily golden as he explored the shoreline to his patch.

His powers of flight have a heritage spanning more than two hundred million years and he arced through three planes of space so smoothly that he could turned faster than the human eye could follow. Binoculars were useless. I saw the insect less as a whole organism, and more as an occasional blur, a momentary pattern, a glittering inference. It was as if we inhabited different atmospheres. Where I wallowed in air, he passed through something finer and lighter. Yet if reminiscent of anything, his twisting fish-like motion back and forth, suggested something sub-aquatic and predatory. When he interspersed those deft quick turns with a slower split-second ellipse there was in that curving moment, before he vanished back into his cave, the unmistakable image of a shark.

Snake

One thing I've learnt from my time at Blackwater is that managing habitat for wildlife is not so much a plan implemented as a prayer offered. And this prayer cost much sweat. For weeks I heaved sodden vegetation, forkful by forkful and barrow-load by barrow-load, onto what's known in our household as 'Slub Mountain'. It's a mound of nutrient-rich waste that had previously been hauled out the dyke or cut from the reed and piled up to rot slowly down. At times it stood ten feet tall but this has gradually collapsed to a heap that is chest high. It's a paradise for those small, dark, ground-scuttling arachnids called wolf spiders. Occasionally a red admiral rests on its sunny slopes, but for long months there was not the faintest trace of its intended occupant.

Last week I glanced as usual in its direction and there, coiled on the crown, was the answer to a slow prayer. I love the way grass snakes move: that effortless pouring forward in sinuous if diminishing lines. That unhurried going away to nothing but the tail tip: it feels less like a willed motion as an involuntary process. This one was sucked steadily into the ground like a brief gutter of dark water emptied by force of gravity. I go back now to repeat the encounter. Sometimes she hardly leaves until I could touch her. Then I found her shed skin shining on the top.

The dorsal scales are oval and diaphanous and look like the popped cells in bubble wrap. The belly scales feel like overlapping pieces of old dried sticky tape that have lost adhesion. Through the mysterious act of renewal (technically called ecdysis) a new snake emerges head-first from its old self. I am left only with a ghost, but I touch the slender tube, rustling now like a bit of old plastic bag, and think of the ground it slithered over, the water it breasted and the male snake that once coiled around. I reflect on the swelling womb that once lay within, nourished by the sunlight, that caused her to answer my prayer and mount that soft-soiled hill to breed.

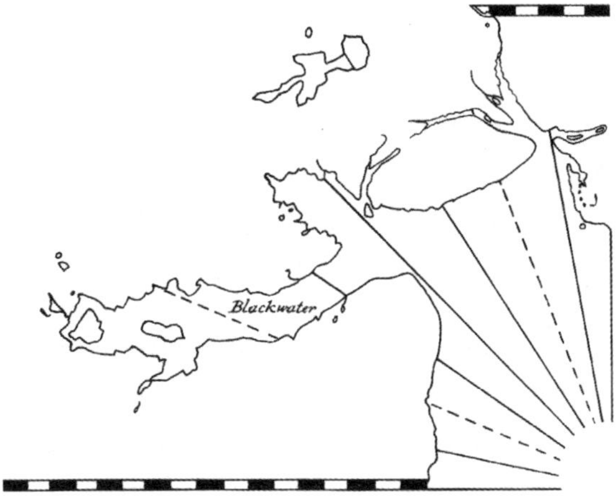

Geoffrey Hill (EIGHT)

Expostulations on the Volcano 47

From lead to mercury the sky; bare trees,
Refined archaic leaf-patterns of slate
Against the sky-tone, veins to arteries:
Mid-November, correctile, intricate,

Under strange genial suns; at least two.
Mute acoustics of light to bring aligned.
Why should Rutland Water, unsung, not glow;
Undulant midland shires, the many-faned?

They have been too long reflective, I grant,
In a bent mirror of longing not theirs
At all; concave to convex or mere slant;
Staggering hermeneutics of arrears,

Barely wrought to fixed legacy. Finish
So; finish with this or that absurd grief
In resolution; fields under varnish
Of new-sliced red earth held cuttingly stiff.

Shall call this *Bacchanal for over-pre-*
pared Piano: nothing original;
Girt evanescent England, its display,
Whichever way I play it, not final.

John Brannigan (ELEVEN)

Leaves

In every village I drove through there was at least one house which flew either the Union Jack or the St George's Cross from a window, or a fence, or sometimes even a flagstaff. The flags were clean, bright and new, unlike the faded hand-me-downs I was used to seeing in the streets of Belfast. Here, in the villages of South Derbyshire, the furthest you could get from the sea in England, patriotic feelings were evidently fresh. The reason was clear: prominent beside the flags were the simple injunctions, often hand-printed, 'Vote Leave,' or sometimes just 'Leave.'

At the roadsigns which marked the end of each village, I could not help feeling that I was somehow, as a passing visitor, also the subject of these injunctions. The villages of England were closing in as well as closing up, and witnessing this withering process was perhaps as undignified as it was unwelcome. In every village I passed, there was a High Street with no shops, a marketplace with no market, an out-of-place building with decorative stonework which professed its former life as post office, bank or town hall. I was not the only one leaving the villages behind, and the dazzling whiteness of the flags seemed defiant, almost sullenly so.

I had come to Calke Abbey to see the Old Man of Calke, an oak tree over one thousand years old that stands in the grounds of an estate preserved by the National Trust as an 'unstately home'. The estate is described as 'overgrown' and 'little restored', kept almost on the cusp of ruin, except of course for the shop, the restaurant, the car park and the neatly signed trails and walks. You could picnic among the ferns and willowherb, amidst the peeling paint and grass tufts of the stables; dining out in an England caught somewhere between splendour and ruin. The new leaves sprouting from the Old Man of Calke seemed also like defiance, a sign of 'carrying on', that famous English phrase which means both stoicism and misbehaviour.

The Old Man of Calke is not marked out or signalled with any of the usual information boards. It is fenced off, with a brass plaque attached to the fence which informs the visitor about when it was given its name, in 2004, but nothing of its longevity or history. It had stood unnamed and, it seems, unremarked, for over a millennium, until a woodland walk was pathed around its trunk, although it had perhaps served to mark the boundary between the woods which had once been home to fallow deer and the tall grasses of the grazing field beyond. As I stood to contemplate its twisted shapes and extraordinary texture, a man and woman came by, pausing only for a moment. They were perhaps too eager not to disturb me, but perhaps also embarrassed into regarding the tree by my attention to it. 'It is the Old Man of Calke,' the woman said quietly to her companion. 'Hmmm. Amazing it's still there,' he replied. They could move on now, it seemed, reverence for the antiquity of the tree duly observed.

I wondered if my own attention to the oak was not also dutiful, a ritual of contemplation reserved for a fenced and plaqued 'feature'. I had not stopped and gazed at another stout and ancient oak barely twenty metres away, nor at what looked like an equally formidable sweet chestnut some ten metres away. Indeed, I did not leave the designated paths. In the distance was the sound of children venturing further into the woods than I. They may have discovered hidden arboreal treasures in the depths of the woods more deserving of awe and wonder

– oaks with hollow trunks large enough to conceal a platoon, yews with sagging boughs capacious enough to shelter a village, beeches tall enough to reach into the clouds.

Perhaps the man was right to wonder at the persistence of the oak, when one thought of all the roof timbers, ship hulls and kitchen tables it might have become, were it not for the eccentric hoarding of woodland and wildlife which ran like a curse through the Harpur-Crewe family who owned the estate for four centuries. The Old Man of Calke did not strike me for its solidity, its 'thereness', but for its image of violence and change. It was certainly impressively wide with a girth of over ten metres, but it had lost its height, the trunk exposed to the sky above. It offered little shelter, as the prodigious growth of ferns, brambles and nettles around its base attested. The trunk looked as if it had been burst open by a bomb. It was hollow at its core. You could see right through its middle to the field on the other side, and, forming this hollow centre, it looked as if it was not one tree, but several trying to grow through each other. One tree was splitting another open, only itself to be burst asunder in its turn. If the oak told a story of the past, as so many of Britain's oldest oaks are supposed to do, this oak told not of permanency, but of violent change erupting from its core.

This oak could surely not have prompted Edmund Burke's image of the English aristocracy, as 'the great Oaks that shade a Country'. Burke was calling upon the Duke of Richmond, who was as shy of the public responsibilities of nobility as the Harpur-Crewes, to be such a 'great Oak'. In Calke, however, it was the very reclusive inclinations of the estate owners to preserve the woodland as a wilderness, untrammelled of civic demands, which provided the conditions in which the great oaks survived.

'Gnarled' is the word most commonly used to describe the carbuncled, moulding, knotted bark of the oak, but good as it is, it is short of the mark. Neither a photograph nor painting would do any better. This is not the gently wrinkled skin of the beech tree, nor the spiralling latticework bodice of the sweet chestnut. One would need to sculpt it in clay to try to understand its crusted folds and twists, its scarred and fissured hide; the oak is a dictionary of textures and colours, as it is an encyclopaedia of wildlife. Its prolonged, dramatic passage towards death, its staging of all the colours and tortured limbs of death, gave life to so many woodland inhabitants. There were cobwebs on this oak which looked as if they might have their own plausible claims to antiquity. And yet, as I turned to walk on, I had to duck under its burgeoning branches of clustered young leaves.

This was the country which Virginia Woolf called 'the very heart of England' in her last novel, *Between the Acts*. Woolf sought to capture the sense of an island about to be cut off from Europe, and chose to set her decaying country house in unspecified inland recesses far from the wartime dangers of the coast. This inner England was the home of its ancient woodlands, with the oak at its symbolic core. 'The English have a loving but proprietorial relationship with the oak,' wrote Richard Mabey in *Flora Britannica*. Oaks marked boundaries, formed focal points for crop-blessing rituals, and became icons of tradition and continuity on aristocratic estates. Carved depictions of oak leaves in English churches represented a survival of druidic practices in Christian symbolism. My thoughts of inner England were interrupted, however, at Mere Pond, by a blackheaded gull as it perched on a branch that arched over the still water. It was perfectly framed in the middle of the pond, the gull and its perch mirrored together below. It looked at home here, an inland bird which could not help remind one of its seagull relations, as if no part of England, however far from the coast, was truly remote from the sea.

Yet insularity had a meaning in Calke Abbey that was not perhaps so easy to appreciate by the coast. After a succession of reclusive owners had gradually receded into the darkest and most meagrely furnished rooms of the estate, closing up and filling rooms with their voluminous collection of fossils, rocks and stuffed birds, finally the house itself had to be arrested in time. The house and grounds were handed over to the government and the National Trust in 1984, in lieu of mounting capital gains tax bills. Since the nineteenth century, the house had been declining, unable to maintain the lifestyle it was built to support. The

National Trust made a controversial decision, that it would preserve the house and park in its found state of arrested decay. In heritage terms, this was experimental. To restore a mansion to grandeur is a difficult and expensive business, but it is even more difficult to suspend the process of decay and preserve that suspended process for all to see.

Calke Abbey tells a story of England in decline, of a particular moment in the early 1980s when living in decay ran its full course, and decay was now to be suspended and made the object of wonder. This was heritage England, the great and fading past of which was newly lamented in television dramas of the 'big house', in the famous 'Merchant Ivory' genre of films and in a raft of government measures to support the heritage industry. Calke Abbey was at the centre of this new surge of support. Edwina Currie, newly elected as the MP for South Derbyshire, made the case in the House of Commons in 1983 for the funding to acquire the house and grounds for the National Trust. It was not, she argued, 'a great collection of Italian works of art', but 'so quintessentially English, so unusual, so complete' that there was 'nothing quite like it'. Changing tack, she claimed that the acquisition would provide 'a centre of new employment in an area which has no new industries'.

Tourism would fill the gap left by manufacturing; service industries would replace … well, service. In the courtyard of the stables, a tall stout man walked over the grassy gravel bent in conversation with his daughter, her hand invisible within his hand. 'Would I have been a servant?' I heard her ask. 'Oh no, precious,' came his reply, an equable Yorkshire voice, 'probably you might have been a governess or something like that.'

The damp-scarred ceilings, flaking plasterwork, rusty kitchenware and moulding woodwork formed the habitat of the last descendent of the Harpur-Crewe family. It was difficult to feel sympathy for him. Calke Abbey is famous for the tunnels and ha-has by which servants were made to enter and exit the estate so as not to be seen, as indeed servants were required to turn and look away whenever their master entered the room. Successive members of the family were devoted to natural history, and the specimens of geology and taxidermised birds surrounded their living spaces and accumulated throughout the house. There were display cases devoted to game birds, birds of prey, woodland birds, and sea birds. There was no blackheaded gull among its specimens that I could see.

The library intimated the interests of the family: it was, as 'the foolish, flattering lady' in Woolf's *Between the Acts* says, 'the heart of the house'. There was hardly any fiction, and literary writing was confined mainly to Tennyson, Hannah More, Herbert's poems; there was a Dickens novel, a three-volume copy of *Rob Roy*, and Queen Victoria's *Leaves from the Journal of Our Life in the Highlands.* Natural history dominated: Gould's *Birds of Britain*, Lowe's *British Grasses*, Lloyd's *Natural History*, Eagle Clarke's *Studies in Bird Migration* and Lyell's *Antiquity of Man*. Local and regional studies were plentiful too: Harvie-Brown's *A Fauna of the Moray Basin*, Oswald Mosley and Edwin Brown's *The Natural History of Tutbury* and Carr's *Stranger in Ireland*. There was a whole room for the donated library of Egyptologist John Gardner Wilkinson. There were anomalous forays into history and politics in evidence – Eyre's *Military Operations in Cabul* and Kaye's *History of the War in Afghanistan* stood out beside the Tennyson and Hannah More – but politics do not suit the recluse. Stanley's *In Darkest Africa* and tales of expeditions in the Atlantic and Arctic perhaps spoke of armchair fantasies of savouring the natural wonders of other parts of the world beyond Derbyshire. 'What remedy was there … in books?' ponders Isa in Woolf's novel. At its height the estate covered vast swathes of Derbyshire, Leicestershire and Staffordshire, and it is said that you could walk the fifteen miles from Calke to Derby without leaving Harpur-Crewe land. They were known as good landlords – interested in social and agricultural improvements, providing good housing and education – but the tunnels tell a different story.

As one navigates the lands and villages surrounding Calke Abbey, some of the placenames make it difficult not to feel as if inside a children's book, an insular land of the imagination: Wicket Nook, Sharp's Bottom, Broomy Furlong, Badger Wood, Coton in the Elms – this last village nearest to the place officially designated by the Ordnance Survey as the furthest point in Great Britain from the sea. Woolf's characters are peculiarly, almost childishly confused about their distance from the sea, wondering if it is one hundred or one hundred and fifty miles away, 'as if the land went on for ever and ever'. It is seventy miles from this part of South Derbyshire to the sea in three directions, to Flintshire in the north-west, to Gloucestershire in the south-west and to the 'Parts of Holland' of The Wash, to the eastern shores, where over three quarters of the electorate voted 'Leave'. I followed the trail of this 'Leave' vote from England's insular middle, eastwards to its porous Lincolnshire Fenlands, to Boston and its shores.

This flat land was certainly not little England, nor inner England. 'I have never been in any corner of this country that felt more remote,' wrote J.B. Priestley in *English Journey*. Its lands were wide open to the sky and the wind. It was hard to find the sea at first, but there was an unmistakeable band of coastal light on the horizon. More flags began to appear as I approached Boston. In the aftermath of the referendum, Boston was announced as the town in Britain which had voted most strongly in favour of leaving the EU Journalists flocked to Boston to decipher the meaning of 'Brexit'. Yet this was no hidden, introverted England, like the one stashed away in the moulding rooms and woodlands of Calke Abbey. Boston was a European town. It had been the second biggest port, next only to London, in the thirteenth century, and one of the few ports on the east shores of England to trade in the Hanseatic League, surely a coastal precursor of the European Union. The Hansa Cog, that most versatile of medieval cargo ships, had been designed to allow it to cross rough Northern seas as well as navigate silt-swollen channels such as Boston Haven. The Guild Hall, with its sturdy Baltic oak beams, testified to this once glorious and prosperous past as the port that H.V. Morton described as 'the Bristol of the East Coast'. It is famous also, of course, as one of the places from which the Pilgrim Fathers left for America, bringing the name of the town with them.

Nathaniel Hawthorne visited Boston in 1857 with his wife, Sophia, taking the slow steamboat down the River Witham from Lincoln instead of the new railway. On his first ramble about the town, Hawthorne observed an 'odd impression of bustle, and sluggishness, and decay' about the port, with two or three schooners moored along the river-bank, another just rigged at the ship-builder's yard and one returning from a foreign voyage. 'An old man on the bank hailed her and inquired about her cargo,' writes Hawthorne, 'but the Lincolnshire people have such a queer way of talking English that I could not understand the reply.' It was a town of some charm for Nathaniel and Sophia, in which they were drawn particularly to St Botolph's Church in the heart of the town, from which the town derives its name, 'by the quick and slovenly English pronunciation' of Botolph's town. Perhaps by the same principle, the locals call the church 'the stump'.

For Hawthorne, however, 'old' Boston was as slow as its slovenly name, or its silting river. 'I could not but contrast it with the mighty and populous activity of our own Boston, which was once the feeble infant of this old English town; – the latter, perhaps, almost stationary ever since that day, as if the birth of such an offspring had taken away its own principle of growth.' Sophia was also struck by this contrast, writing to her daughter that 'this original old town is not in the least like our "Athens"'. Time and place were complex matters here in Old Boston, in what is sometimes called New Holland. Boston sits on the meridian line, directly north from Greenwich, suspended between east and west, and almost suspended in time. The decay which Hawthorne noted had begun before the 'Renaissance' or the settlements in the 'New World', and it has certainly never recovered its medieval prominence. Nor has the town managed to package its history as heritage: there is no well-worn trail of American tourists, no interpretative centre about the Pilgrim Fathers, nor is there even a maritime museum about its history as a port and centre of shipping and boatbuilding. On the road into Boston I had noticed semaphore signalling on the adjacent railway, but this was not evidence of the preservation of the past, merely the indications of a railway which had never been modernised.

Despite Hawthorne's desire to find Boston a remnant of 'old England', it still looks like a European town. The architecture in places is Dutch, befitting its long associations with Dutch traders and workers. The long history of the town's connections with ports and cities around the North and Baltic Seas continues today, with a high proportion of Eastern European migrants from Poland, Lithuania and Latvia. At 12 per cent of the population, Boston is home to the highest percentage of EU migrants in the UK, many of whom work as agricultural labourers and factory workers in the town's food processing plants. As a result, the town has a high rate of employment and a town centre rejuvenated by shops and cafés selling Polish and Baltic food. It is a town of confluence, where waterways and peoples meet. The Witham flows into Boston Haven, itself also scoured by the Maud Foster Drain, the South Forty Foot Drain, and further along towards the sea, the Hobhole Drain. In contrast to the fairy-tale intimations of the place-names in South Derbyshire, the names around Boston spoke of a history of watery origins and navigations – Fosdyke, Eaudyke, Fishtoft, Wainfleet – sometimes it seemed, as I passed Old Leake and Spilsby, almost comically so.

Where Boston Haven leaks out into the western corner of The Wash, the sea teases the land, creeping into lagoons, salt marshes and brackish ditches. The borders of England are entirely fluid here. There are banks and sea walls, the remains of pill boxes and gunmounts from the war, but the mud marshes which stretch for miles must surely have done more to deter invaders. Freiston Shore was once popular as a bathing resort and for horse racing on the beach, the last sign of which is the old coaching inn that still stands surveying the vast flat reclaimed fields on one side, the wetlands on the other. Tractors pull trailers across the arable fields, keeping pace with the work of the hunched crop-pickers with their low-slung baskets. The workers here are almost all from the Baltic states. On the other side of the sea bank, a lagoon is home to a noisy colony of oystercatchers, joined but never outvoiced by plovers, common terns and godwits. The RSPB manage Freiston Shore as a nature reserve, a haven for waders and seabirds.

Freiston Shore derives its name from the village just two miles away, although once the shore would have been much closer to the village. William Stukeley believed the name came from *frith*, meaning a bay, or area protected from the sea. In his *History and Antiquities of Boston*, however, Pishey Thompson disputes this etymology, and argues instead that it was 'originally settled by a colony from Friesland, and was the town of the Frieslanders'. Whatever its roots, the flat lands, dykes and Dutch red farmsteads make Freiston's sea-crossing affinities abundantly visible. Boundaries between sea and land, between country and continent, were uncertain here.

When I entered the bird hide at the lagoon, there was an elderly couple encamped on the benches, surveying through binoculars the birds chattering on the shoreline. They looked up and we swapped polite greetings, remarks about the weather, but within a few minutes, slowly and quietly they rose to leave. It is as if the hide is understood to be a private place of worship, that exchanging greetings is a prelude to changing places. I was left alone to contemplate the clusters of terns, a bathing row of redshanks dipping their ankles in the water and a pair of blackheaded gulls squabbling, it seemed, over nothing. One gull harassed the other, chasing and beating wings, only to be reciprocated by the other. Every few seconds, they would cease and look around, bored, for something else to do. Fighting was better than loneliness, as Brendan Behan used to say, a sentiment which must have struck him now and then as he gazed upon the North Sea from Hollesley Bay Borstal on the Suffolk coast.

The lagoon was formed by one of the sea walls which kept the North Sea from undoing centuries of enclosure and reclamation. Beyond it lay the salt marshes, with shallow channels of mud and seawater running between islands of scurvy grass and sea lavender. It looked like an elaborate playground of moats scooped out of the mud and reeds, just waiting for giant sandcastles to be dumped down on to the corners of the sea wall. Closer to the sea, there was another sea wall, and then the marshy beginnings of the North Sea. There were half a dozen trawlers out at sea, some chugging in and out of Boston Haven, with the sky above inviting a watercolour of grey and cream washes, and the faintest of blues to mark out Norfolk on the horizon.

I walked along the outer sea wall at Freiston as far as I could, until a breach in the embankment prevented further progress. Here was another experiment in heritage, of an altogether different kind. Centuries of land reclamation on one side, and the rising sea levels on the other, had eroded the salt marsh habitat almost to oblivion. At Freiston Shore, three breaches were deliberately made in the outer sea bank by the Environment Agency, to allow the sea in, to open the land back up to the sea and recreate the salt marsh upon which so many invertebrates, fish and birds depend. This was an experiment in 'managed retreat', conceding the shoreline to the sea, and turning the porosity of sea borders into a strength. Glasswort and sea-blite were the first vegetation to make a habitat of the returning salt marsh. Bass, sprat and herring now use the channels and lagoons of the breached shoreline as a nursery area. Wildfowl and waders, as well as skylarks and twits, populate its feeding grounds in their thousands. From the sea wall I watched the unfolding drama of the skies around The Wash, the rain advancing steadily towards me from Norfolk until the sea and the sky were one shade. The trawlers lost their shapes and colours, the land on the horizon thinned into a faint blur. All the borders were dissolving. I left it too late to leave the sea wall to head back to the car. The rain grew to a thick downpour across the salt marsh. 'Once there was no sea,' says Mrs Swithin in *Between the Acts*, 'no sea at all between us and the continent.' Wet through, with every footstep oozing out a marshy squelch, that vision of a sea-less, borderless England seemed to me paradoxically resonant on Freiston Shore.

Tim Dee (TWO)

Neither Sea, nor Land

The Wash has the colour, consistency and mobility of slip, the warm brown muddied water used to keep things wet and moving on potters' wheels. I am wading through a mud bath and as I slosh up to my thighs in the retreating tide the mud seems to have come up from my childhood. The brown cloud I kick up settles eventually as the memory of a thrill won from a dreary summer's day on a wet British beach of not-quite-sand. The water is so murky I can't see my feet. I stumble and lurch, feeling my way down channels of sucking mud, bumping between ridges of slippery mud. I want water, but there is just mud. Who knows where the shore becomes the sea? A stick showing above the wave tops and marking the land end of Peter's fishing net seems impossibly far out. I cannot believe we will be able to walk that far into the water to reach it. But we can, and entangled in the first net ahead of me I can see a fish flailing at the surface as tidewater draws away from beneath it. It has worked; there will be a catch.

We'd had to wait for the tide. We had chosen a neap but the north wind blowing straight down the open mouth of the Wash had pushed water higher up the salt marsh and held it there longer than usual. The tide seemed reluctant to turn. It was raining too. We waited, caught in a great circle of wetness, and Peter talked about his Wash: his family on its shore and how he is drawn to its water again and again, the fish he catches in the spring, the samphire he gathers in the summer, the wildfowl he shoots in the winter. We sheltered in the lee of a man-made bund that has pushed the marsh further out into the sea. A great round-barrow now, this mound is a burial chamber of human ambition, the moraine of an abandoned experiment to create a freshwater reservoir at the edge of the Wash, just one of a succession of interventions trying to keep things still in this extraordinarily mobile place.

All is temporary on the Wash. This is a wilderness (perhaps the last in England and surely the biggest) made of mud suspended in water. Its tides live for twelve hours; it is born and dies twice a day. All life and all energy is in the great estuary's breathing: mud disappearing and mud reappearing, in the passage from the edge of the marsh to the sea, from freshwater to salt, from sea purslane to samphire, from green marsh to inter-tidal mud, from muddied brown sea to more salty grey sea, from sea to sky to cloud to rain. All these zones are porous, each leak into the other. You have only to be on the Wash for a day to realise the futility of human plans for any permanence in the place. What you take to be a fixed horizon is picked up by the wind and disappears. Water vapour condenses just above the fields of wheat and rape at the shore and deliquesces their edges into cloud. A whitethroat flies out over the salt marsh from its grassed nesting bank on the most recent sea wall, singing its dry ratchet song over the slippery green ooze; a redshank agitated by a marsh harrier towers inland over emerald wheat fields calling its bleak mud-flat alarm. Is there anywhere on these islands that has a less defined edge? This is a place that is no place, that is never what it was, or will be. Everything gives and takes, slides and slip.

The Wash is the greatest of the North Sea's jaw bites that open into the body of England. Its huge square yawn looks big enough to drain everything that flows into it, but it gargles instead, holding all the silt of the east Midlands, the Fens and much of East Anglia. To speak of the mouths of the rivers (Witham or Haven, Welland, Nene, Great

Ouse) that drain into the Wash seems absurd; *it* is the mouth. Its thirst cannot be slaked and sometimes it will gulp down what pours in; but just as often it will spit out what it has half-swallowed. One tide the Fens will nourish the Wash, the next they might be force-fed by it. The throat of the great mouth can be either the blue-grey open marine sky of the northern horizon or the black soil of the Fens to the south. The cycle of inundation and retreat is endless. Conducting all the business between the one and the other is the mud, a huge tongue lolling in the mouth. Imagine a whale's tongue grey-brown and wet forever, fifteen miles long and fifteen miles wide.

The conditioning colour here is brown. Everything runs and nothing is fast, but brown dominates from the end of the fields far out to sea. It is a brown like a child's jam jar of water after a busy painting session, a brown that contains all the colours: the slops of the fens draining green and yellow crops, red poppies, ruddy dust carried from Bedfordshire brick pits via a life in the breeding breast plumage of black-tailed godwits, black soil laid into the heart of heads of celery, the polar white of Bewick's swans, brought to the Ouse from arctic Russia, pink-footed geese's pink feet ripening like tundra berries beneath them, the shelduck's umber, the dunlin's dun, even the hated mink's black-brown stole. All these raw colours are washed down as silt, salted by the sea, then join the mud. Add any more you like; it all becomes brown.

Peter and I walk out across the mud and into the water, but it would be just as accurate to say into the mud and across the water. After fifteen minutes of trudge we reach the stick that marks the first of Peter's nets. I look around; I am standing in a sea. The thin line of the marsh and the open mud we started from now seems so distant and so slight on the vast horizon that I laugh. Two stick figures seeking a third have walked determinedly into the water. We must look insane from the shore, I think, except there is no one there. There is no one as far as my eyes can see. We are alone, standing in the lumpy brown water as the tide battles around our legs, the wind pushing water south towards the land, the invisible moon sucking it away north for its needs elsewhere.

In the nets are a bass and six grey mullet. The two small flounders or butts we let go, and like miniature waves we hold in our hands, mud brown above, sky grey beneath, they snake back into the water. The mullet have tangled themselves; Peter unhooks the nylon filament from their bleeding gills and eases their popping eyes of fish panic back through the net. Most of the fish are still alive when we reach them and being released from the nets gives them a little more twitch. Peter takes the wooden priest strung on his waist and hits each mullet very hard three or four times on its head. It is bone-crunching, a sickeningly loud and finite noise amidst the never-ending ripple and blow of wind and water. As he hits them Peter talks to the fish in a soft voice. After each but the last of the whacks, they spasm and their whole bodies clench and flex against Peter's arm before they return to their fish shape and die, and he lays them gently in his shoulder bag. By the time we have emptied both nets the tide is at our ankles.

Gutting is next. Peter turns the mullet belly up, takes his knife and pushes it through the fish, just below its gills. He cuts bones and pulls the blade up towards the skin so the fish is snapped open one third of the way along its body, now he can slide his knife down the fish's belly opening it in a great split that has been the slaughterman's defining stroke for ever. The gut in all its warmth and reek bubbles in the sluice of the split. A green vegetable slush creams out or, from one of the fish, the three blenched grey bodies of shrimps, the mullet's final meal. The viscera spill into the sea. Four herring gulls detect the offal one hundred and fifty feet up in the wind. They call and jilt in the sky but won't come down while we are there; perhaps they have noted it for later. Peter bends to the sea and washes the gutted fish, his knife and his hands. The clouded water clouds some more.

The sky is fine muslin; the gauzy drift of rain from the north lifts and takes the horizon up with it. I look out towards the Lincolnshire shore and can see it twice, layered on itself. A mirage has raised a line of trees, floating them off the ground into the lower sky, as if to emphasise the impossibility of ever arriving there or anywhere else that would be a real edge to this place. Further north Boston Stump, the church tower I climbed this same morning, hangs detached like an abstract painting in the sky, a blurred colour field of brown in grey. I have seen this effect before though not when standing in the sea. The puszta with its oceanic grasses and shimmering reeds at the centre of the great Hungarian plain is an inland dry Wash. It is so flat with such a wide horizon you can see, it is said, the curvature of the earth. I think I saw that but in the same place I also saw giant stretched cows sailing through the air with horns prodding the heavens, a magnified image of what lay beyond the horizon, thrown into the sky and projected on its vast screen, a fata morgana, or in Hungarian a *délibáb*. I have often wondered if flying birds might see things like this, being able to look beyond the horizon they share with us when they are down on the ground, and if so, how disconcerting a giant floating cow might be to them? That way Don Quixote's visions lie, I know, but standing in the Wash looking towards Lincolnshire I am reminded of John Clare, saturated with looking at what was close to hand in front of him, but wandering near the Wash to the borders of his knowledge, getting to the 'edge of the orison', and thinking he might look over the lip of the world. On the Wash you can.

*

I hitched a ride on a fisheries protection boat making one of its regular research trips to collect cockles, mussels and water samples for analysis. We came out of the River Nene and ran across the Wash's fifteen miles of open water whilst the tide lasted then nosed in and out of channels and creeks once it dropped. When we started black and white cows dawdled on the lush banks of the river, turning grass into milk, and a bright yellowhammer, like an ear of corn, rattled his intention to make eggs from the same green. Then, where the river joined the Wash, we left the full ripening of a whole season behind and sailed at first it seemed into nothing, served up onto a pewter plate of water. To begin with it was blankly disappointing: empty water and open sky. Then the picture was horribly distorted: the screaming yaw of military jets squeezed and split everything at once. US Airforce A10 'tank-buster' planes, painted the colour of the dry brown mud of the Tigris and the Euphrates, dropped their dummies with a *phut*, a flash and a little puff of smoke into the wet brown mud of the Wash's southern shore bombing range. They left behind another of the Wash's mirages, a cloud from nowhere, seen by no one.

*

The Wash is having none of this; it makes its own time over and over. The tide makes the day, it is the only clock, and there is nothing else. The brown wave on the brown sea is the mud of the sea floor raised by the tide. The mud of the revealed banks is the sea settled by the tide. The same mud that cradles the ordnance and sucks at your legs is what gives the Wash its teeming life. Within minutes of sailing out onto the wide water the mud invited us in. This begins with an apparent sinking. We were being taught how the Wash fills as it empties. Land emerged from the sea, mud strips, then bars, then banks appeared, like the backs of surfacing animals, an otter, a seal, a whale. Sky and sea both had brown in their blue, as if in readiness to deal with the apparently rising land. A brown streak was visible below the falling water, and then a thin brown seam opened between the sea and the sky, like a desert mirage in reverse, a sliver of land shining in the middle of the wet. A plain became a mountain range. Five miles out from the bombed shore the mud began to rise over us; we sank lower into the world, the horizon loomed, the sky shrunk. The Wash came alive.

First the land and the sea met in the air. Three gannets, an adult and two immatures, birds of the open sea, and big and bright enough to match it, flew in front of me, drawing their long wings through the wind like turbine blades, and moving crazily south towards the green of the Ouse and the great cul de sac. Where had they come from? The teeming gannetries of fish-stew and aggro at the Bass Rock, in the Firth of Forth, or wild, ocean-bashed Hermaness in Shetland? Why were they pulling deeper in towards the land, as it rose through the water;

where were they going? Then three swifts came, like slates skimmed over the falling sea, five miles from the shore, buzzing the gannets, criss-crossing around them, feeding on flying insects in their wake, and as at home out over salt-water as they are around the eaves and crannies of the roofs of Boston. Swifts are nearly legless and gannets use their feet for swimming; both are ungainly on land, and come reluctantly to it only because they cannot lay their eggs in the air or on the sea. Here over the Wash, with its land that is not land, and sea that is not sea, they met. The brilliant gloss white of the gannets and the black ink of the swifts making broad strokes and fine lines across the grey sky and brown sea, signatures from other worlds.

On the ship's navigation chart in its wheel room, the thin edge of true land (only of interest to a sailor in order to be avoided) is marked in yellow, the Wash is coloured green for its salt marsh and inner muds, blue for its sand banks and white for its deepest draughts of water. The chart marks a heart shape of white called The Well; it is the only place that holds open water at low tide. All the mud banks and sand bars have names too; names they carry with them as they drown each tide and as they shift over time. While half the crew go off in a tender to collect samples to be monitored for an apocalyptic list of algal biotoxins known by their acronyms, ASP (Amnesic Shellfish Poison), DSP (Diarrheic Shellfish Poison) and PSP (Paralytic Shellfish Poison), I look out from the deck over the emerging mud-scape to try to identify the banks and bars whose names I have copied from the chart into my notebook. The crew know the mud by its names, though they don't know who did the naming or when. I think of pirate maps of buried treasure and of Polonius trying to describe the clouds. The mud names record intimacies and fears, stories of hard-won triumph, and magic words to invoke and appease. Some are a transcription of a shape, others a description of riches found or hoped for: Inner Westmark Knock, Gat Sand, Butterwick Low, The Scalp, Styleman's Middle, The Ants, Long Sand, Herring Hill, Black Buoy Sand, Thief Sand, Seal Sand, Old Bell Middle, Stubborn Sand, Breast Sand, Pandora Sand, Bull Dog Sand, Scullridge, Blue Back, Mare Tail, Old South, Inner Sand, The Cots, Sunk Sand.

The tide falls further and on the next excursion from the boat I join the crew in the tender and we nuzzle into the side of a mud bank. Farther along in the afternoon haze is a strange sight. Like a stranding of dying whales, a line of eight fishing boats the size of wooden trawlers are strung along the mud, settled there by the retreating tide, and now dozens of yards from the water. This is quite deliberate. For cockle 'hand working', the fishermen run their boats up onto a mud bank and wait for the tide to drop. Then, in a controlled abandoning of ship, they throw ladders over the side and clamber down onto the mud to rake cockles. Their heads lowered and wandering from their boats, on a bank miles out from solid land, the fishermen look as odd as icebound Arctic explorers, set down on uncertainty. But a good crew on a good site can gather two tons of cockles a day and in the salty blur of rising mud and falling water, where there is neither sea nor land, fishing becomes farming. I think of a cockle's foot, its strange unseen shellfish walk through mud and water, and the fishermen leaving their boats to paddle after them.

As the tide falls each mud bank discovers its own geography as intricate micro-landscapes are revealed and come to life. Spitting cockles are thickest where tiny streams of water run through the low tide mud, in little afterthoughts of flow. This is water that is hidden within water for the rest of the tide. At low tide it makes miniature deltas and estuaries, tiny creeks and waterfalls, as it scoops, turns and bends through the brown mud, building soft banks of it for cockles to hide in and tiny beaches of it for Hydrobia snails to land themselves on. Shelduck love these snails and across the revealed mud banks, echoing the stooped cockle-raking fishermen, I can see half-hidden scattered groups of them like lit lanterns, bright white against the brown, on the little beaches slurping up the snails.

Around us on the newly exposed mud waders arrive, tumbling down to it like a film of smoke run backwards. Their landings here always seem like returns, though the water has only just retreated. The sureness of the birds' spellbinding aerial organisation and the accuracy of their touch-downs make you feel they have done it before over and over, as they surely have, though the world in front looks new made, the sparkling mud with its ferruginous glitter and the dappled water that runs from it. There are two hundred bar-tailed godwits and five hundred knot. Like the solitary grey plover that flew over on my previous visit they will be failed breeders already returning south or birds that didn't even make it to their arctic nesting grounds this year. I cannot see them in the summer without being yanked forwards to winter. Behind the leggy gangs of godwits, there are low twisting lines of dunlin, like mud splashes tossed into the air, and wind-surfing oystercatchers are coming in now too. Tighter flocks of knot thicken above the bank, reflecting down the grey brown essence of the Wash as they turn. A storm of joined life, they are like the silver mullet steering through the water below, the grey green Sueda bushes on the distant marsh edge touching one another into a low ridge of wild hedge, the creamy cockles spitting the slip they have filtered for food, stippling the great whale's tongue of mud.

Into this storm people have come, nervous and brazen at once, alone and sticking up into the sky. Somewhere in the Wash is King John's treasure, ditched into mud in October 1216 in flight from the French, and now sunk, buried, or simply lost. On every tide, it seems, it can be found and lost again by those who know where to look. The mud makes rich companions of all who come to it, but noticing this can make us lonely. The waders and wetsuits that we negotiate the mud with allow us a temporary purchase whilst keeping us from it. I look around but there is nothing like me out here, the nearest things are the brilliant garish green fingers of summer samphire growing from the ooze, standing upright in a world of bend and blow. But the samphire thrives on submersions and beachings, a daily drowning and drying. In this world of ripples on the horizontal, where the Wash is a revolutionary shore with everything in it in a condition of permanent change, human upright fixity makes us ridiculous, cut off and as liable to drift as the tower of Boston Stump in the haze, unless we bend to the mud. More knot wheel and mist over me, looking for their mud for their wading, and I remember their namesake Cnut, or Canute, a would-be ruler of the waves, the man who went down to the sea's edge, thinking it tameable but found it not findable, marvellously unbiddable and variously itself, wet, slippery, awash.

Angela Leighton (TWO)

Two Poems for Maggi Hambling

Scallop

In words the sky looks through, this thing
assigns the wind to its carved tune.

Striations of steel, the colour of nothing,
rib the altering wash of the sea.

Far off, you'd think: the fuselage
of a fallen angel, close to,

a cracked valve, hemmed with letters.
It's wavy, flexed to another dimension.

Fantail, vaulting, locket or shell,
it opens like a listening muscle,

as if a phone or ear had sprung
on the grey shingle, set to listen.

Read, if you can, the sky in stencil.
Touch the fluted hardware of a song.

Something, not music, yet most musical,
fills this pleated clef of the sea,

this piece in piecemeal, full of whispers.
Listen. Trace the cut of its sound,

the speaking hollow of its beaten words –
an ear to its shape, an eye to its call:

'I hear those voices that will not be drowned.'

Ultramarine

Cobalt, sapphire, lapis, slate.
In the sack of the waves' heavy arrangements
a face slides, rises, unfolds –
going under again overrun
in the big sea's blurred hold.

Strata of waves at a stroke, a long
thickening sweep that carries over,
the slub of a weave, open texture –
they net a haul in the undertow,
draw a falling, surface-deep.

You might catch it there, varied, thrown.
Faces move over the waters.
Waters move, like shine on paint.
The tides repeat, closing on drowning.
Cobalt, sapphire, lapis, slate.

Jos Smith and Rose Ferraby
(TWELVE)

Warp-land, Holderness

God for his mercy, what a tide of woes
Comes rushing on this land at once!
Shakespeare, *Richard II*

To say that the road ahead is closed, as the red sign warns, misses the point. It's not that the road is closed – it's just not there. The double yellow lines and tarmac come to an abrupt end pointing out towards the horizon. The road has broken off and dropped onto the beach below. Just a toothed overhang between two crumbling curbstones. Below it, a stratigraphy of infrastructure and a brown slope of silt petering out onto the beach. The tide is out. The wet sands seem supernaturally flat from up here. Beyond this, nothing but the North Sea between us and the archipelagos of the Netherlands, Germany and Denmark, out there somewhere in the drained blue. Britain cut adrift.

From the cliffs at Flamborough Head in the north to the River Humber in the south, the landmass of Holderness in the East Riding of Yorkshire is held in the chalk crook of the inland Wolds, a wedge of soft boulder clay gradually slinking into the past year by year, crumbling at its coastal edge onto the one long beach running away to the south. Great Colden was the village once ahead of us at the end of this road, with a Methodist Chapel, a manor house and a pub called The Cross Keys; Great Cowden is the village now behind us. At the end of the nineteenth century, everyone upped sticks and shuffled inland a mile as the land fell from beneath their feet. Are Colden and Cowden the same place? Tense distorts here. The 'new' pub is *still* called The Cross Keys. We'd come here to visit a Travellers' camp on the very edge only to find the site abandoned, weeds creeping into the open doors of caravans. The lane to the sea had traced a diminishing line of dwellings, from tidy, gnome-filled bungalow gardens, to weathered and abandoned shacks, to a television on a threadbare chair under grey clouds. This is a coastline where it pays to ensure you have the latest map.

At Skipsea, another road comes to an abrupt end among caravan parks. To the right is an abandoned amusement arcade, boarded up, with a sun-bleached poster advertising a live music act: 'Rock With Laughter'. To the left is a fish and chip shop. Perhaps it's the sight of these fallen roads, or the memory of what once lay beyond: car after car arrives while we're there, to drain a thermos and pick at a salty pallet of chips staring seaward. Roll up, roll up, seats at the end of the world. A meditation on provisionality.

The North Sea is its own distinctive, landless region of vying interests, unlike the wider oceans. Smaller, criss-crossed with mainland European traffic for centuries, the sea floor crusted with tools, jewellery, ceramics, boat timbers and who knows what kind of weaponry. Over it, wrote Louis MacNeice playfully, Halvers and Olafs 'jostle our Esquires / And blood-lust our conventions'. 'Beneath it / Smoulder the wars,' wrote Ted Hughes. But over it came much of the language we cherish too, embroidered into the landscapes around here – the '-thorpes', '-thwaits', '-kirks' and '-nesses'. For all it feels quiet now, it connects as much as it divides, something it feels timely to remember today as we recede from Europe into an uncertain future.

To the south, wind turbines haunt the waters like a baptismal congregation. Among them, or so it seems from here, is the drilling platform for North Sea gas, running its pipeline inland. The year had been another of the hottest summers on record. A report by the National Oceanic and Atmospheric Administration, published before we left, claimed that all 18 years of the 21st century rank among the 19 warmest in their 138-year record. The vast gasworks at Easington down the coast is where the drilling platform pipes its yield inland. When they began drilling, they calculated the amount of gas against the rate of coastal erosion and sited the processing plant as far inland as was necessary to extract all the gas in good time. But they found more gas. And, due to climate change, the coast has eroded faster than expected. Now they've shipped great boulders in from Norway to protect the plant from the sea, so that it can process more gas for burning which, in turn, will increase the rate of erosion. It is closely watched by an alarming number of armed police who – we're told by a local, half-jokingly – aren't allowed to fire their guns in case the whole place goes up. There is a living fable here somewhere.

'Road Ahead Closed.' Who knows what that sand contains down there, what stories it could tell? The cliff is low but the edge it represents feels more and more severe the longer we think about it. One minute, caravans, holiday cabins, well-pruned gardens ('Our little corner of the Earth,' reads one house sign), the next just sand and rubble. Life ground down to ruins as soon as the land lets go. Ashes to ashes. Amen.

*

The coast of Holderness is the fastest eroding coastline in Europe. On average, over its forty-five miles, it is losing one and a half meters every year. Less in some areas but significantly more in others. The problem is that the land here is a relatively recent deposit in geological terms. Before the 'Devensian glaciation' around one hundred thousand years ago there was no land here, that is to say, the coast was a chalk edge further inland more like the cliffs at Flamborough Head to the north. But a glacier carrying all this clay, silt, gravel and sand edged down across the sea from the north and eventually melted, compacting its soft earth like flesh on a chalk skeleton and it has been gently eroding ever since. Now climate change is working this weakness. Sea levels are rising, yes, but it's the increase in extreme weather events that is really aggravating matters. More such events mean choppier seas and more storm surges, really significant factors in coastal erosion.

Attempts have been made to mitigate against erosion. War-like terminology is employed: we 'hold', 'advance' and 'retreat the line'. Expensive defences have been established by setting out groins, or raising a sea wall, or indeed shipping in boulders from Norway like those in front of the gasworks; but where they hold the line in one place, land to the south suffers greater effects. The drift of sediment usually nourishes beaches. It even forms what is called here 'warp-land', banks that slowly rise out of the water as sand is deposited in tidal layers. But groins that catch this sediment on its way south cause the waves to eat directly into the clays and soils of the cliff instead. And so it goes, dragging down farms, houses, villages, whole seaside resorts.

Something in the region of thirty villages have been lost along this stretch of coast over the last ten centuries with a ribbon of land nearly two miles wide gone since the Romans. It is hard to imagine two miles of land in front of you when you stand on this precarious edge. Time boiled down to space. It has always been hard to mentally square the scale of geological time to the scale of human time but Holderness seems a place where the gap might be bridged. Strata, compacting here and eroding there, are in both cases oddly imbricated with human remains. Quite literally at times: nineteenth-century folktales record nocturnal visits from London body snatchers after cemeteries were scoured by storm surges.

At Mappleton, the beach is scattered with debris – cement and brick, rusted iron reinforcements, rounded and barnacled cast concrete. The remains of a different kind of coastal defence, a differently held line. The shells on the beach are mixed too. Variables of bivalves, razor-clams and military ordnance. Some of the latter date back to the war. Most originate from the field above, marked, as we descended the cliff, with a sign: 'Danger – Unexploded ordnance on the land beyond this point. It may explode and kill you.' The land in question had, to our concerned puzzlement, been deeply ploughed quite recently. Only a decade ago this field was used for target practice by the MOD, the swift, loud descent of planes followed by a rocking BOOM that probably helped the cliff a little along its way. Now these human fossils lie still on the beach. Precariouser and precariouser. We steer our way clear around one of them, risking a photo or two.

Looking up at the cliff from the beach, there are not only terminal roads but once-connected water and sewage pipes jutting out. Electrical wires trail out of plastic piping down the cross section of sedimented strata. In one muddy outcrop, a septic tank is poking out from under a scruff of turf with no house above it.

Of course, you will also see flags. Threadbare, wind-stressed Union Jacks for the most part. Something about the situation seems to prompt these plotland dwellers to raise an unlikely sign of national pride. Not only Union Jacks though. To our surprise, here and there, a German and a Dutch flag as well. From time to time, they all must have to take down these flags, dig and lever the poles from the ground, take a few steps back and replant them.

*

Spurn Point is the southernmost tip of Holderness and one of the strangest places in the country. Walking out towards the lighthouse on the Point, you have to walk a narrow, sandy ridge, a 'carsey' as they say here, with the North Sea on your left and the mudflats of the Humber on your right. This often floods at high tide making Spurn, technically, an island these days, though it has by no means always been an island. The sand is strewn with debris as it is to the north. In fact, much of what constitutes land here has been dragged in the tide from further north. This is true 'warp-land'.

Many of the red pebbles on the beach here are ground-down house bricks from lost houses to the north. The upended stake of a groin lies across the path, its sharp point weathered to a gannet-head point.

Ropes, chains and loops of blue pipe disappear uncannily into the sand as if connected to mysteriously abandoned infrastructure under the beach. Who will hear if we call down them? Anywhere else and this would feel like a playful fiction, but the last century's wars have brought a subterranean architecture of armouries, lookouts and gunneries to this long spit, so you never quite know what's really down there.

Where the seaward beach of the carsey meets the island proper, we climb a huge, collapsed pile of concrete platforms and timbers up into the dunes. We have no idea what it once was; defence against the trespass of water or men? Weaving through the brush of buckthorn and sea holly, the contrast between sea and estuary becomes starker. On one side, waves crash and withdraw, gush and foam around the debris at the tide line. On the other, there is utter stillness, with only the chuckle and chirrup of turnstones pecking at the mud. Up into the raucous noise of the sea, down into the tranquillity of the estuary.

At this moment, it is a place of two worlds held gently apart on this tightrope of shifting sand. The line it cuts is borne out of that slowly flexing tension between river and tide. But it feels momentary too – a shift in weather could plunge us into something else entirely. Cloud shadows bring a deathly chill as we look back up the Humber towards the Grimsby skyline and feel ever so far out on the edge of things. But when the sun comes out, the warmth and the wind together flash and roar and propel us onwards. Each hour seems to emulate the protean history of this strange warp-land. All that provisionality further north seems to translate, to conciliate, into a posthumous space here, the scattering of bones and house bricks, the give and take of the longshore soul drifting.

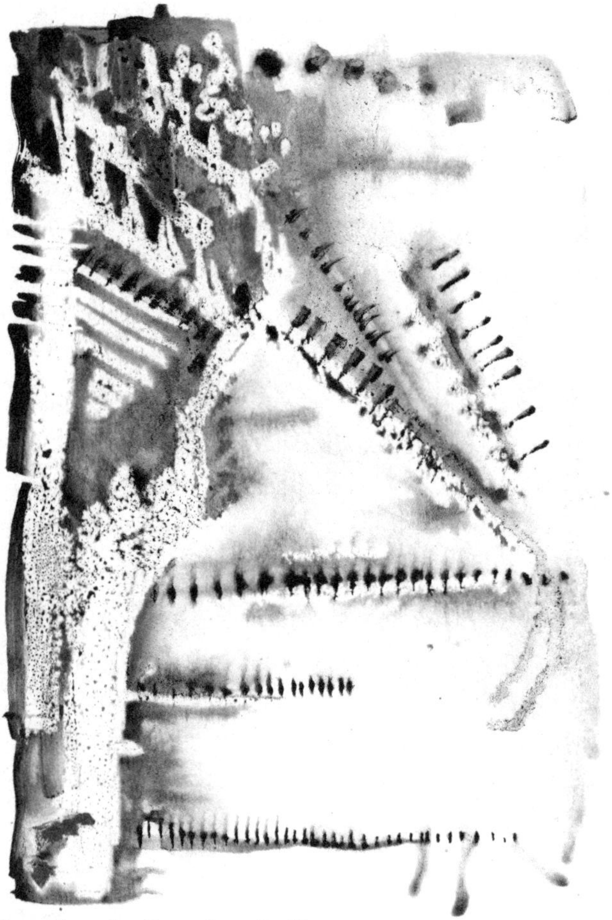

Rose Ferraby, Longshore Drift

> If then we shall shake off our slavish yoke,
> Imp out our drooping country's broken wing,
> Redeem from broking pawn the blemished crown,
> Wipe off the dust that hides our sceptre's gilt,
> And make high majesty look like itself,
> Away with me in post to Ravenspurgh
>
> Shakespeare, *Richard II*

As a place, Spurn Point troubles some of the assumptions that we have when we use the very word *place*. It is the tip of a long, descending swan-neck of a spit stretching some three miles into the estuary mouth of the River Humber. But it is not now where it once was. The whole spit has moved west several miles in the last 1500 years and as it has done so its name has changed. There is some debate about whether it has moved smoothly or whether it has been washed away and reformed again. Either way, it is a place of echoes, rhymes and iterations.

The name 'Spurn' is itself the result of a *linguistic* erosion. It is thought to be the remainder of 'Ravenspurgh' or 'Ravenser Spurn', which emerged from 'Ravenser' and 'Ravenser Odd', which came from the Old Norse 'Hrafnseyrr' meaning 'Raven's Eye' (which, when you see its shape on the map, makes perfect sense). All these different iterations have had places here. But each of them refers to a different longitude and latitude as the spit has moved, warped by the tides. It is a form and a place in rhyming dialogue with itself.

The earliest iteration of this place, and the furthest west, some way out in the North Sea now, was 'Cornu Vallis' when, in around 700, a monastery is rumoured to have been here. We discuss whether the monks came here to be a long way from the bustle of inland life – its conventions and authorities – a little closer to divine silence on the outer edge; or whether they came here to feel closer to Europe, a part of its network of scholars, saints and emissaries. To be in the midst of the comings and goings of the North Sea, the traffic trailing in and out of the Humber. We know, for example, that the Romans travelled up and down the east coast and made landings via the Humber to supply major settlements at Aldborough, York and along Hadrian's Wall, as well as transporting metals from the Pennines back to the heart of the empire.

Better to ask '*when* is Spurn Point?' than '*where*' then. Spurn Head precedes Spurn Point. Ravenser Odd precedes Spurn Head. Some five hundred years after Cornu Vallis had fallen to the sea, Ravenser Odd was founded on the tip of the sandy spit moving west, with the tiniest of beginnings. Around 1230 there was a shipwreck, and from that wooden shell a man aptly called Peter Atte See started to sell things to passing ships. It soon became a thriving town with a regular street plan, a bank and a church. Hull and Grimsby even began to feel sufficiently threatened that they complained to the king. But in 1357, a hugely high tide washed much of the town away and people began to leave. Wavering between island and mainland, it fell into the hands of pirates. Not long afterwards, it is thought to be here that the exiled Bolingbroke made landfall from the Netherlands in 1399. Bolingbroke took the throne from Richard II to be crowned Henry IV, events later dramatised by Shakespeare.

It is Northumberland who rallies his allies to meet Bolingbroke at Ravenspurgh and 'shake off' the 'slavish yoke' of King Richard (Richard is bleeding the country dry to finance war in Ireland). There is an irony that rests on the coast here though. Bolingbroke's father, John of Gaunt, has in the immediately preceding scene delivered one of Shakespeare's most famous speeches, the 'Sceptered Isle' speech. The greatness from which England has fallen is given life in Gaunt's imagery of a nation 'Whose rocky shore beats back the envious siege / Of watery Neptune', a 'precious stone set in a silver sea / Which serves it in the office of a wall / Or as a moat defensive to a house'. This is the 'Isle' as a 'fortress built by Nature for her self / Against infection'. But renewal, in the form of his own son, Bolingbroke, will arrive by sea, and the coast here is, of course, none of these things. Bolingbroke comes from the continent, puncturing these images of fortified nationalism. The image of a past coast that repels is quietly supplanted by the image of a coast that yields to its future. The nation is renewed not in asserting its borders but in relaxing them at this time of instability.

This isn't to comment on the good or ill or otherwise of either Richard II's or Henry IV's reign, but rather to recall the associations of accommodation on this coast – its give. A nation's identity is rarely so demarcated and isolated as some would have us believe. Under most big talk of borders are shifting sands, nocturnal comings and goings, the weft of a deeper, older, quieter 'warp-land'. The surrounding migratory birds are all the immediate reminder we need of this, landing and lifting off in great ribbons that seem the trespassing winds themselves made visible.

*

Walking this warp-land, there is everywhere evidence of slow but decisive change, one era giving way to the next. Beneath our feet, the path leading to the lighthouse is crossed at an angle by train tracks. Tracks leading away to nowhere off to the right ahead of us, under the buckthorn studded orange with berries and out into a line of ruins in the estuary. And behind us, to the left, we see now that the great slabs of concrete and timber we'd been climbing over as we arrived on the island from the sand spit – the inexplicable derelict heap leading out into the sea – are what had once underpinned the railway, on land that is no longer there. The tracks recall the previous orientation of the spit at a ten-past-eight line to its current 6 o'clock sharp. Along the line, ordnance was shipped to the great guns on the southern tip, defending the Humber from enemy ships and submarines. Again, the spit seems caught in a warping tension between fortification and flux; a generation's need to assert and repel as the very ground was giving way beneath their feet.

Among the thirty-odd different, and quite contradictory, meanings given for the word 'warp' since the ninth century are 'to cast forth', 'to fling open', 'to bend', 'to distort', 'to shrink', 'to yield' and of course 'to heap up'. The word itself seems to have warped full circle from meaning to meaning in one long and unpredictable metamorphosis; our own quiet strata on the move as new layers of history settle on the old, shift, drift and settle elsewhere.

*

A flock of redshank come flapping down to a noisy standstill on the mudflats among the eel grass. This grass is fluorescent: rich green at the root rising to something brighter, as close as grass could get to green fire. And the orange legs of the redshank among it sing out. Behind them, a ferry glides inland up the Humber, an amplified voice just audible over the water. On the far side of the estuary, a good couple of miles away, it's almost a continuous line of chimneys, cranes, spires and stacks with the Humber Bridge wobbling in a mirage of light on the river's inland horizon. Gulls settle and lift. The turnstones peel up off the mud in draughts and head back to the flat beach behind us. We walk among hundreds of them sleeping on our way back, at ease on this exposed edge, on this drifting land.

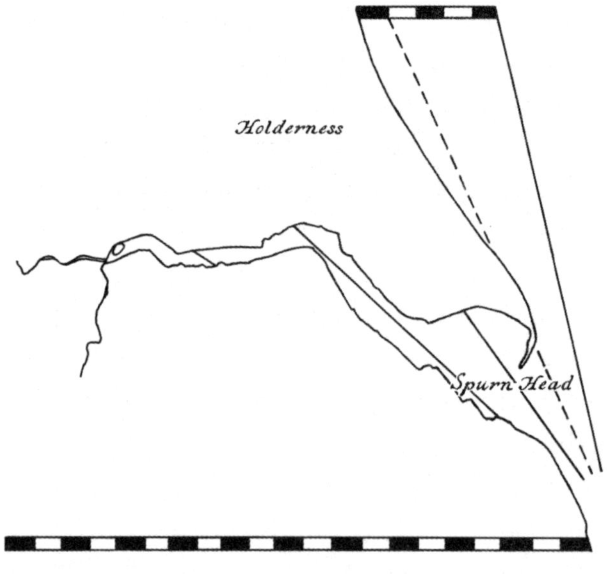

Angela Leighton (TWELVE)

Unquiet Sleepers

The beck, here and there, runs brick-red. A rubric of pawprints on the cinder track shows where a dog, all clarty with mud, took a bitter drink – then bolted, and swerved into a belt of heather. Those stencil marks won't wash away quickly, though they fade as they go … a forensic tease. Ochres and rusts are colours that linger, like something you know under the skin, as if earth's secret haemoglobin might enliven a ditch. That dull red seeps into tarns and pools, deepens the shade of campion or ling, flushes the iron-grey stone in patches. You're reminded of it, seeing the rough, rust-fretted bars of an unhinged gate, that's fallen sideways and makes no closure, but can turn the wind to a phantom, singing.

This land was once threaded with rifts of ore, rich for the picking. Magnetic ironstone, the geologists hailed it, and fast on their tracks came surveyors and speculators, leasers and buyers, drivers and miners. In the space of two decades, from the 1860s to the 1880s, a rural backwater of two hundred people was turned into a busy industrial hub, worked by five thousand. In spite of deep gullies and awkward gradients, the remote moorland was quickly connected by rail and incline to the main routes north: to Ingleby and Middlesbrough, then on to the Durham coalfields. Wagons, called 'tubs', engine sheds and bunkers, haulage wheels and loading hoppers pockmarked the view, as the new industrial power of steam was brought to the unaccommodating landscape, to extract wealth from its ground. Now, only curious walkers pause – in the quiet that has buried so much noise. The hills have healed, covering their scars with bracken and heather, fescue and fog, smoothing their dumps of calcine dust, concealing entries to drifts and shafts, air vents and wells – all the risky underminings of this moorland scene. A hopeful cover of vegetation now softens the raw stone, once unearthed by so much force. Only here and there, like the memory of something hurt and live, that dull stain still leeches out, discolouring the neutral element of water in strangely wounded pools or tarns.

If you walk along the contour of the hill, following the old route of the Rosedale railway, the path is wide and the going easy. This is no picturesque scene of peaks and hollows, but a Rothko canvas of horizontal straight lines drawn by a few simple brush strokes. Above, the heather belt is brown and bare under the sky – a knotty tangle of black roots and stems till late July blesses it with flowers; below, there's bracken, and the dry-stone walls start, brokenly, forgetfully containing their nothing: rough set-asides and sheep-scattered pasture; and finally, in the valley, where the soil is a little deeper, a little more workable, there's a pastoral scene of fields and trees, farmsteads and barns. Your eye might sweep over it all in a moment and get the picture. But now, turn northwards along the flank of the hill, and you find surprising, industrial landmarks: the topless tower of a stone chimney, the regular arches of a row of kilns – Roman, in their look of age-old purpose – then more kilns, high, square constructions built into the hillside, their great herring-boned blocks of stone lined by firebricks, still faintly rouged by the heat they contained. To the right there's a terrace of ruined cottages, and lastly, straight ahead, the gable-end of what were called the Black Houses – a row of railway cottages, once tarred with bitumen as proof against the weather, now only lightly stained like damp. All that's left of them, beside an exposed hearth, is one square aperture looking out across the dale – a folly, it might seem, or some primitive camera for taking the view. Its sculptural open-endedness, framing the slow curve of the valley, giving back what is there in sudden focus, amuses passers-by. Hikers might pause to take a look. Families pose for a selfie in its frame. But at night the sheep use it for shelter, bedding down in the lee of its wall among their own warm droppings.

What is it about landscape? I've returned to this place for thirty years of my life, driven by some need, for its quiet, for the calming indifference of its hills – or perhaps by that instinctive animal hefting that learns, at some level, to return to base. Like the sheep who keep to their allotted terrains, I have gravitated back in a kind of homing. Returns, after all, are the natural way of things here, seasonal or yearly, living and dying. What comes round will round again, following the vast clock of the planets. After the long silence of winter – a silence that throws into sharp relief the sudden cold cough of a pheasant, or the nearly inaudible wing of an owl quartering at dusk – spring brings the dale to life in sounds. Late February brings the first tentative migrants: curlews, that head inland to nest, their faint cue, cue, like a note with nowhere to go, a hopeless tuning repeat, and no tune. But a week or so later it has grown into a flutey, bubbling call, a prolonged coloratura climaxing to each stop. The curlews are joined by lapwings, their slender crested gait, stalking or watching, become a clownish tumbling dance, all flapping wings and whoops and squeals, as the male performs his courtship ritual often late into the night. Snipe, also, might be heard on a still night, high up and invisible, their tail-feathers playing an eerie xylophone – quick scales of notes travelling up and down as they drum the air through which they fall. Warm spring evenings can bring a cacophony of tunes. By late March the first wheatears have arrived, and chit and tut, bobbing defiantly on a moorland stone, then flying, white-arsed, always just a little beyond your reach. And in April, with luck, the shy ring-ousel returns to the heights, its priestly collar showing a point of white on some lonely rowan, or flashing as it flies, swift and low, chuck-chucking over the heather. By late April too, on sunny afternoons the cuckoo starts its routine plainchant of minor thirds in the valley below – an echoing repeat that resonates confusingly, as if a decoy disguised its whereabouts. And finally, those three far-flown birds of summer: homely martins, dipping and chattering along the roadside in search of wet mud for their lintel nests; swallows, with their fantastic appliqué of turns as they swoop and witter to each other, bursting with news; and lastly, in late May, the high tragic swifts, their Greek-chorus of screams underscoring, like a relentless alarm, the whole bright order of summer.

Returns fit the order of things in this place. They mark the year-in, year-out rounding of the planet, while offering a kind of rough consolation for what's lost on the way. For this is also a landscape of no-return, carrying the cost of its human history visibly on its surface – a cost that speaks silently still in the signs that you see. For the engine of wealth took its toll of lives under these monuments. Injured, they died, crushed by wagons, caught by explosives, stunned by falling stones – died often lucklessly, as gangrene, tetanus or septicaemia set in: a boy named John Hugill, twelve years of age, crushed to death between two tubs of ironstone he was hitching for the incline; a man named John Wilcocks, killed inside the mine by a sudden fall of stones; another, Thomas Harwick, completely buried under a collapse of shale; and another, George Kay, slightly injured by a stone falling on his leg, who died nine days later when gangrene set in; and then another, J.H. Dowson, killed when his muffler was caught in the cogged wheels of an engine, lacerating his head. Then another, and another … what is left of that history still tells on these hills, though the lists of names have largely disappeared, except from the specialist records of local history.

And so it happens that a ravaged landscape might become protected heritage, a sad eyesore, a national monument. The lines between them are thin as the grass that hides a railroad and makes a walkers' right of way. What remains of those mines, kilns and chimneys is now protected from the elements, fenced off from passers-by, explained and dated in the tourist brochures – though like all standing stones, they also look like something's tombstone. A hundred years on we can admire the masonry, the weighted symmetries of those hewn blocks, the fine ingenuity of a balanced arch that has survived abandonment, theft and weather. Now the place offers a rest cure for the stressed. *So peaceful*, we might say, dreaming in our own tongues. Our monoglot imaginations can readily ignore the panic of a lamb on the wrong side of a fence, the nightlong wail of ewes when first deprived of their offspring, the miniature scream of a hunted mouse and all the tiny insect palavers, half out of earshot, through which we pass. Only sometimes, perhaps woken in the night by the sudden screech of a barn owl, we might start to hear our own imaginations cry.

The mines finally closed in 1926 with the General Strike, though the decline started some decades before. The workers moved on, leaving long rows of uninhabited cottages, railway sidings, pit shafts, engine houses, piles of calcine waste, broken wagons and rails, till weather and plunder gentled the look of them. Stones could be re-used for dry stone walling, wood reclaimed for fuel or fencing, metal collected for smelting elsewhere. There was, however, one surviving link to that visible past when I first visited the dale in the mid-1980s, searching for a place of escape and succour. Old Bert, as he was known to all, had lived in one of the miners' cottages all his life, and apart from a brief trip to Barnsley to seek work in the coalmines, never ventured beyond a walking radius of his home. He used to recall how, as a boy, he went scrumping for the coal which fell off the tubs – good high-grade stuff meant for powering trains, and therefore worth the risk of a serious accident. Groups of boys would run along the rails after dark, hoping for that windfall of missed diamond. Bert would tell us how, when the mines were working to capacity, the beds were never cold in the terraced cottages, each twelve-hour shift-worker simply replacing another, day and night. But he himself grew up in the slump years, with no work now for a miner's boy, so made shift to live by his country wits. His pantry, he once proudly showed us, was hung with poached pheasants and rabbits, which he'd pluck or skin, then cook himself. The blood-smell of them seeped into his sitting room, like a raw haunting that was hard to stomach. His back garden was a vegetable patch, and his hens – the *yens*, he called them – were cooped by the side of the lane that ran alongside. Bert knew every inch of his home territory, but little of what lay beyond. It was he who told us where to find bilberries before the sheep got to them, in places that – he would spread his hands wide – were '*blae o'er*'. For the rest, he eked out a living by lending a hand to the local farmers, mending fences, humping bales, assisting with the lambing. We would meet him on cold April nights, keeping company with the old shepherd at the door of the lambing shed, in days when waiting on birth meant standing, crook in hand, silently at the ready any time of the day or night, to lend a literally helping hand.

A man of few words, Bert might sometimes come in for a drink, but felt no social obligation to talk and often lapsed into silence. Mostly, he just answered our questions, slowly, thoughtfully, translating our English into his own: curlews were rain-bods, skylarks were skillies, lapwings, lappies. If he didn't understand, he simply declined to answer, while being amused by our ignorance of local idioms and country ways. Only on one occasion did he take me by surprise with a question of his own. As we walked down the road from the local shop one day, he suddenly paused as if struck by a thought, and looking sideways, as if at something far away in the hills, said very quietly: 'Will ye lie wit' me, then?' I thought I'd misheard and stumblingly replied: 'Eh, sorry?' But he only said it again, more softly this time, and further away: 'Will ye lie wit' me?' It was touching, ancient, wistful, a phrase from some long-gone impossible pastoral, almost bookish if it weren't also so matter-of-fact. It was the question of a man who perhaps, in all his eighty years or so, had not had occasion to ask before, or who took his cues from the natural world about him. For myself, all I could do was pretend I hadn't heard or hadn't understood. I clumsily changed the subject, while his slow shake of the head contained all the sadness of a negative, larger than even he might have known. To Bert's credit he never held it against me but continued to bring eggs when there were some to spare, or come in for a whisky and, if not exactly conversation, perhaps just for a different, more shared solitariness.

Returning to those hills, as I still do, to escape my sedentary academic life, to walk, to think, to sleep with the sounds of owls and pheasants, lambs and ewes in my ears, is, I know, a luxury of the city dweller, for whom the landscape needs neither working nor minding, but is a fair-weather option. Yet sometimes, walking along the railway path, once made level for the traction of those dangerous tubs, heavy with spoils, it is hard to forget the cost of this quiet and self-absenting escape. History lurks not far under the national park's tidied footpaths and waymarked routes. It's as if, walking, you might still hear the ratchet repeat of wagon wheels, smell the discharge of coal and steam, catch the calcine dust in your lungs. And it's as if you might still feel, somehow, among the underlying quicks of grass everywhere, those recurrent tumuli of the man-made: those shadows of sleepers, the originals long removed, whose underlay can still be felt like the alternation of something soft then hard, smooth then raised, under your feet. Unquiet sleepers, as the novelist hinted but did not write, can be found here too.

Mick Imlah (FOUR)

Westmorland

Fragments of weather-war. A frost in May
Searing the damson blossom. Hay uncut,
The know-all cocking looks at Morecambe Bay
Where indigo clouds trundle from beaten Ireland.
Late August: oats which swam in the June wind
Laid in bleak patches, mottled, grey-green, drowned.

Geoffrey Hill (SIX)

from The Daybooks IV: ODI BARBARE

XL

Betws-y-Coed dullish red glow Swiss-chasmed
Myriad-black-faceted Blaenau gaping:
Senile grins galls humbles our greed so fancy
    Senile in Bala?

Squatting Brummies sullen mood synthesizers
Adelina Patti who gargled Welsh airs
Where should one brood *Parsifal* but in wild Wales
    Sinister Grail-talk:

Your guess what twists us so rightwing and dotty
Europe's secrets not safe with Sanskrit even
Gwalia hostage to insatiable
    Swoln rhododendrons:

Goldengrove notebooks ripped for late bequeathing
Dyscrasy Publike its own gifts to plunder
Hazardings unscathed by the harsh alignments
      Made for survival:

Make believe Merz | might be collage of rip-offs
Bless the mute parlous for our safe bestowings
Meteor showers sign expropriation
      Cypress's roof-tree:

Hendre Fechan hearth of our hearts' indwelling
Giving song hearth-room and the harp's thrilled diction
Deep penillion woven to snow's curled measures
      Heard past unhearing

XLI

God who holds our memories reft at pre-birth
I would trust intended their restitution:
Sense them sometimes vibrant in music's ratios
      Tighten the grammar

Birtwistle says one myth conceives a lifetime
Long his own time-mythist the seventeen arched
Accrington Town viaduct wired immortal
      Even in passing

Lamentation's triumph rejoicing Orpheus
His detached head that can be turned at pleasure
Speculate these opera cast the shades by
      Lucent obstruction

(Strange to each other in that intimacy
Purgatory even can learn to weep at
Paolo I am not nor are you Francesca
    No such temptation)

There is no narrative but purpose why such
Acts defy endings • Let us reap the darkness
Take to ourselves limping Eurydice's cry
    New to abandon

Lunar fallibilities eyes adjusting
I do not grasp half of what I would tell • No
Tragedy no triumph | a bulging moonface
    Tops the horizon

XLII

Herein public dyscracy given notice:
Not by all non-juring | take Common Law Coke
Held too great an oracle with the People
    England could bear him

Ignorance beats innocence through the checkpoint
Many sit unsaved should I claim exemption
Many lose wagers with themselves as stake-out
    Bugger *what fettle*

Noble lines pre-eminently disordered
How the hierarchies overshot their runways
I have had savant say *monarchical re-*
    Public befell us

Obligation's challenger unjust right • Old
Triumph wired *no triumph no tragedy* • De-
Mystification of our Lords and Commons
    Contra naturam

I would not offload to malignant spheroids
Fate v choice granted we persist and that so
Uningratiatingly light revisits
    Rimming the re-scars:

Ancientry booms if you are Norfolk freehold
Bracken-guarded airfields where now the pigeons
Ponderous wingladen in near-botched take offs
    Rattle the spinneys

XLIII

Lucrative failing no poor oxymoron
Gravely highlight solo polyphony this
Shagged ur-pragmatism of standup comics
    Working rejection

Not at all like self-harmers | much more like the
Scorpion Ibsen my reputed master
Plied with daft fruit there to transplant its venom
    Each to his hobby:

Targeted late laurels a full thesaurus
Whom could you grudge crowned with essential honours
Time's observance high-wrought imagination's
    Body of nerve ends:

May have seen films dire till the planes touch combat
Stand-in tall comrade siphons Fritz off yoúr tail
Vibrant fabrics twanging to fatal eye-flash
Flamers of spirit:

Snap of our poised loves in the breaking consort
Vibrancies signed for by archaic plectrum
Hallelujah stripped off the strapping harp strings
Orpheus in passage:

What is *just reach* apropos *just abiding*
Spell me war's haulage of forgotten ensigns:
Torque me Sopwith Camel around its prop-shaft
Spinning the pilot

WALES

An island is
a rooted boat
and granite vessels
do set sail

GWYNETH LEWIS (NINE)

Gwyneth Lewis (NINE)

Otherworlds

Sea Virus

I knew I should never have gone below
but I did, and the fug of bilges and wood
caught me aback. The sheets of my heart
snapped taut to breaking, as a gale
stronger than longing filled the sail
inside me. To be shot of land
and its wood smoke! To feel the keel
cold in a current! To see the mast
inscribing water like a restless pen
writing a fading wake! It's true,
I'm ruined. Not even peace will do
to keep me ashore now. Not even you.

When I wrote this poem a few years ago, I thought it was about recognising that, having been to sea, I could never again be fully committed to land. Now, I'm not so sure that it isn't about visiting Annwfn, the Celtic 'not-world' that's folded into our own. Cwm Cych in Pembrokeshire is reputed to be one of several entrances to this region and, according to the Welsh medieval tales, the *Mabinogion*, Lundy island is another.

It's difficult to know what kind of world Annwfn is exactly. *Geiriadur Prifysgol Cymru* (The University of Wales Dictionary) defines it as derived from the Latin 'ingenium', with the resultant meaning 'the In-world'. In thirteenth-century Welsh it was the under-world, the nether world, the land of fairies. By the fourteenth, it had changed into 'the abyss; the deep' as a noun but, as an adjective it meant 'not deep, shallow'. In her *Legendary Poems from the Book of Taliesin* (2007), Marged Haycock describes it as 'an +dwfyn', very deep and associated with flowing water or a silver stream.

Lundy has been a romance close to home for as long as I can remember. When we were children, Campbells' steamers ran excursions from the end of Penarth pier to the resorts along the Bristol Channel. Our Sunday School trip, one year, was to Weston-Super-Mare further north. I was too young to remember the day itself but I have a vivid recollection of the ferry pulling away from the pier and our minister waving his handkerchief in farewell. During the summer, you can still take a day trip to Lundy to visit the island from various points on the Welsh side of the Bristol Channel, sailing on 'The Waverley', the oldest sea-going paddle steamer in the world. From Bideford or Ilfracombe on the North Devon coast the voyage usually takes under two hours.

The island stands like a fortress in the Channel, three miles long and half a mile wide. There is only one easy landing place, a jetty built behind Rat Island, a rocky point which gives precious shelter from the prevailing south-westerly winds. Lundy isn't off Brazil or anywhere exotic, but it may be something more interesting. If physicists are correct, and we live in only one of multiple worlds, then Lundy's a threshold between at least two. You don't have to be dead to enter Annwfn, you can pass easily – sometimes too easily – between our world and it, but its physical laws (let alone the moral ones) are subtly different and entirely alien.

*

I was learning to sail in the Bristol Channel off Cardiff a few years ago and so, of course, I listened intently to the BBC shipping forecast, especially for conditions in sea-area Lundy: '… Plymouth, Sole, Lundy, Fastnet, Irish Sea' goes the official weather litany. Lundy, from the Norse word for puffin, was the goddess who ruled the Bristol Channel, with its steep tidal range and shallow, choppy water, brown with silt brought down by the River Severn. The plan with the boat was to make for Brazil. (My husband and I reached Ceuta, a Spanish enclave in North Africa, and from there retreated to Andalusia. That was a long story and has been told elsewhere, in *Two in a Boat: A Marital Voyage*.)

Islands can be a refuge when life on the mainland becomes overwhelming. I've done a fair bit of running away to islands. My first was Nantucket, the tiny island off the Massachusetts coast. I fled there after a failed relationship in New York. Having no money, I waitressed in a seafood restaurant, wore a big plastic lobster on my lapel. I bought a bike and, in my time off, cycled all over the island. I met some fishermen, learned to surfcast for bluefish; I explored the Quaker graveyard and watched sunset every night off the westerly Madaket, evoked in one of Robert Lowell's most famous early poems. Later, doing research at Oxford, I broke the grip of a summer of depression by going to Tiree with some friends. There we drank with the bachelors next door and I walked for miles in the crofters' wellies I still have to this day. On Inishbofin, off the Mayo coast, I fled noise and doing a job I didn't want, by looking at the flotsam beach where whale vertebrae are sometimes to be found.

*

Everywhere looks like somewhere else. The Egyptian geographer Ptolemy compared the passage between Hartland and Lundy to the seaway between Gibraltar and Africa. He marked Hartland Point

Heraclis Promontory on his map of the world, evoking the exit westwards from the Mediterranean, known mythically as the Pillars of Hercules. I had gazed for hours at the actual Pillars from the window of a hospital in Ceuta: the plume-covered Rock of Gibraltar and the Moroccan Mount Acho, with the outline of a dead nymph, pining for Hercules forever. Over the narrow Strait of Gibraltar, Africa and Europe stare at each other. If I were a poor African, I might think about trying to cross this short, but dangerous distance by boat or jet ski or I might risk my life, as many do, by trying to swim across. Due to my husband's serious illness, we had entered a terrifying limbo in Ceuta, not knowing if he was going to survive.

Lundy is the location of one of the most literary gateways into the Otherworld. 'Annwn' or 'Annwfn', the Celtic Otherworld is portrayed in early Welsh poetry. Taliesin's *Preiddiau Annwfn* ('The Spoils of Annwfn') describes King Arthur's raid on an island, 'Ynys Afallon' (the island of apples). Taliesin was the great mythical poet of the Welsh tradition, the shape-shifter and mystic. He was an actual poet but later writers used him as a heteronym for a rich vein of legends. Taliesin's descriptions of the island are often paradoxical. He calls it 'Caer Vedwit' (Miad-fest Fort), 'Caer Rigor' (Petrification Fort), Caer Golud' (Fort of Impediment) and 'Caer Ochren' (the Angular Fort). However, this place is a good physical fit with actual Lundy, which Taliesin also calls 'Caer Wydyr' (Glass Fort). The island guards the Bristol Channel and the dramatic cliffs along its south side might easily be a defensive rampart. The tiny crystals in the island's granite make its cliff shine and scintillate from a distance. This isn't too far from Lundy as the island of the radiant door of Celtic mythology.

The patron saint of Lundy is St Helen, the third-century mother of the Emperor Constantine. She played an important role in discovering the Real Cross. Behind her, mythically, is Sant Elen, the Celtic goddess of travellers and tracks, after whom the Roman road Sarn Helen in the Cambrian Mountains was named. She's also the patron of the elbow and the sudden turn in a road or a river, places which are conducive to entering a different frame of mind.

When King Arthur reputedly staged his raid on Lundy, it's said he suffered huge losses. According to Taliesin,

> Tri lloneit Prytwen yd aetham-ni idi:
> *Three full loads of Prydwen we went into it:*
> nam[yn] seith ny dyrreith o Gaer Sidi.
> *save seven, none came back from Caer Siddi.*

The prize for which Arthur had risked so much was nothing less than the Cauldron of the King of the Otherworld. A magical object, the cauldron turned the death of things into life. The rim of this one was decorated with pearls, heated by the breath of nine maidens and would not boil the food of a coward.

Of all the islands I've been to, Lundy is the most rugged. The living here has never been easy. This is how E.M. Hubbard, who undertook 'A Survey of Trees on Lundy' in 1971, describes the conditions:

> Not only do plants have to contend with high salt-laden winds, strong ultra-violet light and violent storms, but the peaty soil itself is thin, highly acidic, subject to great variation in water content and poorly supplied with mineral salts and clay constituents.

A grown man can be knocked over by the winds on the island. There's a vortex by the Old Light that's so strong at certain times of the year that not even the bravest or heaviest will go through it. You simply go round the other side. Lundy's a cussed place, with a mind of its own, and I like its awkwardness. When planes come into land on Lundy, someone has to make sure that the sheep are cleared from between the grass runway's white stones. One of its Victorian owners posted a notice: 'This island is entirely private property. There are no public roads, footpaths or rights of way whatsoever hereon.' In November 1954, the island itself had its say in the matter. A landslip destroyed both the stone on which it was written and the adjacent lime kiln. Clearly Lundy doesn't take kindly to being part of anybody's plan. It keeps its own world, time and tide.

When the weather closes in, the mainland recedes, and Lundy becomes nothing but a patch of grass in the middle of waves. On a boat, even though you can see the open sky and sea, the vessel itself is often claustrophobic. An island can be small in the same way. There's nothing here except the edge and the weather. No, it's worse than a boat, you can't move it to a more congenial place. And you can't get off. For all its wide views, Lundy is a place where it's easy to become stuck. My favourite prisoner of Lundy was Amelia Heaven, the invalid daughter of the owners. The Heaven family built Millcombe House, the big house of the island. Born in 1833, Amelia or Mille suffered from such poor health during her life that she released her fiancé from their engagement and never married. She, however, wrote most of the family's diaries from 1870 until 1905. She described fog around the island as 'a naked feather bed'. She was so frail that she couldn't be out in the open air for long, and one of the family photographs shows a shelter made for her in the garden. Her siblings mocked it, calling it 'The Ugly', but Amelia protested 'It is the House Beautiful. That is the ugly one up there,' referring to the grand Millcombe. Now 'The Ugly' refers to a small shelter from which you can sit and watched countless ships pass the island.

This area of the Bristol Channel has always attracted rogues and outlaws. In the twelfth century, the de Marisco family used the island as a base for piracy against passing traders with the North Devon coast. A descendant, William de Marisco, was executed by King Henry III in 1242. He was hung, drawn and quartered and a piece of him sent to the four principal cities in the kingdom.

In 1625 a group of Turks took refuge in Lundy and was rumoured to have taken sixty men from a church in Cornwall as slaves. In 1630 Captain Plumleigh reported on the situation to the Lord Treasurer, saying:

> Egypt was never more infested with caterpillars than the Channel with Biscayers. On the 23rd inst. there came out of St Sebastian twenty sail of sloops; some attempted to land on Lundy, but were repulsed by the inhabitants.

In the middle of the eighteenth century, Thomas Benson, who was to become MP for Barnstaple, leased the island from its owners and began to run a black market in galley slaves. He contracted with the government to transport a shipload of convicts to Virginia, but had them brought, instead, to Lundy, where they were set to work, excavating the hard granite in order to create Benson's cave, which was to be used for smuggling. Seven or eight of the men escaped in a boat to Hartland point. When he was upbraided for his deception by the government, Benson retorted that sending them to Lundy was the same as sending them to America.

William Hudson Heaven bought Lundy in 1834 for £9,870, paid with the compensation he received from the emancipation of slaves on his estate in the West Indies. For eighty years Lundy was home to the Heaven family. But even the Heavens found life hard there. The island is a huge granite outcrop, the result of volcanic activity fifty-eight and a half million years ago. This is the same event that created the Shiant Islands in Scotland, a giant plug of molten rock rising from deep within the earth's mantle. Granite quarrying was established on the island but it never went particularly well. From the start, there was conflict between the Heaven family and the rough labourers required to hew and remove the stone. Three hundred men came to work the quarries, many of them fleeing trouble on the mainland. The Bideford County Court judge described the working residents of Lundy as 'the fag ends of society'.

Even Dr Linacre, the company surgeon, who came to dry out on the island failed and had to be replaced. In 1864 George Cauridge, the company clerk, hanged himself. The Victorian Heavens introduced three wallabies. Two were rumoured to have fallen into a well and drowned. A pair of swans, wanted for decorative reasons on Pondsbury water took one look at it and flew back to the mainland. The thousands of visitors who come to Lundy every summer now are hardly the dregs of society. They come, in their anoraks and walking boots, buy cuddly seabirds and Lundy fudge from the shop, then go home to the mainland.

*

They say that if the windows of your house on Lundy aren't rattling, then you know that fog is on its way. In the nineteenth century lighthouse keepers fired guns as fog horns and on one occasion so dense and persistent was the fog that the firing from the westerly cliffs had to last for seventy-two hours.

It was in foggy conditions that the HMS *Montagu*, testing new radio equipment for the British navy, struck a point north of Shutter Rock on 30 May 1906. The commanding officer made his way up to the North Light and greeted the keeper, saying how pleased he was that he'd made it to Hartland Point. The lighthouse keeper pointed out that this was the North Lundy light but the captain refused to believe him, insisting he wasn't on an island at all but on the Devon mainland. Words were exchanged. This didn't help the master at his subsequent court martial.

Fog is a sailor's worst nightmare, as the inability to see puts you in danger in a moving environment. On an island, however, fog has other effects. It changes one's perception of space and one's place in it. Fog on Lundy isn't a straightforward blanketing out of visibility. It often appears in strata. This has created practical problems. The first lighthouse built on the island's Beacon Hill was completed in 1820. It was ninety-six feet high. By 1858 it had become clear that the tower was too high. The owner of the island, Mr Heaven, wrote that 'the Light is not of the slightest use to vessels when most in want of it, in thick and blowing weather, but also in many dark nights, because when the island itself is free from it, the Lighthouse stands so high that it is capped by fog'. The tower was reduced in height but today the two working lights on the north and southern ends of Lundy are both low and the walker looks down at them from cliffs above.

The Old Light is visible from almost every part of the island. It has the breezy but compact look of the Maine lighthouses painted by Edward Hopper. It now provides accommodation for visitors and there's often a deck chair where the old lantern turned, offering the best views of the whole island. At night, the light from Hartland Point sweeps across the wall of your room, six flashes every five seconds, like a regular migraine aura. Nowadays, the two working lights on Lundy are on the north and the south point and one of the hazards of staying in the Castle Cottage is that, during fog, you are very close to the fog horn. It's a high-pitched, feminine sound, like the last of a species calling for a mate who can't answer, because he doesn't exist.

Communication with the mainland and with passing shipping is an important part of an island's activities. The pastor on the island used to let mariners on boats anchored in the Lundy roads know that a service was about to begin in St Helena's church by flying a flag from the castle. The eight bells in the church tower were rung for the first time in 1898. By 1905, when change ringers from the Gloucester and Bristol Diocesan Association wanted to sound the bells, it was found that the salty winds had corroded the iron bearings. It looked as though they would have to leave without striking a blow, but bad weather detained them and the visitors were able to carry out repairs and then ring a complete peal of Stedman Triples, five thousand and forty changes in two hours and fifty-three minutes.

As well as making vibrations in the air, the Lundy bells are eloquent in another way, with inscriptions cast into their metal. These were commissioned by the Reverend Hudson Grossett Heaven, who built the church. I'm always looking for found poems and the mottoes on the eight Lundy bells tell their own story of language and death:

Bell 1	I warn that the hour has now come for prayers
Bell 2	We all sing the praises of God
Bell 3	H.G.H., the vicar, had us brought into being
Bell 4	Charles Carr & Co made us AD 1897
Bell 5	When rung confusedly we announce dangers
Bell 6	When rung backwards we signify fires
Bell 7	When sounding in the right way we proclaim joys
Bell 8	I say farewell to the departing souls

As well as being an obvious danger to shipping, fog on Lundy is known to produce mysterious effects, as described by the nineteenth-century historian John Chanter: 'not a thick, dense, fog but a light, vapoury, transparent mist, in which objects at a few yards' distance appear magnified to three time their actual size. A phenomenon akin to mirage also sometimes appears, and the outline of the Island, as viewed from the shore, and of ships sailing under it, are often lifted and distorted'. These conditions play tricks on the senses. In this sense, Lundy isn't a fixed entity but an island in flux. According to Chanter, it is 'sometimes invisible from the shore, but generally looming dim and mysterious, more or less shrouded in mists, or capped with cloud-reefs; occasionally standing out lofty, clear and distinct, bright with varied hues of rock, fern, and heather, its granite cliffs glittering as they reflect the rays of the morning sun'.

I was told at the Lundy shop that, the last time snow fell here, a rare event, the Devon mainland appeared to be so close to the island that you felt you could step between the two. Indeed, the ability to see Lundy has been used for generations on the Devon coast as a weather forecasting tool. The rhyme goes:

> Lundy high, it will be dry,
> Lundy low, it will be snow.
> Lundy plain, it will be rain.
> Lundy in haze, fine for days.

On the island itself, you learn that visibility is a favour granted to you by the gods of weather. In medieval Welsh mythology, fog on Lundy is one of the signs that a gateway to the Otherworld is nearby. My favourite character in the the *Mabinogion*, is Iarll Niwl, the Earl of Fog. He takes over familiar landscapes and transports you to another world where neither space nor time obey the usual rules.

Perhaps one of the reasons why Lundy is an Otherworld is that it doesn't conform to conventional time and space. Many things about being there took me by surprise. Far from feeling that I was on a speck of land in the middle of the Bristol Channel, I felt as if the island were huge, a vulnerable target in the middle of busy shipping lanes. I kept on expecting tankers to crash into it. The wind pushes everything, ships as well as flotsam and jetsam, towards the towering granite cliffs of the western side. The flag on top of St Helena's Church tower is regularly blown away. Unless washing is hung out to dry in a walled garden, the Landmark Trust's sheets and pillowcases are likely to end up on the north coast of Devon. In 1941 a German Heinkel crashed on the island, with five crew on board. Another tried to land on the Lundy plateau near Dead Cow Point and two crew members were killed but the remaining three survived, to be captured. The following year a British Whitley aircraft hit the cliff about Pilot's Quay and you can still see the engines wedged in the cliff-face.

The more I looked at Lundy, the larger it appeared to me, even though I knew, in my head, that it wasn't very big at all: three miles long by half a mile wide. The more I looked, the more distinct areas I saw. Adam Nicolson has noticed this effect. 'Islands,' he writes, 'are made larger … by the scale of the sea that surrounds them … The sea elevates these few acres into something they would never be if hidden in the mass of the mainland. The sea makes the islands significant, framed by it.'

I was here to try to get my eyes to focus on land again, after years of concentrating on the sea. As an act of will, I turned my eyes from the overfalls at the south-western corner of Lundy and stared, instead, at the rolling moor which is the island's backbone.

Walking on Lundy is never a straightforward matter. I set out from the south to the North Light, thinking that I'd mark my progress by the conveniently named Quarter, Halfway and Threequarter Walls. So far, so scientific. Except that, looking more closely at the map, I notice that the Threequarter Wall is actually two-thirds of the way up the island. The path is lined with granite boulders every fifty yards which used to be painted white to help the lighthouse-keepers not to lose the road in the dark. I made good progress to begin with, but the last quarter of the island seemed endless. By the time I got to the North Point, I was worn out, even though it's less than three miles from the Old Light. On the way back, though, I covered the ground with incredible swiftness, as if space had concertinaed and the gods of the Otherworld had reeled the Old Light closer. It reminded me of Pwyll's attempt in the *Mabinogion* to catch Rhiannon. She's riding a white horse but however hard he tries he can't reach her. This is because two time scales are operating in the same place: the human and that of the Otherworld, and there's a mismatch between them.

A less mystical description of this phenomenon is given by Adam Nicolson writings on the Shiants (islands as we know geologically related to Lundy): 'History does not move here in a single current, sweeping everything up into one comprehensive pattern of change, but in a laminar flow, different sheets of time moving at different rates, one above the other, like the currents in the sea. At the lowest level, the coldest and oldest, there is virtually no movement.'

It seems to me that the church of St Helena has its attitude to time completely correct. The clock above the entrance declares: *Tempus Sator Aeternitatis* – 'Time is the Sower of Eternity' and not the other way around. On Lundy, eternity seems to come down to a terrestrial level, to the salt-blown turf with its tormentil, glaucus sedge and sheep's bit scabious, and the gods of Annwfn walk with their human companions.

There are other anomalies on Lundy. In 1856 building work revealed some ancient graves, containing skeletons allegedly eight feet high. These were then identified with the ninth-century chieftain Hubba who led raids on the area. Another giant is said to have come from Cornwall and, in return for ridding the island of snakes and reptiles, was turned into Constable Rock, a ten-metre-high column of granite. Quite how or why this was deemed a reward is not clear. But, as usual, mythology often hides a kernel of literal truth. Gigantism does happen on islands which are very isolated, such as the Galapagos, when inbreeding results in genetic abnormalities.

When the fog is down and the gods are making all walks impossible, the only place for the island pilgrim to go is inwards. Many visitors comment how they're felled by sleep and spend much more time than usual in that nightly virtual terrain. Perhaps this is why so many people come to the island to change their lives, because it gives them the time and space to take an alternative view of their habitual selves. This portal is utterly reliable.

Fog

Above all else fog shuns
        publicity,
wants intimate islands,
        private seas
(collisions don't matter).
        It has a selective memory:

A lonely fog horn
        cries to mate
with answering sirens
        (too late, too late!).
An island is
        a rooted boat

and granite vessels
        do set sail
through seas of fog
        towards the wail
of mainland lights
        Three ponies stand
at the Half-Way Wall,

dew in their coats.
        Yarrow's furred
with moisture. We are blind,
        steering by what's hard
through white-out. Now
        the voyage is inwards and in words.

Andrew McNeillie (EIGHT)

In Search of Miriam

This is a return journey. At once the phrase reminds me of Dylan Thomas. His comic dialogue of going back to Swansea and asking after his younger self is I think one of his most delightful autobiographical pieces. I have always had a soft spot for it, particularly, because I haunted Swansea too when a young dog. Like Thomas in this, if nothing else, I was once a tyro reporter in the district. I worked the valleys for two local papers, and did 'penny-a-line', often for the Swansea-based *South Wales Evening Post*. Thomas mapped my world, urban, rural, coastal, human, spiritual and literary. He worked on the *Post* in a delinquent way for a while. He was not the best journalistic role model. But that did not deter me as I set foot and set forth.

My high point in the pages of the *Post* was a diary piece they reprinted from the *South Wales Guardian* about a cockle-woman called Miriam Williams. A formidable lady, then aged sixty-two, she was a worthy incarnation of her biblical namesake, Moses's prophetic sister who led the women and sang of the sea in the Book of Exodus. She used to peddle shellfish up the Amman valley in my day. In the course of talking with her I discovered she had been written about before, by

H.V. Morton in *In Search of Wales*. The book came out in 1932, now, as I write, all of eighty years ago. I quoted Morton in my little piece, in a passage I said, surely too generously, reminded me of J.M. Synge and his Aran islanders (I was much preoccupied by Synge's *Aran Islands* in those days):

> The race across the sands is a wild affair. Young and old perched like Arabs on the hind-quarters of their patient steeds, set off at a trit-trot, splashing through the fords ...
>
> Oh yes, indeed, it was a hard life, said Miriam, grubbing away for a few shillings a week in the winter in mussel time, with the wind tearing in from the sea so that you could not breathe, and your fingers frozen stiff as a rope, it was even harder.
>
> ... it was impossible to feel any pity under the sky, with the gulls wheeling and the clean wind blowing and Miriam singing in a loud voice about something that happened in Wales long ago.

Discovering the Morton connection gave my story a depth it otherwise wanted. His book derived from a series of articles in the *Daily Herald* where the account of Miriam and her tribe bore the headline '"BEDOUINS" of the COCKLE BEDS'.

As may be judged from the photograph here, you do not need to be a dyed-in-the wool orientalist to see the resemblance. But Morton had such tendencies. He first made his name in the Middle East and would go on to travel widely there and to write several books about the 'Holy Land'. There is a photograph in his biography, taken just after the opening of Tutankhamun's tomb in 1923. It shows treasures being escorted away under armed guard, led imperiously, on foot, by the archaeologist Howard Carter. Dodging about at the periphery, camera in hand, is Morton, caught by a *Times* photographer. His own coverage of the occasion put him on the Fleet Street map.

*

Last year I had the idea to go back 'In Search of Miriam', to see if, at Penclawdd, down on the Llwchwr estuary, along the famous Gower Peninsula, I could find out what became of her. I made a single enquiry and in next to no time was introduced to her surviving family. They are I found a considerable presence in the local shellfish industry, one now directed more at the European than the home market up the valleys but still continuing there. Proud of Miriam, her daughter and son and other family members made me warmly welcome. Such warmth reminded me of my time in the South. Coal and steel stood at the heart of things then, subject to their own tides of fortune and misfortune, employment and unemployment; and class, community and labour were vital categories. (Don't ask me were they better times. Of course they were and weren't.)

As I Googled up a map I thought of Morton planning his own journey and driving on very different roads, at a snail's pace, to quite another place called Penclawdd than the one I would encounter. I decided to break my journey and to stay overnight in Swansea to give me the greater part of the next day on the Gower. I went online and my search threw up an expensive but unique option, at Dylan Thomas's birthplace, 5 Cwmdonkin Drive (or 'Cwmbonkin' as I found some 'Nogood Boyo' had renamed the road sign with his marker pen). Here was a degree of symmetry I could not resist.

That night I dreamt of the sea and of web-footed cockle women. Every line of Thomas's I knew and half-knew by heart – including the one about 'a double angel' sprouting 'from the stony lockers like a tree on Aran' – seemed to pour in and out of my head, as I lay in the dark, now asleep, now awake, staring at the ceiling, listening to the silence, within the bluster of the wind outside, and the tick-tock and intermittent chimes of a grandfather clock in the front room below. I could have chosen any of the rooms – including Thomas's own cramped one – but I went for the front bedroom, in which the poet first came into the world. Not that the bed wasn't as comfortable as you could wish but I found it hard to sleep with all that was going on in my head. Not only the ghost of Dylan Thomas but everything to do with my time in the valleys, half a lifetime ago, seemed intent on making its own return journey.

It was September, autumnal but not October, the month of the poet's birth, which would have made an even nicer circle. The Gleison mining tragedy had happened just the week before. Everyone was talking about it. It was all over the *South Wales Evening Post*. And inevitably it called to mind shades of Aberfan (9.15am, 21 October 1966), two weeks in the wake of which I'd started my new life as a reporter in the anthracite town of Ammanford. I was from the North. The mining and heavy industries of the South were new to me, as was their living human cost.

Now lying in the pitch-black like a revenant in Llaregub, I saw and heard ghosts from those days. At once among the shades I caught the melancholy gaze of one in particular: Noel Lewis, his balding head blue-veined with coal. I heard him wheezing at his desk beside me, lungs full of dust from his earlier career down the pit. He seemed always to be writing a weekly instalment of his history of industry in the area. I am sure he is writing it still in the next world – an Elysian underworld – and making account of the practice of drift or 'slant' mining, as pursued at Gleison. And he was one of many, and many a younger man, afflicted with pneumoconiosis that haunted the mining towns and villages of those days. They stand now before my mind like fallen figures in faded regimental photographs from the world wars.

*

My original article referred to Miriam's son who'd chosen, to her, perhaps feigned, perhaps real annoyance, to leave school early for the life of the estuary, a life of hardship and hazard, yet also of family vocation and tradition. She herself had done the same, but even earlier, at the age of twelve. She could remember when three women drowned, after mussels. 'It's very dangerous after cockles, but it's worse with mussels because they're farther out. I often came near to drowning when I was young … That's all we had in our village and that's all we've got now. I remember in the 1921 strike when we used to walk to Gowerton with loads of cockles and catch a train up the valley. I never wanted to get out of bed.' So early in my supposed manhood I recorded.

But Jeff Williams, Miriam's son, described its attraction as 'a life on its own' and all he said seemed to celebrate that, no matter what hardship and adversity it entailed, and the inwardness of his life struck me as enviably wide-open, wide-open as the sea itself, and profound in its attachment to a community and a coastal world that reached beyond anything I could have guessed, to far corners of the isles.

There were six of us by the time we were through lunch: my host Marlene Hughes (Miriam Williams's daughter) and her son Richard; Jeff and his wife Elizabeth; and David Tucker, a cousin from America over to research a family history. (Miriam Williams's maiden name was Tucker.) He was pursuing on this trip the life of his grandfather. Walter Tucker was a miner and an autodidact who wrote regularly for the *Herald of Wales* accounts of walks he made in the district. (Some of Dylan Thomas's juvenilia also appeared in the *Herald of Wales.*) How local newspapers served the world in those days, as still also in my time, as mirrors to locality and vigorous, fallible, parochial, narrow, tragic, comical, common life.

David Tucker's mother was Irish, and he was pleased by the thought of his mixed 'celtic' heritage. Tucker is a name you will find in south-west Wales not uncommonly and in Devon (in Ireland too). 'Tucker's Fish' is one of the 'bombed and vanished' shops in Dylan Thomas's 'Return Journey'. It felt strangely like a turn towards returning for me.

My maternal granny was a Tucker. When her Tuckers went to London, I do not know, nor where they went from. But my sense of returning depended on nothing so tenuous as speculative genealogy.

As we ate and talked the conversation turned to Gleison, and Jeff suddenly recalled 'the day of Aberfan' as clearly as if it had been that very morning. '"There's a terrible day," my mother had said, just as to the weather. I took her up to Swansea and on to Ammanford. I went selling … and that was all the news. They were all going off to help, like now to Pontardawe.' One disaster caused us to reflect on another and I think I was the one to raise the spectre of the 2004 Morecambe cockling tragedy. Chinese illegal immigrants, enslaved to a gang-master, had been sent out at the wrong state of the tide, and at an hour – 9.30pm on a February night – scarcely credible. (As chance has it, the cockling scenes in the resulting movie, *Ghosts*, were filmed at Bury Port, not far from Penclawdd.)

'It's a job to know it in the daylight, let alone in the dark,' said Jeff. 'You'd get small rain and fog on a day and you wouldn't know where you are, even on your own patch. You'd see a crowd of carts – so I'll go over there, you say, for safety in numbers. Then of a sudden the carts would be in the air. They weren't carts, they were oyster-catchers. The fog magnifies everything. But can you see your hand in front of your face when it's dark? What hope did they have? They didn't know where they were.'

When H.V. Morton visited Penclawdd he went to the Ship and Castle Inn 'where the people came to go out', Marlene now explained. 'It was six in the morning. People wouldn't speak to him, mind. They spoke in Welsh and the women hid their faces in their shawls.' He had his camera and they turned away from it. Morton tells us the women thought it 'bad luck' to be photographed. That was true enough. But there was nothing superstitious about it. 'They were on benefit, see?' said Marlene. Morton calculated there were some two hundred gathered there. 'Then my mother came. The camera didn't worry her. She was a girl. She would talk but she said to him "I can't speak now … got to go! … the tide won't wait!"'

But in her heyday Miriam would wait, until the others had gone out. That way she could go where she knew the cockles were good and ready and have them to herself. It was all a game of cat-and-mouse with them. She went out last and came back last, so they wouldn't see how many she'd got. H.V. Morton was not the only journalist to discover Miriam. Once she was interviewed by the BBC's Franklin Engelman for his radio programme *Down Your Way*, in which interviewees were asked to pick a favourite piece of music. Miriam chose 'The Last Rose of Summer'.

'Here comes "The Last Rose of Summer" the women joked ever after when they saw Miriam, whether she was going out or coming back.'

But intimacy was at the heart of it all, whether as community or within nature and the life of the shoreland. The people knew the estuary through its seasons intimately, as farmers know their land, and they knew how to tend it. Jeff told how things had been in his youth and younger manhood in the 1960s. You saw into places in more detail from the back of a donkey or from a pony cart. 'You look at the sand and you see where they are.' There was husbandry based on age-old practice. In their season cockles will multiply at an unusual rate. To enable them to do so you must thin them out, just as you must thin a row of carrots, or none will have room to grow. Jeff spoke of 'having it nice'.

In Welsh, the young cockles are called *agen* – a word that means literally 'cleft, slot, or fissure'. 'My mother used to say: "You hear the *agen* singing. When you hear the cuckoo you will hear the cockles rise." Tons and tons of them would appear, a foot high on top of the sand. You could shovel them in. If you didn't take them they'd die. Then they'd become shells. Mussels would fix on them. Mussels create mud and mud gets spartina grass, followed by smaller grass. Estuary becomes marshland.'

Spartina grass was introduced in the 1960s to help 'stabilise' the muddy borders of the river-mouth. It spread beyond control and did drastic damage to the cockle fishing. Fisheries policy in 1965 introduced licensing and policing of practice. Cocklers were forbidden to take the *agen* and the consequences were disastrous. The whole managerial enterprise proved to be against sustainable working. It allowed the demand-driven practice of dredging for cockles. But unlike the traditional hand-rake the dredger destroys the cockles' life-supporting environment. 'The actual beds have to be managed, tended. You have to know when to take cockles – when the "rushes" come in March and to thin the *agen*.' For a while the Fisheries in the 1960s made some gatherers Honorary Officers or inspectors, paying them £25.00 a year for their services. This was an enlightened move. The gatherers policed things differently. 'They *knew* when to take cockles. Cockles replenish themselves very quickly.' But all that went by the board and by the 1980s – that nightmare Thatcherian decade for South Wales and the rest of the isles – and a whole way of life was eroded to the brink of disaster.

When they went selling they went by bus and then walked for miles as far as the Waun (Gwaun-Cae-Gurwen – originally Gwaun Cegerwen, meaning 'white hemlock heath'), north-east on a tributary of the River Amman. The folk put their money out with a bowl on the roadside wall; and the bus drivers went along, stopping at intervals for Miriam and her son to leave the cockle baskets at different points. They then dismounted and walked back, fulfilling their orders. Cockles in the shell are called *cregyn* (meaning '[in the] shell' – *cregynydd* means 'a gatherer of shells') and cooked ones are called *rhuddain* (crimson coloured from boiling). I can taste the anthracite air and their briny estuarine bite at the mere mention of them.

There was solidarity and sociability in that world and respect for the estuary itself, for the fragility of nature as also for its wild force. And there was durance and hardship. Miriam would walk her apprentice son into the ground. To keep the money coming in they had to be adaptable and to move with the seasons. There were cockles, and there were mussels. Jeff remembered the first time they had gone selling winkles. They took them by train to Llandovery. They should have boiled them because, unlike cockles and mussels, winkles are mobile. The next thing they knew they were 'all over the train'.

The occasion's most archipelagically telling story concerned the making of 'Lava Bread', a local delicacy, more properly known as 'laver' from the seaweed *Porphyra umbilicalis* – a dark purplish-red weed that grows attached to stones on exposed beaches where the stones are usually covered by sand, so that the plant appears to grow in the sand itself. In earlier monochrome times, when the railway networks in Britain and, notably, the West of Ireland were far more extensive than they are now, and slow food was the order of the day, gatherers up and down the coastlines of both countries would put their bags of weed on a train, with a label for Swansea. A character straight out of Llaregub, 'Roberts the Lavabread' of Penclawdd would collect, and make payment by registered mail.

This was not so simply a matter of rail networks but of coastal ones, of an extensive seaboard economy. I remember one morning meeting a man on the north shore of Aran gathering winkles – in the winter of 1968 – who spoke of times when the islanders supplied the Billingsgate market, and I recall how much that pleased me, to think of such a far-away place brought near, and worlds joined so simply, regardless of boundary. Seaweed collecting on the islands had similar trajectories and networks, to and beyond the mainland, far afield, mapped also in the itineraries of the jobbers and agents who brokered the trade.

Just so, Jeff told me how his son had once travelled as far as Achill Island off the coast off Co. Mayo in search of laver weed, bringing back fifteen hundredweight in a van, after home supplies had been 'ripped away by storms in September'. At first the journey had threatened to be a disaster, for when he arrived on Achill he found that – as the expression was – 'the sand was in'. The weed was no good. But things proved to be charmed, for overnight the tide carried the sand away. It seemed a miracle. Or he himself went to the 'Knock' and the 'Strand' at Port Patrick in Galloway by train on occasion and later by road. Port Patrick is familiar territory to me. It is to be found in what I call 'McNeillieland'. So here was another piece in the jigsaw of my life geography, a trace retraced, another return upon my visit to the Gower in search of Miriam, another coastal arc in the archipelago.

*

Philosophers today, agitated by a prospect of environmental catastrophe, sometimes speak of seeking to 'live convergently with nature' (as David E. Cooper did in the *Times Literary Supplement*), though what they might mean by the idea is left a little vague. Nature is of course both fragile and red in tooth and claw. It is not a benign entity that wouldn't lay a finger on you ... 'though home and shelter you had none' (to adapt Wordsworth's poem 'Stepping Westward'). Nor is it malign. It has nothing of humanity about it, except it is our invention. A more helpful way of putting it might be to say 'convergently with labour', for it is really 'labour-saving' (now on an impossible scale to redress) that underwrites so much of our present difficulty, that and a concomitant impatience with husbandry; that and a recalibration of seasonality beyond anyone's control. But could we (professional or amateur) 'philosophers' hack it beyond the Symposium, out in the vineyard, out on the shore in all weathers like Miriam Williams? And for how much longer than a summer morning, before sneaking off to the nearest supermarket fish counter?

'We are causing our own problem,' said Richard, 'It's today being greedy at the expense of tomorrow.' But to those like the Williams family who have worked the estuary for generations, it was clear above all, as has been said, that Fisheries management had meant much mismanagement and abuse. In the Llwchwr estuary, an entire ecosystem was destabilised by series upon series of policy initiatives that hindsight soon proved unwise, as foresight by some on the ground predicted it would. (How does the ordinary, local person find a voice in the world?) Cockle beds were damaged irreversibly. Critical decisions had been made centrally by people who knew nothing directly about the natural history of shellfish or shoreland, day in, day out, year upon year, but only as 'science', statistics and regulation.

'The scientist is not *always* right,' said Jeff. Still less one might add are his or her political masters and their attendant bureaucracies – what we now call 'policy wonks'. There was no question but relative prosperity has made us 'greedy and lazy', wanting things 'on a plate' and wanting them *now* as fast food, as out-of-season food, courtesy of supermarket chains only too ready to meet our so-called *demands*, as opposed to anything that could be termed *needs* (even to speak of 'necessity-lite' and not the full-strength commodity).

The practice of seamless provision in the West might benefit poorer economies elsewhere – it depends what we mean by benefit and economy. But beyond doubt, in environmental and spiritual terms, it impoverishes our own. It denies seasonality – however recalibrated – just as recent and current politics tend to silence the proper witness of history, as opposed to the bogus cults of 'legacy' and 'heritage'. Vital structural aspects of resistance and tradition, memory and meaning are airbrushed away. A malleable, uprooted population, with no time to take time even to consider the possibility of pursuing a sustainable way of life, beomes more divorced from 'nature' than ever, and even more divorced from each other: all vital connection, in our great era of 'connectivity', between past, present, and future – Edmund Burke's trinity – broken as never before, not even by the upheaval of the Industrial Revolution.

All the more reason to go in search of the likes of Miriam Williams, for sober remonstrance of resolution and independence, our lives found wanting, in both senses of the term, as we sing in our chains like the sea.

Angharad Price (ONE)

Tynybraich

Tynybraich: the name belongs to a house and a mountain; to a family too, at least in local speech. They have been farming Tynybraich for centuries, my mother's forefathers. There's a genealogy in the family Bible, branches of men's names dating back to 1012.

We came to Tynybraich every school holiday, leaving the quarries of Arfon behind us and heading south. To Dinas Mawddwy, where we learned how to live with mountains, not against them. Turning off the main road, we saw flowers reaching for the car and rabbits running from it. Coming out from Y Ffridd we looked down at the Maesglasau valley and across to Tynybraich mountain, a pyramid of blue extending upwards from the narrow valley floor. In the distance, the rock of Maesglasau, its waterfall our vertical horizon.

We didn't care for the mountain, which we took for granted. We cared only for the house. After all, it was the house that gave the mountain its name. Tynybraich: 'House in the Mountain's Arm.' It was our grandparents' home and we were keen to get there. But there was the steep hill to descend, the brook to cross, the other hill to ascend, seeing nothing ahead but the car bonnet and some sky. Dogs would rush and bark at the sound of unfamiliar wheels.

Only Nan could calm us again. Our mother's mother, waiting for us at the farmhouse door, touched by the smell of food that came through the kitchen window.

She'd come to Dinas Mawddwy in wartime to visit a cousin. My grandfather, Taid, was newly widowed, nearly forty and a father of two. Nan never returned to her home in Cwm Nant yr Eira, the Valley of Snow, in neighbouring Montgomeryshire. On the day they were married she became a wife, a farm wife, a stepmother and a daughter-in-law all at once. Nan began her life at Tynybraich, soon herself to become a mother of two.

Taid insisted she learn to drive. She was to be self-sufficient. At her first outing, with fresh snow on the ground, the car veered off the mountain road and skidded to the edge of the ravine. He straightened the car and forced his young wife to drive back to the house. It was much later that she thanked him for his lesson. For the rest of her life, the car was her means of escape from Tynybraich. Every Wednesday she went to Machynlleth in it, and every Friday to Dolgellau; and to her sister's in Arthog on Saturday night. The car took her to the village on social visits, or in condolence. She delivered meals-on-wheels to old-age pensioners.

She was at her most independent in the car. At election time, she'd draw out her Plaid Cymru poster from the glove compartment. When Tynybraich was out of sight she'd stick it on the windscreen and drive around – a raging nationalist. Returning to Tynybraich, just before Y Ffridd, the poster was folded up and put away. Taid was Labour. There would have been trouble, for there was nothing he liked more than a good debate, and nothing she liked less.

She was an even-tempered woman. The evenness spread out from her. She organised her world evenly around her. Her kitchen table was an even cosmos: planets of plates and saucers, lids of jam jars, Welsh cakes, a Victoria sponge and rounds of bread and butter. Spoons and knives shone like stars between them.

She baked her Welsh cakes every morning, rolling out the speckled dough over the table, a continent whose boundaries stretched outwards from the middle, barely visibly, as the rolling pin moved lightly under

Nan's hand. Our anxiety as the rounds were cut out. Pained again as the golden dough was stained on the griddle. Nan just smiled and carried on. She must have made thousands of them in her life, those golden coins, but statistics would be meaningless. Nan wasn't one to keep count.

The evenness of her handiwork. The swift movement of knitting needles, the controlled loosening and tightening of the wool under her finger. She threw off the stitches carelessly, discarding them as she talked and laughed. But at cast-off and make-up the stitches' uniform tension proved her even hand.

Remnants of clothing were transformed into patchwork quilts. We watched her do it. Her endless patience. Tracing the aluminium template. Cutting up the hexagons. Tacking. Stitching hexagon to hexagon. Time becoming space. Daily life made even.

Nan created a garden for herself at the back of the farmhouse, a patch of mountain enclosed by a wire fence. The Italian prisoners of war helped her, showing how to carve terraces into the earth, as they'd done in their own vineyards. Nan grew flowers and shrubs, in counterpoint to the mountain, like the Latin plants' names and her accent.

But the earth was rough and shingly, unfavourable to horticulture. The mountain tended to take back its own ground. The terraces became steeper. But Nan persisted. The garden was her pride.

Sheep would push through, eating all that was edible, trampling on the terraces, leaving behind them nothing but grassless patches. Of course, she'd been foolish to challenge the mountain. But soon the flowers were back. Nan too held her ground.

She was even in walk and even in talk, and even also in grace. Who could have told that she'd spent her life between two mountains?

Nan watched us playing from the farmhouse window. The mountain had lessons to teach, especially to those of us who'd been reared on marshland. It pulled itself from beneath us, made us somersault through thistles, wool and sheep shit.

Back in the house we found our feet again. The quiet of the hearth. We stared into the fire. Butter melted in a glass dish. Nan would be laying the table.

Then Taid came in cold from the mountain, the stub of a *Players* cigarette between finger and thumb. He wheezed as he approached. Our chatter stopped. Between snatches of breath we'd hear him talk of the mountain.

At the top there were bilberry bushes and pools of water where people had dug for peat. There were larks rising and peregrines falling. The steep Oerddrws Pass, far below, seemed flat. And above there were nothing but peaks: Waun Oer, Foel y Ffridd, Foel Bendin, y Glasgwm, Aran Fawddwy, Aran Benllyn, Cader Idris ... Taid knew all their names.

He'd talk about superstitions. The words were unfamiliar: 'cotton grass', 'the bandits', 'causeway' ... There was that sprig of white heather, and the strange flower that swallowed flies. We couldn't disbelieve him. And yet, we couldn't quite believe him either. Taid's testament was ambiguous, he himself so foreign to us.

After supper he fetched his broken glasses and retired to the parlour to read. He adored debates: books on history and politics. His horizons were broad, you'd think he'd always lived on a mountaintop. We'd look at him as we looked towards the summit of Tynybraich, obliquely and from a distance. And as with the mountain we sought his attention and feared it. The steep banks of his personality: his strict attitudes and his laughter at men's folly.

Of course we didn't know of Taid the shepherd. His daily care for the sheep on the mountain, climbing through the seasons to perpetuate the work of his forefathers.

Between winter and spring, billhook in hand, he'd cut off branches to feed the sheep. At lambing he'd be up there counting, protecting the weak from crows and foxes. A late frost, threatening sleet, Taid would come home with a lamb in his pocket, all damp and slippery, its breath irregular and its head hanging down. It was placed on the hearth in a box lined with newspaper, nourished by Taid with milk from a rubber teat. Nan watched from a distance, new life dirtying the hearthstone.

In spring, if the kitchen light diminished, Taid climbed up to the reservoir at the top of the mountain. It was frogspawn stopping the flow of water down to the turbine. He'd move it away by the fistful, keeping one for the jar which he'd bring back to his children, a transparent treasure. And the kitchen was lit up anew.

Weaning time, and Taid would have to separate the male lambs from their mothers. For days the mothers would bleat, Taid watching them press their bodies against the bars of the mountain gate. With his neighbours he'd gather sheep for dipping and shearing, relaxing at the end of the day with banter at the kitchen table, Nan half-listening as she refilled the dinner plates.

But it was in winter that the mountain demanded most from Taid. Sheep would be trapped under the snow. He climbed up, inserting a rod made of hazel through the thick snow. Prodding and poking, he knew from experience where the sheep sheltered. But there was no guarantee. Finally, feeling the living softness, he'd go down on all fours to release it. Then he'd watch it escape, chunks of snow hanging off the wool, shining in the blue light.

Hours later Taid would return home, lame with frostbite. Nan, relieved, would fetch her husband a bowl of hot stock.

We didn't know how much the mountain had demanded from Taid. My mother's brother had taken over by the time we came along. We were too young to have heard the story of Taid's three brothers, born blind, sent away to a boarding school far away in Worcester, and of two other brothers, dead, as well as a sister dead, his only sister. Taid had been the only one left to work on the farm, to continue as his forefathers had. At eleven years of age Tynybraich had demanded his life.

Gravity's strict lessons, Taid learnt them when he was eleven. Tynybraich tried to possess his life, his education and his wish to study medicine. But he reached a compromise with the mountain, dividing his life between it and his fellow-men. He became a councillor, a Union man, and travelled on business to London and Brussels.

An unwilling farmer, he nevertheless wrote his name in the family Bible, and in local speech, at least, took on the mountain's name. After their marriage, Nan shared that name with him. Tynybraich: covenant of mountain and house.

I only climbed it once, Tynybraich. Taid had been buried many years, Nan a few months. His testament was there at the top: the bilberry bushes, the water pools, the lark and the peregrine, the Pass, the bandits, the cotton grass, the causeway and those peaks whose names I didn't know.

A feeling of trespassing made me leave. In any case I had to go, saying goodbye to my aunt and uncle and turning my back on Tynybraich, driving back to the main road, heading south, towards Cardiff. Tomorrow was work.

I picked my way through thistles, wool and sheep shit. As I came within sight of the house, I slowed down, as Taid himself would have done, and let myself be drawn by the farmhouse's gravity. There was the sound of Nan laying the table.

I wondered at the narrow ledge on which the house stood. The precipice beneath. And I saw, as Taid himself would have seen, the evenness spreading out from it and filling the valley.

Roger Deakin (ONE)

Wood

Approaching Blaenau Ffestiniog, I felt I had landed in a black and white film. Everywhere I looked, the monochrome of slate filled the screen. Yet I knew that somewhere within it, like the glow inside a coal fire in the grate, was David Nash, within his chapel studio filled to the rafters with his works of wood: a furnace of imagination and adventure in a sombre world. Gigantic spoil-heaps of slate, angular mole-hills thrown up by the mines, rose away steeply in silhouette, dwarfing the terraced houses and their gleaming roofs. The steep paths of the quarrymen zig-zag up, or ramp in diagonals across the gloomy, unstable screes that loom everywhere above the town. A ruined viaduct leans out into a void. Tramways and railway tracks run to the cliff-edges of the heaps, buffered by air. After the soft wooded valleys you wind through on your way up, it is a treeless world, except for the odd rhododendron clinging to the slate, or hugging the wall of a roofless winding-house. There is something architectural about the zig-zags, diagonals and monochrome waste-tips of broken slates, discarded like loose change because only those few that split cleanly could be used to roof houses.

Blaenau Ffestiniog hunkers down at the head of a valley in the mountains of North Wales ten miles from the Irish Sea. An odd place for an artist whose name is synonymous with wood to choose to be, but this is the country of Nash's youth, where he and his brother spent all their holidays exploring the Vale of Ffestiniog and the banks of the Dwyryd river from their grandfather's house. There are lanes here he has been walking for fifty years. The irony is that Nash came here after art school to escape a grey world: the suits and money culture of London in the mid-sixties. This is a place of deliberate self-exile, in the working landscape of a Celtic country where they still speak another language. Coming here to see David Nash felt as I imagine it did to journey to remote Cornwall in the 1920s to visit Ben Nicholson and Barbara Hepworth at their studios in the fishing community of St Ives.

Capel Rhiw, the Victorian Methodist chapel where David Nash lives and works, stands almost grandly in a row of slate miners' cottages under the volcano of a spoil-heap on the outskirts of the town. There were once eighteen thousand people and twenty-six chapels in this Welsh Machu Picchu. The chapels were so crowded on Sundays that the congregations overflowed and sang in the streets outside. Nash and his wife the painter Claire Langdown live in the schoolhouse they have converted behind the chapel, which is both studio and a store for all the works that are either in transit, waiting to be despatched to some new exhibition overseas or retained because they're old friends Nash isn't inclined to let go.

I stepped inside to a surprising burst of pagan colour: the warm glow of wood. It is a beautiful, uplifting building with little nuggets of primary colour in the stained-glass friezes of its high windows that beam down blue, yellow and red. I shall not forget the sheer drama of the exuberant throng of Nash's work that fills the tiered space literally to the lofty ceiling, looking over his shoulder as he opened the front door. Moving through the chapel, I mingled with the wooden multitude, 'the congregation', as Nash calls it. It is like meeting the family, an unusually big one, exciting and daunting at the same time: impossible to remember all their names, only a general impression that you want to get to know them all much better one by one in due course. I caught a hint of the impression I often had as a teacher entering a classroom, that the moment before I came in, they had all been deep in conversation.

*

I recognised many of the individual pieces of work: the soaring, high-backed, spoon-shaped *Throne*; the various *ladders*, stairways to heaven made by cleaving the inverted tree in two and joining the opposed halves with carved staves; and *vessels*, symbolic boats carved from a single trunk. There was an Alice-in-Wonderland feeling about wandering amongst all these bowls, spoons, chairs, vessels, stoves and tables: versions of human artefacts plucked from their domestic scale and context, often larger than life, reminders of the ubiquity of wood in our daily lives.

Some of the work I had seen before, in galleries and exhibitions, but encountering it off duty in the workmanlike surroundings of the chapel, a long way from the urban world of culture and the arts, was quite a different experience. Nash now works in a separate workshop and yard up the road where his chainsaws won't disturb anyone, so the chapel and its contents have become, quite consciously, an installation. There was soon to be another international exhibition, this time in Orléans, and several works were being wrapped up and packaged ready for their journey to France, here and at the new workshop. Some were already in packing cases, wood within wood, and stood like suitcases in the hall on the eve of a holiday. Waiting to be wrapped up was a pair of *Ubus*, named after the outsize King and Queen in Alfred Jarry's surrealist play *Ubu Roi*. The wandering, priapic, outward-leaning, etiolated dinosaur necks of these creatures reach upwards from the contrasting solidity of their squat bodies like the branches of the tree they actually are. Nash keeps on returning to this form. Like Nash's various ladders, trees have traditionally connected the earth and sky, and the natural vertical axis, the direction the wood-grain takes the eye, runs through all his work. 'The problem with wood is it's already beautiful,' says Nash. 'How do you make it more beautiful?'

I found myself drawn to one work in particular: the *Cracked Box* of oak. As if entering the wild life of the wood, or at least taking its side, Nash has put as many difficulties in his way in the making of the box as he can. He may work with the skills of the forester, hedge-layer or carpenter but firmly rejects any notion of craft and indeed declined, for years, the open offer of a Crafts Council exhibition. You can feel that resistance, dramatised in his wilful transgression of the rules of carpentry in the construction of the box. Five of its six oaken walls are sawn, perversely, across the end-grain of the tree, anchored to a single wall conventionally machined along the grain. Nash bored out the peg-holes with a two-inch hand augur and carved oak pegs, which he drove in to join up the box. The anarchic work thumbs its nose at the basic rules of woodwork, triumphantly so, because it holds together in spite of the wriggling of the wood as it warps and cracks. The more the wood struggles, the tighter the grip of the oak pegs in their augured sockets. As Nash points out, hand-carved oak pegs make the best joints because their uneven surfaces create greater friction as they are driven in. This is what he calls an 'outside in' work. He made it from green oak outdoors, where the feeling is quite different from working inside the studio, then brought it inside to crack and warp. Things look bigger when they come inside and smaller when they go outside, by a factor of about one third, says Nash.

David Nash, Cracked Box

Nash works in the same tradition of the artist as artisan as Constantin Brancusi, an acknowledged influence since his earliest days, who was a trained carpenter as well as sculptor and also lived at his studio, which he kept peopled with his best works. These days, he works principally with the chainsaw, transformed in his hands into a tool of great delicacy as well as power and scope. He says he is a sprinter by nature, too impatient to see results to work more slowly with hand tools as he used to do until 1977, when he grew impatient with sawing firewood with a bowsaw and discovered a tool that suits his nature.

The chainsaw liberates him to work in bold strokes. It is perhaps the equivalent of the charcoal with which Nash likes to draw, also working fast: he loves its fluidity. The chainsaw lends itself to big, ambitious ideas, enabling him to work on a large scale, quarrying the wood from the tree. He makes no distinction between 'wood' and 'tree' because the green wood in which he works still has a dynamic, organic life of its own and will continue to shift, warp and re-shape itself as a living sculpture. Nash leaves his work unadorned, leaving the marks of the tool on the wood. The chainsaw leaves circular marks, often blackened. The axe leaves roughness and torn slivers. Polished or finished surfaces resist your gaze, distracting it from the essential form. Instead, Nash's grainy, cracked, warped, sawn, fissured, charred, scarred and hollowed works absorb light, involve the viewer, like the bold charcoal drawings that precede them and sometimes accompany them on a gallery wall as a two-dimensional counterpoint to the sculpture's three.

Nash always begins with an idea: it is ideas that excite him and drive the work along. On a blackboard in the little converted shop across the street he uses as his drawing studio, and for seminars and workshops with the groups of art students who sometimes make the journey here, he has chalked up the trajectory of a putative project that begins with *Idea*. He likes the dynamic implications of the word, its forward-tending energy and movement. On the blackboard, arrowed chalk lines lead off in all directions like comet-tails to possible interpretations. There, too, are chalked the names of some fellow artists of his generation whose work and ideas are akin to his: Richard Long, Hamish Fulton and Roger Ackling. *Family Tree*, drawn in pastel in 1995, traces the evolution of consistent ideas and themes in Nash's work from the *First Tower* he built in 1967 on a hillside in Blaenau Ffestiniog. Appraising a life's work to date as a formal tree, Nash represents himself branching out from those early beginnings into the range and scope of his more recent projects, all related in a single living system of thought. There is more than a hint of Platonic ways of thought in all this, and Nash is a strong believer in the notion of ideal forms, returning again and again to the sphere, the pyramid and the cube. Wood often suggests the past, memory and something fixed, so to work as freely with it as Nash does can create fertile tensions. We are accustomed to spheres, pyramids and cubes as sculptural objects in stone, not wood.

Nash chose early on in his career to work in wood, in preference to stone. For him, it offers just the right degree of resistance. Stone has too much and clay too little. Chiselling oak, he feels a balancing strength coming back up his arm. Carving lime, he senses its receptivity, the smoothness of movement through it. He is interested in the past life of the tree, in its relationship with time and the diary it keeps of its life in the annual rings. A tree may live eighty or a hundred years, or for several hundred years, but even then, its life is not so very much longer than a human span when you compare it with stone. Our ability to identify our human lives and history with trees influenced Nash's choice of wood as his sculptural medium. Wood, unlike stone, lives and dies on a human scale. This idea is expressed in the old English folk-saying based on the ancient notion of the Seven Ages, quoted by Robert Graves in *The White Goddess*:

> The lives of three wattles, the life of a hound;
> The lives of three hounds, the life of a steed;
> The lives of three steeds, the life of a man;
> The lives of three men, the life of an eagle;
> The lives of three eagles, the life of a yew;
> The life of a yew, the length of an age;
> Seven ages, from Creation to Doom.

A wattle or hurdle of willow will last for 3 years, so on this reckoning a yew lives for 729 years, a modest but reasonable estimate.

Time and the living forces of the elements within green wood continue to shape the *Crack and Warp Columns* long after the artist has finished work on them. Nash has made a series of them over the years out of a variety of woods from birch to tulip to beech. Lime often creates the best effects, with its energetic warping. Working his chainsaw with extraordinary deftness, he executes a series of tooth-comb incisions that may exceed a hundred into a column of green wood. The impression is of a tall sheaf of papers, all gently levitating, joined together by a solid backbone at the core. Nash says he goes into a sort of trance as he makes the repeated saw-cuts, allowing the rhythm of the work to take over. At any point he might cut through that bit too much and lose the piece altogether. It is like a jazz solo: it has a beginning and an ending and a formal structure but a free, open, anarchic feeling. It is daring and risky. These crack-and-warp columns are quintessential Nash in that they tend upwards like trees, involve a virtuoso chainsaw solo and continue changing shape long after the work is apparently complete, cracking, warping and splitting at random as the element of air enters the sculpture and water evaporates from the unseasoned wood to mingle back into ourselves through the air we breathe. These are, says Nash, air sculptures, where others might belong to earth, water or fire. There is a sense of fragility about them that suggests the sculpture itself might easily evaporate.

Like any other congregation, the sculptures in the chapel are constantly shifting, stretching and discreetly yawning as the wood twists into subtly changed shapes. The crack and warp of green wood is nature at work, continuing where Nash has left off. *Running Table* and *Three Dandy Scuttlers*, sculptures that appear to be making a run for it or dancing on their legs of inverted branches dramatise the dynamics at the heart of everything Nash makes. His aim, he says, is to 'resurrect the tree in a different form'. There is a kind of collaboration between the artist and the living wood that continues well beyond the original hewing.

We drove out to the wooded valley at Cae'n-y-Coed near Maentwrog, the next village, where Nash owns a four-acre plot of mixed woodland inherited from his father. This is where he literally plants and grows his living sculptural work. He began work on one of his best-known outdoor sculptures, *Ash Dome*, in 1977 when he planted twenty-two ash saplings in a ring thirty feet in diameter on a level eminence on the hillside in the Ffestiniog Valley. It was conceived as an act of hope during the dark days of the Cold War. Nash had already made drawings of a lattice of living ash that would enclose a dome-shaped space.

He was trying to find a way to make a large-scale outdoor sculpture that genuinely belonged in its location and would embrace and engage the elements instead of resisting them, as so much outdoor sculpture seemed to do. Inspired by hedges and their half-natural, half-husbanded forms, he was looking for a way of actively collaborating with nature.

From long familiarity with the local hedges, often drawing or photographing the sinuous forms of the laid trees, Nash knew that ash was the most resilient to constant shaping, would lean furthest from its roots and naturally grows into sinuous, idiosyncratic forms. Nash likens the way he is guiding the trees to the way the ancient Chinese potters kept their minds on the invisible volume of space inside the pot and worked up the clay around its shape. He was also attracted by the gradual, long-term nature of the project: its long reach forward and its continuity.

His first ring of saplings was eaten by sheep, so he put up a fence and planted another. He also put in birches as a wind-break, and to stimulate the ashes to compete with them in growth. Then he began to apply some of the techniques of the hedger, pruning and shaping the trees as they grew, grafting on side-shoots, working on the shape every winter, up ladders and even a wooden scaffold as the dome grew taller. At one stage, an elaborate system of guy-ropes and tent-pegs urged the lead growth of the *Ash Dome* towards the centre. He showed me how, in 1983, he made the first bends in the trunks, leaning the trees anti-clockwise by making a series of saw-cuts nearly all the way through the growing trunk on the insides of the bends to allow for compression, binding the wounds with damp cloth under plastic until the cambium layer had healed, guiding and supporting the trees on stakes. Thus he has kinked the trees several times over the years into their wild and graceful dance on the hillside.

As in any collaboration, the trees have their own ideas and Nash must continually work his hedgerow skills to influence them as the sculptor, or choreographer. He admires and enjoys the sense of purpose in each tree, its stroppiness. Again, it is a question of resistance, of arm-wrestling the muscular trees. 'The tree has a purpose, and it will always keep trying to fulfil its purpose whatever happens,' says Nash. I notice that at each place where an ash has been bent or cut it has grown stronger, swelling into a callous like a human knee or puckering into a bump of scar tissue round the little star-cracked crater of each amputated branch. Every one of these details represents a decision, a little setback for the tree to which it responds with redoubled vigour that is certainly defiance and might even be anger, but only adds to the dramatic sense of muscularity and movement in the whole. But Nash has no desire for rigid control: it is the unpredictability of growth that interests him, and he has charted the life of this sculpture by drawing it over and over again, from year to year, through the seasons, even setting up a drawing table on the spot. His drawings of the *Ash Dome* are, he says, 'its fruit'. This is by no means a figure of speech. Sculptors have to make a living just like the rest of us, and the next morning I helped Nash carry a harvest of a dozen or so ash-framed drawings of *Ash Dome* out of his drawing studio to be packed and sent off to a gallery. The effect of the leaning trees is quite different in winter: the lines and the form revealed in the bare trunks and branches most clearly drawn in frost and snow.

In its rootedness, the *Dome* expresses Nash's commitment to a settled life in one place, and a deep rapport with the landscape in which he lives. In hedgerows, sheep will often bite off leading shoots of trees and shape them with their browsing, or branches will fuse together through close contact. As linear woods, hedges have a naturally sculptural quality that is reflected in the dome of ash. But the space enclosed by the trees also suggests to Nash the great hidden, hollowed dome of the slate mine inside Manod Mawr, one of the mountains across the valley. All the leaning trees are *Ubus* of a kind. The curious swaying, zig-zagging habit of the trees in *Ash Dome* is like the tentative, tangential progress of a hare down a lane, reminiscent of Ted Hughes's lines in *The Warm and the Cold*:

> The hare strays down the highway
> like a root going deeper.

*

If *Ash Dome* is about putting down roots, *Wooden Boulder* is an equally radical work about letting go. It is adventurous in every sense, a great gesture of liberation in which Nash has surrendered his work to nature and the elements and set no limits. In the summer of 1978, he heard of a great oak that had recently been felled directly uphill from where we now stood by the stream, and was available to him. Its owners had feared that it might fall on their cottage. Working the tree where it lay over a two-year period, Nash carved a dozen or more sculptures from it. The first of these, a giant oak ball a metre in diameter, was originally intended to go into the studio and dry out. When the moment came to sever the half-carved sphere from the main trunk and roll it to continue carving the underneath, Nash had the idea of using the nearby stream and water-slide to carry the half-ton sphere down to a pool below, then haul it onto a track where it could be rolled along to the road and trundled off to the studio. This is what would have happened, except that the wooden ball jammed itself halfway down the water-slide and wouldn't budge. At first, it looked like a problem until, thinking it over in a Zen frame of mind, David Nash realised it was an opportunity, a happy accident that would transform the work by enabling him to release it back into nature: to shed it like a leaf. He would let it go its own way and be a rock in a stream, with water playing about it, freezing to it, papering it with autumn leaves. From that moment on, it became *Wooden Boulder*, a new kind of work with its own independent life, its own story, and the sculptor as its biographer.

By the following year, the deciduous sculpture had shifted position during the winter spate and settled into the pool beneath the waterfall. Nash had already begun recording its progress in photographs and drawings, and like a scarab beetle, helped it into the shallows to be washed down into another waterfall and the next pool in August 1980. Here it stayed for the next eight years, darkening by the action of the water into the colour of the other stones in the stream. Nash drew and photographed its changing moods and fortunes through frosty or snowy days, engulfed in raging foam during storms or jammed with leaves and sticks. It shifted downstream three more times until, following a massive storm in 1994, it hid itself completely, wedged under a bridge. A scarab once again, Nash winched it out and rolled it back into the stream the other side, where it sat on the stony bed under some trees close to the confluence with the River Dwyryd for eight years until November 2002, when a strong enough flood eventually carried it into the main river. It travelled three miles towards the sea on the tides, and beached itself on a sandbank in the estuary.

In the new setting of wide horizons and reflected sky the sculpture stood out heroically and, like a Celtic saint, it began wandering the waters of the estuary, mysteriously disappearing up creeks, endlessly doubling back on itself in the ebb and flow, moving with each new tide, responding to the moon. By now utterly obsessed, Nash went searching for it in a boat and lost it altogether for a while. 'Capricious' is how he describes its behaviour. He even put out 'Wanted' posters around the estuary. During those chilly winter days of hide-and-seek he studied the tides and pored over charts, mapping the uncertain voyage. Then one January day the great oak-apple reappeared on a saltmarsh and seemed almost settled for a moment until the Equinox tide of 19 March 2003 floated it free. Nash watched from a boat and as the heavy sphere floated 'like a seal', most of its body submerged, rolling slightly as it rode the tide, bumping the bottom, its rough-carved angles smoothed and rounded by so much passage over stone or sand. He had charted its progress whenever he could with his camera as well as on paper. It was just a far-off dot when he last saw it on 30 March. Somebody sighted *Wooden Boulder* floating close to the estuary's mouth a few days later, but it vanished in April 2003. The 'Wanted' posters went up again, to no avail. Nash is still sceptical about the idea that the sculpture is out there in the Irish Sea, perhaps even gone forever, a message in a bottle. He keeps on searching the beaches and creeks of the estuary, quartering it endlessly on board a boat, as he did before. In contrast to *Ash Dome*, which Nash describes as a 'coming', or 'becoming' sculpture, *Wooden Boulder* is a 'going' sculpture.

The very notion of a wooden boulder is a metaphysical conceit, just as the first *Stone Pillar* was in ancient Greece. Until the original Doric column was conceived and built, all temple pillars had been trees, and the fluted stone, with its foliate embellishment below the roof, audaciously mimicked them. Like Dylan Thomas's 'Dogs in the Wet-nosed Yards' in *Under Milk Wood*, it surprises and delights by fusing two hitherto separate elements. In one of his early notebooks, Gerard Manley Hopkins made a sketch of a lasher, a steep, fast-flowing overflow channel on the canal at Wolvercote, near Oxford, and described the racing water as 'running like a wind'. The sudden translation of water into a different element is, again, striking and extraordinary.

We stood on the bridge over the stream where the boulder jammed itself, looking out downriver towards the estuary beyond as Nash told its story. Had it not been low tide, we might have been out in the boat. I had the impression that the searching would go on a long time, whatever the results: it had become part of the work, almost a habit. Claire said later, 'I have never seen a man so happy as when David was out in the boat sighting the boulder far out in the estuary.' We got back in the car and followed the old droving road past the house where

Inigo Jones was born, crossing the Dwyryd by the lovely triple-arched stone bridge he built, with seats of slate set in the triangular pedestrian refuges where people would sit and watch the oak-fringed river on summer evenings. Along the way, we had to run the gauntlet of a farmyard where a pair of sheepdogs savaged the car, as Nash predicted they would, biting at the bumpers as we wound up the windows. He and his brother used to walk this lane as boys, and always hid a pair of stout sticks in the wall to seize as they approached the farm, for beating off the dogs.

I sensed that perhaps *Wooden Boulder* has become an alter ego for Nash: its unfolding story part of his life, the restless thing itself an embodiment of his soul. Something about it reminds me of the Irish story of Sweeney Astray as told by Seamus Heaney. Sweeney, a poet–king, is exiled, naked, into the wild, turned into a bird, flies about Ireland, lives in trees and roosts in the ivy, eating watercress and drinking from the rivers. There is a mythic feel to the story of *Wooden Boulder*. An artist turns a tree into a boulder, which miraculously floats and swims its way over many years towards the sea, where it rolls over like a seal and seems to disappear.

John Eifion Jones (TEN)

Llŷn

Llŷn, the peninsula of Wales that reaches out into the Irish Sea like the arm of a dancing lady, has always been a place apart. A patchwork of small fields and farmsteads punctuated in the misty distance by saintly Bardsey and Garn Fadryn, the mountain which obscures the view to Aberdaron, last hiding place of R.S. Thomas.

I remember it as the province of the smallholder and tenant farmer, a place scoured by the westerly wind, a mosaic of green fields and ploughed earth giving way to swaying gold as the seasons advanced. Many farmers had a small boat to expand their domain and their income. Catching lobsters remains a lucrative sideline, fishing for mackerel the main recreation. The locals shunned the numerous sandy coves which so delighted visitors and their shrieking children. They preferred the rocky natural harbours like Porth Ysgaden which provided anchorage and peace and quiet, and also were the habitat of crabs, another delicacy harvested for good money.

Welsh was the first language of Llŷn, and it remains so today. But locals fear the ancient tongue will be overcome by English, as more second-home owners move in. This is a bitter and recurring theme among modern Welsh poets.

Like R.S. Thomas, my father was an Anglican clergyman, who took up the living of Tudweiliog, on the quiet north coast. In 1960 the place still had a faintly feudal air, an estate village run from Cefnamwlch, the big house hidden away in the trees at the end of a mile-long drive.

Sir William, whom we shall meet later in church, ran the village with a light touch. The land agent lived forty miles away on Anglesey. He turned up every quarter at the village pub, 'The Lion' – but known to everyone as 'The Ring' perhaps because of its circular front garden – when all the tenants duly came by to pay the rent.

Some smallholders lived very modestly. I remember Nou who had just a couple of fields by the Vicarage. Perhaps because of the awkward shape of the fields, or more likely from habit, he still cultivated the soil in a way unchanged since the Old Testament; sowing seed by hand from a cloth sling, and then at harvest time reaping it with a scythe. It probably was hard work, but the rhythmic swing of the blade made surprising progress and it was satisfying to see the golden stooks forming ranks on the hillside.

Small wonder that from this corner we heard the rasping cry of the corncrake on still summer mornings. These elusive birds disappeared from Wales soon after.

In high summer the main cash crop was the English. A few farms practised a form of transhumance whereby the family decamped to the barn or stables and the most rudimentary accommodation to let out the house – which was only a degree more salubrious – to English visitors.

More farmers, however, discreetly planted caravans in small clusters in fields near the sea, attracting families from urban Lancashire on an annual migratory cycle. They did not come from Coronation Street, but quite higher up the social scale for fresh air, sea and a quiet break. But I don't recall great social interaction. The visitors were another crop, rather like the familiar Friesian cows, who if they were well-housed and well-treated would pay a better return.

The tourists of course did not understand a word of Welsh, but none of the resident English spoke it either. The attitude then was that it was too difficult and obscure even to attempt. That has altered somewhat now.

As soon as the visitors left, it was threshing time. This was when Dic Wenallt, father of my best friend, came into his own. He was an agricultural contractor and owned a threshing machine, a huge contraption rather like a giant wooden omnibus with all sorts of pulleys and belts attached. This would be trundled around the farmyards in turn on threshing day. It was all hands to the pump then, with neighbouring farmers all turning out to help – to load, rake, winnow, keep an eye on the slipping belts, sack the grain and stack the straw. Upwards of twenty men was not unusual and all would then sit down at the big farmhouse table to a threshing tea, small boys included.

In my recollection it was execrable. Men had been threshing wholesome corn all day, there were organic pigs in the yard, and the freshest milk in the dairy. But we dined on white sliced Mother's Pride with a slick of margarine and perhaps some wet slices of processed ham and a bowl of tomatoes. There'd be home-made fruitcake if you were lucky. Farming really was an export industry, you rarely consumed the product – apart from milk – but lived on factory food.

Harvest was Dic Wenallt's busy time. But otherwise his passions were his boat and the engine shed.

Dic was for the most part a plain and practical man but he displayed one Epicurean trait. His Saturday treat was mackerel, fried. But he insisted that to maintain full flavour the fish be cleaned and gutted in seawater, which he brought home in an old oil can containing the lobster catch.

And there were plenty of oil cans around because Dic needed them in 'cwt 'r injan' – the engine shed.

The black corrugated shed housed Dic's lathe and tools, but 90 per cent of the space was taken up by the injan. This was the engine of an old Hawker Hurricane plane, salvaged after the war and now ingeniously converted into a power station to supply electricity to the Wenallt. It could probably have lit up half the village, but its maximum demands stretched to four lightbulbs, a television and a washing machine.

At full throttle, the ground shook, the garden shook, the outside privy shook and the machine pounded through your ribcage. Nevertheless 'cwt r'injan' was a social centre. There Dic, my father in his clerical collar and black raincoat buttoned to the top, and one or two other locals would assemble in the evening. It was standing room only, you could not hear yourself think above the pounding warplane engine, the concrete floor quavered. But here the company chose to put the world to rights, over pipe smoke and endless Players cigarettes.

The Wenallt was unusual in that the engine's resources were harnessed purely for domestic comfort. Most of the farms had static engines, but they were first installed to power the milking machines, lighting the house was an afterthought. It all changed in 1964 when Tudweiliog was connected to the National Grid.

'That day it felt like the village had died,' Dic's widow, Beth, recalled years later. 'It was totally silent … and we were so use to hearing first Ty Hir's engine start up, and then Tyddyn Difyr and Ty'n Ffynon. The village changed forever that day.'

For centuries, the centre of gravity in Llŷn lay beyond the peninsula on Bardsey the windswept island a mile off Aberdaron, known in popular legend as the island of twenty thousand saints. The first of them was Cadfan, who established a Celtic monastery here in 516. It became Llŷn's most enduring landmark, a place of prayer and contemplation for more than a thousand years and a major place of pilgrimage in the Middle Ages. Three pilgrimages to Bardsey were the equivalent of one to Rome itself. It is testimony to the extraordinary reach of the Tudor government that remote St Mary's Abbey was shut down in 1537, when Henry VIII decreed the dissolution of the lesser monasteries.

A handful of farmers scratched a living here into living memory. But the island has always exercised a pull for contemplatives. The Welsh artist Brenda Chamberlain lived here through the 1950s in a house called Carreg Stone. Some of the murals she painted are decaying on the walls, one wistfully depicts a boat on a warm beach in the south of France. Nowadays the RSPB are the tenants of Bardsey and Manx Shearwaters, choughs and migrating seabirds are the main inhabitants.

There are fewer pilgrims than in the Middle Ages, but the place still attracts the still and the watchful, among them R.S. Thomas.

> There is no time on this island.
> The swinging pendulum of the tide has no clock;
> The events are dateless.

The only way to get to Bardsey still is by a small fishing boat from Aberdaron or Pwllheli. And on stormy days, the island still feels a world away rather than a mile offshore, cut off by the fierce sea currents. As recently as the Millennium Year a party of seventeen trippers were stranded there for a fortnight, a timely reminder that this has always been a place beyond reach.

The evidence of Bardsey's importance as a centre of pilgrimage is still to be found all over Llŷn in its medieval churches. There are more than two dozen. For the most part these are squat and low, hidden away and built close to the ground, an unconscious echo perhaps of the earthbound pagan gods of the Celts. Heaven-ward soaring Gothic was not for them.

A notable exception is the majestic church at Clynnog Fawr – once again an unmistakable landmark for everyone travelling west into Llŷn thanks to a new by-pass which unexpectedly enhances its place in the landscape. This marks the start of the thirty-mile northern route over the Eifl mountains. Travellers can follow in the pilgrims' steps in the churches at Pistyll, Nefyn and notably Llangwnadl. It was here that St Gwynhoedl set up an altar by the river in the sixth century. By Tudor times the church had expanded into three aisles to cope with the pilgrim traffic. S GWYNHOEDL IACET HIC, reads an inscription on a pillar. Restorers found his tombstone in 1940. The field next-door is still known as Cae Eisteddfa, the field where pilgrims sat and rested.

On the southern route, the medieval visitors left their mark at Abererch, Llangian and Llanengan. The roodscreen and the bell here were saved from the plunder of Bardsey in 1537. The Sun Inn opposite is still on hand with good food and beer for weary travellers. The landlord has a key and a proud awareness of its place in history.

The two routes meet at Aberdaron where light-filled St Hywyn's sits right at the water's edge, the point of departure for Bardsey, blasted by sand and salt spray. Elderly villagers recall an echo of the Middle Ages here in the early 1950s, with a procession of hundreds walking through the village reciting Cranmer's Liturgy at the end of a diocesan pilgrimage. Typically, strong winds grounded the bishop and the Cross-bearing party for days.

My recollection is that the pilgrimage trail ran thin in the godless sixties. R.S. Thomas arrived here at what must have been the nadir of Christian belief in 1967 and gradually the practice has picked up again fulfilling the poet's prediction:

In cities that
have outgrown their promise
people are becoming pilgrims
again, if not to this place,
then to the recreation of it
in their own spirits

Nowadays, pilgrimage routes across Europe are gathering strength. They are fortified here – or perhaps challenged – by the bleak doubting lines of the foremost religious poet of postwar Britain. Last summer the parish organised weekly meditations in St Hywyn's punctuated by readings from the poems Thomas wrote at Aberdaron.

On retirement, the poet shifted his ground just a couple of miles over the hill to Rhiw, a scattered settlement of cottages hunched into the rocky hillside. But it commands one of the finest views in Wales, a panoramic sweep across the water from the peaks of Snowdonia right along the length of the Cambrian coast. It also shelters Llŷn's brightest jewel, the Mediterranean-like garden of Plas yn Rhiw. Both are there thanks to the generosity of the Keatings, three daughters of a prosperous Midlands industrialist. Here they created their earthly paradise and then bought large tracts of the headland below to preserve it from caravan parks, a projected nuclear power station and other modern benefits. The Keatings showed a great love and generosity towards Wales, but they did not speak Welsh of course.

That is the paradox of Llŷn. The Welsh overlooked the view. The English overlooked the language.

Change in the peninsula was, for the most part, slow in 1960. The village children spoke only Welsh until they went to Botwnnog, the grammar school at the centre of the peninsula. Founded by a local boy who became a Tudor bishop, it has been the crucible of learning on Llŷn – moulding the minds of everyone of promise raised on the peninsula since the early seventeenth century. In my time Pritch, the Welsh master, a man with dark burning eyes and a temperament scratchy as his Welsh tweed jacket, schooled us in the art of 'cynghanedd'. He produced one outstanding success in Alan Llwyd, today the master of this complex verse, balancing stress, alliteration and rhyme within each line, in the following manner:

> Ai diwedd hil yw ei dyddiau heulog?
> Do sunlit days mark the end of a race?

and:

> Nid gwlad gwlad heb dreftadaeth,
> Nid cenedl yw'r genedl gaeth

> A land is no land without a hinterland of heritage,
> A people in chains cannot be called a nation

Botwnnog was a big leap from Tudweiliog village school, ruled by green-suited Mr Davies aided by his handbell and cane, wielded with at least a weekly frequency. Tudweiliog children were considered 'bright' in the peninsula's intellectual order, but the playground was still a rough place to be if your Welsh was not up to scratch. The older farm boys could be very prickly about outsiders. As an incomer from Montgomeryshire with brittle Welsh, I suffered their rough aggression and raw fists.

At the end of the school lane the R'Efail, blacksmith's smithy, was still a busy place, a black sooty cave pierced by a blazing fire, but welding farm gates or repairing machinery, not shoeing horses, was the work by now. The other place of industry was the Gweithdy, a green corrugated workshop up the lane that was Thomas Henry's Joinery. Domestic carpentry – window frames, doors and the like was their stock in trade – but they also made coffins whenever one of the villagers died. As boys we would fall silent and glimpse with reverent dread when we saw the men working on an 'arch' (coffin). When business was slack Thomas Henry, Tommy Gwelfor and Gruffudd Hughes kept busy lovingly building a fishing boat for themselves.

There were two shops in the centre of Tudweiliog, the stone-built Post Office was the main trading hub. Business was slacker at Old Mrs Roberts's shop but it was a mecca for schoolchildren with its selection of Penny Arrow toffee bars, Love Hearts and Sherberts. The discovery of bubble gum triggered a brief trading frenzy as these sickly pink squares were packaged with colourful cards depicting flags of the world. On the back were a selection of phonetical phrases stereotypical of the country. Thus: 'Do you like my new sombrero?' (Mexico). 'Beware! The green snake is highly poisonous' (Thailand). 'Sothach,' Mr Davies the School branded it, as he fought a losing battle against the craze. He need not have worried. Many of us just threw away the gum and polished our life-saving phrases in the playground.

Another focal point of village life was the doctor's surgery, held in the terraced cottage next to the Post Office. Patients gathered in the tiny back parlour soberly exchanging pleasantries whilst all the while avoiding the really interesting subject – the ailments – until later. 'Poor old Tom looks terrible. He can't be long for this world, surely,' – 'Bobol annwyl! Mrs Evans hobbling along with that horrible swollen leg and no shoe. It doesn't look good at all.'

The doctor held consultations at the table in the front parlour amid a riot of heavy Victorian drapes, china figures and coloured glass. The young Dr Thomas cut a dashing figure in his brown suede shoes and yellow socks. It gave me confidence in modern medicine at an impressionable age. He had been in the Navy and drove a convertible.

Sundays were a day apart in those days. The main event was Matins at the church. A few minutes before 11 o'clock a wide black Hummer glided up, chauffering Sir William and his wife from Cefnamwlch, followed by another black limousine with lesser family connections. Mr Dodd the organist made up the church parade in his green Ford Poplar. He had been a tea planter in Ceylon and retired to equally remote Aberdaron, still taking delivery of the *New York Saturday Evening Post* every week.

Sir William was driven to church by Mr Howard, who was the loyal factotum at Cefamwlch, where his wife was the cook. Perhaps he had been Sir William's batman. During the week, Howard – as he was universally known – drove around in a canvas-topped Land Rover, greeting everyone with the Churchillian V-sign – although the war had been won more than fifteen years earlier.

Sir William Wynne-Finch (Eton and Scots Guards. M.C.1916; Served Egypt and Sudan), Lord Lieutenant of Caernarvonshire and Custos Rullorum, was kindly and soft-spoken. With his military moustache and dark pinstriped suit he was the epitome of *noblesse oblige* in this faraway place, respected but a well-liked man. He and his American-born wife sat in the front pew and effectively led the congregation. When Sir William stood, the villagers shuffled to their feet; when he knelt the parish fell silently to its knees.

Or rather the Anglicans in the parish did so. The Methodist chapel down by the council houses was an even bigger draw on a Sunday morning in those days.

But a small band including Mr Davies the School were Annibynwyr and worshipped in the Sunday afternoon quiet at Berseba, the Independent chapel on the edge of the village, near Nou the Sower's cornfield. This tiny white-washed chapel attached to a plain stone cottage must have been one of the smallest in Wales. I can find no pictures of the interior, and no record of its history on the web. Even the Ancient Monuments people seem to have got there long after it was converted into a holiday cottage. I still remember passing by and hearing the faint echo of an unaccompanied Welsh hymn through the small high window. I thought too little of it at the time, but it must have been sustained by intense devotion.

That devotion is gone now. And Berseba's story might serve as an easy parable for those who fret about the future of the Welsh language and its erosion by English settlers. Too easy. What of the Welsh themselves? My old school contemporaries nearly all remain in Llŷn as farmers, craftsmen, businessmen, teachers. I was the exception, the one who left. But it is they, not I, who keep the culture alive. But what of their children – a doctor, a barrister, postgrads. Will these professionals stay in rural Wales?

As Alan Llwyd put it: 'Enill gradd a cholli gwreiddiau' – gaining a degree and losing your roots.

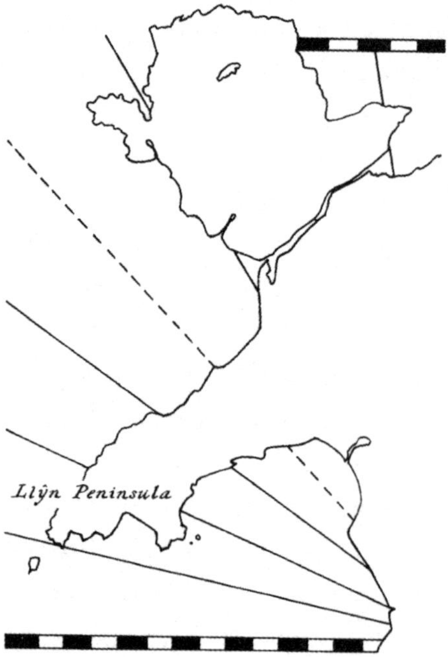

Robert Macfarlane (ONE)

Island

Low evening light glowed in the bow waves. The wind was strong, and the boat was heeled over at 20 degrees to the horizontal. The sails were tight, the sea grey, agitated. All three of us onboard were braced against wires and wood in order to keep our footing on the sloped deck. I was at the helm, trying to hold a steady course towards the island. I could feel the current pushing us sideways, forcing a sly lateral slide north, towards the distant rocks of the mainland, upon which broke a line of fine pale surf. Above the mainland hung two thin layers of cloud, black over white: a sign of disturbed air.

Early evening, early summer, off the westernmost tip of the Llŷn Peninsula. We had left harbour late, knowing that the wind was high, and darkness three hours away at most.

The boat was moving nearly eight knots over ground, and had settled into a steady battering bounce over the waves, when there was a crack, and a fierce white flapping, like a swan taking off. The boat slewed round to leeward and slowed, as though the water had suddenly thickened, and we were all jolted forwards. Cold spray broke up and over the starboard side and slapped my face. I could hear a noise like an irregular drumbeat.

The stay-sail had torn out from the deck, near the bows. The thick pin that clasped the sail in place had sheared through under the wind's pressure, and the sail was lashing almost free, secured only at the mast-head. The heavy metal spool fixed to the sail's loose lower end was flinging about and pounding at the fibreglass deck.

John, the skipper, issued brief and exact orders. He took the helm, brought the boat round into the wind, and then left me to keep it there. Wave-water soaked the deck. Jan, John's wife, edged out along the boat's bucking side, caught the spool and lashed it to a railing. The sail was lowered, and we wrestled it back from the wind and rolled it, so that it could be laid flat along the deck and taped down.

The final hour passed in the quiet that follows a crisis. With less sail up, we moved slowly. Four knots over ground, rarely more.

The island, to the south-west of us, was silhouetted against the setting sun: a big back of cliff and crag, rising five hundred feet out of the water, then tapering off to a long shallow arm of land. On the arm stood a tall lighthouse, its opal mirrors glinting every few seconds.

We sailed at last into the wind-shadow of the island's cliffs, and the single sail slumped, airless, from the main-mast. Then, by way of welcome or miracle, though of course it was neither, the low sun broke fully through the clouds, and turned the sea silver, and we motored into the small sheltered harbour on the surface of that bright water.

As we drew close to the shore, the air filled with a high keening noise, which grew in volume the nearer we came to land. I thought that it must be an acoustic effect of the wind – quick air singing in the boat's tight wires – and I looked around at my companions, unsure if I were the only one hearing it. As it became louder, I realised that it was not a single note, but a braid of dozens of notes, each of a slightly different pitch. Then I understood. Seals! Seals were making the sound, the hundreds of seals who were hauled out on every rock and kelp-hung skerry in the bay, and on its curved shoreline. They were giving off noise without seeming to, as bees do, or water. They were of many different colours: grey, black, white, fawn, fox-red and leather-brown. As we passed close by three smaller females, I saw that their fur was elegantly marked in swirls and contours.

John rowed me ashore in the dinghy, running it up onto the pebbled beach in the dusk light. I moved off alone inland, down the island's thin south-western arm, passing through the plainsong of the seals, prospecting for a place to sleep.

*

The island's name is Ynys Enlli, which means 'Island of the Currents'. The name is well given, for several fierce tide races meet around Enlli. A tide race occurs when a rising or falling tide drives the sea rapidly through a channel. The water in tide races, especially at points where two or more races converge, behaves erratically. At the turn of tides, it can achieve a sleek calmness, but when the tides run, the water seethes and there is a submarine twining of currents. Where the races meet, waves stand up like shark-fins, and bubbles rise in spreading gouts, as though the seabed itself were being stirred.

Tide races can also reach into apparently open water. When a race meets a headland, as it does at the tip of the Llŷn Peninsula, it is deflected outwards. The distance of the deflection depends upon the speed of the race: a quick race can reach out a menacing arm for miles. It is easy to see how early navigators, caught in the pull of such a current, ascribed supernatural malevolence to certain headlands and peninsulas.

Ynys Enlli was among the many remote places of the west and north-west coasts of Britain and Ireland to be settled between around 500 and 1000 AD. During those centuries, an extraordinary migration occurred. Monks, anchorites, solitaries and other devout itinerants began to travel in their thousands to the bays, forests, promontories, mountain-tops and islands of the Atlantic littoral. In frail craft and with little experience of seamanship, they sailed out across dangerous seas, in search of something we might now call wildness. Where they stopped, they built monasteries, cells and oratories, dug cemeteries for their dead and raised stone crosses to their God. These travellers were known as *peregrini*: the name derives from the Latin *peregrinus*, and carries the idea of wandering over a distance, and gives us our word 'pilgrim'. Before coming to Enlli, I had plotted on a map the known routes and landfalls of these migrations, and I had ended up with a tracery-work of what are still among the wildest parts of Britain and Ireland.

This Celtic Christian culture of retreat originated in the Ireland of the fifth and sixth centuries. Begun by St Patrick in the 430s, and inspired by the desert saints of the preceding centuries, the practice of retreat spread to what are now western Scotland and coastal Wales: a centrifugal motion, carrying men to the brinks of Europe and beyond.

It is clear that these edgelands reciprocated the serenity and the asceticism of the *peregrini*. Their travels to these wild places reflected their longing to achieve correspondence between belief and place, between inner and outer landscapes. We can surmise that the monks moved outwards because they wished to leave behind inhabited land: land in which every feature was named. Almost all Celtic place-names are commemorative: the bardic schools, as late as the seventeenth century, taught the history of places through their names, so that the landscape became a theatre of memory, continually reminding its inhabitants of attachment and belonging. To migrate away from the named places (territories whose topography was continuous with memory and community), to the coasts (the unmapped islands, the anonymous forests), was to reach land that did not bear the marks of occupation. It was to act out a movement from history to eternity.

From the early years of Celtic Christianity, Ynys Enlli was renowned as a destination for the *peregrini*, and the first monastery is thought to have been built there in the sixth century. For all its difficulty of access, however, it is among the least remote of the monks' habitations. You wonder at how the monks reached and settled landscapes such as the Garvellochs – the islands off the Argyll mainland where, over a thousand years ago, people lived in clustered mortarless huts shaped like beehives – or Skellig Michael, the rock fang that juts seven hundred feet out of the Atlantic, nine miles west of the Kerry coast. The uppermost slopes of Skellig Michael are riddled with cells, hewn out of the rock by the monks who landed there in the sixth century. The cells, which were used for penance and meditation, face out onto the Atlantic. Below them, the rock swoops away so abruptly and steeply that it is hard to believe you are even on land, and not hovering above only air and sea. There, with the ocean extending away from them, and nothing on the horizon to abbreviate or delay the eye, the monks were free to consider infinitude.

George Bernard Shaw travelled to the Skelligs in September 1910 in a clinker-built rowboat. The journey out took two-and-a-half hours in calm weather; the way back was longer and more unnerving. Rowing in thick mist and darkness, compassless and moonless, over tide-races and currents, Shaw's guides steered by instinct and knowledge alone. The following evening, sitting by the fire in the Parknasilla Hotel in Sneem, Shaw wrote a letter to his friend Barry Jackson about his experience on Skellig Michael. 'I tell you the thing does not belong to any world that you and I have lived and worked in: it is part of our dream world … I hardly feel real again yet!' For Shaw, as for the monks who once lived there, on the Skellig you were brought to think in ways that would be possible nowhere else. It was a place for deep dreaming.

The sea-journeys that the *peregrini* made are extraordinary to contemplate. We had difficulties reaching Ynys Enlli in a thirty-three-foot ocean-going yacht. Shaw had feared for his life returning from the Skelligs in a well-manned rowboat. Yet the monks had got to the Skelligs, and had made longer, riskier voyages – to Iceland and to Greenland, over the rough seas of the North Atlantic – in far more exposed and unstable craft.

The boats in which they travelled went by different names in different traditions: the coracle or curricle in Wales, the carraugh in Gaelic, the knarr in Norse. Their shapes differed, too – the curragh was generally long and thin, with a snub nose and squared-off bows, while the coracle was lenticular. What they shared was a method of construction. Their hulls were of ox-hide, which was oak-tanned, then wetted and stretched over a framework of bent wood and wicker. As it dried, the hide shrank around the framework, setting it rigid. Once it had set, it was caulked with tallow. What these craft had in common, too, was a logic of motion. They were designed, in their lightness and their shallow draft, to slide over the currents and the tide-rips, to slip up and over waves. This was their talent as vessels: they possessed a kind of maritime guile, barely displacing water, moving over the sea with the delicate touch of a pond-skater.

At last light, near the tip of Enlli's southern arm, I walked through a field of dead sea-pink, the compact plant that grows so well in the saline conditions of coastal margins. The crisp heads of the flowers, on their stiff stalks, vibrated in the breeze, so that in the twilight it seemed as though the ground were shivering. On water to the south, I could hear the clatter of a cormorant taking off. I could see the glimmer of the cabin lights of the boat, swaying in the bay, and briefly wished I were there with John and Jan: hot food, a glass of whisky, the company of friends.

I glanced back towards the mainland. It was visible only as a line in the dusk, wire-thin. The monks would have launched their boats from the coves of the peninsula. Even now and even in summer, if the weather is poor, it can be two to three days before it becomes possible to reach the island. When the winter storms set in, Enlli can be isolated for weeks at a time. The monks would have gauged their timing carefully. The long wait for flat weather. The watching of tides.

Then the launch, feet crunching in the pebbles, splashing in the water. The boats lurching even in the swell of the coves, and then tacking out into the open sea of the Sound, the currents stacked in descending storeys beneath them.

How exposed they must have felt, I thought. Yet perhaps they did not, perhaps their faith was so absolute that it resembled fatalism, which is a type of fearlessness. Certainly, many of them – unnamed, unchronicled – died there in the Sound, drowned by wave and current. 'There is an island there is no going to / but in a small boat,' wrote the priest-poet R.S. Thomas, whose parish of Aberdaron looked out onto Enlli:

> The way
> the saints went, travelling the gallery
> of the frightened faces of
> the long-drowned, munching the gravel
> of its beaches …

We can know little for certain about the *peregrini*. We know few of their names. Yet, reading the accounts of their journeys, and of their experiences on places like Enlli, I had encountered a dignity of motive and attitude that I found salutary. These men were in search not of material gain, but of a hallowed landscape: one that would sharpen their faith to its utmost point. They were, in the phrasing of their own theology, exiles looking for the *Terra Repromissionis Sanctorum* – the Promised Land of Saints.

A long Christian tradition exists that considers all individuals as *peregrini*, in that all human life is seen as an exile. This idea was perpetuated in the 'Salve Regina', the chant often recited as a last night-prayer. *Post hoc exilium*, the prayer declares; all will be resolved after this exile. The chant, when sung, sounds ancient and disquieting. It is unmistakably music about wildness, an ancient vision of wildness, and it still has the capacity to move us.

Much of what we know of the life of the monks of Enlli, and places like it, is inferred from the rich literature which they left behind them. Their poems speak eloquently of a passionate and precise relationship with nature, and of the blend of receptivity and detachment which characterised their interactions with it. Some of the poems read like jotted lists, or field-notes: 'Swarms of bees, beetles, soft music of the world, a gentle humming; brent geese, barnacle geese, shortly before All Hallows, music of the dark wild torrent.' Others record single charmed instants: a blackbird calling from a gorse branch near Belfast Loch, foxes at play in a glade. Marban, a ninth-century hermit who lived in a hut in a fir-grove near Druim Rolach, wrote of the 'wind's voice against a branchy wood on a day of grey cloud'. A nameless monk, responsible for dry-stone walling on the island of North Rona in the ninth century, stopped his work to write a poem that spoke of the delight he felt at standing on a 'clear headland', looking over the 'smooth strand' to the 'calm sea', and hearing the calls of 'the wondrous birds'. A tenth-century copyist, working in an island monastery, paused long enough to scribble a note in Gaelic beside his Latin text: 'Pleasant to me is the glittering of the sun today upon these margins.'

Gleanings such as these give us glimpses of the nature of faith of the *peregrini*. They are recorded instants which carry purely over the long distances of history, as certain sounds carry with unusual clarity within water or across frozen land. For these writers, attention was a form of devotion and noticing continuous with worship. The art they left behind them is among the earliest testimonies to a human love for the wild.

*

Ideas, like waves, have fetches. They arrive with us having travelled vast distances, and their pasts are often invisible, or barely imaginable. 'Wildness' is such an idea: it has moved immensely through time. And in that time, two great and conflcting stories have been told about it. According to the first of these, wildness is a quality to be vanquished; according to the second, it is a quality to be cherished.

The etymology of the word 'wild' is vexed and subtle, but the most persuasive past proposed for it involves the Old High German *wildi*, and the Old Norse *willr*, as well as the pre-Teutonic *ghweltijos*. All three of these terms carry implications of disorder and irregularity, and as Roderick Nash has written, they bequeathed to the English word 'a descriptive meaning of wilful, or uncontrollable'. Wildness, according to this etymology, is an expression of independence from human direction, and wild land is *self-willed* land. Land that proceeds according to its own laws and principles, land whose habits – the growth of its trees, the movements of its creatures, the free descent of its streams through its rocks – are of its own devising and own execution. Land that, as the contemporary definition of wild continues, 'acts or moves freely without restraint; is unconfined, unrestricted'. This basic definition of wildness has remained constant since those first appearances, but the values ascribed to this quality have diverged dramatically.

On the one hand, wildness has been perceived as a dangerous force, that confounds the order-bringing pursuits of human culture and agriculture. Wildness, according to this story, is cognate with wastefulness. Wild places resist conversion to human use, and they must therefore be destroyed or overcome. Examples of hostility to the wild are ubiquitous in cultures ancient and modern, Eastern and Western. 'Except for the true civilisation builders,' hallelujahed the American preacher and writer James Stalker in 1881, 'the very land in which we live would still be an undiscovered wilderness! These men see teeming cities, and thriving factories upon the desert, where others see only sage brush and alkali plains ... these men have tunnelled our mountains, have spanned our great rivers, and opened our mines of wealth!' The Old English epic poem *Beowulf* is filled with what the poet calls *wildéor*, or savage creatures. In the poem, these monstrous dragon-like beings inhabit a landscape of wolf-haunted forests, deep lakes, windswept cliffs and treacherous marshes. It is against these wild places and *wildéor* that the civilisation of Beowulf's tribe, the Geats – with their warm and well-lit mead halls, their hierarchical warrior culture – sets itself.

Parallel to this hatred of the wild, however, has run an alternative history: one that tells of wildness as an energy both exemplary and exquisite, and of wild places as realms of miracle, diversity and abundance. At the same time that the Beowulf-poet was writing his parable of the conquest of the wild, the monks of Enlli, Rona, the Skelligs and elsewhere were praising its beauty and its riotous fecundity.

Even earlier than the *peregrini*, indeed, evidence can be found of a love for the wild. It is there in the Chinese artistic tradition known as *shan-shui* or 'rivers-and-mountains'. *Shan-shui* originated in the early fifth century BC and endured for two thousand years. Its practitioners – T'ao Chi'en, Li Po, Du Fu, Lu Yu – were usually wanderers or self-exiles who lived in the mountain-lands of China and wrote about the wild world around them. Their art, like that of the early Christian monks, sought to articulate the wondrous processes of the world, its continuous coming-into-being. To this quality of aliveness, the *shan-shui* artists gave the name *zi-ran*, which might be translated as 'self-ablazeness', 'self-thusness' or 'wildness'.

Pilgrims and walkers, they explored their mountains in what they called the 'dragon-suns' of summer, and in the long winds of winter and the blossom-storms of late spring. They wrote of the cool mist that settled into valleys at dawn, of bamboo groves into which green light fell and of how thousands of snowy egrets would take off from lakes like lifting blizzards. They observed the way winter light fell upon drifted snow, and how shadows hung from cold branches, and wrote that such sights moved them to a 'bright clear joy'. Night was especially marvellous to them, because of the clean luminous presence of the moon, and its ability to silver the world into strangeness. Beauty did not always connote benignity: Li Po so loved the moon, it is said, that he drowned while trying to embrace its reflection in a river. Nevertheless, reading the poems and viewing the paintings of the *shan-shui* tradition, you encounter an art in which almost no divide exists between nature and the human. Form imposes itself on content so absolutely that these artefacts do not represent the world's marvels, but partake of them.

*

A hundred yards from the black-rock headland that marked the end of the island's peninsula, I searched for a sleeping place. The night air was loud with the pennywhistle piping of oystercatchers, and the gulls' yowls. It felt exciting to be out there in the dark, among the birds and with the sea surging and sloshing all around me.

The ground was uneven, and sloped down to a set of cliffs that were cleft by big wave-channels. Finally, I found somewhere I could sleep; a body-length patch of grass, on a terraced bank, above a deep gorge-like inlet. The bank tilted slightly inwards; there was no danger of me rolling off it in my sleep. I could make out the shapes of seals moving through the water. Sweeping above me were the beams of the lighthouse, long thin spokes of light opening out into the darkness, turning in slow predictable yellow rotation. It was warm enough for me not to need the bivouac bag I had carried, so I laid out my mat and sleeping-bag on the grass.

The noise began at around midnight, or that was when I woke to it. Birds were falling through the air above me, screaming while they fell, leaving long curved trails of sound as they plunged. I could hear them landing with soft thumps on the ground around me.

Every few seconds, one of the plunging birds and one of the turning lighthouse beams would coincide, vertical through lateral. I began to see them, here and there, momentarily outlined in the light – birds, with arrow-wings swept back from their little bomb-bodies, so that even as they disappeared, my eye retained an image of their streaking forms.

Shearwaters. Of course – they were shearwaters. Migratory, long-travelling, long-lived birds, which nested in burrows, and which waited until the cover of darkness before coming into land. Their name is given for their habit of gliding low over the water, wing-tips skidding the waves and striking droplets from them. The longest recorded wave-top glide of a Manx shearwater is one and a half miles. They are remarkable, too, for the distance of their pilgrimages. In a single day, they can cover as much as two hundred miles. When the breeding season is over, obeying impulses beyond our cognition, the shearwaters of Enlli will fly thousands of miles to spend the rest of the year at sea in the South Atlantic.

Ynys Enlli, like so many of the islands and marshes on the east and west coast of Britain, is a refuge for migrating birds. Hundreds of species stop off during their search for undisturbed feeding grounds. Tides and currents of birds, sweeping seasonally north and south, dispersing and returning, linking remote place to remote place.

Around 2 o'clock, the shearwaters settled. I lay in the quiet dark, watching the light beams turning silently above me, until I slipped back into sleep.

I woke to a still dawn. The sea, breathing quietly to my south, was pearly, with a light low mist upon it. The sky was pale with breaks of blue. The splash made by a black-backed gull diving fifty yards away sounded like a stone lobbed into the water nearby. I sat up, and saw that dozens of tiny dun-coloured birds were littering the rocks around me, making a high playground cheeping. Pipits. They gusted off when I moved.

I clambered down the shallowest side of the gulch, to the sharp angled rocks at the sea's edge, and washed my face in the idle water. On a rock-ledge, I found and kept a heart-sized stone of blue basalt, beautifully marked with white fossils: coccoliths no bigger than a fingernail, the fine fanwork of their bodies still visible. I set a thin shell afloat, carrying a cargo of dry thrift heads. As I placed it on the water, it was sucked out away from my fingers on an invisible back eddy, bobbing with the gentle swell.

Two big seals were hauled out on the rocks on the far point of the gulch. They watched me, and when I neared them they began to toil off their perches. Then they slipped into the water, rolled onto their backs, and sculled past the mouth of the gulch, gazing at me. They both dived. One disappeared. The other surfaced close to me, his thick head rising like a periscope. His big liquid eyes locked onto mine, and he watched me with a calm intransitive attention. For ten seconds or so we stared at each other. Then he ducked his head under the water with a splash, as though to rinse it, and disappeared.

Seals have long figured in the folklore of the Atlantic fringes as possessors of an uncannily double nature: in-between creatures, half-human and half-marine. In the 1940s, the writer David Thomson travelled between the westerly sea-communities of Ireland and Scotland, gathering stories about the seals. Everywhere he went, he found that the stories told were the same: of the capacity of the seal's gaze to compel and hold its subject, of seals stepping from the sea and becoming humans and humans slipping into the form of seals. The seal was a living reminder, he noted, of how close we are to animals, and of our aquatic ancestry. 'Land animals may play their roles in legend,' he concluded in the book he wrote about his journeys, 'but none, not even the hare, has such a dream-like effect on the human mind as the seal.'

I walked back to the shingle-beach on that still morning, past the burrows of the shearwaters, over the soft moulded grass, back through the field of thrift. I tried to imagine the conversations the monks would have had with one another about the places in which they dwelled: their discussions, implicit and explicit, about what it meant to be in affinity with the land they occupied. I admired the ways in which their spirituality found expressions and correlations in the physical world. In the view over a low-misted sea from a headland. In the fall of light upon the margin of a page, or a bay. In feathers rocking down through still air like snow, or snow rocking down through still air like feathers. Of course there were physical discomforts to their lives in these places; of course there would have been disagreements, dislikes, currents of bad feeling between the men themselves. But these ascetics had desired and celebrated an affluence which was beyond the economic, and which found its forms in the clearness of the air over the sea, or the shoaling patterns of a flock of seabirds in flight. Henry David Thoreau had written about such ideas of value. A lake, he said, a hill, a cliff or individual rocks, 'a forest or ancient trees standing singly', 'such things are beautiful, they have a high use which dollars and cents never represent'.

Much had changed since the time of the *peregrini*. Plastic flotsam washed up in Enlli's coves and gulleys. Rib-boats with twin engines thumped over the water near the mainland. There were problems with sewage, piped out into the Irish Sea from the Welsh coastal towns, and with chemical pollution which, on certain days, set the water foaming like shampoo on the rocks. And I could not have survived on the monks' island, could not have lived on it even for a month, probably – the draw of the city, my own routines, my needs for libraries, luxuries, connection, variety. Yet aspects remained of what had attracted the *peregrini* there, centuries earlier, and it felt somehow right to have begun my journeys in a landscape where people had, in the past, lived companionably with the wild.

Later we sailed back across the Sound to the mainland, at the turn of the tides, passing as we did so over water that was plump and gleaming, as though it were covered in a sheeny surface membrane beneath which the upwelling current seemed to pause and tremble.

*

John moored the boat a hundred metres offshore, near a point jutting west towards Enlli, facing a small bay. To either side of the bay rose jagged high cliffs, complicatedly recessed, and cut into by caves, off which bird cries pinged. The boat rolled on the subtle green swell, snapping its anchor-rope tight with each roll, so that water sprang from it. Its mast, seen from the stern, ticked from side to side like a metronome.

I dived in. Blue shock. The cold running into me like a dye. I surfaced, gasping, and began to swim towards the cliffs at the eastern side of the bay. I could feel the insistent draw of the current, sliding me out to the west, back towards Enlli. I swam at a diagonal to it, to keep my course.

Nearing the cliffs, I moved through different ribbons and bands of temperature, warm, then suddenly cold again. A large lustrous wave surged me between two big rocks, and as I put a hand out to stop myself from being barged against them, I felt barnacles tear at my fingers.

I swam to the biggest of the caves. Holding onto an edge of rock, and letting the swell lift me gently up and down, I looked inside. Though I could not see the back of the cave, it seemed to run thirty or forty feet into the cliffs: cone-shaped, tightening into the earth from its mouth. I released the rock, and drifted slowly into the opening. As I crossed the shadow cast by the cave's roof, the water grew cold. There was a big hollow sucking and slapping sound. I shouted, and heard my call come back at me from all sides.

As I got deeper in, the water shallowed. I swam breast-stroke, to keep myself as flat as possible. I was passing over dark-red and purple rocks: the voodoo colours of basalt, dolerite. The lower sides of the cave were lined with frizzy green seaweed, which was slick and shiny where the water reached it, like wet hair.

Farther back into the cave, the light was diffused and the air appeared powdery. The temperature had dropped, and I sensed the whole gathered coldness of the unsunned rock around and above me, pulsing out into the air and water.

I glanced back over my shoulder. The big semi-circular mouth of the cave had by now shrunk to a cuticle of light. I could only just see out to the horizon of the sea, and I felt a sudden involuntary lurch of fear. I swam on, moving slowly now, trying to sense the sharp rocks over which I was moving.

Then I reached the end of the cave, and there, at its very back, and in its very centre, lifted almost entirely out of the water, sat a single vast white boulder, made of smooth creamy rock, and shaped roughly like a throne or seat. It must have weighed five or six tons. I climbed awkwardly out of the water, slipping on weed, and sat on the rock, while the water slopped around its base, and looked back down the cave to the curved rim of light, all that remained of the world beyond.

Remembering the white rock now, it seems like a hallucination. I cannot explain really what it looked like, certainly not what it was doing there, among the red and purple basalts. Nor could I conceive of the might of the storm-waves that, over the centuries, must have brought that boulder to the cave, and then shifted it deeper and deeper in, until finally they had heaved it into that position, placed perfectly at the centre and the back of the cave.

*

That afternoon the sun returned, filling the air with low warm light. We climbed steep cliffs near the cove, above deep sea water which would catch us if we fell, and gathered the rock samphire that grew in vertical fields. We perched in little nooks and sentry holes, facing out to the setting sun, and talked to each other across the cliff, and chewed on the samphire's pale green leaves, relishing its saltiness.

As dark was finally falling, we returned to the cove off which the boat was moored. It lay at the mouth of a small steep-sided valley, cut by a stream. The valley's two banks were thick with small trees – ash, elder, rowan – hung with wild honeysuckle, and bindweed, whose almond scent gathered in the air and moved with the wind in currents through the dusk, and whose white trumpet-shaped flowers shone in the fading light.

The cove's beach was formed of hundreds of thousands of stones, some as round and smooth as eggs. Several old rusted tractors with black plastic bucket seats were pulled up to either side, near the cliffs, ready to haul fishing boats out of the water. Where it was sandier, near the water, three wading birds moved forwards together in a line, swinging their beaks from side to side in arcs as they advanced, like a team of metal detectors. We moved boulders to make seats, and sat for a while, watching the sun complete its combustion over the western sea.

When it was fully dark, we lit a birch-wood fire in a pit of stones beneath the westernmost cliff edge of the cove, and sat round it, drinking, eating, talking. The orange re-popped bright sun-flares out into the darkness. Resin hissed, and wood cracked as it tore itself along its grain. Sparks rushed in flocks into the darkness, before passing out of sight. The sea hushed on the shingle. Time became measured by the fire's failing and flaring. Later in the evening, I walked across the cove. I looked back through the dark at the fire, to see its orange sway, and the figures, visible only as shadows, moving about it.

By two in the morning the fire had dulled down to a pyre of embers, which pulsed black and orange with the light wind. The night was moonless and tepid. It was then that I saw the glimmering of the water. A line of blinking light – purple and silver – rimming the long curve of the beach. I walked down the edge, squatted down, and waved a hand in the water. It blazed purple, orange, yellow and silver. Phosphorescence!

I left my clothes on the stones and waded into the warm shallows. Where it was undisturbed, the water was still and black. But where it was stirred, it burned with light. Every movement I made provoked a brilliant swirl, and everywhere it lapped against a floating body it was struck into colour, so that the few boats moored in the bay were outlined with luminescence, gleaming off their wet sloped sides. Glancing back, the cove, the cliffs and the caves all appeared trimmed with light. I found that I could fling long streaks of fire from my fingertips, sorcerer-style, so I stood in the shallows for a few happy minutes, pretending to be Merlin, dispensing magic to right and left.

Then I walked out into the deeper water and slipped forward and swam in a squall of tangerine light. I rolled onto my back, and sculled along the line of the shore, looking back at the land, and kicking my legs so that complex drapes of colour were slung outwards. What was it Thoreau had written about a similar experience at Walden Pond? 'It was a lake of rainbow light, in which, for a short while, I lived like a dolphin.' I remembered Roger describing how he had stood one night on the beach at Walberswick, in Suffolk, and seen dozens of swimmers out in the phosphorescent water, their bodies 'striking through the neon waves like dragons'.

It was dark in the cove, and there was little loose light in the sky, and I realised that I could not see myself, only the phosphorescence that surrounded me, so that it appeared as though I were not there in the water at all: my body was unclear, defined only as a shape of darkness set against the swirling aqueous light.

It is now understood that marine phosphorescence is a consequence of the build-up in the water of minute bioluminescent organisms: dino agellate algae and plankton. By processes not entirely understood, these simple creatures ignite into light when jostled. They convert the energy of movement into the energy of radiance. For their phosphorescence to become visible to the human eye, the collaboration of billions of these single cells is required, from each of which light emanates.

The existence of these plankton, long remarked upon by sailors, especially warm-water sailors, has produced some extraordinary phenomena. During the Gorda Basin Earthquake, which struck California on 8 November 1980, witnesses on the coast saw vast areas of the ocean light up. In the 1970s, several sea captains navigating the Indian Ocean and the Persian Gulf reported the sight, in calm seas, of vast phosphorescent wheels with luminous rotating spokes, up to two hundred metres in diameter, trembling in the wake of their ships. Sometimes these wheels appeared to be below the water and sometimes they seemed to hover just above its surface.

In 1978, while crossing the Persian Gulf, under a starry sky in which stars were falling with long green tails, the captain of the Dutch vessel *Dione* saw several such wheels. There are no pre-twentieth-century records of this phenomenon, and it is generally assumed to be a function of the turbulence caused by the ships' engines. It has also been proposed that the wheels' apparent transcendence is due to the still water acting as a kind of lens, projecting the phosphorescence onto a thin layer of mist hanging just above the water's surface.

In 2004, a father and son were sailing in the Gulf of Mexico when their yacht was capsized by a gust of wind, sixty miles offshore. They clung to the hull, as it was carried on the powerful currents of the Gulf. After night fell, the water became rich with phosphorescence, and the air was filled with a high discordant music, made of many different notes: the siren song of dolphins. The drifting pair also saw that they were at the centre of two rough circles of phosphorescence, one turning within the other. The inner circle of light, they realised, was a ring of dolphins, swimming round the upturned boat, and the outer circle was a ring of sharks, swimming round the dolphins. The dolphins were protecting the father and his son, keeping the sharks from them.

When at last I left the sea, and came out onto the beach, the light-filled water shed from me onto the stones, flashed and vanished. I walked slowly inland, fading back into darkness as the water ran from me, and then lay down and slept by the low embers of the fire.

AFTERWORDS

‘a redundant light-house keeper, striking a match in a storm’

ANDREW MCNEILLIE (ELEVEN)

James Macdonald Lockhart

'Things Foreknown'

I was driving too fast. It was the end of winter; snow on Ben Cruachan and the last ferry for Mull left Oban in half an hour. Daft to think we could make it. But the A85 through Glen Lochy was an empty runway and I was anxious not to miss the ferry. It was only when we reached the bottleneck at the Pass of Brander, where road and loch are pressed together and Loch Awe narrows and sharpens like a heron's bill until it's finally squeezed into a river, that my gentle friend yelled at me to 'Slow down, for Christ's sake! Better to miss the ferry than the next bend in the road ...' My friend never yelled at anyone. I slowed down, mumbled sorry, and as we dropped the final half mile into Oban, we saw the red and black-topped funnel of the CalMac ferry pulling clear of the harbour.

If *Archipelago* is a ship, as Andrew McNeillie often referred to the journal in his generous, supple, subtly subversive editorials, then my first glimpse of it was seeing the ship leave harbour and, in a hot panic, running after it along the quay, jumping ropes and lobster creels, yelling for the ship to wait, to come back for me. For the journal was already in its third outing when I heard about it and, hearing its name, seeing the crew who manned it, the ethos which floated it, I immediately knew I wanted to climb aboard.

Seamus Heaney, who might be said to guide the many guiding spirits of *Archipelago*, caught it best, that peculiar experience of coming upon something for the first time which is already known, in the opening lines to his final poem in the 'Squarings' series from *Seeing Things*:

> Strange how things in the offing, once they're sensed,
> Convert to things foreknown.

Archipelago made sense to me as soon as I sensed it. Here was a journal – a vessel – which tilted the angle at which we viewed the islands we call home. Suddenly the map had a new perspective. The view felt reoriented. Perhaps more than anything it is a journal which has brought the fringes of the British and Irish archipelago more sharply into focus. *Archipelago* is a project which has helped to dispense with the view that these places are somehow marginal, peripheral. 'Remote from where, exactly?' is an *Archipelago* refrain. 'Remote from ourselves' is one answering echo which can be felt, more than heard, through the dozen years the journal has been going. I feel that echo, for instance, in Michael Longley's poems which feature regularly throughout the journal. Longley's delicate attentiveness to the natural world serves as an almost shamanistic bridge to a world we have virtually, catastrophically, lost touch with.

Never setting out to organise itself thematically (*Archipelago* always navigated by the stars rather than charts), each edition relied on a certain serendipity, a negative capability and the editor's astute instinct of where to steer. This approach to assembling the journal allowed for themes, places, voices to settle, to form patterns, quietly, organically. Pieces spoke to one another, set the pages of the journal echoing. It takes a great editor to achieve this effect, to balance, to judge the heft of the thing, before setting it afloat. Several issues in, I was asked by Andrew McNeillie if I would assist him with editing *Archipelago*. I did what I could from the sidelines, but really my role was to look on and watch a master at work.

Nor did *Archipelago* set out to be, as the inaugural editorial put it, 'a scholarly or an agitatedly political' journal. Again, this instinctive resistance to a type allowed the scholarly and the political, as with the journal's thematic strands, to settle and manifest in different ways. If the term 'remote' has become blurred with overuse, *Archipelago* could be said to have salvaged it by drawing our attention to the word's Latin origin, *Removere*: 'to remove, take away'. People, communities, languages, wildlife have all been removed from many of the landscapes *Archipelago* travels through. As such, it is a journal intuitively concerned with the politics of place, the history, its legacy – the 'board nailed across the window' in Heaney's translation of Sorley MacLean's great poem, 'Hallaig' (p. 145 above) – of many of these landscapes. It is also a project which acknowledges that the terms we use to name this cluster of islands, whether that is Great Britain, Britain and Ireland or the United Kingdom, don't always fit, or fit awkwardly.

This resistance in the fabric of the journal to be too neatly pigeonholed also produced one of my favourite irregular-regulars of *Archipelago*, the 'Ghosts' series, portraits of somewhat neglected figures from art and literature. Here was the 'scholarly' settling differently. Ian Niall, Richard Jefferies, W.H. Hudson, David Thomson are some of the names this series of essays reached for. Each portrait a vivid resurrection, a stand, to use the poet and critic Ian Hamilton's phrase, 'against oblivion'. Other ghosts move through the pages of *Archipelago*, ghosts in the landscape and in literature: Edward Thomas, Ivor Gurney, Eric Ravilious, artists whose work haunts the landscape as much as the land inhabits their work. 'Larkin's shade surprised me,' Heaney writes in 'The Journey Back' at the beginning of *Seeing Things*. The 'shades' which move through *Archipelago* surprise you with their immediacy. Here is Jasper, the young man in Ronald Blythe's 'Family Circles', 'immensely tall and fragile … his voice would descend in a run of rough barks', whose funeral, aged just thirty-three, Blythe takes. Here is David Thomson passing through a Roscommon hedge as if slipping into another world.

Archipelago has always been a respectful, attentive traveller, treading lightly, giving prominence to the languages, the literature, the art and culture of the distinctive districts of the archipelago. One of the ways this respectful approach manifests itself is in the quality of the journal's production. *Archipelago* is a beautiful object; that cover image of gannets diving over the curve of the earth, the British Isles aslant, slipping, as if no longer attached. The topography of the journal's interior is just as striking: poems with the space and silence around them to breathe on the page; Gaelic poems with their translation like a reflection; essays made less essayistic by the photographs which grow out of them; Norman Ackroyd's etchings, bringing the weather with them. Each edition of *Archipelago* always felt like it had been put together with craftsmanship and love.

My yell from the quayside for the good ship *Archipelago* to wait, I sent in the form of an essay I had written. The essay was not right for the journal but something in it gave Andrew McNeillie pause to, if not come back to port for me, then at least drop anchor a while and wait there in the offing till I could swim out to the ship. Andrew asked if I might write something else. And I found myself stood dripping on the deck of his ship, nervous of the crew going about their work, watching how they worked, learning from them. I watched poets – Angela Leighton, Alice Oswald, Kathleen Jamie, Meg Bateman, Sinéad Morrisey, among them – riding the ship's bow wave like dolphins. Tim Dee showed me how to really look at birds. Robert Macfarlane's encouragement made me feel that I wasn't a stowaway. Then Andrew appeared from his engine room with a warm-hearted grin and told me to get on with my work. I'll always be grateful to Andrew that he paused long enough to haul me aboard. I've been writing for the journal on and off ever since. I have learnt a great deal from reading it. I always want to write for it.

We missed that ferry to Mull and had an impromptu night out in Oban instead. I miss *Archipelago*, hauled up in a dry dock since Issue 12. I miss the way a new edition would arrive through the letterbox, carefully packaged, with a handwritten 'thank you' note. Then opening it to hear the sound of storm petrels in a Shetland broch, the calls of choughs on a Cornish cliff. With each edition these islands became vaster, more nuanced, more intricate. Perhaps the ship needs to rest in dry dock for a while. Perhaps the journal is less like a ship, more like a shipbuilder, crafting a vessel – part currach, part kayak – with the agility and buoyancy to glide across our islands' many seas. The vessel's log: the map of a constellation.

Andrew McNeillie

Andrew McNeillie

Archipelago: *A Life*

For those not familiar with the publication, each issue of Archipelago *carried an 'Editorial' in which the editor figured himself as the Skipper of a fishing boat that eventually became known as* 'The Good Ship'. *His contributors were his crew, their contributions its catch. Their publisher was the Skipper's own* Clutag Press, *his office* 'The Wheelhouse' *in honour of W.S. Graham. This is the story of where* Archipelago *came from.*

Archipelago was conceived not at sea where you might expect it to have been but in Barcelona. I first thought of it on stepping out of Irati, a Basque tapas bar, in the autumn of 2005. It happened in an instant, a seemingly unpremeditated moment, a rush in conversation with my future son-in-law John Sullivan, after several tapas and as many or more glasses of Rioja *tinto*.

As swiftly are we all conceived. A good lyric poem can write itself like that without need of revision. As time has proved, *Archipelago* was 'a good poem'. Both lyric and epic (in that epics speak of nations), it never seemed laboured in its making. Though like any work of length by multiple hands it had its peaks and troughs, its triumphs and its one or two errors of judgment, along the way. Beware the weak moment. Spare no feelings. The Spanish poet Luis Rosales, one of the Generation 36 writers of the Civil War period, had lines for it: 'Knowing I have never erred in anything / but in the things that have mattered to me most.'

Subscribers and readers are an easier party, and it is for them that I'm attempting this essay. They don't miss deadlines and have always been lenient towards me when I have. I hope they won't think I'm making too much of too little.* Perhaps I'm asking a lot by going the long way round via Holyhead. But 'longest way round, is the shortest way home', said James Joyce and I believe him. Whatever else, it is the readers' story. They're the Lloyds underwriters to 'The Good Ship'. This is my tribute to them and my gratitude. Without them *Archipelago* would have sunk to the bottom of the deep. There'd have been nothing to salvage but a fond hope and a hole in the bank account, of which there's never any shortage.

I saw what *Archipelago* was to be and described it as we walked to No. 5 Carrer (or Calle) Aribau, where my daughter and her man had their apartment, up the hill, in a pleasant district, nearer the Via Augusta than the bustling, lower Gran Via end. Not a short walk, and more than long enough for me to outline what I found I had in mind. When I'd done, I remember falling silent, almost certainly to my companion's relief, for the remainder of the way, exploring to myself what I'd imagined or what had rather imagined itself seemingly out of nowhere.

I told it in almost the same words on returning home in a 'credo' or manifesto, a proposal I'd promptly circulate to potential contributors. Some of you will know what I had to say well enough. There was a time when I knew I could count on you to stand by your bunks and recite it word for word. But now you probably need to look it up

* I'd never have thought to attempt this essay were it not for Jos Smith and his chapter 'Fugitive Allegiances: The Good Ship *Archipelago* and the Atlantic Edge' in *Coastal Works: Cultures of the Atlantic Edge* (OUP, 2017), of which he was co-editor with Nicholas Allen and Nicholas Groom. It opened my eyes to what 'The Skipper' had been up to.

in Issue 1 and peruse it quietly in your armchair. Otherwise, for your interest and mine, here's the document I circulated, to Seamus Heaney, Derek Mahon, Robert Macfarlane and a good many others. As you see, it isn't quite identical with the 'Editorial' version in Issue 1:

> **ARCHIPELAGO** is to be a literary journal in the ordinary sense, in that it will contain writings in non-fictional prose, and verse. Extraordinary will be its preoccupations with landscape, with documentary and remembrance, with wilderness and wet, with natural and cultural histories, with language and languages, with the littoral and vestigial, the geological, and topographical, with climates, in terms of both meteorology, ecology and environment; and all these things as metaphor, liminal and subliminal, at the margins, in the unnameable constellation of islands on the Eastern Atlantic coast, known variously in other millennia as Britain, Great Britain, Britain and Ireland etc; even, too, too readily, the United Kingdom (including the North of partitioned Ireland), though no such thing ever existed, other than *in extremis* during wartime, but in the letter. But while the unnameable archipelago is its subject, its vision is global, and its concerns with the state of the planet could not be more of the hour.
>
> In spirit and letter **ARCHIPELAGO** will assert, in an unrepentantly secular sense, that prayers of praise or celebration are as worthy as, perhaps even more worthy than, prayers of petition, and it will be committed to hearing both, where quietly composed, with thoughtful craft. Among its prophets will be such visionaries as Job, Ecclesiastes, William Blake, William Wordsworth, John Clare, Henry David Thoreau, Herman Melville, Gerard Manley Hopkins, D.H. Lawrence, David Jones. Above all it will be a literary journal, with literary values, for the common reader, not a scholarly or an agitatedly political one, in the ordinary senses of such terms.
>
> The aim is to solicit contributions from established and emerging writers, and initially to produce an annual issue of around 64pp, to sell at £11.00 plus £1.50 p&p. As the project progresses, and dependant on success, biannual publication is envisaged and it is hoped this might be achieved in year two. Proposed consultants and collaborators: Robert Macfarlane,

Tim Robinson, Damian Walford Davies, Patrick Crotty, Marina Warner, and Julian Bell.

The journal will find structure and shape around poems and non-fictional prose pieces (of about 4000–5000 words) that bear un-programmed correspondences, within the field-force of ideas described above. Each issue will seek to pay homage to the work of an exemplary practitioner, whether established in the canon, or one whose work has fallen from the living record. There will be illustrations.

ARCHIPELAGO will set sail flying the following flags:

'One generation passeth away,
and another generation cometh,
but the earth abideth for ever.'

'All the rivers run into the sea; yet the sea is not full;
unto the place from whence the rivers come,
thither they will return again.'

ECCLESIASTES 4, and 7

'From where will a renewal come to us, to us who have devastated the whole earthly globe?'

SIMONE WEIL

*

How prescient, how visionary was Simone Weil (1909–43). How timely, as it's proved, was the Skipper's conception.

Not all that was proposed came about, and not all those mentioned became involved. Not all those invoked figured in the log either. I called it a journal and since then a magazine. Strictly speaking, it was neither. It was more an annual anthology of specially recruited new writing. But the main thing is that it held to its course and ideals. It cohered. We were never short of writers to sign up for a trip, and never short of readers to welcome them back, enough to make the venture pay for itself, staying well in the black to the end.

I wanted there to be a bite to it, and certainly for it not to be just a poetry magazine. It had to have range and openness, and to be preponderantly non-fictional prose, leavened by poems. Established writers known to fame might help lift tyro exponents or neglected practitioners above the parapet. It had to be a mix and take the odd risk. It had to be about place and landscape, nature and the wilderness. It had to be carried off with a certain humour and it had to allow ample space to the visual, the image.

When Derek Mahon responded to the manifesto, he said how welcome it was to have the prospect of a publication 'with an agenda'. Seamus Heaney felt the same and after a fashion became a patron. When he bought a copy he'd send a cheque for £300.00 or £400.00 or thereabouts. In the year of *Archipelago*'s conception, Clutag Press had published *A Shiver*, a pamphlet of poems by Heaney. So he was already on board. Thanks to Richard Ovenden (now Bodley's Librarian) and Chris Fletcher, the Press had the good fortune to be adopted by the Bodleian Library. They were interested in acquiring its archive and do so still in more or less annual instalments. They hosted events at the Library, in Convocation House, particularly in connection with *Archipelago*. At the first of these – a series of readings – Seamus Heaney spoke impromptu in praise of the venture, contributing to what would become the first 'Bodcast' podcast. It was an occasion that brought Heaney and Norman Ackroyd together for the first time.

A fundamental part of the agenda was also to give literary and visual pleasure, material pleasure by means of high production values that none the less steered clear of the precious or deluxe. The medium is also the message. In this *Archipelago* was enabled beyond words by Adrian Lack of Senecio Press, a vital collaborator from start to finish. A perfectionist and uncommonly committed, he checked and double-checked and checked again every feature of page design and typography, and tweaked every image to the utmost towards best possible reproduction. And as to appearances and practicalities, Gail McNeillie designed our Corncrake logos (from a drawing by Julian Bell, taken 'from the death' in the Pitt Rivers Museum) and our web pages, typeset every issue barring the last two, and with John Sullivan hosted and handled all digital matters gratis.

I don't mean to be merely dutiful here. This is an engaged, at times, thanks to the Skipper, an off-the-wall essay, not a glorified set of acknowledgments, as *Archipelago* readers might expect, and as you'll see in due course. But it needs to be clearly stated: such a publication as *Archipelago* is a collaboration, not a one-man band; it is an orchestration; it is a moveable feast and a community. And it is more than the sum of its parts in its order of service and balance struck between contributions, one against the other by subject, by form or genre, by image. It becomes its own forcefield, and every issue creates its own dynamic. To borrow a notion from Joseph Brodsky: every issue restructures time. If that is true, then the twelve issues taken together knock a hole in time forever.

The moment in Barcelona was the start of it but not of course its beginning. Like a river, such a thing has as many beginnings as there are raindrops in a cloud. I hardly know where to begin. There's no doubt there were presences, visible and not so visible, that made a difference. Among them surely was the conversation about 'the Isles' that grew up around the framing of the Good Friday Agreement. Norman Davis's popular-unpopular historical survey *The Isles* was published in 1999, a book of four-nations perspectives. I fell upon it keenly when it came out as it promised to articulate a view I could never recall not holding. It had its odder moments, if I remember, but its heart was in the right place for me. That is, on the other side of the planet from the 'national' story as told traditionally and still by those unable to get over the idea that Britannia no longer rules the waves – who can't acknowledge that the 'union' is and ever was divided in multiple directions and fractured at innumerable levels, socially and politically, and that the official history doesn't serve. That devolution cannot go too far. Nor true community come too near. Nor has the official British story ever served but superficially across the spectrum of who/whom. For example, in the course of the toxic Brexit debate, it was not 'Britain' that wanted to 'leave' but England and, it seemed, Wales. The 'English' have since emerged as an aspiring political entity for the first time in centuries. Make of it what you will.

The manifesto spoke of the 'unnameable archipelago' of Britain and Ireland. It did not do so to espouse a particular cause but to acknowledge political complexity. Further, if you remove a name from something habitually associated with it, you shake things up, just a little. And rather on the principle that Nature abhors a vacuum meaning rushes in to stimulate thought afresh. We find new ways of looking at things across borders and over walls of sea. Terry Eagleton's 'West Is South' in Issue 2 caught the idea exactly.

Well, *Archipelago* did what very little it might on this front and sideways, in a minor key, not in a buttonholing in-your-face manner. That was never its business. Its business was to explore and to observe the wilderness limits of place in the unnameable archipelago, from multiple points of view and a wide range of interests and concerns. Perhaps nothing makes the point better than the map on its cover, the first thing the reader sees, commissioned in just about every detail from the artist and writer Julian Bell. Its gannet's-eye north-west point of view more or less drops the unnameable south-east, the seat of wealth and power, Hugh MacDiarmid's 'Megalopolis', over the far horizon. It makes not only a political point but also an environmental one with its scarcity of fish in the waves below.

Less clearly the case than *The Isles*, in chronological terms, and more local to me, in my then job as Literature Editor at Oxford University Press (uncharacteristically, for me, at the heart of the English establishment), there was John Kerrigan's *Archipelagic English: Literature, History, and Politics 1603–1707* which eventually came out in 2008. *Archipelago* 1 was published the year before. Had I seen a version of *Archipelagic English* or discussed it with its author before the autumn of 2005 when I had my Damascene moment in Barcelona? I don't think so. I certainly don't recognise any obvious mechanism of cause and effect. But I do think *Archipelagic English*, a work of canonical adjustment and national re-ordering of a deep-rooted and intriguing kind, must have played at least a subliminal part in the ongoing emergence of the ideas behind the magazine. Kerrigan's cover also plays with the map of Britain and Ireland (and includes the Shetlands), Britain more or less reclining on its east coast, with Ireland's west coast at the top of the frame. Did I have any part in that? At any rate, I would have signed off on it, as the book's editor. All is present and correct in the Kerrigan cover image (barring the Channel Isles), while *Archipelago* for its part omits them, and the Shetland archipelago too, on the argument, as urged by MacDiarmid, that it is really a part of Scandinavia.

Then there was the hinterland of what was called the 'new' nature writing. Writing about place and landscape, nature and the wild, 'the environment' and soon enough, in the wake of the brilliant Ian Sinclair, 'the edge', from the Hackney Marshes to the scrublands of Nowhere. It was I think the environmental, eco-sensitive element in the best of this work that justified the epithet 'new'. Roger Deakin was for me the finest of them, and Robert Macfarlane hard on his heels. Tim Dee altered the picture radically too, as a writer and a filmmaker. Mark Cocker re-grounded our affair with nature in scientific observation. Kathleen Jamie made influential findings along telling sightlines. But Robert Macfarlane, above all, was deeply influential in the venture, as moral support as it began, but fell away as his own very different world grew. I took him out to supper and sought his reassurance that what I had in mind might work.

When Issue 1 came out, not only was he in its pages, it was launched at his College, Emmanuel. It was on his advice and through his influence that we received a subvention of £1000 a year, for five years (Issues 2–6), from the Ashden Trust, an eco-charity under the Sainsbury umbrella. We weren't really environmentally *engagé* or zealous enough in the right style for the Ashden agenda, so with good reason the grant wasn't renewed. I was grateful to them but not sorry to say farewell. Independence is always best and essential to difference. Avoid patronage. Avoid being tied to an institution – like the plague. That is, to allow you to follow your instincts without looking over your shoulder. Let the likes of Hugh MacDiarmid, Dylan Thomas, Sydney Graham and Brendan Behan be your heroes. Live and die for it. Don't sell your soul to anyone, certainly not the management, or any other party.

Not only was Macfarlane a contributor, but he played midwife to the inclusion of a piece in our first issue by the – by then – late Roger Deakin, to whom I was once introduced over a pint of beer in Cambridge shortly before his untimely death. He seemed in that brief moment a mesmerising and extremely genial man. But now when I recall the occasion I see a ghost. The ghosts accumulate. They haunt the rigging. They rattle the fish boxes below decks. I hear them like Hamlet's father in the cellarage. One of them down there, Mick Imlah, left us cruelly soon. Seamus Heaney and more recently Richard Murphy and Derek Mahon have joined him since. I mark their going here, and draw breath, as they do still, but through their works.

Robert Macfarlane and I had originally discovered each other's existence, some time not long after 1997, when he wrote to me asking if he might reprint in an issue of *Oxford Poetry*, I think it was, a poem of mine called 'Wishlist' that seemed to strike a chord with him:

> The iceberg that makes it round the world.
> The complete works of Anon.
> A cape and stars above the sea.
> The camel through a needle's eye.
> The Life of William Shakespeare by Himself.
> The first of day. Her louch look.
> The sweetest fuck.
> The nesting bird.
> The omertà of old age.
> The light at the heart of the pyramid.
> The song you have by heart.
> The harbour light at dawn.
> The sound within the poem.
> The curlew on the moor.
> The wild-goose skein.

The raven rolling in a windy sky.
The world turned upside down.
Tête à tête *avec* Owain Glyndŵr.
Genius-in-waiting.
Winter lightning.
The last word of the old order and first of the new.
The Republic of Scotland.
The Republic of Wales.
Vision and revision.
Hindsight as foresight.
The reader read.
The people's voice.
The happy couple.
The oar's puddle.
The Tower of Babel.
The lighthouse bell.
A millpond sea.
The dune's crest in the moving air.
The tribe's oral tradition.
The other as me.
The one in B minor. The next line.
The coelacanth's mating ritual.
The girl who never returned your love.
The end of all that. The end of all this.
A new poetics. A new prosody.
The poet guilty as charged.

A 'louch look' is a come-hither. He would later point me in the direction of Norman Ackroyd. I had seen an early Ackroyd etching on a wall in my sister's house long before but had yet to discover his mania for islands and the wilderness. When he heard about *Archipelago* and saw it at last, he rejoiced in it, saying it made him feel no longer alone in his nesomaniacal pursuit. Issue 1 contained only one of his works – a version of 'Ailsa Craig'. Almost every subsequent one included several.

His work helped define the magazine, becoming its staple and mainstay, to the extent that the publication came to feel like a collaboration between us, an honest resistance to virtual culture and its material consequences – about as far-flung from these things as are Muckle Flugga, St Kilda or Skellig Michael.

Then there were the bird people and more besides: Tim Dee and Mark Cocker, again; and the lyrical precisian of observation in the field, James Macdonald Lockhart; and many another of different pursuit. We were joined by Katherine Rundell, whose career was taking off in so many directions it was hard for her to make time to write for us but she managed it, a little, and that was a less that meant more. (Otherwise I note the absence of women here, an imbalance I tried always to redress in the magazine, but never to my satisfaction, until perhaps Issue 12.)

As for the new nature writing, I really took my measure elsewhere: from Tim Robinson and his self-confessed work of reparation in the world west of the Shannon. This was only natural. We had the Aran Islands in common. There's a radical politics implicit in Robinson's work – his writing and mapmaking – that's grounded (rooted is the radical word) in true dwelling and philosophy, regarding time, space, place, language, the environment and the colonial legacy. But it's one that expresses itself in a jargon-free prose that serves no academic agenda, a prose that is artful and literary, giving us 'stones of Aran' where Ruskin gave us 'stones of Venice', and which pursues compelling, Proust-like mysteries of memory and record with extraordinary precision, tenacity and wit. Nor does his work have anything whatsoever to do with writing to order for university managers, or for publishers and their marketers. Or with the calculations and speculations of the literary agent.

Homogenisers all, killers of the Word, and vain and inglorious debasers of our cultural currency. They would iron everything out to meet the market, those opportunistic Jacks and Jills in office, according to the Skipper of 'The Good Ship', who has just entered, stage left. As most of you know he's a haunted, some would say a slightly deranged character, with a touch of Melville's Ahab about him. If he has a leg to stand on, it's not always clear that he has two. But on he presses in pursuit of the whale that is truth and revelation. In the dynamic between us, I discover a point of view, a take on things, that is more his than mine, created by the dynamics of fiction. 'What are the people?' he asked me the other day. 'The people are as rain through the hands of politicians ... They are adversity in the face of laughter.' Who can't agree with him that politics comes nowhere close to what we are and what being alive is and what life on earth is for? In his view it's just machinery, stuff for earnest rude mechanicals, honest lawyers, disingenuous ideologues, dishonest chancers, weather-cocks, expenses fiddlers, to embroil themselves in. Fear not, he says, there'll never be any shortage of them, the worthily well-intended, the ambitious busy-body, the cunning operator, the hubristic backwoodsman, the sly turncoat, the out-and-out gobshite and mediocrity.

Just so there'll never be any shortage of such folk to dismiss the Skipper as a suitable case for treatment. But if there is a last laugh they won't have it. What mark do they make? Who remembers any of them for long? They confuse means with ends and end up meaning nothing. How quickly they diminish to less than Lilliputian proportions. A good one passes through the political landscape as rarely as Halley's Comet crosses the sky. (Or not so often, mutters the Skipper, now from the wings.) How soon we see that the emperors have no clothes. Naked we come into this world, naked we leave. That's what the seven-sided sea teaches in its compelling drama, to the end of time. '"Vanity of vanities," saith the Preacher ...' That's the Skipper's position. Whenever I suggest to him that the world's a more complicated place than he seems to accept, he looks at me with pity. He'll assert that one person, one vote is a right we must all be ready to die for at the barricades. But otherwise he looks awry at life's tragic spectacle.

NEVER A JOINER OR A FOLLOWER BE, he proclaims, adapting an old saying, as he steps aboard, every time we cast off. The only community he holds dear are his crew and his readers (even then he has his moments). Apart from that, he's inclined to say, 'Wherever more than two are gathered together, look for trouble.' Something he tells me he learnt from James Joyce. Or, no less characteristically, looking up from the pages of *Moby-Dick* or *Les Fleurs du Mal*, he might say: 'Mystery and regret are also characteristics of the beautiful.'

He's no stranger to melancholy. We should never be so inattentive as to overlook his belief in the natural obscurity of things. He's a bundle of contradictions. To him self-contradiction, according to his auto-didactic reading, is one of the fundamental Rights of Man. Someone told me she thought of him not as Ahab but as the Ancient Mariner. But what is his trouble that he holds us with his glittering eye and skinny hand? What has he seen with his famished gaze? Being born west of the Severn and the Dee and knowing the world west of the Bladnoch, he has travelled west of the Clyde and knows the world west of the Shannon. It all seems to have deranged him, shipwrecked him far away, in the lost lands of the Native Americans, somewhere off Cape Cod, Nantucket or Nova Scotia, settled him in the hillbilly Appalachians, starved him near to death in Chubert, poor soul. Here you might see him in something of that light, in lines from our co-authored lengthy excursion 'Meditations in a Boatshed':

> 'Lower Away', though waves be steep,
> join those in peril on the deep,
> seeking refuge from disaster
> somewhere not in the hereafter.
> Let go fore and aft, and say farewell.
> Follow the *Pequod* if you will
> or play it safe along the coast
> to put in somewhere in the past
> where the drowned hurl against the rocks
> in yarns of storms and tragic wrecks.
> Or say good riddance to the last
> of England at its very worst,
> the dark side of its bill of lading
> black as Ahab's soul out whaling,
> a tale a million times as thick

as a million copies of *Moby-Dick*.
Put a good ship to good use
its good name still might come off worse:
the *Windrush* scandal a disgrace
as shocking as the Dreyfus case –
seen off with a resignation,
whitewash for a troubled nation.

Oh why not embark at last
and go barefoot before the past
first round one cape then another
shriven by the wildest weather?

'Barefoot before the past,' that's the Skipper's trouble, and some say his mistake. But we neglect the past at our peril. It is the yardstick to conscience. And as Thomas Mann asked, 'Is not the pastness of the past the profounder, the completer, the more legendary, the more immediately before the present it falls?' What might it be to bury the past? To restore the world to 'factory conditions', as the mobile phone option has it? It hardly bears thinking that we'd be so foolishly naive. Otherwise, I think it safe to say the Skipper's incapable of systematic thought. At times he's nothing short of crazed. One night we were out on the Porcupine Bank and I had to wake him, as we were ready to haul. Startled and staring wildly, he turned in his bunk, and cried out, 'I appeal to every thinking man to show me what remains of Life.' He was quoting Charles Baudelaire. But you never quite know where you are with him. If ennui and even monkish *acedia* sometimes plague him, there's seldom a dull moment when he's around. I count myself fortunate to have spent time in his company, if not to have known him well.

While I insisted that *Archipelago* was to be a literary magazine and not a political one in any strident sense, still it had a political edge. The Skipper himself was ever a dissenter, with a radical Scottish view of the social order written into him at his father's knee, pretty well Burnsian in sentiment; and a Welsh non-conformist tradition, a mindset absorbed from infancy – subconsciously, osmotically, blindly – and none of it in thrall to any form of institutionalised religion. Stand on your own two feet was his injunction. Have no intercessor of any kind between you and your maker or your fellow citizens. 'People obeying rules laid down by somebody else,' he agreed with John Berger's mother, 'is not the same as respecting life.' Insofar as this relates to me, I thank the influence of my father's native wild spirit. His scepticism was liberating. As was his contempt for the dour Presbyterianism that had been brow- and otherwise beaten into him as a boy. I have him to thank that I was never Christened, neither blessed nor wounded by clerics. The language of religion might enthral us but let no man of god seek to contain us or put us asunder. And no other order of man either, no patriarchy, no unelected hierarchy or other parcel of stuffed-shirt rogues. We'll never rid ourselves of them, but we needn't serve them and must oppose them where we can. And so the Skipper takes his stand, closer in spirit now to the William Blake of 'The Marriage of Heaven and Hell' than to Robert Burns and 'Tam O'Shanter', closer as well to Charles Baudelaire, though nature was not Baudelaire's bag. He was more attuned to the painter Edgar Degas, who famously said that landscape artists should be arrested and charged with molestation.

Norman Ackroyd

When I told Norman Ackroyd about Degas's opinion, he laughed with delight. But what is landscape and the art of landscape can hardly be better addressed than through the work of that 'force of Nature' Norman Ackroyd, as Douglas Dunn has called him (Dunn an *Archipelago* mainstay, especially in the earlier issues). Norman Ackroyd's name has become for a broad public one synonymous with the British and Irish Isles and a particular form of artistic practice. At etching he is the acclaimed modern master, a virtuoso, working at the outer limits, somewhere beyond the Ultima Thule of what might be done with light, air, water, acid, copper, ink and paper. Latterly, too, we have become increasingly aware that he is also a master of watercolour.

A butcher's son, with an artistic mother, from very humble origins in South Leeds, and so a Yorkshireman, he is among those rare beings, like D.H. Lawrence (Lawrence a hero in the Ackroyd household), who lift our hearts by showing just how, given half a chance and an inspired work ethic, genius will out. What we call genius is nothing without extraordinary native talent, obsession, critical focus and hard work.

That Norman Ackroyd is obsessed and driven, though in a most genial way, is obvious. And his focus, that all-important element, is, as the expression goes, 'out of this world'. He sees straight into and seizes things instantaneously as from mid-air, transmuting onto paper and into art what's always fleeting before eye and mind: the sea, sea-light, the sky in all its weathers, forms in nature and place, things waiting to be found and made new, if you are a seer, if you are an artist. That is, if you 'live in the eye', as John Keats put it, while in the Lake District. The eye is different from the mind.

It has often been said, and was said of Ackroyd early on when he was a student at the Royal College of Art, that he is a visual poet. It is the recent and contemporary poets that spring to mind for me whenever I come to dwell on the nature of his achievement. I think at once of Richard Murphy, who showed the way for a new generation of nesomaniacs – myself among them. He is the poet of Inishbofin and of Cleggan, of High Island (which he once owned) and Omey. I think too, of course, of Douglas Dunn – Dunn another miraculous product of the working class – author of *St Kilda's Parliament* (1981), with whom Ackroyd has collaborated so profoundly in *A Line in the Water* (2009) to make one of the most beautiful books I own. I think of Derek Mahon's great archipelagic and coastal poems that give such powerful voice to our alienation. I think of Heaney and of Michael Longley (another mainstay in our pages), the bard of Carrigskeewaun. I think of Sorley MacLean, George Campbell Hay, Iain Crichton Smith, Norman MacCaig, George Mackay Brown, W.S. Graham and of course MacDiarmid. I think of Angus Martin. And I think of R.S. Thomas (who as a young man went on a Celtic pilgrimage to Galway and Connemara) and of the painter Kyffin Williams, another visual poet, who went to Patagonia (Chubert) and brought it back to Snowdonia.

We associate Norman Ackroyd with the wilder extremities of the archipelago, the far coasts and islands. But like the swallow, the cuckoo and the corncrake, the shearwater and petrel, he is a migrant bird in these places, a bird of passage, rather than a resident. He travels out from his workplace in the urban heart of the metropolis. He doesn't inhabit a studio so much as a workshop, a place somehow redolent of the Industrial Revolution, and its Northern history, with its heavy machinery, its wheels and levers, its metals and acids, its sense about it of a vital past still put to use, integrated into the present.

It is central to bear this matter in mind. Not only does it speak to Ackroyd's urban, working-class origins, the environment in which he feels most 'at home', it should also prompt us to recognise that for him 'Britain' itself is not only where he lives and belongs, it is also an island. It is not a mainland. He is of an island people. He takes his stand upon it, like stout Cortez above the Pacific in Keats's poem. In this respect, and now with the death of the late Poet Laureate Ted Hughes, with whose vision Ackroyd's own has much in common, I call him the last surviving King of Elmet.

It is from that vital vantage point high up in Yorkshire that he likes to describe the arc of the archipelago, from Muckle Flugga – where, long ago and literally, he saw the light(house), in a far-flung Damascene moment – round to Dursey Head off south-west Ireland, to Bishops Rock and on, via Brancaster Roads and the Farnes, back again to Orkney. Not the monarch but the maker of all he surveys and has given to us, in our need to know and acknowledge where we belong and what we come from.

A trouble with the visual arts is that you cannot talk about them in their own language. They move on silence and give pause to speech. The achievement of any artist is within the integrity of the individual work, in its innovation, its absolute moment, brought and held together in the process of its making, in the dynamic of its emergence or 'continual arrival', to borrow an idea from another important archipelagic poet,

W.S. Graham, yet another great maker, sprung from a 'set-in bed' in a tenement in Greenock.

To generalise across the work of a lifetime is to risk doing that work no good service. But there is a general question here, in the case of Ackroyd's oeuvre, that insists by its very nature that we broach it. Usually I'm inclined to distrust the idea of an extended artistic 'project'. It often refers to something more *voulu* than organically compelled, and what metal it began with soon beats so thin you can see right through to the idea behind it. The *voulu* spells death, I remember learning, in the long ago, from Bernard O'Donoghue.

A huge artistic project is however what Ackroyd has bequeathed us. It is tempting to regard it as record. But works of art, poems and paintings, are not made 'for the record', with the exception of some civic and public genres. At any rate, they are not documents. Documentary might be a work of art, but documents are the stuff of evidence merely, the materials of the historian, not concerned with aesthetic value. We need to look at what goes on in an Ackroyd etching just as we look at what's going on in say the work of his friend and inspiration Francis Bacon. Think of those reflective and refractive glassy surfaces in Bacon's work. The risk in any art of landscape is that we tend to see it as representation, not from a formal and textural point of view. There is a further risk in considering a typical Ackroyd: that we can tend to think his work is monochrome. But his etching is also a subtle art of colour, however muted and subdued the range and modulation in hue.

Of the four Ackroyds I own, my favourite is *Inishbofin Sound*, currently hanging in our stairwell, near the top of the stairs. It is as fine an example of his practice as you might find. In this case, the light from a stairway window, falling at a glance, suits its shadowy energy, its eruptive turbulence, its storm-gloom, its boisterous sea-turmoil, its fineness of spray and air or sky, its powdery-seeming and quite impossible texture – its paradoxical air of evanescence, its no less paradoxical solidity and groundedness.

I have been at sea on Inishbofin Sound, and visited the island too. The image captures the spirit of such a place in wild weather. But even given weather to match, you would be hard put to hold *Inishbofin Sound* up from a boat and locate its subject or discern the artist's physical point of view. But whether or not you could, Ackroyd's art isn't about that. Beyond what I've said about it so far, by way of impressionistic criticism, *Inishbofin Sound* is I think at heart and most significantly about forms, peaked or pyramidal forms and masses (wave and shore and elevated land), and how these essentially triangular elements, on the right of the picture, relate to a tilted, more-or-less oval land-mass to the left. The two areas are held apart, and conjoined, by a third, in the form of a softened, slanting V-shape of spume, cloud and light. It is as if a minimalist post-cubist abstract has been exposed to the weather, left out in the wind and rain to acquire a patina from a somewhat chiaroscuro nature.

The weather is always a medium in Ackroyd's work, the weather in literal meteorological terms, and the equally fugitive and variable or fluid weather of the etching process. Ackroyd snatches at things twice, first in nature, then in the workshop. He does sometimes etch *en plein air* or indeed *en pleine mer*, in the wild. Otherwise he uses sketchbooks, working with watercolour, graphite, ink. However many stages, and in the workshop there can be many, the result is pure invention, true creation, something that is a thing-in-itself, delivered into the world on its own terms, at some point in a dynamic that reaches beyond the artist's immediate sense of possibility, to carry him over into something else, to extend or be extended by his own vision, and to hold us spellbound by that 'thing in itself' and leave us wondering how on earth it can have been made.

But suppose for the sake of it we refer to Ackroyd's achievement, as something on a huge scale, that is 'for the record'? What is it recording? What has it recorded, except the artistic vision of a man with a passion for islands, coasts, the high seas, places apparently without people in them?

For myself, I tend to think of the whole in other terms, rather more as a large orchestral piece of sea-music – and I see its importance as a 'collection' as that rare thing, the major expression of a *zeitgeist*, of the spirit of an age in which the majority of people 'belong' nowhere, having been uprooted by history. Today, what happened to so many in the wake of the Industrial Revolution, Enclosure and Clearance, is now propelled into new dimensions by the next such development, the Digital Revolution, a revolution that also tends to demote the vital materiality of work such as Ackroyd makes.

Now many people sense their loss, yet it is in the majority of cases the loss of something that personally they never had. Nor is it about Eden, or Paradise Lost, still less Regained. It is more what I think both Norman Ackroyd and Ted Hughes tell us all about. It is about Wildness Lost, and Wildness Regained, by the highest means of art.

Yet this isn't the whole picture. For Ackroyd is also a consummate latter-day antiquarian and student of topography, an impassioned studier of maps, those potent springboards to imagination. The edition of historical maps of the Hebrides assembled by Finlay MacLeod can hold him rapt in reverie at every turn of the page. On his studio wall there is a large map of the unnamable archipelago, its margins littered with the kind of red dots you see in galleries to indicate that a work has been sold. They mark terrain in which he has found forms of place and weather to reinvent into art.

In my lexicon, landscape is framed out of place. The two aren't one and the same, as sometimes contributors to *Archipelago* have seemed to believe. Landscape is found and designed, whether aesthetically or for mere practicality. It is a format. It is descriptive. It is analytic. Place resists design and contradicts analysis through time. Place is where we live and it is how we live with all our garbage and dross. It is like something you see seething under a microscope, or the view backstage, drama without apparent unity, or the constellations from behind. Order here is temporary and in the making. It is always becoming and never achieved. It improvises. It mends and makes do. It consumes all before it. Its laws are the laws of nature. You need to be a scientist to find its rationale. The laws of landscape are our laws of proportion and order. When it sails too close to place, landscape puts itself in peril. Landscape has a quality of stewardship, but the laws of stewardship and husbandry are not laws of place. They converge on and colonise place. Landscape is colonised place: it is the picturesque. It is scenery. It is a bourgeois, not a labouring man in a tied cottage. It is Wordsworth's *Guide to the Lakes*, a key work none the less, powerful and neglected. Place is what we call 'nature' and it has no vocabulary, no language, it can't shrug off, not even that of the scientist. It is a subconscious condition. Mind is a place, not a landscape. It is not fixed, except upon ideals, on *idée fixe*, on appetite for knowledge and improvement which is change. We have more in common with place than with landscape. Landscape is solace. It pleases the eye. It pleases the senses. It is a commodity. It is something we bring with us and set up like a painter's easel. It has a price on it. It is property, stage property, theatrical backdrop, the framed view, the perfect scene, pastoral in the many versions of that species. It is beauty. It is both elation and delight, and mystery and regret.

The Irish Sea

The view of the archipelago I hold is one heavily inflected by the history and politics of Ireland, a country I first visited at the age of four and one to which, I have since discovered, I owe the totality of my Y-chromosome, barring a dash of Viking, and a microscopic smudge of Anglo-Saxon. Does genetic makeup play a part in our bias? Is there something like a cultural magnetic field that draws us in, to home to a people and land we feel peculiarly akin to? The poet Geoffrey Hill believed so, as to Wales, from which he was partly descended. I think that way madness lies. None the less, I number more Irish folk among my friends than any other variety. I think it has something to do with talk and focus. No doubt having spent my formative years in my father's house played a big part. As did the fact that the house in question stood (questioning indeed), in Wales, and that we dwelt too among the colonised, as our most intimate friends, more than with the colonisers and language assassins of those days.

When my mother's waters broke I washed ashore at Colwyn Bay, or hard by, in the mouth of Afon Colwyn, a child of the new peace and of Clement Attlee's government, a child of the Irish Sea. The evening there set directly towards Seamus Heaney's Glanmore. My own shipping forecast told another story: from Great Orme's Head to Mull of Galloway. My father's McNeillie and McGarva Galloway Irish family farmed as tenants, not landowners, at the northern end of that sea. His maternal forebears were McDougalls and Munros, from Argyll via Govan. Before her line was dispersed to work for the railways, my mother's family farmed similarly at Winmarleigh, not far from Morecambe Bay, above the Irish Sea in Lancashire. Their name was Hoyles, by chance a very old Welsh name.

The Irish Sea and its reflected light filled my life and flooded my dreams as I grew. My eye rested on it or registered it in the skies above from dawn to dusk. It blew through my sleep, rocking my cradle, and on stormy nights woke me up. I would draw the curtain aside in the dormer window of my attic bedroom and look into it. On some such nights in the crazy turmoil a ship would loom at anchor in Llandudno Bay, its lights and bulk blurred by rain, shielded from the worst of the westerly by the Great Orme. I always wished I was looking the other way, from ship to shore, at the smudged lights of the town, the blowing lights on the hill. I swam my first strokes in the Irish Sea. I fished in it obsessively. I stared at it in distracted reverie, on the rebound later in adolescence from the poems of Dylan Thomas, 'The Lovesong of J. Alfred Prufrock' and Baudelaire's poetry of voyage and departure. I breathed it in. I tasted its salt. The brine of it was in my blood. When I licked a cut made by my knife or a fishing hook or the sharp spike of a bass's dorsal fin I tasted my origin.

It was a great thrill on clear summer evenings to make out two or three specks that were the Isle of Man away to the north. I had seen Man close-up to the south, from the Machars of Wigtownshire. I had sailed to it from Llandudno Pier on a red-stacked steamer of a Liverpool shipping line. When we moved to live high above Llandudno, I could take in the Conwy Estuary and the Lavan Sands beyond from our bit of land and limestone bluff. And there were Anglesey and Puffin Island, riding at their moorings, and the Great Orme's head, almost an island, against which the below-sea-level town huddled and climbed a little as if from harm's way.

Lavan

Already your long low tide draws me down
And your *trompe l'oeil* of sailing through sand
Runs my loss against those mussel banks
At the mouth between island and mainland.

At mere memory of your name I drown
And all that sails in me looks to the lifeboat
Whether *Tillie*, *Annie*, *Isabella* or *Lilly* –
And *What-Ho!* herself and the Menai Light.

From the saintly life of the headland I
Take spare comfort, grateful for small mercy,
The life of the head and the brain-cell
Flashing intermittent signal blindly.

Blind as in faith, on the sea of language,
The eighth sea with its own ports of call,
A mirror world in the world's image.
Here I come again by Lavan to make landfall.

Tillie, *Annie*, *Isabella* and *Lilly* were the names of successive Llandudno lifeboats. What's in a name? Everything. That's why it's deemed ill-advised to rename a vessel, as in 'The Good Ship':

Never rename a vessel
but leave memory to trawl
in her wake. Tragedy
furrows the seas. Weather
holds true to its lunacy.
Boats founder. Souls grieve.

While she changes
by repair as she ages:
a heart transplant in
the engine department,
new winch-gear and sonar –
to say nothing of you.

Know her by name.
Feel the ballast there
as she soars and plunges
to the grounds that are
the grounds of her being.
Know her through time.

Call to her as she is now
and as you remember her
who caught your heart
long ago. And see her home
as you used to when
you were both young.

The Great Orme and the Conwy estuary were territories I knew intimately through my passion for fishing, for nightlining, for fishing off the rocks for mackerel, for digging bait, and in the river mouth retreating on an incoming tide, up to my waist, fishing a lure for bass that now are no more in the threadbare sea that enters the river there, bridged, tunnelled, barraged and marina'd out of all wildness, except the waters there will still suffocate and drown you if given half a chance.

I knew it too from aboard the aforementioned *What-Ho!* – a vessel of the 'Nobby Cutter' class owned by our local fishmonger Mr Arundell who sailed her out of Conwy when Conwy was Conwy still and the ghost of Owain Glyn Dŵr haunted its ramparts. For a time, in my teens, I went as a summer-holiday deckhand aboard the *What-Ho!* She was the original 'Good Ship', the dream and rough-and-ready immediacy of setting sail and making landfall, the betwixt-and-between, the sea-womb.

Mr Arundell fished for the shop. We dragged a trawl off Penmaenmawr and round north-east Anglesey mostly for plaice, flounder and thornback skate, a few dogfish inevitably, but not the quantities of plastic you'd get today. We were relatively low on catches of plastic. For us Thomas Carlyle's 'sea-green incorruptible' still washed as it doesn't anymore. We also trolled lines for mackerel, generally as we moved from one ground to another and beyond Anglesey – Ynys Môn (Môn Mam Cymru: Môn Mother of Wales), as she's known in Welsh. I found the shifting perspectives hypnotic and compelling, the turning distances, as we made our to-fro, erratic way. There's an air of completion and mystery, peace and solitude, to coasts and mountain skylines and islands seen from a distance at sea, and I revelled in it as we went out through the strait, east of the Penmon Light, with its tolling bell, the lighthouse that has written on its side: NO PASSAGE TO LANDWARD, words of warning more generally worth heeding in life.

Just as I was, Nobby Cutters were born of the Irish Sea. They are much associated with the Isle of Man. Around the turn of the nineteenth to the twentieth century they were the boat of choice for Morecambe Bay prawn fishermen. Nobby rigs and proportions, sail-plans – symmetries – varied according to required use. They were generally decked with a cockpit aft and fished with a beam trawl, as was the case with the *What-Ho!* In some configurations and rigs, decking apart, there is little to distinguish a Nobby Cutter from a Galway Hooker, especially a hooker of the *bád mór* (big boat) variety. Indeed, according to Richard J. Scott in his wonderful little study *The Galway Hookers: Working Sailboats of Galway Bay* (1983), some twenty Nobby Cutters were built in Connemara, Galway and Aran, between 1898 and 1904, as a relief initiative for the Congested Districts. I only learnt this relatively recently, and certainly knew nothing of it when I was sixteen, or nineteen when I first saw a Galway Hooker plying across Galway Bay. Now it has since all begun to rhyme together for me and to join up into this yarn from which I weave *Archipelago*'s Odyssey.

I was hooked deep and for life by the whole business, not least: coming in after nightfall on a late autumnal tide, nudging forward, under the stars, her keel crunching over mussel beds, frenetic waders piping her to harbour; and skinning the thornbacks – a tough task, on a cold night, raw on the hands, but an intoxicating wonder to a starry-eyed youth.

It was all above and below sea level. The skies were full of the sea. The seas were full of the sky. It was all osmosis and porous, limestone being our rock-bed (as it is on Inis Mór), not the granite they quarried across the way at Penmaenmawr, to the south of which rose the granites of eastern Snowdonia. It was where nevermore met evermore and intermingled. Here were archipelagic beginnings aplenty, when I was 'a windy boy and a bit'.

Theatres in the Round

An island is an open-air theatre in the round, with the sea in the wings, or the sea for audience, constantly heckling when not roaring approval. At any rate, no geographical feature is more clearly complete. The sea goes all the way round the island, an Aran islander once explained to Tim Robinson, in a classic bull. The very idea contains and delays departure, that's why an island makes such a compelling literary and dramatic figure. Consider those dramatic island tales from Homer to Shakespeare, Defoe to Golding. We might say the sea holds life up to closer inspection. Dramatis personae on small islands are fewer and more clearly defined as community, and the sea as an agent of tragedy lends drama to their survival. Their worlds are theatres in the round.

An island contains and integrates by nature, and the sea renders the whole unique. Islands considered in this way are the 'One' with a capital 'O' created out of the opposition where extremes meet. Darwin found this for natural history. Norman Ackroyd saw it for himself when he went on a commission to the Galapagos. Just so islands integrate the human. Unique concentrations are formed. But isolation isn't absolute. Viewing the Hebrides from an aeroplane, that most modernist of vehicles, in the 1930s, for the first time, Hugh MacDiarmid spoke of seeing them 'at one and the same time in their individual completeness and in all their connections with each other and with the mainland'. As John Donne didn't quite say, we can: 'No island is an island, entire and of itself,' for each is a part of the archipelago. Each is part of an arpeggio.

I came upon MacDiarmid in any significant measure a few years after I discovered Synge. He post-dated my sojourn on Aran. But by 2005 I was a devotee. And being a circumstantial reader, I was especially fascinated by his time on Whalsay in the Shetland archipelago, where he stayed in the greatest conceivable hardship from 1933 to 1942, another inexplicable meteor of working-class origin. Not for him the academic grove, the cloister or the creative writing school, no more than for Sydney Graham. Seamus Heaney was right to call it 'the most moving [period] in the whole of MacDiarmid's life'. The vast body of work MacDiarmid produced on Whalsay, in both in poetry and prose, included *Stony Limits* (1934) and *The Islands of Scotland* (1939), an unlikely volume in the Batsford Guide series. These two provided a vital touchstone for keeping me, and *Archipelago*, real and humbled, as work to take bearings from.

One thing that 'real' must manage in our context is the minority perspective. The periphery or 'the outskirts' have always to hold out against the imperial or imperious centre. 'Outskirts' was Joseph Brodsky's preferred term when considering the case of Derek Walcott on the island of St Lucia in his essay 'The Sound of the Tide'. It's an essay that should be on every *Archipelago* reader's list. As we might expect, MacDiarmid was sharply alive to the matter. He took a strong line regarding 'the Megalopolis' and the assumptions of its denizens and politicians that they hold the centre, and that by virtue of their location and number they are entitled not only to their power but to a belief that their vision of the world is superior.

'The idea that by going to islands one cuts oneself off from the resources of civilisation is one against which I cannot protest too strongly,' wrote MacDiarmid, the man who lamented vehemently, and often, the near total absence of intellectual company and resources on Shetland, who now and then protested that he was quite out of touch with what was going on down there across the sea in Glasgow and London. In spite of which he puts his case on the issue in a paragraph of free verse called 'In the Shetland Islands':

> I am no further from the 'centre of things'
> In the Shetlands here than in London, New York, or Tokio,
> No further from 'the great warm heart of humanity',
> Or the 'general good', no less 'central to human destiny',
> Sitting alone here enjoying life's greatest good,
> The pleasure of my own company,
> Than if I were one with the crowds in the streets
> In any of the great centres of population.

I call this heroic solipsism. Readers of *Archipelago* will recognise the genre, I am sure. Heroic solipsism is our modus operandi, our ground bass, our challenge to the existential order and to authority. MacDiarmid in this piece isn't just skirmishing. He makes an ever-pressing point about the meaning of democracy and by implication the voice of islanders and place of island life in the scheme of things.

It should hardly bear saying, but I'll make the point none the less: the writings of Synge and of MacDiarmid are very different in literary character. But both wrote vital prose about and made a poetry out of islands. Synge's prose is felt and expertly measured, though it did begin as journalism. His Aran Islands book is a work of art, a masterpiece of the genre, a subtle exercise in the art of self-effacement and, as W.J. McCormack says in his life of the playwright, 'a testimony to Synge's unclassifiable intellect and imagination'. The figure of drowning at the heart of his one-act tragedy *Riders to the Sea* and the terrible fact of drowning are held up to each other without redundancy or excess.

In contrast with Synge's account of the Aran Islands, MacDiarmid's contribution to the Batsford Guides is hardly a guide, and it is no work of art. It is extremely MacDiarmidian: impassioned, volcanic and didactic. You are dragged into a vortex, or several vortices, when you embark on it and are thrown this way and that way as MacDiarmid turns the world and a myriad assumptions upside-down and inside-out. He is full of statistics and analyses and undigested chunks of quotation, but also a redeeming poetry.

For all that, both MacDiarmid and Synge in their markedly different ways offer radical critiques of the economic and social realities of their chosen places of stay, visit and visitation. And in the opening paragraphs of MacDiarmid's 'Island Funeral' (first published in the Batsford Guide), a poem of extraordinarily measured diction, plain depiction and evocation, his world and Synge's appear to overlap in a literary mystery and puzzle of seeming appropriation, which no one has yet succeeded in solving. (I wonder if it doesn't derive indirectly from the 'Man of Aran' movie that MacDiarmid might have read about, or perhaps managed to see.) Anyway, Synge and MacDiarmid make a strong pairing, if an odd couple. They are both subversive writers whose geniuses were profoundly enabled by experiencing island life. They also knew their Karl Marx. They're both patron saints of *Archipelago*, though not for that reason.

Island life off the west coasts of Ireland and Scotland can't be understood without attending to the language question. This was an area in which *Archipelago* could only fail, though it nodded in the direction through a number of contributions: Gaelic verses with *en face* translation (Sorley MacLean translated by Seamus Heaney, for example), extraordinary poetic adventures between Irish and Scottish Gaelic by Rody Gorman and a couple of essays (on place names, in particular), if no more. Translation is a gesture, but in what direction can be a question of challenging dispute. I decline to get any distance into the cultural fray here, or that around the differences between the indigenous islander's view of island life – or life itself otherwise – and that of the interloper. Of course I'm aware of it – how could anyone not be? – I was a blow-in once (I might ask to have that on my headstone, but then we're all blow-ins when it comes to that, *sub specie aeternitatis*), and I am also aware of problematic territorialisms generally, what in the old days Marxists, after V.I. Lenin, used to call 'the who whom' of it. I'm far more interested in the fact that what we might ever know of a place, whether we're native to it or not, is a profound question. 'It is not down in any map; true places never are,' says Herman Melville's Ishmael in *Moby-Dick* (1851).

But to return to the matter of language. We may look for help here to Máirtín Ó Direáin, the Árainn-born Irish-language poet, and his poem 'Homage to John Millington Synge' (written in the 1950s): 'The words you gathered then,' he declares, 'Will live on in an alien tongue.' With a nod at Shakespeare's *Macbeth*, he sees Synge's contribution as a kind of holding operation, 'till Coill Chuain comes to Inis Meáin' ('till Cowan's wood' …). But, of course, he's hardly writing in a spirit of optimism. For Ó Direáin it is all too late; 'the ways of [his] people decay', he says, and 'The sea no longer serves as a wall.' Though it's true that while the sea-wall and the language-wall are both broken, and now overridden by the internet, they still serve as significant barricades to cultural invasion. Though nowadays, for certain, with the threat of rising sea-levels it does seem to be all too late and a matter of time before the sea serves not as a wall but as a lid on our coffin.

Ó Direáin applauds Synge's achievement unreservedly, but ultimately we know translation is impossible beyond approximation where poetry or the poetic are concerned. And all, or the greater part of the rest is a matter of lingua franca, economics and cultural dominance.

As Ó Direáin points up in his 'Homage' poem – Synge didn't 'listen to the tale of the stones' – for him, 'Greatness lived in the tale of the hearth.' As I've already said, Ó Direáin's poem alludes to Scotland via Shakespeare's *Macbeth* but doesn't it now also evoke MacDiarmid's 'On a Raised Beach', and MacDiarmid listening to the stones? Listening that is to the cosmic, the infinite.

Just so MacDiarmid, in his great existential soliloquy about 'Being and non-being', seems to nod at Hamlet's suicidal preoccupation in his 'To be or not to be' speech when he writes in 'On a Raised Beach' ('ataraxia' means a state of unperturbedness or of calmness):

> I am prepared with everything else to share
> Sunshine and darkness and wind and rain

And life and death bare as these rocks though it be
In whatever order nature may decree,
But not indifferent to the struggle yet
Nor to the ataraxia I might get
By fatalism, a deeper issue see
Than these, or suicide, here confronting me.

I think two things, one possible: that Ó Direáin, who was a serious writer and intellectual, might have known 'On a Raised Beach'; and, almost certain, that MacDiarmid was mindful of *Hamlet* in writing his poem. Though one should remember too the boatman's fear, when asked to ferry MacDiarmid to and leave him on East Linga overnight, that the poet might be suicidal.

Listening and hearing are at the heart of Synge's narrative. Often as we read we note him hearing Gaelic through floorboards, through a broken window or in the next room. Such moments serve to signal to us the way Synge is placed somewhere between two languages, two worlds. He is the intermediary between two cultures – the European and the beyond-the-pale peripheral reputedly ancient Irish, descended from the mythical (Irish and Greek) Fir Bolg, or 'bag men'. He is the translator between two languages, his ear to the wall. He is, in the Coleridgean, Hopkinsian, MacDiarmidian sense: where extremes meet, extremes to be reconciled, to be integrated, given distilled lyric expression in and by art. As to hearing and representation, the Irish-English of Synge's plays has been scorned by some Irish speakers – notable among them the satirist Brian O'Nolan – as a deplorable kind of stage Irish patois. But not so by Brendan Behan, another Irish speaker who made his debut as an Irish-language poet, and a playwright who admired Synge's plays, who knew and wrote about Árainn.

Again Declan Kiberd, in a detailed study of Synge's approximations, has established that Synge's language is grammatically highly informed and idiomatically accurate. Seamus Heaney was more pointed when he called it 'a new mandarin idiom', but, coming from where and when he did, we might expect him to be so. None the less we might say Synge had heard the language thoroughly. The key here for me lies in the matter of hearing and listening, in Synge's passivity and honesty in setting down what he hears (whether pretty atrocious folk ballads or distinctive poetic expressions) and what he sees, to say nothing of his artistry. As I've said, the figure of drowning so central to 'Riders to the Sea' and the terrible, devastating fact of drowning are held up to each other without redundancy or excess. They are, as Kiberd would say, expressed. They are written from observation and experience if not bereavement.

But interlopers or blow-ins – and *Archipelago* itself is a blow-in many times over – must tread with care. The Irish-speaking, Árainn-born scholar and daughter of a family that earns its living from the sea, Deirdre Ní Chonghaile fully acknowledges and applauds Synge's triumph. She takes no narrow view by any measure. But she sees, too, the cumulative effect of cultural representations of drowning as serving established, fatalist attitudes in island communities and among those who fish the seas. She would bring us to earth here, to look more roundly at what drowning and loss at sea mean in reality, psychologically, for island and fishing communities, and she would draw our attention, as she does in the last issue of *Archipelago*, to a pressing need for positive action to improve safety at sea for the fishing industry and emergency provision for island communities. However figurative his world, the Skipper has been a sea-goer in his time and has personal reason for agreeing with her.

Song

i.m. Myles Joyce and Iain Munro

On a long night in the pub
when the sea ran fast in the Sound,
I sat with Myles who was drunk
but sang as well as he could
and held his arms out to sing
while one either side took a hand
to pump it out of him.

Over he sang and again
and up and down we pumped
as if to keep us afloat in the drink
that seized us in its swell
as the song rose and fell.
And what he sang was grief
and of his own survival.

'Three days and nights,' he sang,
'three days and nights adrift
with a dead man before
we were washed up ashore
on the coast of County Clare.'
All of fifty years ago
when I was young, you know?

Little did I think then
I'd have such a song of my own one day
and feel his grief again
year in year out come May
and learn the hard way that
what never can be mended
will ever have its say.

For now, the islands of the tattered archipelago with its ragged edges, like the edge of an indecipherable flag that has frayed on the wind, still remain to themselves, in their own language, just, and in the languages of weather and season, as hard of access as the sea and its storms still can – and do often – render their shores. The wall of the sea might be broken but strait is the gate, narrow is the eye of the language needle. And then, still, we must accept, you can't stop time, you can't live in the past, but you can try to live in creative sympathy with it, with history and tradition, and with the present. *Archipelago* attempted this. Synge achieved it. His two works of prose and drama are his homage to Aran, if not reparation.

As I have already suggested, for any sense of what reparation might be we need to go to Tim Robinson. But before him in the scheme of things was the example of Robert Flaherty's movie *Man of Aran* (1934), with which I say a terrible beauty was born. Flaherty on Aran was hardly listening and what he heard was distorted sound, both musically and elementally.

In Flaherty, a vision of Aran island life is imposed from outside, not expressed from observation and listening. Of course the film is a fiction, but it is fiction posing as documentary. 'Fuck the Man of Aran,' an acquaintance with whom I used to fish for mackerel off the perilous easterly point of An Sunda Caoch (Blind Sound) exclaimed to me, regarding his wife's annoyance that he wouldn't go with her that night to a showing of Flaherty's film in the village hall at Kilronan. And one understands what he meant. Flaherty's film has been much applauded as a pioneering docu-drama, as was his earlier *Nanook of the North*, but in both cases fictional elements vitiate the documentary art. Film buffs applaud its technical innovation. But *Man of Aran* is profoundly unrealistic, and exploitative. MacDiarmid found 'fake glamour' in representations of the Hebrides. Flaherty doesn't quite give that. Rather he gives us fake hardship, undoubted heroism but in fake or mythic circumstances. Flaherty's cast of islanders risked their lives to perform tasks at sea neither they nor their forebears would ever have attempted, in dangerous waters, off the far west of Inis Mór, at a most turbulent and treacherous strait, around the mini-archipelago of the Bhranóg and Iarthach islands. (I have crossed it in a curragh myself, on a low night tide and a Guinness wake.) That no one drowned in making the film is a miracle. Other scenes in the film too were hardly true to life. Synge would I think have been amazed if not appalled.

The film did not itself sound the death knell to traditional ways of life on the big island and certainly not to social hardship. But it surely played some part in turning a tide in the lives and minds of at least some of the islanders. The islands had been a magnet to scholars of the Irish language and the antiquities, for decades if not centuries. This had made them aware of their difference. Now they had been thoroughly romanticised across the world. Those involved went to premiers and publicity events. Some of them subsequently became 'stars' of local celebrity, caught up in performance whenever you met them, as I did in my time – Tiger King, on the road, or Maggie Dirrane passing – a draw too for the growing tourist trade. They were stage islanders – 'slebs' as they'd be today, if not on 'Love Island'. The community did not necessarily like it or sell their souls to it. Always insular and inward, they now learnt to distrust the outside world more than ever. Indeed, there is something about them resembling what MacDiarmid found on Shetland, 'a secret radicalism' … 'a hidden preservation of their real lives and an outward accessibility to current conventions' (*Islands of Scotland* [1939], p. 89). That they could mostly conduct their private lives in Irish made the difference. The sea was one wall, broken though it might be, and the Irish language a powerful line of defence still, Máirtín Ó Direáin's vision notwithstanding.

An interesting epilogue to the *Man of Aran* story may be found in the case of two later interlopers, the American photographer George Pickow and his famous folk-singer wife Jean Ritchie. They visited Inis Mór in the early spring of 1952, staying at Cillmhuirbhigh to the west, just beyond the mid-point of the island, where Flaherty had his headquarters in what have since become known as the 'Man of Aran Cottages'. Pickow took a series of photographs, on the road and in domestic settings. There is a collection of his work in the Hardiman Library at Galway University. Cillmhuirbhigh is where I made my stay for little short of a year, in 1968–69, renting a leaky old cabin from the Hernon family of that village.

Among the villagers caught by Pickow's lens are several people I knew, and came to know well. Among them Annie Hernon, photographed variously at a spinning wheel, weaving a *crios* or belt, and before a great hearth. There's a photo too of a ceilidh in the same room. Another image shows Tom Hernon, who became my bosom crony, at the sticks of a curragh. But where was the hearth? I didn't recognise it when first introduced to the Pickow collection, and it took me a while to find anyone who could tell where it was. It was not in any Cillmhuirbhigh home, I was certain. And I was right, for it was in Robert Flaherty's purpose-built studio, now restored and a B&B business, but derelict in my time and infested with rats. The islanders were performing for the benefit of Pickow. Pickow might have photographed them as they actually lived and worked, for they lived a truly De Valeran hard life, fishing and farming the stony acres of the island. But he preferred them staged, and the people were willing to go along. A close look at the image of Tom Hernon in a curragh shows it to be a prop. It isn't on the sea. He is rowing in air. Not even in 1952 did the Hernon family live quite as they are portrayed by Pickow. They are being exploited, and at the same time they are exploiting an opportunity bequeathed them directly by the *Man of Aran* movie. As MacDiarmid says in *Islands of Scotland*: 'A sense of actuality will serve us better than any artificial allure,' but artificial allure is what we have in this case.

Tim Robinson

It took a Yorkshireman, Tim Robinson (his mother was Scottish), and his Irish partner Máiréad to turn all this about; to speak back to Synge and beyond; to redeem the time lost to colonialism, commerce and banality; to explore the meaning of place in all conceivable dimensions, at the heart and soul of which stands the Irish language. All of this I think holds its ground against the view that wants to class Robinson as a 'tea planter' by other means.

Robinson read mathematics at Cambridge. He had a hard-wired intellect. After adventures as an abstract artist, he and Máiréad visited Aráinn, were bewitched by the place and in 1972 returned to live there, settling finally at Fearann an Choirce, about midway between east and west of Inis Mór. They stayed for some twelve years, a period comparable in duration with MacDiarmid's on Whalsay, and studied and learnt Irish to a high standard. Robinson was a philosopher and theorist, and a literary writer of skilful artistry and great erudition worn lightly. To my mind he has no peer in the literature of place, except Henry David Thoreau. As in Thoreau's case, a political point is never far from the surface of his work. And what he achieved, for Árainn, and subsequently for Connemara and for the Burren in Co. Clare – indeed, for Ireland and the world – is breathtaking. I will restrict myself here to his Árainn writings, more or less, writings and maps, for perhaps the most important and exceptional thing about Robinson to note is that he was also a mapmaker, founder of a little operation that came to be known as Folding Landscapes, based in Roundstone, in Connemara. His prose accounts of Árainn are underwritten by his work as a cartographer. That work speaks inevitably to the British Ordnance Survey, to place names, to language and history, to the work of the great Irish dramatist Brian Friel and such plays as most notably *Translations* but also *Faithhealer*, with its litanies of place names that so affected Norman Ackroyd when he saw that play at the Royal Court. Friel, by the way, was a great admirer of Robinson, knew him personally and visited him in Roundstone.

Robinson reversed the colonial legacy. His maps recover and discover the Gaelic placenames of the islands in their true spellings, names for places and features of the landscape where an outsider might be forgiven for imagining there to be no need for names. 'What's the future of a place if no one remembers its name?' he asked somewhere. Infinite, is perhaps the answer, and truer than fiction. Those of you who come from the Scottish islands will be familiar with the place-name phenomenon. I once published in *Archipelago* a fascinating piece by a Lewis man, Angus Macmillan. It explored the Gaelic origins of place names in Galloway, origins blurred or buried beyond knowledge or hearing by phonetic approximation and custom. By talking with the islanders and trusting evidence only when he heard the same thing independently from two out of any three persons he questioned, Robinson recreated the islands for the islanders themselves, working in extraordinary detail, with infinitesimal scrutiny. Taken together with his prose accounts in *Stones of Aran: Pilgrimage* and *Stones of Aran: Labyrinth* (which is to say, outer and inner, in all cultural dimensions), his work, his 'poetical view', as George Mackay Brown rightly called it, 'takes in almost everything about the place, its geology, its birds and flowers and seaweed, history and folklore and place-names and the contemporary scene'. That last element, 'the contemporary scene', is crucial, and it is of course where friction might arise between outsider author and native islander – and indeed to some degree friction arose, as it was bound to. But walking Inis Mór with Tim Robinson, as I once did, I quickly found how warmly, how completely, he was venerated there by all and sundry, especially those who knew him, whether as children or adults, in his time. Robinson taught Ireland's Aran Islanders their place, so to speak, and put them in it, but of course benignly, as a scholar who relied on their various and uneven individual knowledges to assemble an encyclopaedic map and cultural history of their world. He looked in Rome to find Rome and found the closest likeness to it possible, rather more thoroughly than John Ruskin, who looked in Venice for Venice, stone by stone. He built a new seawall against the attritions and complacencies of progress.

And I would add, as to Robinson, a most modest man, that once at an event in Galway I heard him tell a member of the audience, who'd asked him a question of a quite uncontroversial kind about his work as a whole, that he (Robinson) saw it as 'reparation'. (On hearing which his questioner was so moved he welled up with tears.) Folk east of the Shannon perhaps do not know or appreciate how continuous communal awareness of loss can be and how the past, and certainly not the recent past, is not another country there. I doubt the denizens of the English Megalopolis have any idea or care in this regard. Didn't Boris Johnson once ask why Leo Varadkar wasn't called Murphy 'like the rest of them'? At a similar event, and in a very different context, one of pastoral irony, I once heard an Irish Garda – a policeman formerly stationed on Inis Mór – remark how Robinson's maps had revolutionised the administration of taxation on the island in the matter of land ownership, and also the ownership of cattle. As to the spirit of 'reparation', and restoration, we could do with more of that in the wilder corners of the unnameable archipelago. In the Skipper's view, at least, reparation should evict 'heritage' and 'legacy' from the cultural lexicon and consign them to Myles na Gopaleen's catechism of cliché.

Ian Niall

If Synge gave me Ireland via Aran, MacDiarmid returned me to the land of my fathers. In this return I have been inspired by Alan Riach, a vital contributor to the magazine, and by the painter, also a contributor, Alexander Moffat, who knew MacDiarmid and all those great makers of poetry he has depicted in his magnificent *Poets' Pub* (1980) collective portrait. These include Sorley MacLean, Norman MacCaig, Iain Crichton Smith and George Mackay Brown. Though not poor George Campbell Hay, author of the most inspirational of sea-going fishing poems 'Seeker, Reaper' and much else of archipelagic focus.

And then there was my father himself.

In the beginning was my father, and the word was with him. By the time I was conceived he had published three novels with an international London-based publisher, the first a shock *succès de scandale*, in the naturalistic manner of Zola and Upton Sinclair. It drew attention to a controversy over the living conditions and morality of the labouring poor, the cotfolk of the Machars of Wigtownshire (part of what has long been called 'Little Ireland'). Serialised in a Sunday paper, it scandalised many in Scotland in 1939, and joined a controversy that reached as far as the House of Commons. The story's hero exits whistling 'The Wearing of the Green', a provocation to Unionist Scotland, maybe, but a genuine reflection too of the racial complexion of 'Little Ireland'. Its author began it when he was nineteen and he was twenty-two when it came out. By the time I was born on 12 August 1946, John McNeillie had finished a fourth novel, and this would prove another start to my archipelagic story. It came out under a pen name.

My father became Ian Niall, the future nature and rural writer; and he would be distinctly 'old' nature, in that his nature was red in tooth and claw, though he came to align himself differently in later life. Nor was he ever cloistered or sheltered by a university. Though he left school at seventeen to be a news reporter, he ended up in wartime North Wales, drawing his pay from a precision-tool engineering firm – a small business owned by a family called Ratcliffe, one ever on the brink of going under – as well as from his pen. Neither amounted to much but just about equalled each other. So we were relatively better off than most of our neighbours, certainly better than Stanley Valentine who lived next door and worked in a butcher's shop, the black sheep brother of the great Welsh nationalist Lewis Valentine, whom we knew. My father also knew Valentine's collaborator and fellow, sometime inmate of Wormwood Scrubs, the playwright Saunders Lewis. He was no nationalist himself, of any colour, though he would vote Plaid Cymru as an expression of his love for Wales and the Welsh people.

As I say, I was born just before Ian Niall came into the world, but not to the same reception. *No Resting Place* was published in 1948 and it was a hit, promptly reprinted. A tale of Traveller folk – the Kyles – told non-judgmentally from their lawless and brutally violent point of view, it was turned into a film, an art film, directed by Paul Rotha and produced by Colin Lesslie, at the Arklow Studios and on location in Wicklow, starring Abbey and Gate Theatre players, with Michael Gough miscast in the leading role, a major flaw in the integrity of the project. Wolfgang Suschitsky was the cameraman (later director of photography in Joseph Strick's version of Joyce's *Ulysses*). It has some fine lingering moments and cameo performances. It won praise at the Venice Film Festival, and from Winston Churchill no less. The wartime leadership apart, my father was no fan of Churchill. In the 1930s he wanted to have him hanged from a lamppost. A copy of the movie was required at Balmoral, of all unlikely places. Unusual to note, the adaptation from the novel bears close resemblance to its source, much of its dialogue coming verbatim from the book, with some interpolations in Irish. But Michael Gough is the fly in the Irish ointment.*

In the wake of the film, when I was four going on five, we all went on holiday to Greystones in Wicklow on the proceeds. There we met all kinds of people my father had got to know during the making of the film, including at least one man who had 'walked Frongoch' with Michael Collins. And we were reunited with some old friends who'd

* For a full account see 'No Resting Place: The Movie' in *Ian Niall: Part of His Life* (Clutag Press, 2007) by Andrew McNeillie.

returned to live in Ireland from North Wales. I remember the experience vividly and have written about it elsewhere.

His original editor at Putnam, having heard that a book about the Traveller people was in the writing, sent him a set of the works of J.M. Synge in little golden-spined volumes, all, I think, bar one under the imprint of Maunsel, Dublin. He thought my father might benefit from Synge's play *The Tinker's Wedding* and presumably essays in which 'tinkers' occur in the collection *In Wicklow and West Kerry.* John McNeillie quickly came to revere Synge, but his Kyles were based on people he had watched and known and studied for himself in childhood and youth in the Machars of Wigtownshire. He had their speech and their defiant attitude in his head. He was too, for sure, socially closer to them in his origin and language than was Synge to his peasants and Travellers. He knew their ways. He would make a big hit soon enough, with another defining book for him: *The Poacher's Handbook: For the Man with the Hare-pocket and the Boy with the Snare* (1950). The skills of the poacher had featured vividly in both *Wigtown Ploughman* and *No Resting Place.* Now they were described in an enchanting, lean, lyrical prose (this was no common 'handbook') as practised by real-life characters (Francie McGinn, Butcher Murphy) and by the author himself.

As I say, in the beginning was my father and not just the word but the way was with him. He would decline an invitation from some special military people in Hereford to go to teach them survival techniques. It was hardly his world, though he had belonged during the war to one of those secret GHQ Auxiliary Units, trained in irregular warfare to blow things up and generally frustrate the course of a Nazi invasion. Instead, and after a fashion, schooling me from about the tender age of eight, gradually year by year, he taught me to be a hunter and scavenger, a provider for the pot. I was the boy with the snare in his pocket (the pocket of his imagination too), a purse-net, a nightline and all the other tricks and tools of the trade at his disposal. It was a different world then. Above all I had developed in me a heightened instinct for it, an eye for the lie of the land, for a piece of water, for a stretch of shore, for the habits of fish, flesh and fowl, and an appetite and patience and a spirit to endure in their pursuit. I was a consummate moocher, at a cost to my schooling. That was all my love and hankering, all my alienation, away from the road conventionally taken, to the sea-road. It served me well on Aran. As a boy I adored my father and aspired to be like him. You can have too much of a good thing but none of any of this, and certainly not *Archipelago*, would have been, without him and his take on the world.

Then, as by now clearly you know, there was John Millington Synge, and the word was with him. For among those golden little volumes my father received in 1946 was *The Aran Islands*. So reading Synge in my teens would change my life, giving it that vital archipelagic turn that took me at the age of twenty-two to live on Inis Mór, in November 1968, for a little short of a year. I have told that story, but how it came to be told is a much longer story, all germane to the life of *Archipelago*, for there would have been no *Archipelago* without it either.

Richard Murphy

Not least also there was Richard Murphy and his first collection of poems *Sailing to an Island*. I encountered it in Green's bookshop, on Nassau Street, Dublin, in 1965. I was nineteen and on my way home via Holyhead to Llandudno. It was one of those defining moments. Thanks to J.M. Synge, I had the day before sailed from an island in the shape of Aran after my first, life-changing exploration of what the islanders nowadays call 'the Rock'. They were different times, PDE (Pre-Digital Era) for one thing, and it was an utterly different world, as was Murphy's Cleggan of the fifties and sixties. Galway was a wild west town. There was great poverty and hardship to be seen in its streets and in the wider country and in parts of Inis Mór, little short of nineteenth-century poverty.

Not being Irish and not being wired into the contemporary literary scene in Ireland, I had not heard of Richard Murphy before. His book's remarkably affecting sea-green book jacket of yet simple design, on its inside flap, told me next to nothing about him.

With Richard Murphy's *Sailing to an Island*, it declared, 'we add a new poet to our list. There will be, we are confident, a warm welcome for this sensuous yet strictly disciplined verse inspired mainly by the land, the boats and the people of the west of Ireland'.

That's all it said. Nor did it really matter. The poems – especially the trio of the title poem, 'The Last Galway Hooker' and 'The Cleggan Disaster' – told me all I needed to know. I was spellbound by them as I stood reading them in the shop. They still spellbind me, of course, more than fifty years later. I board them with a lifetime's baggage of associations.

Poetry is not sociology or mere document of historical interest. Nor are its effects dependant on knowledge of a poet's biography, though I agree with Louis MacNeice that literary criticism should always be partly biographical. In Murphy's poems I found an art rooted in the hard and dangerous work of fishing, and of sea-tragedy, a world moored among fishing boats and fishermen, chandlers, boatwrights and repairers, boatmen. A world of which I'd had a taste and knew at first-hand, a little but enough, in Conwy, if not Cleggan, and across the river at Deganwi, where our boatyard was, boats there dumbly speaking to me always of 'symmetry' and 'art within immensity', to borrow into English the words of Charles Baudelaire. I have a poem in memory of the men there. Among the nameless others it refers to, I would mention 'Wee Boy' here. There is all the difference in names and naming. They speak to the true poetry of place.

Block: A Pulley Used in Running Rigging

I cannot put it down
Or knock it into shape
That world and time
Inside my head
Once no less real than
Today and as ordinary
As daylight delayed in a rhyme.

I'm beached by the flood
Caulking my dreams
Haunted by such men
As Johnnie Rogof, Jackie Craven
And other names
No one remembers
Hauling nets in all weathers.

I think of them and the pulley
To their hopes
That drew them to sea
And the stars' rigging
Taut as ever aloft
About their obscure lives
In that Welsh estuary.

Sufficient unto the day their lesson
Their names signed nowhere
As if written in water
And no thought spared
But to immerse in that world
An example to all and no one
Hauling fish into oblivion.

The point about Richard Murphy's sea-poems is surely that they hold us in their rhythms, imagery and story-lines while simultaneously calling us not only to history and place but to material circumstance, to Cleggan, to Bofin, to Galway, to the folk, and all the rest of circumstantiality – to the Irish Sea and Conwy if you will. They take us out of the bookshop, out of our daily lives, away from the land and into their actual world, a world too of common folk, ordinary folk like ourselves. (If you don't think yourself ordinary, kindly leave the page.) None the less, it's in their ship-shapeness, their crystal-clear and resonant prosody, that they defeat time and will survive. As Joseph Brodsky put it, 'prosody always survives history. In fact, it hardly needs history; all it needs is a poet', and Murphy was just that.* And he was a poet of islands. Like Synge and MacDiarmid before him, he was an agent of 'the archipelagic turn' and was in fact the unacknowledged legislator in my adventure and the book it became, a book that very nearly didn't happen. I mean the book *An Aran Keening*. Let me give it a heading of its own.

Lazarus

As I keep saying, it's hard to say when and where anything begins, but a wake begins with a turn of the screw, wind in a sail or a pull on an oar. Or it begins with a corpse.

If my wake and waking began in the Irish Sea in North Wales, then it resumed on almost the exact same line of latitude, at the edge of Galway Bay, in my time on Aran.

Fifty years on that time still haunts me in the small hours. When for whatever reason I can't fall asleep at night and I lie in the dark staring at the ceiling, I comfort myself by recalling those days, every minute fraction of them. Over and over, round and round, to and fro. I see things, folk and occasions, wild adventures, stirring catches of fish, clearer in my mind's eye than yesterday. It is as if the ceiling were a movie screen and my head a reel of film with my eye for a projector's shutter. And I have the cinema to myself. The projectionist and the manager have gone home. The usherette went on ahead, leading the way with her torch pointing its cone of light behind her. While my wife sleeps beside me – the one I'd left behind, the one to be – in one of those old-style double kissing seats. Think of it all in monochrome but nothing black and white.

*

---

* Joseph Brodsky, 'The Keening Muse', on Akhmatova, in *Less Than One: Selected Essays* (1986). Brodsky says: 'and Akhmatova was just that'.

Had I not been running out of money, I'm sure I would have stayed on for as long as it took to be running out. Sad to say it's a tide that never comes back on its own, a one-way ticket. I'd survived on the island on what I had saved from my pay since I was twenty. Up to that point I could barely live on what I earned. What I saved was of course a finite amount and had no guarantor but myself. So I had no choice that autumn but to wave goodbye. To stand astern and see the islands out of sight beyond a subsiding wake. To lose myself in the throng aboard what was a Galway Fair Day sailing, our hold full of sacrificial cattle, a fitting way to end an Odyssey. I had little money left and less than I thought. I sailed from Kilronan, Inishmore (note the spellings), the length of Galway Bay aboard the *Naomh Éanna*. It was heartbreak house on water, comforted by Nurse Guinness.

Nothing in my life so far has managed to displace or surpass my time on Aran. 'One thought fills immensity,' as William Blake said. It wakes me and I wake it. In the end I count fish as others count sheep to fall asleep at last. I could count stones in drystone walls. I could count waves on the sea. I could count grains of sand in the dune. But there was no shortage of memorable fish in those days to see me into oblivion now. Morpheus, eat your heart out.

I can find my need for what Aran has become for me in childhood longing and melancholy and in my father's voice and character. But it's the allure of the place itself, its layers of history, its timing, its measure, its seasons in and out, its weathers and tidal flows; its birdlife and botany, and its shorelife, its microclimates, its pace and its past and its folk; its walls and stones; calms and storms that draw me there – its sheer, asymmetrical beauty, its shadow of its former self, its bleak wilderness severities. I go to rather than from. I have never gone anywhere 'to find myself' or to lose myself. I'm not interested in myself. I'm interested in the phenomenon of being. I discover things I didn't know about the island each time I visit. I also discover ever more angles on my time there and on the mysterious nature of memory.

I had passed, or not exactly passed, a Christmas on the island (I spent it in Galway Hospital). I celebrated my twenty-third birthday there, at Kilmurvey, on 12 August 1969. I was a belated youth in protracted negotiation with adulthood. He had no time for the world's busyness and business. Nor had he any interest in Paris or Woodstock. In those days for him the world was everything that was not the case. It had to be other or it wasn't worth the candle, indoors or out of doors, or as he'd come to learn to say, he must go his way, boots or no boots. He had a point.

I've not changed my view that much since. 'The fox condemns the trap, not himself,' said William Blake.

Who does not tend the machine now and toil at the screenface to one degree or another in the course of earning a living? Who isn't lost to process, hurrying to nowhere, tending the machine, keeping it running to what end, from day to day, year on year? To pound the treadmill in the gym, to keep fit, but fit for what? Launching an upgrade with yet another product 'going live' in a merely mechanical, however ingenious, version of life. Who doesn't stoke the boiler? Who doesn't oil the wheel? Who doesn't know the mills are still dark and satanic? Who doesn't serve the god of illusory progress and still the poor are always with us? 'What can be more absurd than Progress,' exclaimed Charles Baudelaire. 'Is not work the salt that preserves mummified souls?' For work more aptly these days read employment. As the Australian poet Les Murray, no stranger to our pages, said: 'In the midst of life, we are in employment.' 'Work is another kettle of fish,' as the Skipper in his wisdom knows.

But as to progress, who doesn't Google to see where they're going ahead of going, and so compromise the immediate experience of elsewhere?

Throw away your digital gadgets, your phone, your Google Maps. Let them sink to the bottom of the ocean. Go dark. Go off comms. Revive *non serviam* for first principle. Don't line the pockets of Zuckerberg. Revive the steam-age letter. Use pen and ink. Refuse to serve or finance the machine. Revive silence, exile and cunning. Don't read the newspapers. That was Kierkegaard's advice all that time ago, and it wasn't his worst idea, as John Berryman said. Remember what

Charles Baudelaire had to say: 'In the numerous lists of the *rights of man* that the wisdom of the nineteenth century returns to so often and with so much satisfaction, two rather important ones have been forgotten, namely the right to contradict oneself and the right to *go away*.' I copied that down from somewhere and much prefer it to Philip Larkin's '*chucked up everything / And just left*', a move Larkin's poem found itself unable to endorse.

*

I scraped home to North Wales and into frosty disapproval. So I soon took the road again and from necessity entered wage-slavery. For a while, I worked in the packing department of a computer-parts warehouse in England. And so I served the machine at a very humble level. Then Harry Houdini came to the rescue and got me in, as a 'mature' student, to read English at Magdalen College, Oxford. I have to say it took some courage to go. I had not been drilled for it. My contemporaries were six years my junior. I felt like a schoolboy in the sixth form whose mother had sent him to school in short trousers. Magdalen had been Richard Murphy's college, but he was a serious contender, a Demy at the age of seventeen, that is, on the college foundation, like a Fellow. Yet he threw it up and ran away to the West of Ireland to write poems. Who could not applaud that? His father threatened to have him certified insane. So back Murphy went to Oxford, to be stripped of his Demyship, rather as a cashiered soldier is stripped of epaulettes, badges, medals.

Bernard O'Donoghue

Among my teachers at Magdalen, arriving in my second year, was the poet Bernard O'Donoghue. He wasn't known then for writing poems, or, it seemed, remotely aspiring to. But he was ever a dark horse. You didn't know him. He eluded you. He was about six months my senior and had begun to climb the academic ladder, a very slippery slope, especially for an Irishman in Oxford. He had very neat, polished shoes, I remember, and sharp creases in his trousers. His shirt was close-fitting and had some fancy decorative stitching down the front. I thought him disconcertingly dapper and said so to him later. But he wasn't really so. It was the job, and he had to try it on for size. In those days he liked to play bar billiards, drink in the pub, watch 'Match of the Day', sing Irish songs and music-hall songs such as 'The Bold Gendarmes' (after Joseph Locke) or play Irish tunes on a tin whistle. He had an impressive repertoire. He was a bachelor and often lovelorn for a girl called Amanda.

It is fair to say of that time that Philip Larkin was his god and Larkin's philosophy his religion. Seamus Heaney hadn't really got going for him by then. Together with a flatmate, Dave Williams, he lived out of a black frying pan in a top-floor flat in Oxford's Parktown crescent, long before that phenomenon became millionaires' row. Dave Williams had been at Hull as an undergraduate. He was as bald as Larkin, to whom he was also devoted. A tall man, a policeman's son, he was a benign presence studying unhappily, T.S. Eliot and Mallarmé, under the supervision of a mismatch of a don, one of Oxford's eternal man-boys to whom he couldn't relate, a common enough experience in that place in those days.

Bernard could be scathingly humorous and looked on the world with a sharp eye and a sharp mind, offset by jokes, many of them with a slow fuse, and so a bigger splash. Myles na Gopaleen was a favourite with him, as he was with me, and Bouvard et Pecuchet not unknown to him. He was an endless fount of little stories from West Cork, out of the parish of Millstreet. He was learned. Learned Bernard, I called him and call him still. He had plumbed the depths and scaled the heights of Dante in the original, from hell to paradise. He knew his business. But he wore it lightly and self-deprecatingly, even as if it wasn't to his great credit. Even as if it didn't set him apart from us, his abysmally ignorant students. For a while, and because he had freakish mathematical aptitude, he had dallied with the machine and gone into the computer business, such as it was at that time. Which was light years from what it has since become in the digital era. But he soon came to his senses and returned to the scholar's cloister. An architectural feature most suited to medieval studies. One of his party tricks involved having someone read a sentence at random, ideally a long sentence, perhaps from Henry James. Then, to everyone's astonishment, at the very moment the sentence came to an end, he would say how many letters it contained. His gift for this was like a poem in that it had no practical application but was startling to observe.

For my part I could count without using my fingers, though I hardly read without saying the words to myself. (Wake up there, in the back.) I could count beyond twenty (unlike some people I'd heard about) but that was the extent of my talent for number, if not entirely for numbers, though almost, in the poetic sense. I could string sentences together – on paper, at any rate – and in drink. I was too shy to say boo to a goose normally wherever more than two were gathered together. This inhibition would be the bane of my life for years yet to come. Silence is best, age tells me, trying to be wise, yet I don't heed it. I'm as phatic now as the next man, as you see. I'd been a news reporter on local papers in the mining valleys of West Glamorgan, and in Liverpool; and I'd worked last in the Radio Newsroom at the BBC in London, keeping the company of the likes of John Simpson, playing midwife to John Humphreys, on which relatively well-paid London-weighted labour I'd built my Aran fund. I wish I could have floated it on the stock market and made a killing, but I knew nothing about finance, just speculation.

Meeting Bernard at this time, with his extraordinary gifts as a teacher, was crucial for me. He was negative capability personified. He gave you confidence. No one was more Irish. He'd had no choice but to leave Ireland at sixteen. After his father's death, his mother took the family to Manchester. His father had dropped dead beside him at a Gaelic Football game. His last word as he fell, a cry of 'Bernard ...'

This was the unsounded depth in the poet to come, the poet whose accumulated work is a soft-spoken epic of Irishness in our times. He took great interest in my time on Aran and, in a sense deeper than I knew, understood far more about it and around it than I might ever know to this day. He was an Irishman and scholar of the medieval world, and Aran was naturally a part of his cultural territory. If he was not an Irish speaker, he certainly knew a good deal of the language in a scholarly way. He took what for me seemed an entirely disproportionate interest in a little Aran poem I'd written, on the model of an Anglo-Saxon riddle (examples of which I'd encountered before I went to Aran in Richard Hamer's *A Choice of Anglo-Saxon Verse*):

> Spring slips him in through a gap
> In a stone wall, a secret agent
>
> Bargaining with the underworld
> Against sleep, a bomb
>
> With a slow time-fuse, an old man
> Winding all our clocks on, and back.

The answer to which is a corncrake (*Crex crex*). And this was typical of him to find more in such a thing than anyone else might, and to know why. He was my best reader.* I suppose in our distinctly different ways, we both had a 'slow time-fuse' in common. But he was in another league by a long chalk, and on his way to becoming an Oxford don, an expert in medieval literature and much more besides.†

*

After my farewell wake in 1969, I next went to the island thirty years later, to write a postscript to my time. Let's not forget, we arrive with a wake, just as we leave with one. Waking is such sweet sorrow but it is not all goodbye … There is pleasure in good riddance just as

* To see his take on the poem (and for very much else) consult his *Very Short Introduction to Poetry* (2019), from OUP.

† John Fuller who'd been instrumental, with Emrys Jones, in getting me into Magdalen, would print a postcard version of 'Corncrake' on his Arab Printing Press with a line-drawing of the bird by Julian Bell.

there's sorrow in farewell. But waking is arrival too, and awakening, continual arrival as Sydney Graham would say. What poignant beauty there is, though, in staring into the aerated waters and seeing their roiling turmoil thunder and spread like lightning, to die away. To renew over and over with every turn of the screw, every billowing of the sail.

I sailed as I had the first time from Ros an Mhíl in Connemara to Cill Rónáin and Árainn. There is a world of difference in those spellings. Just so there was a world of difference in the absence on the island of the corncrake by then and evermore since.

But I didn't go aboard a trawler into the eye of a storm, as I had in November 1968, when the waves were so big they drowned a wake at birth, cut it short the moment it began.* Or even sooner, as the propeller turned mid-air on a high peak. Just so those waves would snatch the breath out of you, if you were swept overboard. Nor could I sail from Galway harbour either, aboard my sainted darling the *Naomh Éanna*, a vessel I wake here again in my heart's parlour, a vessel of harrowing outline and beauty in the nostalgia stakes, if unstable and a handful in hard weather. If I may remind you: 'The symmetry of boats speaks of art within immensity.' Baudelaire would have known what I mean when I speak of the *Naomh Éanna* plying through the immensity of Galway Bay in all weathers, on a dawn sailing, best of all. She has featured in several poems I've written, most recently, one imagining:

The Naomh Éanna*'s Last Voyage*

for Michael Muldoon

Who saw her leave, who watched her
turn south that time and wondered

* The trawler was the *Ros Ronain*, a relatively small vessel. I didn't know her name at the time but learnt it very recently, in October 2019, from the fisherman and remarkable folk historian of Inis Mór, Micheál Joyce.

had she lost her mind, her bearings …
her skipper shipwrecked
when something in him hit a rock?
And left him crying: 'It's all too much.
A sailings, B sailings … standing off
for the folk to row their emigrants out,
towing their cattle and horses,
as if we were on the South Seas
only paying our way with letters and groceries,
Guinness canisters, bottled gas – un-
stable, labouring in hard weather,
many a miracle she never capsized …'

Who saw her go? running for her life,
using those white ships from Japan
for cover, the tuna longliners, bound
for the ends of the Earth beyond.
And who didn't? by every tide, and every
sailing since, coming home or leaving,
on her turbo-charged replacements.

Instead I'd go aboard one of those replacements, the turbo-charged *Draoicht na Farraige* ('Magic of the Sea'), that left behind her the wildest wake you ever saw, strong enough to go twice round the world as fast as Puck the fairy. Fairy, ferry and *farraige* – the sea, the sea. Magic of words, words, words. All we have and to hold, to tell our tale, till depth do us part.

We might like to think it's not what's changed but what hasn't that is the bedrock of place and self. But there is no fixity across generations and no single self but selves. There's no one *genius loci* but many, for all is in the eye of time and the beholder who misremembers, misinterprets, and so invents, in spite of all best efforts not to. Provisional is the nature of reality. It's in the missing our hits are made by what we must omit and what we can manage to put into words or execute.

Slippage is the order of the day. So it is with place. Ask Heraclitus. As everybody should know by now, but few in office will say, today's decision is tomorrow's error.*

All of which is to say, I went back to a changed world, as how could I not? Most importantly it was a world transformed by the cartography and writings of Tim Robinson. He and Máiréad had settled on Árainn in 1972. Around three years after I left.

It was a world transformed materially too by the approaching Celtic Tiger. Soon it would ruin again, as it rode the tide of boom and bust that will always return, and turn again like Dick Whittington, to where the streets are paved with hubris and the money always runs out, never to come back on its own. Whatever money is. Hubris the most ridiculous vanity of vanities and one that infects so many.

*

I remember when Robinson's *Stones of Aran: Pilgrimage* was published by the Lilliput Press, in association with Wolfhound Press. What names! They still raise my heart with hope and fear. I remember seeing in a newspaper a photograph of Robinson's publisher, Antony Farrell. It was Lilliput's second publication. And it was my Nemesis at last. My territory had been usurped, and in a manner far beyond my capacity, by a work universally acclaimed. It was surely, and sure enough, a work from the hand of a genius. I would not read it. I could not bear to look at it. The day of its birth was a cold, dark day for me. Not, I think, that I felt quite as territorial as Robinson did about Leo Daly's Inis Mór novel *The Rock Garden* (1984), the existence of which he never acknowledged in his writings, although Daly

* Recently, and by a tale that's too long to tell here, but one concerning poetry, and Brexit, I was invited to coffee with Governor Carney, in his office at the Bank of England. He sat me down at a very old, square table – one dating from at least the eighteenth century – and as we sat he said, 'This is where all the mistakes are made.' But then he's Canadian-Irish, descended from Co. Mayo (an old map of which hung on the wall nearby), and not your usual dry-stick governor material.

had done Robinson great kindness in alerting Antony Farrell to the existence of the manuscript that became *Stones of Aran*.*

Now my wake lengthened and my waking intensified. I didn't know how to draw a line under it. I was like an albatross scouring the ocean as if without end. I was like the Ancient Mariner, forever telling my story to whomever I might stop and hold with my skinny hand. The word 'closure' hadn't yet entered the catechism of cliché then. But I refused to sully my mind with it. I had a typescript in my drawer, like a corpse in an unsealed coffin. I had been keening over it for years. The undertaker had been unable to finish with it. It was way past rigor mortis. Decomposition had long set in, in my mind, composition and decomposition, the doom of the struggling author. Not that anyone ever thought it alive but its maker. No one with a bone in their body, anyway, it seemed. It could find no publisher but equivocation, except from Bernard O'Donoghue, who gave it its title but wasn't a publisher.

Then, speaking of bones, honest enough, I literally broke a leg. I did so by mishap on a judo mat one night. In consequence I sat convalescing on the sofa with my leg up on a chair. It proved a lengthy convalescence too, as the hospital managed to give me a potentially fatal infection – osteomilitis – that took forever to eradicate. I underwent several debriding operations in a handful of nil-by-mouth days, a major skin transplant, a bone-marrow transplant, diving down again and again to the bottom of the sea that is general anaesthetic. I might not have resurfaced at any point along the way. But I surfaced every time like an irrepressible cormorant.

Now at last I had time on my hands to look about me. I had mortality on my mind too. A sense of urgency set in. And, having nothing better or worse to do, I asked my wife if she could bear to bring me the corpse

* *The Rock Garden* (1984) was Lilliput's first book. An Irish speaker, Daly was devoted to the Aran Islands and summered on Inis Mór over some thirty-five years, chronicling it in his own pictorial history *Oileain Arann: The Aran Islands* (1975). Antony Farrell tells me that Daly knew Robinson 'when he was drawing the dole and sign-painting on the island, and he and Máiréad, I think, wanted to put those memories in a back drawer'. A German translation of *The Rock Garden* (*Der Felsengarten: Stimmen der Aran-Inseln*) appeared with Editions Caro in Berlin in 2017.

from the drawer. She did. I couldn't have her attend my wake and burial before I'd finally finished my book. I was forever writing it for her. I looked at it and I tried once more to breathe life into it, and to make it look presentable at least. I called it 'Lazarus', in unsure and uncertain hope. The likelihood was I would do it to death once more.

Fishers

Of men and of women. Fishers was a restaurant on St Clements in East Oxford, at its best in the late 1990s, and I was often there, entertaining authors (and myself) on plastic supplied me by Blackwells the publisher. Lunchtime O'Booze used to frequent it regularly. Those were the days still, and it was that kind of place. They'd decked it out, literally, with sea-going furnishings: compasses; lamps and lights; lifebuoys; lengths of rope; a stretch or two of net; porthole windows; air scoop vents; concave deck benches, once intended to double in a disaster as life rafts (ideal for cosying up on, and for destroying your posture) &c, &c.

Angela was the mistress of ceremonies, and her lover the proprietor. They raided Billingsgate before dawn. They had their own van come up from Looe in Cornwall. It brought the freshest catches anyone might serve so far inland. As a small harbour, accessible only to smaller vessels that worked round the tidal cycle of a single day, Looe enjoyed a quicker turnaround of fresh, and therefore for a restaurant fresher, fish than other ports whose boats were at sea for days and weeks. At its height, in those years, there was nowhere better to go than Fishers. It was hail-fellow-well-met. It buzzed like a gannet rock. It made me think of Aran. And it served wines of the finest nectar for loosening the tongue. It was a theatre in the round where all were players and the script improvised from the menu and the wine list. Could anyone wish for more, unless it was a one-way ticket from Galway to Kilronan, ideally for December or January, on the cusp of a gale, boarding in the dark of 6 am?

It was the only place to take Terence Brown, then Professor of Anglo-Irish literature at Trinity College, Dublin. I'd recently been responsible for publishing his biography of Yeats. His next book, I hoped to persuade him, would be a short cultural history of Irish literature. We were still talking at 4 pm and still putting away a bottle when the subject of J.M. Synge and *The Aran Islands* entered the conversation. What choice did I have? I played my card and told Professor Brown about my time on Inis Mór, which led, as sure as death follows life, to the corpse.

'I'd like to see it,' he said, without so much as holding his nose. He'd clearly had more than his share of the bottle. All too eager to get it out of the house for an airing, if only for the round trip, I mailed it to him, post-haste. I think it was October. It might have been September. Anyway, I heard nothing more from the professor of Anglo-Irish literature all the long way down to the year's end. I knew how busy academics are. Besides, everyone has a typescript in their drawer they're all too ready to foist on anyone foolish enough to agree to see it. So what? I'd just about accepted that the corpse was a dead duck and forgotten it. No professorial pathologist was going to see it rise from the slab and say, 'Call me Lazarus'. as if it were Ishmael, whose name means 'God hears'. Lazarus means 'God helped'. Whatever the risen corpse might say, God had so far neither heard nor helped. How could I expect a mere mortal to? I had never believed in miracles.

Christmas came. I had to fly on St Stephen's Day to Chicago or New York or one or other North American big city, for a meeting of the Modern Languages Association of America, a huge gathering of academics, a job marketplace for them. In those days the meeting always straddled the year's end and the year's fresh start. It was de rigueur for academic publishers to attend. It was hard on family life, and hard on one's mind-body equilibrium. On one of these trips I had a remarkable mid-air encounter, described in a poem I called 'American Wake':

> Heading for America, on St Stephen's evening,
> A vision from below swam up to haunt me:
> The islands in the bay's mouth, gliding.
> The day was turning thin, no sign of habitation,

From that height, or hint of colouration, yet
From the cast of light I knew, if one asked there,
'Will it rain?', the question was her answer.
It seemed a miracle to me that I should see them:

I never take a window seat (to speed escape
On landing) but stood up just to stretch my legs,
And by some gift or grace of timing, glimpsed
Them, through a port-hole: the parting glass,
Raised between us, and since who must go, and who
Must stay? the moment made me wonder.

I'd generally fly back on New Year's night. We were expected to work through jetlag, so if it was a weekday, I'd roll up at the office on 2 January, or someone purporting to be me would.

Lo and behold, what did I find in my inbox but an email from Professor Brown. The corpse was the last thing on my mind, except that I felt a bit like one. My first thought was that the learned man had spent the festive season mapping out the new book I wanted in my list. I clicked to open the mail. What was it? In huge letters allowing no more than a word per screen, it scrolled down to say: 'IT'S / BLOODY / MARVELLOUS!' He meant the corpse. He meant Lazarus. What's more, Lazarus had already crossed Dublin and been checked over by Antony Farrell who wanted to publish him. Terence Brown, it turned out, was a director of the Lilliput Press. Had I known that, I am not sure I'd have sent him my typescript. I'd had enough wounds from publishers already. Even harder to credit, I was adopted by Terence's agent, a South Walean by the name of Jonathan Williams – 'Agent Williams', a Dublin legend with a fine tenor voice. It was some morning's work. I stood back and looked at my day job with more than usual revulsion.

Squawk

The Irish Times of Saturday, 10 March 2001 carried an almost full-page, illustrated review by Tim Robinson, entitled, in language nodding at John Ruskin, 'Faithful to the Last unto Aran'. The book in question was *An Aran Keening* by Andrew McNeillie, which the Lilliput Press had just that week launched at the Irish Writers' Centre in Dublin. Seamus Heaney turned out for it, though he'd only that day stepped off a plane from visiting Derek Walcott on St Lucia. There were some eighty people there, including my wife's Wicklow relations. There was a great bash in a house somewhere near the centre of Dublin, with Guinnesses and U2 people and god knows who wasn't there. It was a miracle, however late in the day.

I had anticipated the Irish would be hard on me, as an outsider stepping on such hallowed ground. But they weren't. When I said as much to Bill McCormack, whose biography of Synge was then in the making, a poet who signed himself Hugh Maxton, he took me aback. He said no. You are home. You have come home. I liked that, having always had as you know a fatal attraction to Ireland. But it was hardly true that I was home, still less home and dry. As you know, I was conceived in the Irish Sea and delivered into this vale of tears on its North Welsh shore.

Now Antony Farrell and I were on our way to Roundstone, via Kenny's Bookshop in Galway, that same Saturday to have dinner with the Robinsons –Tim and Máiréad. We'd spent the night before staying with friends of Antony's in Carlow. At the first service station we came to, we stopped and bought a copy of *The Irish Times*. We knew the review was to appear that day but didn't know – or at least I didn't know – what the verdict would be. It was a butterfly-stomach moment for me. The reviewer was none other than Tim Robinson. Would the master of the subject – the Man of Aran par excellence – like my book?

I was bound to worry and fear the worst. But as it turned out I needn't have. He paid it many a fine compliment and introduced the germ of what remained a standing and much-elaborated joke between us, down to his last days. Nodding at the literary history of the place and the celebrated authors associated with it, he said: 'We will all just have to move up, like cormorants on a rock when another arrives with widespread wings, and, without graceless squawking and pecking, make room for a worthy addition to the canon.' As you might sign a letter or email with 'love and kisses', ever after that day we always ended our communications with 'love and squawks', or indeed just 'SQUAWKS!!!'

Now I began to go back to Inis Mór regularly, sometimes twice a year and re-entered the labyrinth again and again, finding ever-new threads, one way and another – the labyrinth as Tim called it in his second book – that led me back and led me on. This is the story of those threads, those loose ends, that ravel and unravel in a wake of pages, a litter like a flock of gulls trailing the good ship, all of them vital to what would become *Archipelago*.

Now, for farewell, I leave you in the capable hands of Bartley Beatty 'The Ferryman':

How would it be, do you think?
There would be mist, I'd say,
shielding the shore, first forward
then aft, as if to ease you
between being alive and being
dead; if there is death there

and not just after-life, as I've heard
is what's in store with Dido
and that crowd Aeneas saw
or Aengus as they call him here.

The sea would be a millpond
I suppose and the light ghostly.
I've made such crossings before
and on a one-way ticket too
in which Bartley Beatty made
a little tear as I stepped aboard
nodding and asking how things were.
Not bad, considering, I might say
after a lock-in at the Castle
just a short step from the quay

where one evening Anthony
Hernon missed his step between
the boat and the wall
and so jumped his turn
for the sea-road home.
There were so many Bartley thought
he had a job for life
after serving his time
on the platform of a London bus
as if he'd been invented by Louis MacNeice.

But they laid him off.
To make ends meet he drove
a taxi in Galway, ferrying drunks
out into the sticks
to far-flung bungalows down
fuschiad lanes by little loughs
in barren bogs, places so remote

they could have been
on the far shore of the Styx
for all you might know.

*

Meanwhile remember, please, for now and ever after: when folk say farewell, be sure to fare well.

FAREWELL

Acknowledgments

The editors would like to thank all the contributors and executors who have granted permission for their literary and visual work that was first published in *Archipelago* to be reproduced in this volume. Poems in copyright by Ivor Gurney are reproduced with kind permission of the Ivor Gurney Trust; Angela Leighton's poems are reproduced with permission from Shoestring Books and Carcanet; Mick Imlah's poetry was subsequently published in *The Lost Leader* (London: Faber, 2008) and is reproduced with permission of his literary executors, Mark Ford and Alan Hollinghurst; Seamus Heaney's poetry is reproduced by permission of his estate, and Faber & Faber. Heaney's translation of 'Hallaig' was first published in a pamphlet published by Urras Shomhairle (The Sorley Maclean Trust). Bernard O'Donoghue's 'Geese Conversations', first published in *Archipelago* and then in *Farmers Cross*, and 'Ballybeg Priory', first published in *Archipelago* and then in *The Seasons of Cullen Church*, are included here by kind permission of the poet and Faber. Douglas Dunn's 'Botanics', first published in *Archipelago* and then in *The Noise of a Fly*, is also included by permission of the poet and Faber.

All reasonable efforts have been made to secure copyright, and if the editors have made any error we will be happy to address it.

The editors are very grateful to the Willson Center for Humanities and Arts at the University of Georgia for their invaluable sponsorship, and many thanks to the English Faculty of the University of Oxford for their support.

The editors would also like to thank Andrew McNeillie for his generosity in support of this publication. The selection included in the Reader was made solely by the editors, who are very grateful to Malcolm Sparkes for creating the series of coastal maps.